THE FIRST IRISH CITIES

THE FIRST IRISH CITIES

AN EIGHTEENTH-CENTURY TRANSFORMATION

DAVID DICKSON

YALE UNIVERSITY PRESS
NEW HAVEN AND LONDON

For Fred

Published with assistance from the Annie Burr Lewis Fund.

For information about this and other Yale University Press publications, please contact:
U.S. Office: sales.press@yale.edu   yalebooks.com
Europe Office: sales@yaleup.co.uk   yalebooks.co.uk

Set in Minion by IDSUK (DataConnection) Ltd
Printed in Great Britain by TJ Books, Padstow, Cornwall

Library of Congress Control Number: 2020943247

ISBN 978-0-300-22946-2

A catalogue record for this book is available from the British Library.

10 9 8 7 6 5 4 3 2 1

CONTENTS

ILLUSTRATIONS

PLATES

ILLUSTRATIONS

ILLUSTRATIONS

FIGURES

MAPS

TABLES

ACKNOWLEDGEMENTS

The idea behind this project began a long time ago and many people have shaped it, knowingly and unknowingly. I owe a particular debt to generations of graduate and undergraduate students at Trinity College Dublin who have challenged arguments and bounced off ideas over many years in our study of Irish urban history, and whose enthusiasm and insights have been so enriching. Among the many individuals who have generously helped along the way, I am greatly indebted to Toby Barnard, David Brown, Richard Butler, Andrew Carpenter, Christine Casey, Mary Clarke, the late Maurice Craig, the late Bill Crawford, Louis Cullen, Rowena Dudley, Paul Ferguson, Susan Flavin, Alison FitzGerald, the late Desmond FitzGerald, Norman Gamble, Raymond Gillespie, Patrick Griffin, Brian Gurrin, Richard Harrison, Cathy Hayes, David Hayton, Jacqueline Hill, Susan Hood, Aidan Kane, James Kelly, Liam Kennedy, Máire Kennedy, Magda and the late Rolf Loeber, John Logan, Breandán Mac Suibhne, Eve McAuley, Ian McBride, the late R.B. McDowell, Ivar McGrath, Edward McParland, Anthony Malcomson, Jane Maxwell, John Montague, Bob Morris, Timothy Murtagh, Niall Ó Ciosáin, Cormac Ó Gráda, Ciaran O'Neill, Jim Smyth, Tom Truxes, Brendan Twomey, Patrick Walsh, Kevin Whelan and Christopher Woods.

Many have helped in the search for images and in arranging permissions: in this regard I am enormously grateful to Hannah Baker, Alec Cobbe, Éamonn de Búrca, David Davison, Sarah Gearty, Catherine Giltrap, Rob Goodbody, James Gorry, Arnold Horner, Sylvie Kleinman, William Laffan, Mary Lombard, Eamonn McEneaney, Edward McParland, Aidan O'Boyle, Diarmuid Ó Gráda, Finola O'Kane, Ruth Thorpe, Brian Walker, Bernadette Walsh and Rose Anne White. I am particularly indebted to Matthew Stout for map-making and to Robert Towers, who played a critical role in the early development of the project.

ACKNOWLEDGEMENTS

I would like to acknowledge my appreciation to the following institutions for their support and help in the course of the project: Adams Fine Arts Auctioneers, Dublin; Cork Archives Institute; Cork Public Museum; the Crawford Art Gallery; Davison & Associates; the Department of Early Printed Books and the Glucksman Map Library in Trinity College Dublin; Derry City & Strabane District Council; Dublin City Libraries; the Gorry Gallery, Dublin; the Highlanes Gallery, Drogheda; the Irish Architectural Archive; Limerick Civic Trust; the National Library of Ireland; National University of Ireland, Galway and the *Duanaire* Project; the Public Record Office of Northern Ireland; the Royal Irish Academy Library and, associated with it, the *Dictionary of Irish Biography* and *Irish Historic Towns Atlas* projects; the Royal Society of Antiquaries of Ireland; the Waterford Treasures Museum; and Whyte's Fine Arts Auctioneers, Dublin. I would also like to acknowledge the financial support provided by the Trinity College Arts and Social Science Benefaction Fund and the Grace Lawless Lee Fund, and to thank my former colleagues in the Trinity College Dublin School of Histories and Humanities for their support, encouragement and boundless generosity. Warmest thanks are due to my publisher Heather McCallum, to Marika Lysandrou, Percie Edgeler, my copy-editor Eve Leckey, and the editorial team at Yale, and, not least, to my anonymous referees for exceptionally valuable and constructive comments. Finally, profound thanks to my ever-supportive family who have, as always, sustained me in ways that only they know.

Dublin, March 2020

ABBREVIATIONS

AH	*Archivium Hibernicum*
Anal. Hib.	*Analecta Hibernicum*
BL	British Library
BNL	*Belfast News Letter*
CAI	Cork Archives Institute
CARD	*Calendar of the Ancient Records of Dublin*, eds. John and Lady Gilbert, 19 vols. (Dublin, 1889–1944)
CEP	*Cork Evening Post*
CHI	*Cambridge History of Ireland*, ed. Thomas Bartlett, 4 vols. (Cambridge, 2018)
Coll. Hib.	*Collectanea Hibernica*
CSP Dom.	*Calendar of State Papers (Domestic)*
CSPI	*Calendar of State Papers (Ireland)*
DEP	*Dublin Evening Post*
DHR	*Dublin Historical Review*
DIB	*Dictionary of Irish Biography*, ed. James McGuire and James Quinn, 9 vols. (Cambridge, 2009)
ECI	*Eighteenth-Century Ireland/Iris an dá chultúr*
ECS	*Eighteenth-Century Studies*
EHR	*Economic History Review*
Eng. HR	*English Historical Review*
ESTC	Eighteenth-Century Short Title Catalogue
FDJ	*Faulkner's Dublin Journal*
FJ	*Freeman's Journal* [Dublin]
FLJ	*Finn's Leinster Journal* [Kilkenny]
HC	*Hibernian Chronicle* [Cork]

ABBREVIATIONS

HJ	*Historical Journal*
IAA	Irish Architectural Archive, Dublin
IADS	*Irish Architectural and Decorative Studies Journal*
IESH	*Irish Economic and Social History*
IHS	*Irish Historical Studies*
IHTA	*Irish Historic Towns Atlas*
IMC	*Irish Manuscripts Commission*
JCHAS	*Journal of the Cork Historical and Archaeological Society*
JCLAHS	*Journal of the County Louth Archaeological and Historical Society*
JEH	*Journal of Economic History*
JGAHS	*Journal of the Galway Archaeological and Historical Society*
JHCI	*Journal of the House of Commons (Ireland)*
JKSEIAS	*Journal of the Kilkenny and South-East of Ireland Archaeological Society*
JRSAI	*Journal of the Royal Society of Antiquaries of Ireland*
JSAH	*Journal of the Society of Architectural Historians*
NAI	National Archives of Ireland
NHI	*A New History of Ireland*
NLI	National Library of Ireland
NMAJ	*North Munster Antiquarian Journal*
NS	*Northern Star* [Belfast]
NUI	National University of Ireland
ODNB	*Oxford Dictionary of National Biography*
Proc. RIA	*Proceedings of the Royal Irish Academy*
PRONI	Public Record Office of Northern Ireland
QBIGS	*Quarterly Bulletin of the Irish Georgian Society*
QUB	Queen's University, Belfast
RCB	Representative Church Body of the Church of Ireland Library
RIA	Royal Irish Academy
RSAI	Royal Society of Antiquaries of Ireland
TCD	Trinity College Dublin
TKAS	*Transactions of the Kilkenny Archaeological Society*
TNA	The National Archives (Kew)
TRHS	*Transactions of the Royal Historical Society*
UCC	University College Cork
UCD	University College Dublin
WHM	*Walker's Hibernian Magazine*

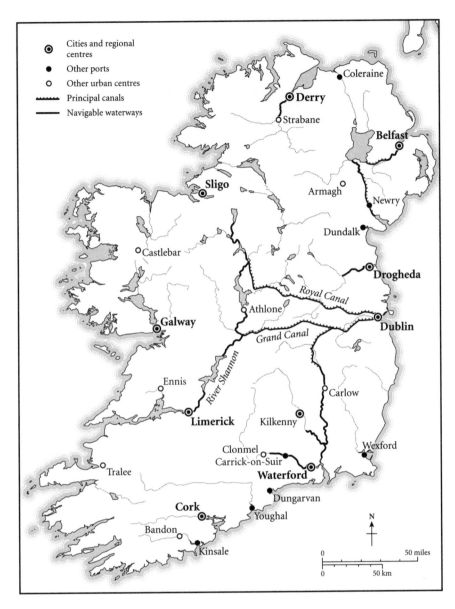

Map 1 Irish cities and regional centres [Matthew Stout]

INTRODUCTION

Most of Ireland's larger towns are close to a millennium old and the Viking seaports a little older, yet the urbanization of Ireland has, by European standards, been a slow process. Only since the 1960s has more than half the island's population lived in towns and cities. Furthermore the process of town and city growth in Ireland has been noticeably uneven. The first official census of 1821 indicated that the proportion of Ireland's population living in towns and cities of 5,000 inhabitants or more was just below 10 per cent, low by west European norms but somewhat ahead of what Peter Clark has characterized as 'outer northern Europe', namely Scotland, Ireland and Scandinavia. But in the century after that census, a time of wider European urbanization and industrialization, not least in Scotland, most Irish cities and towns lost population at the same time as the country's huge exodus of population to Britain and America continued. That pattern of urban decline was highly unusual and was not reversed until well into the twentieth century. However, what is even more distinctive is what had preceded the 1821 census: a cycle of unusually strong Irish urban growth over the previous two centuries and one in which the largest Irish urban areas became, by European standards, very sizeable cities indeed.[1]

There had been an earlier cycle of urban growth in the thirteenth century when Anglo-Norman control of the island was at its strongest but, outside the south-east, towns in the colony had remained very small. However from the early fourteenth century, perhaps before, the urban share of Ireland's modest population was slipping back, and it probably stood at less than 2 per cent in the wake of English re-conquest of the whole island *c.* 1600, a time when many western and southern European cities were greatly expanding – until war, plague, famine and rural demographic decline halted that process in the early seventeenth century. Yet it was at precisely that moment that the first signs of

1

post-medieval growth appeared in Irish port towns and regional centres, and although almost no urban community was spared the effects of sword and cannon in the civil wars of the 1640s and 1689–91, or the associated scourges of plague and famine, urban growth was surprisingly strong in the intervening years of peace, helped by several waves of immigration. In addition, large numbers of villages and small towns were established during the seventeenth century in port hinterlands, on a scale not found anywhere in Europe apart from the Slavic borderlands and parts of Scandinavia. These new towns were essentially colonial enterprises: they were closely related to the transformations in the power of the English state in Ireland, in the ownership of Irish land, and in the exploitation of that land, all of which unfolded during the century.[2]

Following this, the 'long' eighteenth century – from the 1660s to the 1820s – was an era of deepening if unsteady commercialization of what had been a largely pre-market economy and, related to this, the transformation in size and function of a handful of very old urban centres. Six long-established ports around the Irish coast graduated during the period to become active participants in the North Atlantic trading world – Drogheda, Dublin, Waterford, Cork, Limerick and Galway – and they eclipsed equally ancient neighbours, Wexford, New Ross, Youghal and Kinsale. In the north of Ireland, Belfast, an almost entirely new colonial settlement created at the beginning of the seventeenth century, challenged its much older neighbour Carrickfergus to become a sophisticated and wealthy urban community.

North Munster and south-east Ireland inherited the most developed medieval urban system, and Kilkenny, the *de facto* capital of that region, became the only city of the interior to stand comparison (in scale and economic diversity) with the principal port cities. By contrast, the north-west had almost no medieval urban legacy, and no major city emerged there during the long eighteenth century. The ports of London/Derry[3] and Sligo trailed far behind the Leinster and Munster cities in terms of population and scale. However, these centres developed strategically important urban functions during the eighteenth century within their respective hinterlands – west Ulster and north Connacht – and for that reason they merit inclusion in the top group of urban communities.

⊰⊹⊱

Since early Norman times the principal port towns had served as bridgeheads for colonial immigration and as walled sites of defence, enjoying fiscal and chartered privileges in return for maintaining military capability. These communities, both those of pre-Norman origin (Cork, Dublin, Limerick and Waterford) and those established in the first hundred years of the Norman lordship (Drogheda, Galway and Sligo) were ethnically mixed throughout the medieval era. But over many generations the leading burgher families cherished their English origins and in later times embellished their heroic record in defending the interests of the English Crown against supposedly 'rebelly' neighbours, although in truth their relations with neighbouring lordships were often intimate and collusive.

From the late sixteenth century these 'Old English' urban elites, Catholic but loyal, were challenged by an assertively Protestant and centralizing government, and they were gradually disempowered – financially, legally and by *force majeure*. The struggle ended in their wholesale defeat and expropriation at different points in the seventeenth century, and their replacement by 'New English', French Huguenot and Dutch migrants. And this new urban elite that stepped into Old English shoes proceeded to recycle the same colonial ambiguities, albeit articulated now in primarily religious terms.[4]

The elite present in most early modern Irish towns and cities was heavily dependent on the goodwill, support and spending power of the rural land-owning caste scattered across their hinterlands, families who often had influence with government and the judiciary, and who had deep pockets (and some of whom were direct stakeholders as well, owning substantial urban property). The gentry's influence was particularly evident in the capital city: from the mid seventeenth century a large proportion of resident Irish landowners and their families routinely wintered in Dublin – for business, politics and recreation. Thus the capital city's economy was for 150 years hugely affected by a bounteous inward flow of rent-derived spending power.

Many of the elements of what Peter Borsay has christened an 'urban renaissance' in England were adapted and adopted in eighteenth-century Ireland: the gradual assimilation of the 'rules' of classical architecture and the rise of brick over stone as the standard building material; the tentative introduction of building controls and street planning; and the appearance of purpose-built market houses, assembly rooms and dedicated public spaces. 'Improvement' was indeed the catch-all fashionable ideology of the era that covered the presence of two quite different sets of policies and processes: what can be termed 'hard' improvement – policies affecting the physical appearance of a town and its facilities – and 'soft' improvement – policies that promoted order, industry and enlightenment among its inhabitants.[5]

Hard improvement was always presented in a positive light, although the redesign of public space had mixed social consequences: sometimes the drive to 'improve' an urban environment required the decanting of low-status families and the expulsion of dirty industries (like brickmaking) from customary locations. The impact of *soft* improvement is harder to measure, but variations in the provision of schooling, urban literacy, associational culture, the consumption of print and the formation of reading clubs and circulating libraries may give some clues. But what impulses were driving soft improvement? Was there indeed an elevation of 'urbane' over local 'civic' culture and the creation from within of a novel appetite for metropolitan tastes and fashions as, it would seem, had transformed the social character of early modern English towns? Toby Barnard has suggested that 'the inhabitants of [Irish] towns, especially the ports, were ideally situated to learn and practise the latest fashions' from the world outside, and that they were 'first to receive and then to spread the attitudes and accessories of gentility'.[6]

A.C. Hepburn in his study of a number of 'divided cities' in the nineteenth and twentieth centuries has developed the concept of the 'contested city' to describe urban centres where 'two or more ethnically self-conscious groups – divided by religion, language and/or culture and perceived history – co-exist in a situation where no group is willing to concede supremacy to the other'. Typically the struggle for dominance occurred within social classes, even within particular occupations, but such contests could be both a source of conflict and of innovation.[7] Belfast was one of Hepburn's European case-studies: does the 'contested city' model have earlier and wider Irish application, or was Victorian Belfast, as many have liked to think, unique?

As the first attempt to synthesize a broad field of research, this study has been shaped by the highly uneven state of knowledge. Furthermore, the sources available for the study of eighteenth-century Irish urban history are far thinner than exist for almost any other part of western Europe. However, modern scholarship on architectural history, print, theatre, music, science, high culture, politics and urban morphology is now fairly abundant and of a high order, but the study of urban economies, social relations and material life has been the work of very few hands. And there has been a notable absence of theorizing.[8]

Therefore this book, while building on the researches of a great many, can only be a preliminary skirmish into an exciting but under-studied branch of urban history.

The physical morphology of Irish cities from the era of war and siege in the seventeenth century to that of spreading suburbs a century later can now be reconstructed – thanks not least to the heroic work of the *Irish Historic Towns Atlas* project – but the diverse demographic patterns remain more opaque, although seismic changes in religious composition stand out (Chapters 1 and 2). The economic functions of cities are somewhat clearer, and the contrasting ways in which foreign trade lifted some cities more than others illuminate a variety of issues on Ireland's place within the first British empire (Chapters 3 and 4). Dublin's commercial primacy is a central part of the story, but its status as a great pre-industrial manufacturing city is equally striking (Chapter 5). However, outside the realm of economics, it is the long history of the rival confessional communities that cohabited in the cities that provides a key to understanding urban culture (Chapter 6).

The battle to control and develop urban space, to mitigate the effects of growth, and to adapt new concepts of urban form is a major theme in Dublin's eighteenth-century history, and contrasting Dublin's 'improvements' with the more tentative provincial initiatives is highly suggestive (Chapter 7). Dublin led the way with the emergence of a remarkable print culture, and eventually this resonated in provincial centres but less clearly so in rural Ireland (Chapter 8). Dublin was also a cockpit of social conflict: the weakness of traditional remedies of social control led to an enhanced role of the state (via the army) in enforcing urban security and in creating professional policing for the capital (Chapter 9). But it was only in the tumultuous 1790s that there was a wider challenge to existing power structures, and a focus on that decade reveals the scale of social change underway, not least in the transformed civil status of Catholics (Chapter 10). But it is only from the 1820s, the end of the long cycle of growth, that a full sense of what was accomplished and what was now lost becomes evident (Chapter 11 and Conclusion).

1

THE WALLS COME DOWN

John Ferrar in his history of Limerick published in 1767 reflected on the ending of the city's final siege in 1691: 'May it be the last this city will ever sustain, for who can look back without horror on the calamities and misfortunes it occasioned, or how can we be sufficiently thankful when we compare that period to our present peaceful and flourishing condition?' The achievement of a hundred years of peace from the 1690s to the 1790s was indeed one of the defining characteristics of eighteenth-century Ireland. The power of the state may sometimes have been challenged at the edges but, compared with previous centuries, common law and the peaceful enjoyment of property prevailed, and for those with a stake in the status quo, risk was perceived to be external and overseas, not (in the first instance at least) emanating from any domestic quarter. A measure of this change was the disappearance of defensive walls from most of the larger urban centres. These walls were old and by Continental standards quite tame structures, both in height and in mass. Bastions, towers and elaborate gatehouses were unevenly spread, the wall circuits small and the areas they enclosed modest. This was a legacy of the diminutive size of the largest Irish towns in preceding centuries (see Appendix 1).[1]

Some city corporations and (where they existed) military governors found residual value in maintaining city walls long after 1700, whether it was to control the night-time movement of strangers, to define the jurisdictional boundaries of municipal authority, or as a means of taxing goods in transit. There was also the memory, drawn from two cycles of civil warfare in the seventeenth century, of the value of walled spaces as places of refuge in times of military emergency. But by the mid eighteenth century extramural growth was now so pronounced that it undermined the case for their retention: city boundaries stretched far beyond the line of old walls, tolls could be collected elsewhere, and threats to nocturnal peace came from within, not outside the city. Thus by 1800 both entry-gates and much of the connected walling had vanished from Irish cities. However in the once-walled neighbourhoods the footprint of defence works had an after-life, visible in the layout of central streets, their width and orientation.[2]

In their prime, city walls had defined the intangibles of civic identity and corporate prestige. Did their passing contribute to the dilution of such sentiments? Yair Mintzker, surveying this process in eighteenth-century Germany, has argued that the disappearance of city walls was a deliberate and often controversial process that reflected the progressive subjugation of city communities to the princely state and its military priorities. In the case of Ireland the old port cities had enjoyed a comparable degree of autonomy from the English Crown in the fifteenth and sixteenth centuries, but by identifying with the old religion and the Counter-Reformation they began to find their liberties under challenge from the state, particularly after the short-lived urban recusancy revolt of 1603. Thus the symbolism of Irish city walls was already compromised long before demolition began.

However, urban defences had continued to shape military outcomes in the course of the seventeenth century. The immediate prologue to the century of peace and defortification was the Williamite War (1689–91), the last conventional war fought on Irish soil. It was the final chapter in more than a century of destructive regional conflicts and was the first occasion when heavy cannon were deployed on Irish soil. City walls and urban sieges featured prominently in the conflict and several walled towns, as often before, became places of emergency shelter. It was also the last occasion when civic leaders and the urban population at large shouldered much of the responsibility for their own defence, coming at a time when state authority was temporarily in total abeyance. This was particularly the case in the northernmost city of Derry.[3]

One day in September 1733, shortly before the winter sitting of the Irish Parliament, two great tapestries were unfurled in the House of Lords chamber in Dublin. They had been ordered five years previously to adorn the upper house of Ireland's new parliament building, the magnificent 'pile majestic', and they revealed strikingly colourful images of *The valiant defence of Londonderry* (1689) and *The glorious battle and victory of the Boyne* (1690). The chief advocate for a new parliament house, Speaker William Conolly, was now dead and the immensely gifted young architect of the building, Edward Lovett Pearce, had only weeks to live.[4]

Conolly, the country's wealthiest commoner, had been no aesthete, but he trusted those like Pearce who were, and he was ultimately responsible for two of the most important building projects in eighteenth-century Ireland, Castletown, his country house 12 miles west of Dublin that was 'fit for a prince', and the new parliament facing onto College Green. Neither building was completed by the time of his death but everything, including the tapestries, continued more or less to plan. Initially there were to have been six tapestries, each to celebrate a key event in the two-year struggle between James and William – and between Catholic Ireland and Protestant Ireland – including one tapestry that would have recorded the sieges of Cork and Kinsale. But only two tapestries, perhaps on a vaster scale than originally planned, were executed. They were produced by Robert Baillie, a tenant of Conolly, who had revived tapestry-making in Dublin and imported Flemish and French artisans, one of whom, John van Beaver 'the famous tapestry weaver', was the principal designer. The inspiration was presumably the venerable Brussels tapestries that hung in the House of Lords in Westminster celebrating the English defeat of the Spanish Armada, and it was probably Baillie who suggested an Irish adaptation.[5]

If indeed it was Conolly's choice, the decision to memorialize Derry's siege ahead of other turning-points in the two-year 'War of the Two Kings', James and William, was not surprising. Conolly's rise to great landed wealth had begun in post-war Derry where he acted as law agent for the Corporation and for the London-based Irish Society, the principal landowner in the city. Later he sat as MP for Co. Derry from 1703 until his death in 1729. It is entirely plausible that he would want to privilege the image of 'his' city in the new chamber. But, more importantly, Derry and its siege had already developed unique symbolic importance for those who sought to own the Williamite victory, namely the Irish Protestant establishment.

DERRY

The 'little city' that had been created in the 1610s as a City of London project was set on 'the island of Derry', a lozenge-shaped hill overlooking the River Foyle. Its substantial walls enclosed an urban site of some 13 hectares, soon to be dominated by a substantial Anglican cathedral that was built at its highest point. The town attracted at first a modest settler population of English and Scots, but much larger numbers crowded in as refugees during the Confederate Wars of the 1640s. In the chaotic early years of that conflict it remained an outpost loyal to the English Crown, but in 1648 a commander whose allegiance was to the English Parliament gained control. The following year, in a strange twist, the city was besieged by the Scottish army in Ulster for some seventeen weeks, before being relieved by the Ulster Irish commander Owen Roe O'Neill. The Scots may have failed to capture Derry in war, but over the next generation the city became an increasingly Scottish Presbyterian stronghold, even within the walls, some threatening the Anglican bishop that 'ere long [they] would have their church and pulpit from them'. The bad blood between kirk and church was etched deep. And the Ulster Irish were there too: in 1660 a third of those within the walls were listed as 'Irish', as were two-fifths of those resident in the suburban lanes.[6]

In 1688, when the government in Dublin headed by the Earl of Tyrconnell was actively supporting the Catholic King James and purging the Irish army of its potentially disloyal Protestant soldiery, the areas of English and Scottish settlement in Ulster grew restive. Armed resistance was slow to form, and when it did Derry city once again became a place of refuge. Resistance within the city came from below: a 'mob' of thirteen apprentice boys closed the gates against Jacobite solders ('Highlanders and Ulster Papists') as they arrived to fill the garrison, a move 'that extremely surpris'd the graver citizens of the town', many of whom disappeared to safety. It was from such small beginnings that Derry became for the next six months, in Tom Fraser's estimation, 'the heart of the unfolding contest for the future of Europe'.[7]

The conventional estimate is that up to 30,000 defenders and civilians were penned within the city, and that the death toll during the siege reached 10,000, not including Jacobite losses; even if these figures are greatly exaggerated, there was appalling civilian carnage (especially of the refugees) from famine and disease. Almost immediately after the event, a narrative of demotic defiance and of heroic and very costly resistance was fashioned in print and in printed image. However, bitter controversy erupted as to who deserved most credit for resisting James and the Jacobite regiments.[8]

George Walker, one of the governors and an Anglican cleric, produced a graphic, elegant and highly self-serving account of the fifteen-week siege and its seemingly providential conclusion after a small flotilla had broken through the Jacobite boom across the River Foyle. John Mackenzie, dissenting chaplain in Walker's regiment, produced a minutely detailed riposte that emphasized the overwhelmingly Presbyterian affiliation of the common soldiery who had formed the backbone of resistance, and he documented how they, 'the multitude', had rebelled against the authority of the Council of War when it had sought terms with the Jacobite enemy.[9] Another veteran of the siege and in its later stages the military governor, John Mitchelburne, was slower to write; he had also been one of those resisting peace terms and had flown a red flag, the conventional colour of defiance and no surrender, from the cathedral tower. A professional solder and an Anglican, he turned to print to make his claim for recognition, eventually retelling the saga as a tragi-comedy (this despite losing his wife and children during the siege). His play, first published in London in 1705, became a standard text, being reprinted at least a dozen times in Belfast, Dublin, Newry and Strabane, and it was still circulating in chapbook form in the early nineteenth century.[10] The drama existed out of time, as John Gamble noted as he journeyed through Co. Derry in 1812: 'the wars of William and James . . . in Ireland, where accounts of them have been handed down from father to son . . . are as fresh as if the events had only occurred yesterday, and the Siege of Londonderry is talked of with much less reference to distance of time than the Siege of Boston is in England'.[11]

As Conolly grew rich in the decades after the wars, Mitchelburne, like other Derry veterans, remained a luckless supplicant, denied financial reward or even military back-pay; he remained in Derry until his death in 1721. Unlike the two other governors of the besieged city, his portrait was not included in van Beaver's tapestry. Yet he was probably the key man responsible for the first local commemoration of the siege in 1718 (flying a crimson banner over the city cathedral on the anniversary of the closing of the gates) and he left money in his will for this gesture to be continued. Also, he seems to have been the first to draw on the continental sexual metaphor applied to cities that withstood siege and resisted capture (notably Venice and Dordrecht), bringing the conceit of 'the maiden city of Ireland' to Derry: 'her vestal chastity did never fail/And force and bribes in vain did her assail'.[12]

The 'maiden city' trope, with its themes of treachery, bravery and providential liberation, resonated within both elite and popular Protestant Ulster society, indeed was amplified by the early nineteenth century. The walls of Derry at that time came to have almost sacred meaning and they remained as the defining physical feature of the city, shaping a local sense of exclusive community. The 'greatest part' of the Catholics resident within the city were

Figure 1 Inside Derry's walls: Shipquay St leading up to the Exchange at the top of the hill, rebuilt after the siege, *c.* 1693.

driven out beyond the walls in December 1688, and a ban on Catholic residence within the walls far outlasted the crisis, although it was only acted on at moments of renewed threat (notably in 1744, when rumours of King James's grandson raising his banner in Scottish Highlands reached the city). Indeed even at the end of the eighteenth century there were reportedly only two Catholic households inside the walls. But outside the ramparts, the Catholic presence began to grow; by the 1780s it was large enough to support the first post-plantation place of Catholic worship, the Long Tower chapel, which nestled close to, but outside, the walls.[13]

SLIGO AND GALWAY

For all their totemic significance, Derry's walls had probably been obsolescent even when they were built in 1611–14. They helped to protect the city in the brief siege of 1649, but if Jacobite commanders had possessed greater artillery and siege engines to pound those walls in 1689 they would surely have been breached. Sligo, the other regional centre in the north-west, never had the protection of walls, even though the early modern town was repeatedly ravaged – in 1574, in the 1640s, and in 1689–91. A small band of beleaguered merchants had mooted the idea of building a town wall in the late sixteenth century, but because the site was immediately overlooked by hills their case to government met no response. Yet Sligo as an open town grew to become a regional centre of trade during the seventeenth century and it attracted several waves of Scots and English immigrants. It was eventually enclosed in 1689 after it had been taken, abandoned, and re-taken by the Jacobites: General Luttrell oversaw the construction of an earthen rampart and palisade, and these helped keep the town in precarious Jacobite control for most of the war. Despite its modest scale, Sligo was always seen as a strategic prize, 'the key of Connacht', 'the centre of a great amphitheatre of mountains which surround it'. It was and would remain a frontier town, to be protected not by walls but by great forts and professional soldiers (and by the 1730s it was the sole location in the provinces for a full cavalry regiment). The stone tower-houses of its first merchants, dating back to an era of late medieval prosperity, had almost all been lost in the repeated attacks on the town, and eighteenth-century Sligo was built almost entirely anew, albeit following the old street plan; however the ramparts of 1689 left no mark.[14]

Urban defences influenced the course of the war in 1691 in the case of both Galway and Limerick. Four centuries old, Galway was the smallest and most isolated of the Old English ports, but one that may have been even more successful than the southern ports in establishing *de facto* autonomy from Dublin in the fifteenth century. Surrounded by water and marsh on three sides, its topography gave it a measure of natural security; even its corn mills were located within the walls. However, with advances in military technology it was exposed to artillery attack, and there was a series of attempts to strengthen its defences during the seventeenth century, both within and outside the walls. In the half century before 1641 its Catholic merchant elite, the fourteen 'tribes' of Galway, had enjoyed an Indian summer based on overseas trade, notably with France, a prosperity evident both in the substantial acquisition of property in several Connacht counties, and in their sturdy 'marble' houses within the walls. The public improvements to the town undertaken in the 1620s and 1630s suggest a well-developed sense of civic identity. Their response to the collapse of government authority in 1641 was notably muscular, and between 1643 and 1651 they were involved in erecting three substantial bastions along the landward-facing wall. Thanks to these and other 'modern' fortifications, the town managed to withstand an intermittent Cromwellian siege for nine months in 1651–52, despite being ravaged by repeated bouts of bubonic plague and shaken by internal divisions over strategy when 'old and young citizens did not agree; civil and martial were at odds; men and women [were] in contestation . . .'[15]

Galway was the last town in the country to seek surrender terms from the all-conquering Parliamentary army. For some that simply marked the end of the royalist cause in Ireland, but the terms of capitulation were unusually generous and left the Corporation and freemen intact with their privileges and with two-thirds of their property. This deal was eventually overturned by the English Parliament when, nearly three years after the surrender, the garrison commander was bluntly instructed to put the government of the town 'into the hands of the English and Protestants' and expel all Catholic freemen. One reason for the *volte face* was that in 1643, in the early days of the English Civil War, the English Parliament had used the prospect of large-scale confiscation of property in Confederate-supporting Irish towns as a means of raising loans in London: Galway, Limerick, Waterford and Wexford had been selected as targets. The sums raised from 'adventurers' had been modest, but nevertheless the wholesale forfeiture of urban real estate captured from Confederate or royalist garrisons was part of the Commonwealth agenda in the 1650s, and it was a key element in the radical remodelling of corporate governance in previously Catholic-dominated towns. How far this was implemented in the complicated case of Galway prior to the collapse of the Commonwealth in 1660 is unclear, but there was a later memory of how leading Galway families, 'the best and greatest merchants in the kingdom', were hastily scattered into 'smokey and miserable huts and barracks in the country'.

The Galway Catholic elite managed to recover much of their power and wealth after 1660, but this was more through the recovery of substantial freehold lands outside the town than by trade within, for their expectation of regaining formerly owned *urban* property was (here as elsewhere) dashed by the terms of the Act of Explanation (1665). The famous 'bird's eye' map of the walled town (the first such image of an Irish city) was printed abroad at this time: it represented an elysian Galway at peace (with the arms of the fourteen leading families emblazoned around its base). But by the 1660s the map was more an act of recall than of celebration. Governance of their now desolate town had passed to new settlers, while old money was finding its way into fresh rural land speculation.[16]

James II's accession brought representatives of the old families back into civic office, and for a while they ran the town again. They busied themselves in

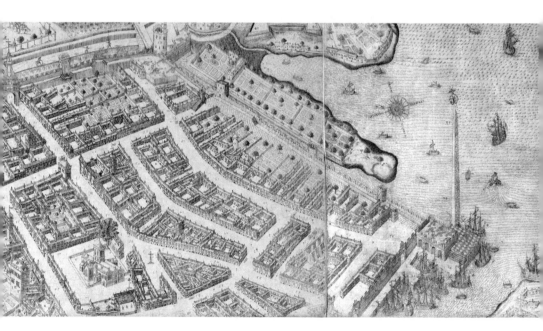

Figure 2 Galway's walled town from Abbeygate St and St Nicholas's Collegiate Church southwards, via High St, Quay St and St Augustine St, to the small medieval quays.

re-organizing urban defences in 1689, including the demolition of all houses and thatched cabins 'near and adjoining the walls', more in hope of standing outside the coming conflict than being part of it. The province of Connacht remained safely under Jacobite military control for most of the war and it was only in the summer of 1691 that Williamite forces, driving westwards after their great victory at the battle of Aughrim, threatened Galway. Protestant inhabitants had been shuffled out to the western suburbs across the Corrib, and the walls and fortifications of the town were strengthened early in 1691 under the direction of French military engineers, albeit on a more modest scale than in the 1640s. Thus when the Williamite army arrived in late July the town was in a position to play for time and to threaten to prolong the war by another year, helped by a stock of over forty cannon and a large if ill-fed garrison. But it had become a sickly, despondent place and, despite strong French disapproval, there was no appetite among civic leaders for a long siege; indeed there had been multiple peace feelers sent to the enemy, and there were no disaffected common soldiers anxious to hold their town to the last, as in Derry. Powerful walls and a functioning citadel gave the negotiators the leverage to extract decidedly favourable terms of surrender within two days, and the terms, unlike those of the 1650s, were interpreted fairly generously, although it required intense political lobbying over the next decade in Dublin and London for the Galway signatories to secure their properties.[17]

Galway in the next half century remained a heavily militarized community, with the town showing little sign of physical change or 'improvement'. Its citizenry remained overwhelmingly Catholic in affiliation. Some of the descendants of the old mercantile families conformed to the Established Church, many more became part of a Galway commercial diaspora that reached at least a dozen trading centres on both sides of the Atlantic. In the penal law of 1704, a specific clause required all existing Catholic householders in Galway (and Limerick) to give security for good behaviour and excluded any Catholic newcomers; 756 adult males in Galway complied. But in 1708, following reports of the attempted Jacobite invasion in Scotland, the mayor expelled all Catholics from the walled town (including those who had given securities) for a month, an action that was briefly repeated in January 1716 during a similar scare. That was the end of such after-shocks, and thereafter a sympathetic Corporation connived at the large Catholic presence in the town. By the 1730s Catholic parish chapels, friaries and convents were all visible within the walls. And when a somewhat eccentric military governor, Stratford Eyre, highlighted the degraded state of the old fortifications in 1747 and argued for their full restoration to help police its supposedly disaffected citizenry, the Irish government was not convinced, trusting in the town's three modern barracks to keep the peace. From the 1760s the walls were quietly left to decay.[18]

LIMERICK

Limerick city, like Drogheda on the east coast, inherited two walled elements, together making the shape of an hour-glass: Englishtown, located on the southern end of King's Island on the River Shannon, was overlooked by the imposing cathedral and royal castle, and Irishtown, the old suburban quarter lying immediately to the south, was attached to it by a single bridge over the Abbey River, a distributary arm of the Shannon; Irishtown was laid out on rising ground and had been fully walled since the fifteenth century. Larger than Galway and in every sense less exclusive, Limerick's main street in the seventeenth century was lined with battlemented stone houses that stood four- or five-storeys high; most of them were in Englishtown. It was long regarded as the most impregnable city in Ireland, but as a sign of what was to come, the Dublin government built a bastioned redoubt outside Irishtown in the 1590s. The city withstood five sieges during the next century, including two during the Cromwellian re-conquest: the second – in 1651 – was an appalling six-month ordeal causing the deaths of many thousands inside the city and was only brought to an end by the devastating combination of plague, Cromwellian artillery and a garrison mutiny. Irishtown appears to have been particularly affected.[19]

Reconstruction of the battered city after 1660 was tentative as Old English, New English and Dutch merchants competed for commercial dominance, but with its excellent berthage and Atlantic access, Limerick was a strategic prize in any conflict. Thus when Tyrconnell's government fled Dublin after the battle of the Boyne in July 1690, their immediate destination was Limerick, even though it was more than a hundred miles away, and the city remained the Jacobites' political and military stronghold until the end of the war. Their French military advisers were convinced that such an awkward site could not resist the oncoming Williamite juggernaut, but they were over-ruled: the defences around Irishtown were greatly strengthened, and the large suburbs outside the southern gates were destroyed 'to create a field of fire'. In the event, these 'hurried improvements' worked, and King William's 1690 campaign

Figure 3 Possibly the earliest brick houses in Nicholas St, Englishtown, Limerick.

ended in humiliation outside the walls of Limerick, a consequence of bad weather as well as clever Jacobite tactics. Irishtown's walls were indeed breached, but the attack was repulsed with the help of civilians. Indeed here and in Derry there were reports of women joining in the fighting, throwing stones or otherwise assisting the soldiery.

A year later and after substantial investment in fortification works under French direction, a second and longer siege dragged on for five weeks: after a crescendo of 'cannonading and bombarding' and of bitter recriminations over defence tactics, the Jacobite leadership in the now partially destroyed city surrendered. The 'Articles of Limerick', similar to those granted in Galway, allowed the Jacobite army to march off into exile and brought the Irish war to an end.[20]

The failure of a now entirely Protestant Irish parliament to ratify the peace terms in full (specifically the article relating to religious toleration) gave the Treaty of Limerick and the events surrounding it an enduring notoriety. Thirteen years later, as in Galway, all Catholic residents in Limerick above the status of labourer were required by the penal law of 1704 to give sureties for good behaviour, and new Catholic residents were excluded from the walled areas. About 350 men gave sureties, but the operation of the law left much to the discretion of the city's mayor, and local arguments over the meaning of the clause continued for decades; only occasionally, as in the 1707 and 1715 Jacobite invasion scares, did it lead to temporary exclusion beyond the walls. By the 1720s the status of Catholics and the security of the city had become enmeshed in local Corporation politics: the victorious Tory faction led by Major General Thomas Pearce openly supported Catholic merchants, while berating their opponents for allowing the city walls to fall into disrepair. Nevertheless, during the anti-Jacobite panic of 1745, Catholic merchants feared that once again they might be 'turned out of town', even though the 1704 restrictions were quite forgotten by then.

Limerick's walls remained intact and the gates were policed for another generation. However, housing density increased markedly within the walls, brick replacing stone, and the old suburbs expanded, notably on King's Island, sweeping over the old and ill-maintained defence works. One result was that in the 1760s the Corporation began the piecemeal demolition of the walls. Some sections survived, but unlike the case of Derry, they carried few glorious memories. By then Limerick had three operational barracks, including the reconstructed Castle barracks. Between them they were able to hold more than 1,100 men, making the city the largest garrison in provincial Ireland.[21]

CORK

In September 1690, ten days after King William's return to England after humiliation at Limerick, the capital of north Munster, his commander-in-chief, the Earl of Marlborough (who was Tyrconnell's brother-in-law) set sail from Portsmouth, having hastily assembled an 82-ship armada. The mission was to seize Cork, the capital of south Munster, and thereby weaken communication lines between the Jacobites and their French sponsors.

Cork before the Confederate wars had been similar to Limerick and Waterford: an Old English urban community enjoying strong commercial links with France and the English West Country, and a record of hostility towards the new religion and, more obliquely, towards New English settlers in their midst. Since the 1580s the latter had infiltrated much of Cork's hinterland, and New English merchants gained a strong foothold in the nearby ports of Kinsale and Youghal in the decades leading up to 1641 – but not in Cork city itself. There, nearly every building in the city and suburbs was still owned by an Old English family in 1640, in what was a bustling, expanding town dominated by a small knot of inter-connected families. The Confederate wars changed all that: after the outbreak of the 1641 rebellion, thanks to a large garrison, military control of the city remained in royalist and therefore Protestant hands. But Protestant disillusion with the royalist cause led in 1644 to a tactical switch of allegiance to the English Parliament. This in turn led to the wholesale expulsion of its 'Irish and Catholic' citizenry that summer, a poor return for their huge financial outlay in support of the royalist cause over the previous three years. It was indeed a highly controversial action by the garrison commander, the Earl of Inchiquin, but it set the precedent for urban 'cleansing' in other cities over the next dozen years. Some of the empty Cork 'city' houses were taken by the 'English' inhabitants of the suburbs, and many of those displaced from the city travelled no further than Cove Lane or Shandon (where, it seems, a Catholic chapel was established in 1645). Some of the expelled were briefly re-admitted in 1649 when the garrison's loyalties changed again, only to be ejected once more when the city surrendered quietly to Cromwell later that year. From 1649 the island parishes for the first time became overwhelmingly Protestant, with some of the new residents having Munster roots, but many of them were immigrants.

By 1661 the 'English' constituted 65 per cent of tax-paying adults within the walls and 46 per cent of the city and suburbs overall. In the following quarter century, this essentially new urban community was responsible for a commercial transformation of the port, making Cork a far busier place than either Limerick or Galway. The old merchant families managed to recover some of their city properties in the 1660s, but they played only a secondary role in the boom.[22]

In military terms Cork remained a vulnerable site. The old walled city was a mere 14 hectares on the low alluvial ground between channels of the River Lee, with a central stream intersecting the city and a secure wharf within the walls offering protection to trading vessels (see Plate 1). Despite being overlooked both to the south and north, the city had seemed well protected, guarded by its fourteen mural towers, two great gates overlooking the bridges, and walls that were higher and more substantial than Limerick's. Periodic flooding severely tested the walls, and the suburbs, which had been extended onto the nearby hills, only to suffer spoliation in the 1640s, were always at risk in wartime. And the cycle of mushrooming growth followed by suburban destruction was to be repeated once again in the second half of the century.

In the age of artillery, Cork was peculiarly at risk. After the shock of Spanish invasion at Kinsale (1601), early improvements in the city's defences had focused not on strengthening or extending the walls but on fortifying the approaches, beginning with the great fort on Haulbowline island (1602–04), and including a series of modest fortifications near each headland at the Harbour mouth some 20 kilometres downstream. In the 1620s the bastioned Elizabeth Fort was erected on an elevated site beside the city's southern approaches, while at the same time the two city gatehouses were repurposed as gaols. Little more was done to strengthen Cork in the Restoration period, the regional focus being on a massive investment in fortifications overlooking the naval station at Kinsale.[23]

In 1687 the remodelled Corporation of Cork passed back into Catholic control. The Jacobite governor, Roger MacElligott, was determined to hold the city for James despite large numbers of disaffected Protestants still residing there. But once Marlborough's flotilla appeared in the Harbour, to be joined by Dutch and Danish Williamite forces arriving from inland Munster, there was little prospect of a successful defence. MacElligott was urged to burn the city and withdraw; instead he burnt the suburbs, which by that point housed around double the population of the walled city, and tried to strengthen the city's defences. He held out for a mere six days of destructive bombardment and, after some prevarication, was forced to surrender on disastrous terms: his officers ended up in the Tower of London and the rest of the garrison fared even worse. Marlborough promptly departed to greater things.[24]

Given Cork's importance over the next 125 years as a strategic source of naval provisions and of foodstuffs for overseas consumption, the city's defences remained surprisingly weak. Its location, tucked deep inside Cork Harbour gave it natural protection, but a report in 1733 on the state of the walls discovered a huge degree of encroachment by private building, with no fewer than thirty-six houses partly built on the footprint of the walls. From the 1760s on, military engineers fretted over Cork's vulnerabilities to external attack in wartime, and it was only in the Revolutionary and Napoleonic era that large-scale marine fortifications were constructed in the lower harbour.[25]

The walled city on the marsh retained its Protestant character for most of the eighteenth century. Remarkably, land access was limited to the two narrow bridges until a third one was built in 1760. Outside, the extramural parishes became overwhelmingly Catholic, a pattern of segregation almost as marked as in Derry. However, the walls of Cork, having neither defensive nor symbolic power, were untidily dismantled, some becoming quays, some recycled into adjacent buildings. Only the two great gates survived as landmarks, both rebuilt to be massive gaols for city and county in the 1720s.[26]

WATERFORD AND KILKENNY

The third of the great Munster ports, Waterford, 13 kilometres from open sea, had once been the most substantial city in the south of the country and its walls the strongest, enclosing an area of 23 hectares, but its housing stock was mainly plaster and timber, unlike the stone tower-houses of Cork city and Limerick. With up to fifteen gates, twenty-three mural towers and sections of its defences double-walled, it was still regarded as the second city of Elizabethan Ireland with a superb anchorage along the river. In the late sixteenth century its defences were considerably modernized, and an impressive new artillery fortress built downstream at Duncannon signalled the strategic importance of the approaches. The city's thirty or so 'tribes' were then at the peak of their commercial influence and political autonomy, maintaining intimate links with Bristol and strong Continental connections, and enjoying a sophisticated material culture. But in the early seventeenth century, Waterford became the loudest centre of Catholic resistance to the Crown's religious policies, and this led to the total suspension of the city's charters and liberties in the 1620s, lasting some years. At the same time, a new citadel was built by the government to the west of the city with, perhaps menacingly, four cannon mounted on a platform facing into the city. But after the outbreak of the 1641 rebellion the city's leaders only came out in support of the Confederate Catholic cause many months later and after intense civic turmoil.

Waterford was subject to two Cromwellian sieges (in 1649 and 1650), the first successfully resisted, the second, a two-month siege, ending in a brisk surrender on terms. The Cromwellian regime began to expel the Catholic population beyond the walls in 1651 and to install a new set of burghers. As in Galway and Limerick, they partially succeeded in the first aim, and completely so in the second: an entirely new cadre of families took control of the Corporation when civic government was revived, and a large number of well-connected Waterford trading families decamped, principally to Saint-Malo. In the Restoration years some of these returned 'with much more experience in traffic and commerce . . . [than that] of all their predecessors', but most did not. The city's economic fortunes recovered somewhat, with both old and new families involved in overseas trade, but its physical expansion was much less dramatic than that of Cork, its old streets being 'narrow, thrust close and pent together', and there was limited overspill beyond the walls. Thomas Phillips, the great military engineer, gave a pessimistic assessment in 1685 both of the city's defences and of those at Duncannon, and he argued for a massive fortification on the heights over Passage village downstream.[27]

Here the transition back to Catholic control in 1687 was relatively easy as it reflected the religious division of wealth. After the Jacobite defeat at the Boyne, Waterford was hurriedly prepared to resist the Williamite advance. Suburbs were destroyed and the city garrisoned. But the governor (John Barrett, a Corkman) surrendered the city at the first sight of a Williamite army in order, it was said, to win good terms for his own regiments, but a less than satisfactory one for the civilians. Nevertheless the properties, real and personal, of the defendants were not on this occasion forfeited.

Waterford thereafter remained a religiously mixed city, with Catholic worship inside the walls tolerated from the 1690s and Catholic merchants holding a substantial share of the city's trade; unlike Cork, there was no suggestion of religious segregation. The most dramatic physical change in the early eighteenth century was the removal of the walls along the river, a process that commenced in the 1690s, thereby creating the 'noblest quay in Europe' (Mark Girouard's accolade), which eventually stretched for more than a paved mile along the river-front and became the city's most striking feature.[28]

Waterford enjoyed a defining attribute that it shared with only one other Irish city: a prime location near the estuary of a complex river system. In the case of the similarly endowed Derry, there was little potential for upstream competition from other towns (even with a canal, Strabane posed no threat to Derry's overseas trade). But in Waterford's case, there were no less than four other urban centres set close to navigable water across the city's hinterland: to the west some distance up the Suir valley was the walled town of Carrick, which became a kind of industrial satellite of Waterford; further west again and just beyond the Suir's navigable limits was the strategically located walled town of Clonmel that experienced its own seventeenth-century horror story with the Cromwellian siege of 1649. Trade along the Suir was traditionally conducted by the many 'flat-bottomed boats, that carry from fifteen to twenty tons; and the most water they draw when loaded, does not exceed four feet, [and they] . . . carry up goods to the towns of Clonmel and Carrick'.[29]

Water transport was always faster and cheaper for bulk goods, and this kept the rivers busy. Waterford's ancient rival in overseas trade was New Ross to the north-east, the medieval town lying up the easily navigable River Barrow and enjoying direct access to Waterford Harbour downstream of the city. But New Ross's great days were past and by the seventeenth century the only urban centre in the region comparable in size and wealth to Waterford was Kilkenny: lying far up the more modest River Nore, it was designated a city by James I in 1609. It was already well established as the seigneurial capital of the Ormond lordship and possessed no less than three sets of walls, two on the west bank enclosing High Town and Irish Town, and one on the east, St John's. Irish Town (or St Canice's) on the north side remained a separate corporation, the personal fiefdom of the bishop, with only the modest River Breagagh marking the boundary. Uniquely in Ireland, Kilkenny became a city of commercial consequence despite its inland location, being more than 25 kilometres above the navigable limits of the Nore at Inistioge.

Having enjoyed the prestige of hosting the Confederate assembly of the Catholics of Ireland for half a dozen years, Kilkenny had its nemesis in 1649 when, plague-ridden, it surrendered to Cromwell after a six-day siege, its burghers paying over a punitive fine. Civic government continued for several more years before an attempt was made to expel Catholic property owners, in some cases to distant counties to the west. But this was executed even more imperfectly than elsewhere, and in 1660 precisely half the population within the walls and almost all those outside the walls were listed as 'Irish'. For the most part, the old families got a foothold back in the city in Restoration times, and all benefited from the Duke of Ormond's expansive project to transform Kilkenny Castle and environs into a French-style palace quarter. Catholic chapels were rebuilt although, despite attempts to reopen worship within the walls, they remained in the suburbs.[30]

Kilkenny navigated the fleeting Jacobite ascendancy without dire consequences. Indeed, both James and William stayed briefly in the city, and some 500 Catholic inhabitants signed an oath of loyalty to the new regime. There was no talk of clearing the town of its Catholic citizens again, and it remained a strongly Catholic urban community in the eighteenth century. Its complex system of walls and gates was only slowly dismantled, and a visitor to the city in 1779 was struck by the fact there were still nine gates standing. The most dramatic change in Kilkenny's evolution was the collapse of the house of

Ormond and the forfeiture of the Butler estates, coming after the second duke's flight to Jacobite exile in 1715. Yet the political and economic impact of the golden years associated with his grandfather, the first duke, continued to be felt in Kilkenny far into the eighteenth century.[31]

DUBLIN

The three east-coast ports of consequence, Dublin, Drogheda and Belfast escaped physical destruction in the Williamite war, but in each case it was a close call.

Dublin's capacity to withstand siege had not been tested since the early sixteenth century, and indeed the small walled heart of the city – encompassing the royal castle, one of the two cathedrals, and the commercial core on the south bank – had not been captured since the twelfth century. But in the chaos after the sudden outbreak of the 1641 rebellion, the extreme defencelessness of the city was obvious: the walls were 'much decayed and have no flankers' and the castle was little better, with 'no modern fortification', and the 'crazy' towers were reckoned likely to crumble when the ordnance mounted on them came to be used. The city was isolated militarily by 1642, becoming a vast refugee camp for a mixed population surviving under the royalist flag. Parts of the suburbs, including much of the south-west Liberties, were deliberately razed. The city was threatened with full-scale assault by a Confederate army in autumn 1646 but in the end, despite there being only a makeshift garrison, the city was not attacked. The political complexion of government in Dublin Castle changed the following year after the peaceful royalist surrender by the then Earl of Ormond to a sea-borne Parliamentary force, but two years later a combined royalist/Confederate army led by Ormond returned in strength to reverse the handover. The Parliamentary garrison was outnumbered, but at that point the military governor, Michael Jones, expelled all Catholics from the city (who promptly set up camp in Finglas). Ormond's army approached within a mile of the city walls, but was taken by surprise and heavily defeated by Jones's agile tactics. Dublin's old walls were not a factor in Jones's victory, but what may have helped was the huge earthen rampart erected by the Irish government in the early days of the war: 8 feet high, it was erected around the city on both sides of the Liffey, enclosing the much swollen suburbs on the north, the south and the east of the walled town, and was 'reinforced by at least 18 bastions positioned at regular intervals'. In all, it was nearly 4 miles in length (and once again it involved the destruction of houses lying outside the new defensive line). These works gave some protection from enemy cannon and allowed the government to manage the huge influx into the city; they also marked the line beyond which Catholic inhabitants were briefly expelled in 1649.[32]

Dublin's emergence as undisputed first city of Ireland had begun in the sixteenth century. This was tied closely to the rising power of the state and, by extension, of English authority over the island as a whole, militarily, legally and administratively. From the first decade of the seventeenth century the once-dominant Old English families lost ground on many fronts, religious, commercial, fiscal and constitutional, as New English and Dutch merchants became the local great traders, and Dublin Castle, with its broadly New English agenda, was increasingly the arbiter of the city's future. That process had already transformed Dublin by 1641, but the long-run effect of the rebellion and the Commonwealth regime was to accentuate the process. Catholic households had still formed a large majority in every city parish in 1630 except for two near the Castle that lay inside the walls. The religious balance was changing even before 1649, and although the Catholic expulsion was mitigated during the 1650s, Protestant households formed four-fifths of the total in every parish within the walled city in 1660, and formed just over a half the total in the suburbs on the north side.[33]

By then Dublin was well on the way to become 'a little London', a centre of fashionable seasonal residence, a financial hub and the busiest port, but also now a 'metropolis without fortification'. The first signs of extramural property speculation were evident in the Restoration period both north and south of the old city. And although the city's first Custom House (built c. 1621 on reclaimed land) lay downstream of the city, the business heart was still located within the walls: the premier merchants were based along the old spine from High St to Castle St, or down nearer the river on Cook St. Even the retail markets that operated outside the walls along Thomas St did so within the zone protected by the extra-mural St James's Gate. Dublin was still a city of cage-work and highly combustible houses, but a sign of things to come was the construction of a formal entrance to the city from the east. At the instigation of the Earl of Essex (Lord Lieutenant, 1672–77), Essex St became the new point of entry from the quays, and it was dominated by two sets of arcaded buildings ('piazzas'), small malls for new-style shops.[34]

After James's accession in 1685, the Corporation and the Jacobite government veered towards an increasingly assertive promotion of Catholic interests within the city. With a new charter and a Catholic majority in the line-up of aldermen, Protestant control slipped away quite quickly. The city's large Protestant population began to take ship in 1688, but about two-thirds of them stayed behind, and Anglican churches remained open until very near the end of Tyrconnell's government. With armies of the rival kings resting on the island for nine months before the first decisive engagement at the Boyne, the city's defences were hardly touched, and there is little evidence of defence planning. Indeed there had been almost no investment in the city's defences since the 1640s; Essex had championed the idea of a giant citadel to the east of the city in the 1670s, and there were plans for something similar on St Stephen's Green in the early 1680s; meanwhile major sections of the walls were taken down. In what would have been the ultimate exposure of Dublin's weakness, there was also a strong possibility at the time of the Jacobite retreat after the Boyne that the garrison would systematically set fire to the undefended city before retreating westwards. This plan was overruled by James himself. Instead, Tyrconnell's government withdrew hurriedly, leaving its Protestant citizens to take charge again and prepare a welcome for William.[35]

In the following century defensive concerns had little bearing on Dublin's growth. Plans for the great citadel to guard the bay never materialized, and although the construction of a giant fortress was begun upstream on a corner of the Phoenix Park *c.* 1709, the project was abandoned shortly afterwards. In the city itself at least three of the principal mural gates were dismantled around that time and the remaining walls were smothered or despoiled by private building and neglect. And of the great earthen rampart there was no sign on eighteenth-century maps. With a Protestant majority until the mid century, there was no sense of any internal threat to the city.[36]

DROGHEDA

Drogheda, a serious rival to medieval Dublin, maintained its very extensive system of walls encompassing twin towns lying north and south of the River Boyne far longer than did any other city in the south of Ireland. Millmount, a medieval fort high above the south bank, reinforced the sense of ample defence. Yet during the seventeenth century the town, a critical stopping point on the road from Dublin to east Ulster, was subject to three sieges, one of which in 1649 was devastating. With its rich north Leinster hinterland and its close but more troubled relationship with south Ulster, Drogheda had all the marks of a wealthy town with deep roots. Its Old English merchant community had close ties with the Old English gentry of Fingall and Meath and – like them – it remained for the most part Catholic in religion. However, in 1641 the town did not follow the 'Pale Lords' into an alliance with the Ulster rebels, and was instead placed under a three-month siege by Confederate forces. A precursor of events in Derry in 1689, the town was then relieved by sea when a downstream boom was breached. Drogheda remained a government outpost throughout the 1640s; its governors were royalist, then parliamentary, then royalist again in their allegiance. It was the garrison's particular misfortune to be the first Irish town to be targeted by Cromwell's vast army in 1649, and the refusal of the then (English) governor to surrender led to the slaughter of over 2,000 soldiers and an unknown number of civilians. Yet, despite the notoriety of this event, post-Cromwellian Drogheda was not as profoundly 'reformed' as were the Munster cities: it remained a religiously mixed town with some wealthy merchants and, unlike the Old English 'tribes' of Waterford and Galway, a small number of the dominant pre-war families managed to retain substantial urban assets after 1660.[37]

The Boyne was the preferred Jacobite line of defence in 1689 against the Williamite army that had landed in Belfast Lough, and Drogheda itself became the first Jacobite rallying point. But when the rival armies eventually met the following summer, 'the glorious battle' took place around the fordable sections of the river 5 kilometres upstream. The Drogheda garrison was not involved, but when it was challenged a day after William's victory, the Jacobite governor's ploy was to force the town's Protestants out 'under the section of wall earmarked for bombardment'. However, his officers insisted on prompt surrender and were granted easy terms: 'the inhabitants were assured they would not be deprived of their possessions', which it seems was honoured, and just a few years later the town struck one visitor as 'a handsome clean English-like town'. Indeed, the Corporation actively opposed any tincture of Scottish influence and resisted a proposal to build a Presbyterian meeting house in the town.[38]

Drogheda's capacious walls stood for another century, not for reasons of sentiment but because there was ample unbuilt ground within the circuit available for development, and perhaps also because of their unusual solidity (see Plate 2). Millmount, now a large barracks, continued to loom over the town. The gates on the north side were still being locked (late at night), and it was only in the 1790s at the time of the town's greatest expansion, that piecemeal demolition of gates and walls began. However St Laurence's, the great east-facing barbican gate, survived, a powerful symbol of the town's medieval wealth (see Plate 6).[39]

Belfast by contrast had few symbols or scars from the past at the start of the eighteenth century. It was from the beginning a proprietorial town, established around the riverside castle by Arthur Chichester, soldier, politician and plantation projector. In 1603–04 he had secured huge lowland land grants in south Antrim, including parts of the north shore of Belfast Lough around Carrickfergus and at the mouth of the River Lagan. But Belfast (unlike Bandon, a similarly scaled plantation town in west Cork that was strongly fortified) was not tightly managed, and Chichester did not invest in either walls or other defence works, although his own castle (near High St) was heavily defended, and for good measure he kept total control of the new corporation. Located beside the lowest ford across the still wooded River Lagan, Belfast grew rapidly in the early seventeenth century, an open settlement and a revolving door for immigrants from Scotland and England. Its vulnerability was revealed when the Ulster rebellion erupted in 1641: at first 'most of the inhabitants fled or [were] flying' to the security of Carrickfergus castle, 18 kilometres away. But within a year an earthen rampart with a 'wet ditch' and large bastions was thrown up to protect the town from the Ulster Irish. In fact, the predators turned out to be the Scots. Initially garrisoned by regiments loyal to Dublin and English rule, Belfast was seized by trickery in 1644 by Robert Monro, the Scottish army general in Ulster. Over the next four years it became in effect a Scottish town and, even though Scottish military control was ended in a similarly bloodless stroke in 1648, the legacy of those years was profound.[40]

It was nominally a royalist enclave in 1649 when a section of Cromwell's army arrived at the ramparts shortly after the fall of Drogheda: there was a four-day stand-off, possibly a skirmish, before a surrender on easy terms. It was later claimed that 800 Scots were turned out of the town, together with their wives and children, but any such expulsion (if indeed it occurred) was only temporary. The Chichesters had had no role in the town since 1644, and they did not recover control till 1656. During this time there was a marked influx of Scottish traders, and some became remarkably successful Restoration merchants and shipowners (see Plate 3). But the subsequent permissive attitude of the Chichesters towards Presbyterianism was critical in deepening this Scottish ascendancy.[41]

In 1689 the Williamite army entered a town remarkably unscathed by war. Yet five months earlier a Jacobite army, sent from Dublin to overawe east Ulster, had caused panic as it approached Belfast: 'the whole inhabitants and merchants (a few excepted) transported themselves and families into Scotland and other parts', abandoning the town. But Thomas Pottinger, a veteran Presbyterian merchant who had been appointed sovereign of the reconstituted Corporation by Tyrconnell, stayed behind and almost singlehandedly (or so he claimed) managed through diplomacy and largesse to secure the town from looting and destruction.

Belfast's status as a Presbyterian stronghold was – if anything – enhanced after the embarrassments of 1689. But then after two decades of growth there was a palpable brake on the town's expansion: bitter disputes erupted over the governance of the town following the legal exclusion of Presbyterians from civic office in 1704, and the long withdrawal of the Chichester family compounded the malaise. It is striking that in an estate map of the town in 1757 the ramparts of 1642 (now tree-lined) still defined its boundary. But the innate strengths of Belfast – its location within a growing Ulster proto-industrial economy, its potential for physical expansion as a port, and its restless and unrestricted merchant community – were revealed in the great revival of its fortunes evident from the 1750s.[42]

LEGACIES

Irish cities in 1700 were therefore a mixed lot. A history of destructive siege warfare, over now but not forgotten, was by no means unique to Ireland. Not far away, Colchester and Dundee had had their own recent experience of horrific sieges.[43] But the Irish tally was very high: every one of our ten urban communities had experienced at least one siege or blockade since 1641, and eight had endured multiple sieges and/or blockades over that time; the same number (or more) had seen the forced movement of urban populations, some temporary, some permanent, some a short distance, some to distant parts, and all very imperfectly executed. And the suburbs in at least five of the ten were systematically razed on at least one occasion after 1641, an indication that most extramural housing was probably of timber or mud-wall construction and easily cleared (although the inner Cork suburbs, wilfully destroyed by McElligott in 1690, seem to have been more substantial).[44]

Unlike Puritan Northampton, which had its walls pulled down in retribution by Charles II in the early years of the Restoration, the walls and earthen ramparts of Irish cities faded slowly and uneventfully. By the mid eighteenth century five of the ten centres had, it seems, demolished substantial proportions of their gates, bastions and stonework defences, and by 1800 only Drogheda and Derry still possessed prominent walls.[45] But did the passing of these reminders of the past really matter? Local resistance to their removal in early nineteenth-century Derry suggests it could matter a great deal where a particular set of walls was freighted with historical meaning. But Derry apart, no urban community at this time articulated much concern about legacy monuments: thus medieval market crosses, the historic centre point of several towns, disappeared without notice from eighteenth-century Galway, Kilkenny and Waterford, and the medieval cathedrals in Cork and Waterford, by then Anglican places of worship, were totally demolished in the course of the century without a murmur. Yet in most cities, motifs from the municipal past were conscripted to legitimize and enrich corporate material culture: the ancient armorial and other heraldic devices – the city gates or castles – were inscribed on the maces, banners and paintings, the freedom boxes and other silverware which together formed the conspicuous trappings of Protestant urban elites, who saw no irony in honouring their civic past with these time-honoured symbols.[46]

2
PEOPLING THE CITIES

Dubliners who purchased the first printing of John Rocque's map of the city in 1756 or those who read the first *Dublin Magazine* in 1762 were treated to a re-issue of the diminutive map of the city that had been produced in 1610 by John Speed, and they were invited to wonder at how Dublin had changed 'in little more than a century and a half, from the lowest ebb of wretchedness and contempt, to almost the summit of elegance, extent and magnificence'. Readers could now share an urban world transformed. Such civic self-congratulation was a mid-century conceit, but reflections on the striking physical growth of Dublin, Cork and later Belfast became almost commonplace. One writer, commenting in 1788 on the 'prodigious' growth of Dublin over the previous thirty years, suggested that 'the above increase ... would be an alarming circumstance did not the great provincial cities of Cork, Limerick, Belfast etc. increase in the same, or rather in a greater proportion, which is by no means the case in England'. And another enthusiast for Dublin's 'amazingly extensive' increase of buildings, writing in 1793, saw it all as positive: 'no city can increase in size if the wealth of the country did not supply the means'. But no one probed the causes of the growth of the cities, although there was some awareness of its environmental effects, notably in the writing of John Rutty, Dublin apothecary and polymath (1698–1775), who sought to establish the links between weather, economic activity and the changing patterns of disease in the capital city.[1]

Pre-industrial cities across Europe depended for their survival on attracting a constant flow of outsiders to come and settle. People came for a great variety of motives and faced very uncertain outcomes. Irish evidence on this phenomenon is exceptionally thin and oblique at best, and any attempt to get a sense of the underlying demographic processes at work before the first national census of 1821 must rest on the interpretation of shards and archival fragments.[2] By

English or west European standards, both central and local government were underdeveloped and so the gathering of social data (or what might later be interpreted as social data) was very late in coming; most of the limited demographic information that we have for the period comes from Church of Ireland sources, and what is extant is but a fraction of what was available before the destruction of the Public Record Office of Ireland in 1922. Only at the very end of the eighteenth century was there a rigorous investigation of any city population, that of Dublin in 1798 by the Reverend James Whitelaw. In his commentary on the results he sought to understand, and if possible to reverse, the huge social contrasts within the capital city, but he threw no light on where his Dubliners had come from. Whitelaw's census marks the beginnings of urban social enquiry in Ireland, but only his abstracts survived the events of 1922.[3]

For comparative purposes we have to start with the 1821 census. An immediate problem arises as (other than in the case of Dublin) little effort was made in the published census schedules to distinguish between strictly urban populations and the total population resident within corporate boundaries, which included many residing in unambiguously rural areas, and this sometimes (as in the case of Cork city) added considerably to official 'urban' totals. The 1821 totals in Table 2.1 try to take account of this problem and eliminate the non-urban element.

The only earlier point of comparison for the 1821 civic totals is the nation-wide return of poll taxpayers of 1660/1. This was generated by an unusually

Table 2.1
Urban Population Estimates: 1660/1 and 1821

	Estimated civilian population 1660/1	Civilian population 1821
Derry	2,349	9,313
Sligo	1,415	9,283
Galway	n.a.	27,775
Limerick	3,964	43,978
Cork	7,627	80,114
Waterford	2,508	26,514
Kilkenny	3,802	23,230
Dublin	34,800	227,335
Drogheda	3,570	18,118
Belfast	1,708	37,390

Sources: 1660/1: *A Census of Ireland circa 1659*, ed. Séamus Pender, with introduction by W.J. Smyth (2nd edn Dublin, 2002); *Census of Ireland, 1821*.

Note: Smyth's suggested median multiplier of 2.9 (Pender, *Census* (2002), p. xiv) has been applied to poll-tax returns to generate civilian population estimates. For fuller analysis of both series, see Appendices 2 and 3.

ambitious direct taxation initiative overseen by William Petty, physician, administrator, and Cromwellian surveyor extraordinaire, who alone in seventeenth-century Ireland had the organizational capacity or the curiosity to complete such a project. But the poll-tax returns are highly problematic: there are uncertainties as to how far enumeration procedures were standardized, and it is impossible to determine whether the collapse of the Commonwealth/Protectorate government in May 1660 and the restoration of the monarchy affected local population movements.[4]

Two things are strongly suggested by a comparison of these two data series: that all Irish cities and regional centres witnessed powerful long-term growth of population, albeit at rather different rates; and second, that the rank order remained surprisingly constant over a century and a half. If we take the 1660 series at face value, a comparison with 1821 suggests a growth rate of around 1.3 per cent per annum over 160 years, which can be compared with a rate of around 0.75 per cent for the top ten British cities each year between the 1660s and 1801. The highest growth rates appear to have been in Belfast, Cork, Limerick and Waterford; those below the mean were Drogheda, Dublin, Kilkenny and Sligo, with Derry trailing at a rate less than half that of its east Ulster rival. But the growth trajectories were probably quite dissimilar, Dublin and Cork witnessing their most rapid growth in the century *before* 1760, all the others an acceleration in the sixty years *after* 1760. In rank order, Dublin and Cork stand out as first and second cities in both series, and the pole position of Limerick (3rd of 9) and Waterford (6th) did not change either. However Derry and the secondary Leinster centres of Kilkenny and Drogheda seem to have lost position. Dublin's primacy in 1660, slightly larger than the other nine centres *in toto* (whatever assumptions are made for the missing data for Galway), had slipped significantly by 1821; by then the capital constituted around 44 per cent of the aggregate population of the ten centres, and it was to lose even more ground before the trend was reversed late in the nineteenth century.[5]

MORTALITY

Behind this superficially benign scenario lie a number of issues: were cities a healthier environment than the small towns and rural locations from which migrants were drawn? And if not, why did they continue to come in numbers sufficient to swell every city? Bubonic (and possibly pneumonic) plague in its horrific mid seventeenth-century visitations affected first and most severely Irish cities and large towns, notably Galway and Dublin (although it was not restricted to the towns). Plague never reappeared after the 1650s, but the fear remained. But, plague apart, we can assume from the abundant comparative evidence from England that urban life expectancy in Ireland remained significantly lower than in the countryside, particularly for infants and children. The strength of this 'urban graveyard' effect in England has been questioned, but it was probably a near-universal feature of pre-industrial urban life in good years and in bad. Yet, as we have seen, when war or harvest failure brought crisis in the countryside, people flocked to the towns and cities: in the eighteenth century the worst years for rural Ireland were the late 1720s and the first half of the 1740s. At both times the existence of large-scale relief schemes in the cities (and the near total absence of poor relief outside) led to a major influx of malnourished and often diseased migrants, whose presence heightened indigenous urban mortality. But in the worst of times, as in 1740/41, it is unlikely that death rates in the southern cities reached the devastating heights so evident in their hinterlands: the Church of Ireland burial registers for Holy Trinity in Cork and St Peter's in Dublin suggest only a modest elevation in 1740 (37.5 and 40.2 per cent above the 1736 to 1745 decennial average), and even less in 1741 when famine fevers were at their most virulent outside the cities. But the rural crisis was fully reflected in the busy register for St Mary's in Limerick (recording, it seems, the interment of all comers): burials there in 1741 were almost three-fold (265.6 per cent) above the decennial average. However, even in more normal times Irish coastal cities had their particular health dangers. As international ports they were the gateways for new pathogens, and as the location for large concentrations of unskilled male labour engaged in seasonal port-related work they provided excellent sites for the transmission of infection into the countryside.[6]

Smallpox emerged as the single greatest cause of urban death in late seventeenth-century Europe, and its devastating impact on children and young adults only began to lessen in the final decades of the eighteenth century (whether because of mutations in the virus, the early impact of inoculation, or through a process of endemicization).[7] There was ample evidence of this in Ireland. In Derry, in the first half of the eighteenth century infant and child burials regularly made up two-thirds of all interments, the proportion occasionally flaring up in some seasons to 90 per cent, reflecting the lethal impact of smallpox and, more occasionally, influenza and measles epidemics. Belfast also suffered huge losses from smallpox, as in the awful summer of 1733, and the death toll in St Patrick's in Waterford was significantly greater that year than even in the famine years of 1740/41. The Dublin bills of mortality, published weekly for more than a century from 1661, had they survived, might have provided a fuller picture (even though they were gathered exclusively by Anglican parish officers). But for a few years between 1682 and 1755 they do survive, and they highlight the occasional horrors of smallpox epidemics: in 5 of the 23 years for which bills survive, smallpox accounted for more than 20 per cent of all deaths, and in the second half of 1696 'when the smallpox did rage in Dublin' it accounted for over 40 per cent of all deaths. Such rates seem to have been significantly higher than in contemporary London (which in most respects was a more deadly environment for the young than Dublin, or presumably any Irish city). In the years 1712 to 1718 and 1724 to 1731, children aged under 16 made up over half of all recorded deaths in Dublin, with the figure reaching 58.7 per cent of the total in 1714 and 61.6 in 1730 (see Appendix 4).[8]

The virulence of infectious diseases ebbed and flowed for the next half century, with seasons of acute food shortage in the countryside often followed by an epidemic peak in the cities, as in the disastrous summer of 1740, or the hungry summer of 1745 when, John Rutty recalled, 'the small-pox were [sic] brought to us [in Dublin] by a conflux of beggars from the north [of Ireland], occasioned by the late scarcity there, whose children, full of the small-pox, were frequently exposed on our streets'; and in the following months up to 27 deaths per week in Dublin were attributed to smallpox. But then in the relatively favourable years 1752 to 1754, the under-16 cohort contributed only 41.7 per cent of the burials recorded in the Dublin bills. In Dublin's great industrial parish of St Catherine's, child burials between 1729 and 1742 in the Church of Ireland cemetery had been close to this (averaging 40.5 per cent), but again the recurring epidemics of the early 1730s brought a child mortality peak of 60.6 per cent of recorded burials in 1732.[9]

There are other shards of evidence confirming the pernicious levels of infant and child death in the city environment. The huge Dublin Foundling Hospital, established in 1730 for abandoned newborn babies from town and country, became notorious for its exceptionally high death rates; it seems that more than three-quarters of the thousands of infants that were taken into its care over the next sixty years perished either within its walls or in the care of its country nurses. Foundling hospitals in London and Paris had a bad, but not quite so notorious, record and whether the vast toll of infant death in Dublin reflected high child mortality rates occurring outside the hospital, or simply a greater degree of neglect within the institution, is unclear. It was not until the early nineteenth century that survival rates in the Foundling nursery fell below 30 per cent of the intake. Probably all that can be taken from the desperate history of the hospital is evidence of a marked change in public attitudes: from indifference in the 1750s to isolated campaigns of reform in the 1760s and 1780s, to a full-blooded parliamentary exposé in 1797 of 'facts [about the hospital] which carry a complexion of more than average cruelty', finally leading to reform of its governance and a marked fall in infant deaths. But at the other end of the social scale it is striking that in St Thomas's parish in the north-east quarter of Dublin, then the most fashionable parish in the city, infants and persons designated as 'son' or 'daughter of' perished in alarming numbers in the 1760s and 1770s: they constituted 54.8 per cent of the total Church of Ireland burials between 1766 and 1769, 49.8 per cent in the 1770s. However, in the 1780s there were signs of real improvement, with the young then forming only 35.7 per cent of burials.[10]

A further hint of the heavy burden of child loss in the cities comes from Eversley's longitudinal study of the demography of Irish Quakers, based on the reconstitution of some 1,300 families, at least two-fifths of whom were based in Cork, Dublin, Limerick or Waterford. Eversley's results indicate a rise in infant and child mortality rates from around 275 per 1,000 in the second half of the seventeenth century to over 350 in the first half of the eighteenth century, falling to just over 300 in the second half, and then a very marked improve-ment after 1800.[11] Quaker families were generally of high or middling status, but evidence from Dublin's maternity hospital, the Rotunda, in operation from 1745, illuminates the experience of lower-status urban families, or at least of the newborn. There was a striking improvement in perinatal survival rates between 1760 and 1800, from a situation where 20.5 per cent of live births were being lost in the first week during the 1760s, falling to 16.9 per cent in the 1770s, then to 7 per cent in the 1780s, continuing to decline to 3.6 per cent in the 1790s, with further more gentle improvement in the following decades. Maternal mortality in the hospital remained stubbornly high for much longer.[12]

FERTILITY

If life expectancy for the young in the cities was unfavourable for most of the eighteenth century but improving in the final decades, what of fertility levels?

But here we have even fewer shards of evidence. The Dublin bills of mortality imply huge changes in the ratio of baptisms to burials for a scattering of years between 1666 and 1754, ranging from a trough of 2.40 burials for every baptism registered between 1712 and 1718 to near parity (1.04) in the years 1752 to 1754. If indeed Protestant Dubliners (making up roughly half of the city at mid century) had such contrasting demographies between the 1710s and 1750s, then something remarkable had happened. Allowing for great imperfections in the data, there is at least the suggestion that the capital in the 1750s may have had the capacity to sustain its numbers without immigration, in stark contrast to a far more adverse environment in the 1710s. Wet-nursing, where it was practiced, may have raised fertility and reduced urban mortality rates within the social groups involved, and it seems to have been accepted practice among professional as well as upper-class families until the end of the century.[13]

In Thomas's study of the Anglican registers for Templemore parish, which included all of Derry city and its extensive city Liberties, spanning the century 1654 to 1750, he found that city burials exceeded city baptisms in every decade after 1670, and that in the first four decades of the eighteenth century burials were running 1.72 times ahead of baptisms. However they reached parity in the 1740s, after which there is a gap in the register. When it resumes in the early nineteenth century, Derry baptisms were far in excess of burials. Less complete Anglican registers for other cities in the *early* eighteenth century echo the Derry pattern, with burial registers recording much heavier business than did the baptismal ones.[14]

Was the apparent natural decrease in Dublin and Derry evidence of depressed fertility in both cities, or simply confirmation that *burial* records encompassed all denominations, or at least all Protestant denominations, while *baptismal* returns related exclusively to the Established Church? If we pursue the former line of argument, what might have reduced overall fertility levels in the cities? A lower proportion of the adult urban population in conjugal relationships might have been one element, reflecting the presence of large numbers of soldiers, unmarried servants and older apprentices, leading to a somewhat higher age of first marriage, at least for males, than applied in rural Ireland. But if there were increasing numbers of servants and apprentices, were these predominantly male? We lack specific occupational data even in the 1821 census to identify servants and soldiers, but the number and gender of servants were noted in a small number of earlier private censuses: in Captain South's census of Dublin in 1695, 17.1 per cent of the city population were classified as servants, but in

James Whitelaw's 1798 census the proportion had fallen to 10.7 per cent. In 1695 females accounted for 56.4 per cent of servants (a much lower proportion than in contemporary London), and a century later the figure had risen to 65.3 per cent (a factor here may have been the increase in journeymen living independently outside their employers' households).[15]

In Sligo 12.5 per cent of the urban population were listed as servants in 1749, and 63.7 per cent of those were female; in a 1779 census of Lisburn, Belfast's old rival up the Lagan, 11.5 per cent of the town's population were returned as servants, with near gender parity. But in a pioneering study of the demography of the small cathedral city of Armagh in 1770, Clarkson was surprised to find that only 3.5 per cent of the population were servants or apprentices. He also found that the city had a very modest mean household size of 3.9 individuals (4.1 for Anglican families, 3.9 for Presbyterians and 3.8 for Catholics). Such a finding might suggest the after-effects of a recent epidemic (of which there is no evidence) or, more plausibly, 'a supply of cheap cabins and plenty of jobs [that] enabled young newly married couples to establish households of their own', in other words a young town where the economy was booming and where servants were not required.[16]

Derry provides some fascinating evidence on fertility change: Thomas has produced evidence of a dramatic fall in female age at first marriage, dating from the years after the trauma of the siege. In the four decades *before* the siege the average age of Anglican brides was 27.6 years; in the four decades beginning 1690 the average had fallen to 22.7 years. The sample size is small, but it is tempting to see this acceleration in family formation as a sign of a post-war replenishment of a devastated community by young migrants setting up new households. And for a period after 1690, the time of first conception after marriage seems to have shortened as well. More generally, the trauma of a year or two of economic hardship caused by high food prices or artisan unemployment (or both) was reflected in a temporary fall in live births: thus in St Patrick's parish in Waterford, the near-famine conditions of 1728 saw live births in the parish more than halved, while during the subsistence crisis of 1739 to 1741 live births fell by more than two-thirds below the decennial average (in both 1740 and 1741).[17]

However, the only rigorous analysis of urban fertility in eighteenth-century Ireland comes in Leslie Clarkson's study of Carrick-on-Suir, Waterford's industrial satellite, for which a remarkably detailed census for 1799 survives. It was no longer a prosperous textile town, with evidence of a very considerable absence of young men (away to war or to the Newfoundland fisheries), yet his findings show that this town, reporting a population of 10,907, had an impressive mean household size of 6.3 persons (a census of Drogheda the previous year gives a mean household size of 5.4). Clarkson has estimated a high age of female first marriage (25.9 years), which was probably several years later than that in the surrounding countryside, but it was close to that reported for urban Ireland in the 1841 census (26.6 years). The Carrick census implied an infant mortality rate for the town of 365, about 14 per cent higher than the all-Ireland urban infant mortality rate in 1841, and that more than 70 per cent of all infants and children were dead by the age of 10. We have no clue as to the typicality of these findings, but they do suggest that even in the deeply troubled state of Carrick in 1799 it was nevertheless a town full of children, with 36.7 per cent of the population under the age of 15.[18] That was substantially higher than was reported in Dublin in 1695 (28.4 per cent), in Sligo in 1749 (30.8 per cent), in Lisburn in 1779 (31.2 per cent), or presumptively in Kilkenny in 1731 (where the under 10s were 18.5 per cent, as against 25 per cent in Carrick). But the Carrick child ratio is very close indeed to that reported for all Irish cities in 1821 – apart from Dublin – a hint that the force of the 'urban graveyard' effect may now have been weaker.[19]

MIGRATION AND APPRENTICESHIP

Derry in the 1690s and Carrick in the 1790s suggest contrasting demographic profiles. Derry in the post-siege generation drew in migrants from its north-west hinterland and from Scotland, and new family names populate the Anglican registers. Carrick by the 1790s was a town of declining economic opportunity, perhaps a stepping-stone for country migrants with greater ambitions, but when the town's woollen industry was at its peak half a century earlier, its petty manu-facturers would have depended on a ready supply of short-distance migrants. Indeed we can be confident that no Irish city or regional centre, given the demo-graphic balance sheet, would have grown at any time in the eighteenth century without attracting a constant inward flow of young migrants, and that in the first half of the century, and possibly later, the majority of residents of Irish cities were migrants.[20]

In the seventeenth century there had been repeated attempts on the part of the state to orchestrate migration from England to Irish cities as part of the wider colonial agenda. Sometimes this was successful, as with the initial peopling of Derry; sometimes it was an utter failure as with the Commonwealth's attempts to plant the devastated town of Galway in the mid 1650s with artisans from Gloucester and Liverpool. Indeed all the various attempts to clear the larger walled towns of their Catholic citizenry were predicated on the misplaced belief that adventurers, soldiers and their families from England would quickly fill the vacuum.[21]

A later and less coercive strategy was the series of parliamentary statutes, introduced first in 1662, then reactivated in 1692 and 1703, to remove all economic barriers to civic freedom for foreign craftsmen of the reformed faith, a move that boosted the immigration of Huguenot craft families in the 1680s and 1690s, and of English skilled migrants over a longer period. But most seventeenth-century and all eighteenth-century migration to Irish cities occurred independent of state policy or parliamentary statute. Proprietorial initiatives were rare, although the third Earl of Meath sought settlers from Yorkshire for his Dublin estate in 1683. Even the massive Huguenot migration, while strongly endorsed by governments of differing political colours, was largely shaped by private initiative. And in the short run it had real impact: in the first half of the eighteenth century there were around 900 French-born families or families of recent French extraction in Dublin, constituting well over 5 per cent of the city's population, and significant Huguenot communities were established in Cork and Waterford. They constituted the last wave of external Protestant migration into urban Ireland.[22]

The Irish regions that supplied migrants to the cities greatly varied over time and between occupations. Before the 1841 census revealed the birthplace of urban residents, we have only a few hints as to the geographical origins of migrants. The 1821 census gives one important clue about the origin of migrant Dubliners: the three contiguous counties surrounding the capital, Kildare, Meath and Wicklow, had the lowest population densities in the whole country, and migration to the city was one ingredient in that pattern. But for the eighteenth century we have to turn to the few apprenticeship registers extant for Dublin and Cork. Craft apprenticeship in Ireland in its legal definition was very similar to the English institution, an apprentice being party to what was conventionally a seven-year contract. A down payment was required at the commencement of the term, for which the master undertook to impart the necessary skills and training, to provide bed, board and clothing, and to act *in loco parentis*.

A gradual fall in the age of apprenticeship in seventeenth- and eighteenth-century London (from a median entry point of 17.4 years in the sixteenth century to 14.7 by the early nineteenth century) had obvious ramifications on family formation and youth culture there, but we lack such age-specific data for Irish apprentices. Indeed we do not even know the age of the thirteen apprentice boys of Derry who closed the city gates in 1688. There are other instances of gangs of Protestant apprentice boys engaging in muscular protest in the late seventeenth century, notably in Dublin where they were involved in violent protests in 1671 over the construction of a new bridge, and in attacks on a Catholic chapel in 1678 and on Huguenot immigrants on May Day 1682. But references to eighteenth-century apprentices imply that they were little more than children, younger than university freshmen, and not at all like the adult and far less biddable journeymen, who were young men in their twenties; one Dublin writer in 1795 assumed that 15 was the typical entry age to apprenticeship.[23]

The longest time series on apprentices comes from the Dublin Company of Goldsmiths, a guild that was re-established in 1637. It was always a high-status craft, and master gold- and silversmiths could command a high apprenticeship fee, perhaps ten times that which a master hosier or shoemaker would receive. Between 1660 and 1800, 869 youths were apprenticed by Dublin masters (although in the eighteenth century only a fifth of them advanced to become free of the guild).[24]

The overwhelming majority of apprentices came from within Ireland and principally from Dublin city itself (see Table 2.2). Dublin's dominance as the main source of apprentices became more pronounced in the eighteenth century

Table 2.2
Origins of Apprentices to the Dublin Company of Goldsmiths: 1660–1800

	1660–1699 (no.)	Percentage of those with origins specified	1700–1800 (no.)	Percentage of those with origins specified
Dublin city and county	51	46.4	394	66.1
Other Leinster counties	30	27.3	117	19.6
Ulster counties	6	5.5	34	5.7
Munster counties	4	3.6	25	4.2
Connacht counties	2	1.8	11	1.8
Britain	16	14.5	13	2.2
Other	1	0.9	2	0.3
Unknown/unclear	44		119	

Sources: F. Berry, 'The Goldsmiths' Company of Dublin', in *JCHAS*, viii, 53 (1902), 29–50;
Alison FitzGerald, *Silver in Georgian Dublin: Making, selling, consuming* (Abingdon, 2017), pp. 45–7.

(as did London in England), whereas the importance of nearby Leinster counties receded. But the small numbers coming from further afield, specifically south Munster, tell of a rival pole of attraction: Cork city. The large handful of apprentices coming from England and Wales in the second half of the seventeenth century was not maintained after 1700. In the case of the Goldsmiths Guild, overall apprenticeship numbers peaked in the 1750s and fell quite sharply in the final decades of the century.[25]

Dublin's St Luke's Guild, dominated by printers and booksellers, reveals a fairly similar picture for the later eighteenth century: the dominance of Dublin and the near absence of apprentices from the other three provinces (see Table 2.3). Interestingly, the far more voluminous evidence on the origins of craft apprentices coming to early modern London has revealed a striking contrast between the sixteenth and early seventeenth centuries, when many came from the distant shires, and the eighteenth century when the recruitment field was increasingly restricted to the metropolis and adjacent counties.[26]

Very few of the masters in this Dublin guild would have been a match for the established goldsmiths, and admission fees were doubtless lower among stationers and much lower among cutlers and painters, whose apprentices were overwhelmingly drawn from the city. No less than 26.9 per cent of goldsmiths' apprentices in the eighteenth century had fathers who identified as esquires, clergymen or gentlemen, whereas the figure for stationers' apprentices (18.3 per cent) was significantly lower.[27]

Table 2.3
Origins of Apprentices in St Luke's Guild, Dublin: 1740–99

	A. Stationers' faculty (no.)	A. Percentage of those with origins specified	B. Cutlers, painters' faculty (no.)	B. Percentage of those with origins specified
Dublin city and county	97	61.4	81	80.2
Other Leinster counties	44	27.8	17	16.8
Ulster counties	2	1.3	2	2.0
Munster counties	8	5.1	1	1.0
Connacht counties	5	3.2	0	1.8
Britain	1	0.6	0	0.0
Other	1	0.6	0	0.0
Unknown/unclear	126		42	

Sources: Register of Apprentices, St Luke's Guild, Dublin: NLI MS 12,131; Mary Pollard, *A Dictionary of Members of the Dublin Book Trade 1550–1800* (London, 2000) pp. xxx–xxxii.

Most such apprentices came from Protestant families, reflecting the exclu-
sionary by-laws adopted in all Dublin guilds by the 1690s, but there were many
Catholic master craftsmen who, on payment of a quarterly fine, were permitted
to trade and to enjoy some or all of the economic privileges of guild membership. These quarter-brothers took on their own apprentices, presumably co-
religionists, but there was a statutory maximum of two on the number of
apprentices that they could register at any time (although there is no evidence
that this was enforced). Catholic teenagers can have formed only a small proportion of those entering formal apprenticeship in any of the Dublin guilds, yet in
some of the lesser trades engaged in personal services – such as hair-dressing –
Catholic non-freemen seem to have outnumbered those who had come through
formal apprenticeship. These controls were weakening around mid century,
notably in the textile trades, and indeed it was pressure from below, from journeymen, that put a brake on deregulation.[28]

One group that had traditionally been outside the formal discipline of guild
membership in Dublin were the traders and craftsmen who chose to locate in
one of the neighbourhoods beyond the Corporation boundary, whether in the
well-watered 'Liberties' in the south-west of the city or in the small neighbourhoods nestling around the two Anglican cathedrals. The south-western Liberties
of Thomascourt and Donore, owned since the Reformation by the Brabazon
family, earls of Meath, had seen great expansion in the course of the seventeenth
century, and immigrant traders and craftsmen, Dutch, Huguenot and English,
had been particularly prominent there. These Liberties remained the great centre
for the city's textile workshops and preserved a strongly Protestant character
until well into the eighteenth century, but their status as a zone free of guild
control – over apprentices in particular – mattered less and less. Indeed many of
the leading figures of the Liberties were freemen of the city, and the Weaver's
Guildhall (built in the 1680s, then rebuilt in the 1740s by Huguenot James La
Touche) was located on the Lower Coombe, inside the city but only a few paces
from the Meath Liberty.[29] There were also 'Liberties' in this sense in Cork (the
manor of St Finbarre's lying around the cathedral), and in Limerick where the
old St Francis Abbey properties lying just outside the walls of Englishtown were
owned by the Sexton Perys and were believed to provide cover for Catholic
traders flouting the laws of the city (a claim unconvincingly rebutted by the
ground landlord).[30]

In Cork, where the individual trade guilds were much weaker, the Corporation
itself maintained a register of apprentices, a partial copy of which survives (see

Table 2.4

Origins of Cork City Apprentices: 1729–56

	Number registered	Percentage of those of known origin
Cork City	124	57.4
Cork county	45	20.8
Limerick county	18	8.3
Tipperary county	9	4.2
Other Munster counties	8	3.7
Other Irish counties	9	4.2
England, Scotland, Minorca	3	1.4
Unknown	29	

Source: UCC Archives, U 55.

Table 2.4). It is not clear whether Catholic apprentices were included, but the family names suggest a substantial minority may have been Catholic; the register was limited to apprentices attached to freemen of the city, in other words, to Protestant masters. The register demonstrates how much more limited Cork's migration field was, even at a time when the city's commercial influence extended well beyond the province of Munster.

With the total eclipse of Kinsale and Youghal as major ports, Cork city held a near-monopoly of attraction across south Munster for those who could afford the apprenticeship fee. Possibly Norwich, England's second city for much of the early modern period, offers a parallel: apprentice origins there were overwhelmingly local, with surrounding parishes and the smaller towns of East Anglia acting as the major supply source.[31]

SUBSISTENCE MIGRATION

Apprentices from outside the cities, whatever their eventual fate, were 'betterment' migrants, usually backed by limited family resources or helped by city relatives. Some returned to practise their craft at home; most stayed. However, the majority of city migrants were less well endowed: young women seeking domestic service, young men seeking employment outside the regulated trades in construction, food and drink preparation, street-selling and porterage. And often whole families were displaced and uprooted by loss of tenancy or extreme want; it is likely that such migrants were principally drawn from the most marginal sectors in the countryside, not from the relatively comfortable ranks of the tenant farmers. Michael Smith has observed how, in a global context, decisions about local migration by individuals and households were [always] strongly conditioned by economic hardship. Research from a political economy perspective in many regions and time periods supports the conclusion that members of poorer peasant households – typically those without land – are and were far more likely to move locally or regionally than members of wealthier households.[32]

Some Irish commentators saw the growth of cities as the cause, not the consequence, of rural depopulation: 'large cities, by draining the country of its produce, destroy small farms and small towns ... Such ... will be the effect of the present system of enlarging Dublin', suggested one writer in 1793. But 'push' factors were certainly in operation too, and we can infer that new arrivals to the city who came without resources – 'subsistence' migrants – were disproportionately drawn from the cottier/labourer segment of rural society and that on average they probably travelled longer distances than 'betterment' migrants. Yet supporting evidence is weak. In a review of the operations of the Dublin workhouse c. 1726, a new category of unattached pauper was spotted:

the vagabond youth of both sexes: many of these their parents were not able to keep, but more I believe [there are] who have run from their parents lest they should be put to country labour, and it's one cause why hands are in the country so much wanting. These kind have either brothers, sisters, cousins or some neighbours' children, formerly their acquaintance, who [are] now at service in Dublin. These sort of relations do both shelter and support the vagabond youth and out [sic] of their masters' house or stables; and the girls lurk in cellars as the boys do in stables. Thus a very wicked brood increases.

The boys, it was believed, lived as news criers, porters or shoeblacks, and if tighter controls on unattached youths were imposed, they would simply quit town. But doubtless many stayed (see Plate 4).[33]

In the years of catastrophic harvest failure, the arrival of new waves of 'the poor' into Dublin was noted and dreaded; thus in 1729 it was reported how 'the poor throng in crowds' to the city, and that those in the countryside who had 'eased them out' should bear some responsibility for their relief. In 1745 William Colles, one of the promoters of the first Kilkenny workhouse, established in

1743 to curb the huge growth of street begging, explained how this phenomenon had come about:

> Great numbers of poor people of this city and the country and villages adjacent having been reduced to beggary by the great frost [of 1740] and the calamitous summer which succeeded [it] found on the return of plenty that they got by begging as much as would maintain them in idleness in as good a manner as they could maintain themselves by working.

In time of trouble they had come to town and learnt to survive. The opening of the Limerick workhouse in 1774 also came shortly after a severe economic downturn. During its first twenty years of operation there were 2,747 poor and distressed admissions, and just over half (51.9 per cent) of those who declared a previous residence came from outside the city; only a very small number identified as a farmer (1.8 per cent of those declaring an occupation), whereas over 8 per cent of the males identified as a labourer (and around two-thirds of these had out-of-town addresses). It is surprising that although urban workhouses were coming into existence elsewhere in Munster – in Ennis, Cork and Waterford – during these years, 36.1 per cent of the Limerick admissions were from other Munster counties and 7.7 per cent from elsewhere in Ireland: for the poorest the city's drawing power evidently extended far beyond the lower Shannon. The intake had a nearly even gender balance, although it was disproportionately male in older cohorts, but with an over-representation of women among young adults and in the years of rural crisis.[34]

The register of Limerick workhouse demonstrates how one city – at an expansive moment in its history – was an open door to the rural poor. A different insight into the variegated inflow of migrants to a place like Limerick comes from an analysis of surnames: the 1660 poll-tax returns included a crude frequency measure of Irish surnames in the various cities and towns enumerated. In the case of Limerick, Cork and Waterford these can be compared with the surnames that appear in the first trade directories published in 1787/8. The 1660 data suggest a surprising degree of surname variety already present in each city with the dozen most common names in each place attached to only a tenth of the 'Irish' population (7.9 per cent in the case of Limerick, 8.9 per cent in Cork, and 11.6 per cent in Waterford). Of course the exceptional post-war environment may well have heightened the number of strangers in or on the edge of these towns at that point. But a century and a quarter later, Lucas's

Figure 4 'The poor house [the House of Industry] on the North Strand, Limerick'.

Directory gives a not dissimilar picture, with the dozen most common surnames attached to 10.2 per cent of directory entries in Cork, 15.4 per cent in Limerick and 17.1 per cent in Waterford. In each city only about a quarter of the top twelve surnames of 1660 were still in the top rank in 1787 (in Limerick: O'Brien, Hogan and Ryan; in Cork: Murphy, Barry and MacCarthy; and in Waterford: Walsh/Welsh, Power and Murphy). Most but not all of the other top names of 1660 were still there in 1787 but only in single figures, sharing their cities with hundreds of other family names that had not, it seems, featured in the 1660 listings.[35]

Catholic baptismal registers survive for a few eighteenth-century urban congregations and can also offer some useful information. Whatever their other limitations, they reveal the constant turnover of family names: a study of the Catholic registers for Ennis, the substantial county town of Clare, notes how fewer than half the surnames appearing in the 1744–48 baptismal register reappear in that for 1785–1800, implying 'a large turnover ... and much coming and going in the intervening years'. And we can assume that larger and less isolated centres witnessed even greater turnover. From early in the century there is tantalizing evidence from Galway: of the 756 adult Catholic males who gave sureties under the 1704 legislation (most if not all of them merchants and traders), only 176 were still there in 1731: almost half of the total were dead, and another 176 were dispersed at home or overseas.[36]

THE CHANGING CHEMISTRY

The most compelling evidence on internal migration to the cities is however hiding in plain sight: the changing religious composition of most Irish cities (see Table 2.5). Thanks to the recurring fascination of the eighteenth-century state in the country's religious demography, we have fairly rich pickings on household and/or population totals at parish level broken down by religion, which were collected at various times during the century. These returns are incomplete, unstandardized and sometimes error-strewn, but sufficient urban parish data survive to plot, in general terms, the changing religious profile of each city.

The 1660 poll tax again provides a baseline and the 1834 Education Inquiry returns a terminal point (no official Irish census included a question on religious affiliation until 1861).[37] The most extensive religious data for the eighteenth century come from the 1760s; these returns are a mixed bag, but taken

Table 2.5

Religious Composition of Irish Cities: 1660–1834

Percentage 'Irish'/Catholic inhabitants in certain urban parishes

	[1] 1660	[2] 1724–49	[3] 1757–71	[4] 1834
Derry	38.1		20.6	51.9
Sligo	73.4	52.3		75.7
Galway		[63.0]		96.6
Limerick	47.3		69.7	90.9
Cork	56.4		59.2	82.3
Waterford	43.4		71.5	82.9
Kilkenny	75.2	75.7		93.4
Dublin City	26.4		63.2	72.4
Drogheda	51.1		65.9	89.8
Belfast	37.9		6.5	32.2

Sources: see Appendix 5.

Note: In column *[1]* 1660 figures relate to civilian adults levied for poll tax; the convention of equating the figures given for 'Irish' inhabitants as the Catholic population has been followed here. In column *[2]*, data for Kilkenny date from 1731; data for Galway (houses), 1724; data for Sligo, 1749. In column *[3]* all data come from 1766, except Drogheda (households) (1764), Belfast (1757), and Derry (1771).

in the round they stand comparison with the other series. Coming so soon after the Cromwellian urban clearances, 'Irish' poll-tax payers in 1660 were present in far greater numbers in most cities than had been planned or permitted, forming more than half the adult population in four of our ten centres and less than a third in only one – Dublin city. In the following century of urban growth, 're-catholicization' was greatest in Dublin, less in Cork and Kilkenny, while in Sligo, Belfast and Derry the process was apparently going in the reverse direction. The very similar values and trends for Limerick and Waterford between 1660 and 1766 are reassuring and entirely plausible, whereas the values for Derry and Belfast are more suspect. In the case of Dublin, where the evidence is richest, Fagan has suggested that the Catholic share of the population was around 33 per cent in 1715, but that it increased sharply from that time, so that Catholics may have been in a majority there by 1750 (although not yet a majority among heads of household). Catholic parish registers, such as they are, give a more ambiguous impression: baptisms in the large parish of St Andrew's in the east of Dublin city were fairly stable in the 1740s, rose sharply in the 1750s, then showed little growth over the next thirty years.[38]

Between the 1760s and the 1820s, the era of maximum demographic growth for all centres except Dublin and Cork, the rate of religious change was strongest in Drogheda, Sligo, Cork and Kilkenny, less rapid in Waterford and Dublin itself. In St Peter's in Drogheda, the principal Catholic parish for the town, baptisms in the period from 1785 to 1794 were more than double those in 1745 to 1754, suggesting a rate of growth of 1.86 per cent per annum (considerably ahead of estimates for the town's overall growth). But it is the absolute values that tell the clearest story: the implication here is that at least three-fifths of the residents of seven of the ten urban centres were Catholic by the 1760s, and that by the 1830s seven out of the ten were three-quarters or more Catholic.[39]

Derry and Belfast followed a different trajectory, the former only achieving a Catholic majority by the 1830s, the latter – despite huge immigration – remaining more than two-thirds Protestant. Belfast reflected what had once been the general pattern everywhere else: a distinctly Protestant movement to the cities. In Dublin's case, it seems likely that Protestant migration up to c. 1750 was sufficiently large to boost Protestant numbers, by which point they may have reached 60,000 in a city of around 125,000, stabilizing at or around that level until after 1800. Protestant numbers in Cork city continued to grow up to the end of the eighteenth century, and may have been growing even more strongly in Waterford and Sligo at that time. But this was almost certainly not the case in Limerick or Galway, where Protestant numbers, never large, were falling in absolute terms long before 1800. Such a shift may reflect no more than the changing religious composition of urban migrants, but there is also the possibility of differential fertility levels within the cities.[40]

Reflecting the exclusionist policies of the 1650s and after, Catholic demographic dominance was first evident in extra-mural parishes rather than inside the walls. This was still the case in Kilkenny and Limerick in the 1760s, and dramatically so in Cork, where Catholics then formed only 45.3 per cent of the population within the three island parishes, but in Shandon and St Finbarre's, north and south of the old city, they constituted 75.3 per cent. Cork's suburbs often attracted highly negative comment: to the French traveller Aubry de la Mottraye in the 1720s, Blarney Lane on the north side was the worst of the worst, 'habitée par les plus pauvres gens et les maisons ne valent pas mieux que des hutes de percheurs [recte pêcheurs]'. Such neighbourhoods, the natural focus for migrant workers, were disease hotspots (see Plate 5). The leading Cork physician of the period, Joseph Rogers, observed that in that area adjoining the city's multiplicity of slaughter yards the death rate from smallpox in the epidemics of 1718–1721 had been a third higher than elsewhere in the city (confirming evidence from London that smallpox took its heaviest toll among migrants to the city).[41]

The thatched cabins in Cork suburbs were also a perennial fire hazard; the worst incidents were in the 1760s when over 220 houses were destroyed in two South Parish fires (only to be replaced by the same 'straw-roofed hovels'). The dense lanes in St Francis Abbey in Limerick were also hazardous: 'above eighty cabins' were destroyed in a night fire there in 1755, and over forty cabins on Ballybricken common in the suburbs of Waterford were burnt down in 1809. Suburban clusters outside Kilkenny and Sligo remained quite modest, but the ribbon development of single-storey housing was visible outside the old defensive boundaries of every city. A survey of Derry city in 1738 found that within the walls there were very few cabins (single storey mud-walled houses), but that outside the walls 275 of the 330 houses were reckoned to be cabins. But there could be gradations in the quality of cabin: a tantalizing report on suburban property on St Stephen's Island in Galway in 1684 noted that 'all the houses in the North suburbs[,] at least 200[,] are on that land and more likely to be with little garden plots, I mean Irish houses of the better sort . . .' Belfast was sometimes regarded as the only large Irish town without cabin suburbs, but in a survey of 1757 there were several areas on the northern and western edges of the town where there were 'only low thatched dwellings of a mean appearance', and even in 1780 'falling cabins and tapered houses, all tumbling down' were noted on one of the approaches to the town. It seems these were swept away in the rapid expansion towards the end of the century.[42]

In the case of Dublin, there were almost no one-hearth houses within the city at the time of Rocque's survey in 1756, but nevertheless he plotted hundreds of small houses on the roads and lanes on the northern and western approaches. When a circular road arcing across open ground on the north side was being planned in 1763, one of the local landowners protested that cabins would spring up along the proposed new road, making it a 'filthy suburb'. However, most of the small suburban houses depicted by Rocque had some land attached, presumably garden plots producing vegetables. It was a rather different story in the densely settled markets and manufacturing districts of the city itself: mean household size was already high there in the early eighteenth century, averaging 12 per house in St Michan's parish in 1723, and Arthur Dobbs claimed that in some houses 'in the trading part of the city' there were families in every room 'oftentimes on each floor and in the cellars'. These houses were however modest by comparison with the monumental terrace houses appearing in the fashionable suburbs directly east of the old walled city and on the Gardiner estate across the Liffey. With the relentless increase in such houses it is no surprise that by 1766 the Protestant proportion in Dublin's extra-mural parishes was greater than in the old city parishes, a pattern even more evident in 1834.[43]

That pattern was part of a larger story evident in every Irish city (see Plate 6). The older urban norm was one where low-status and generally Catholic migrants were clustered in rudimentary houses thrown up along suburban roads and lanes and exposed to the full vagaries of war and climate, while higher-status residents dominated the inner streets and occupied much larger houses of stone or brick. But by the late eighteenth century this situation had shifted; some central neigbourhoods were congested with 'roomkeepers' and courtyard tenants, and older housing was now being divided and subdivided. It was a very slow process, as Nuala Burke's study of the Aungier estate south of Dublin Castle has revealed, with high-class housing being first adapted for bourgeois occupancy or commercial use, and several generations passing before such property was transformed into tenements. Whitelaw's census of 1798 provided graphic confirmation: in the western parishes, both those that had lain within the walls and the neighbouring old parishes in the Meath Liberty, there was an average of

13.3 persons per house; elsewhere in the city the figure was 10.7. And the suburbs now had positive associations: from Drumcondra to Harold's Cross, Glasnevin to Blackrock, a string of satellite villages were appearing up to 6 kilometres from the centre of Dublin, salubrious retreats for the city's professional and business elites and, more importantly, busy centres of mill-based employment.[44]

The shift of poorer families from the periphery to the urban core was less clear-cut in provincial cities, and indeed it seems that by the early nineteenth century nearly every large provincial town (outside east Ulster) had a congested cabin quarter some distance from the business centre. In Cork the old city centre remained socially mixed and the island parishes relatively prosperous, although the highest status streets were those developed late in the century – notably the South Mall and St Patrick's Street – which lay on reclaimed land east of what had been the walled town. In 1834 the island parishes taken together were still registering a Protestant share of over 30 per cent, although this was slipping. Only in the special case of Limerick did the old walled city become the principal zone of congestion and deprivation, becoming ever more evident as Newtown Pery grew and expanded.[45]

WATER IN DEMAND

The great migration into the cities since the seventeenth century, unplanned and unmanaged, placed recurring pressure on basic urban amenities. Water supply was the most critical. In Dublin two medieval watercourses had provided separate supplies to the city and the Meath Liberty, and beginning in the 1660s a network of street pipes was constructed and extended to give direct supplies to basement cisterns in low-lying locations. By 1705, 758 houses in 52 streets lying within the city's jurisdiction had an intermittent supply of water, a logistical achievement far in advance of most Continental cities at that time. But the system was breaking down by the 1720s due to growing demand, wastage and adulteration of the water courses – by paper and small woollen mills along the Dodder. This prompted the construction of an extensive reservoir, the Basin, on the city's south-western edge near James St, large enough to hold ninety days supply. But after recurrent shortages in the next decade, a great waterwheel was built on the Liffey at Islandbridge to raise water and augment the growing demand on the north side. Then in the 1760s summer water shortages prompted the Corporation to take over the Grand Canal, then under construction reaching into the south Midlands and, although the arrangement did not last, for almost a hundred years the Corporation came to depend on canal water to fill a growing number of city basins. Compared with the residents of other cities, eighteenth-century Dubliners who could afford it were well provided for; the standard had been set by technical advances in the supply of water to eighteenth-century Londoners, which now influenced developments in Dublin.[46]

Cork Corporation was much slower to provide piped water. However a local consortium built a pumping engine and small reservoir above the Lee in the 1760s, but it took more than a decade for subscribers to benefit. In Limerick, local MP and landowner Edmond Sexton Pery funded the excavation of deep wells and the erection of water-pumps to service fountains in both Englishtown and Irishtown in the 1770s. Belfast had a rudimentary piped water system from 1678, but the system was unable to cope with the late eighteenth-century growth of the town. In December 1791 it became a crisis: 'the poor are likely to perish for want of [water]' and the affluent were carting their water into town. A voluntary body, the Charitable Society, at first provided water carts for the town, then took on the challenging task of renovating the network in 1795; it remained the local water authority for many decades.

Elsewhere, private springs and artesian wells sufficed. But for the vast majority of urban populations, even in Dublin, water remained a scarce resource, purchased in the street from water carts or carried a distance from river or canal. Prompted by an aristocratic campaign, the Dublin Paving Board built ten ornate public fountains around 1790 that alleviated the deficit, a rare instance where conspicuous philanthropy and real need coincided (see Plate 7). There was talk in Cork about the necessity for public fountains as well, but not until 1815 did the Water Company, ever fearful of its revenues, agree to provide free water to a public fountain in Nile St. But these fountains probably had marginal impact on welfare. In the growing commentary from the turn of the century on the state of the urban poor, the complete absence of personal hygiene and the pervasive stink of human excrement in the courts and back lanes, were recurrent themes, pointing to a collapse of older sanitary practices and the dire consequences of the now extreme overcrowding.[47]

3
THE KEYS OF THE KINGDOM

Whether the sea-ports of Galway, Limerick, Cork and Waterford are not to be looked on as the keys of this kingdom? And whether the merchants are not possessed of these keys; and who are the most numerous merchants in those cities?[1]

The readers of Bishop Berkeley's *Querist* (1735) of course knew the answer. The Catholics were gaming the system. In his long litany of rhetorical questions, Berkeley was criticizing the follies of this system in that it was creating huge wealth for the owners of cattle and land but was keeping the majority of the country's population in dirt and idleness, a system that was officially committed to the religious reformation of Ireland but was turning a blind eye to the accumulation of Catholic wealth in the cities.

Berkeley was however mixing truth with half-truth: the seaports of the south and east were indeed lynch-pins in an economy that had become highly export-dependent. They were the conduits through which trade passed, where goods were assembled, processed and despatched, and where financial services (wholesale credit and the paper surrogates that had developed for the transmission of money) were available. And 'merchants' did indeed possess the keys. Across western Europe and the North Atlantic this was the classic era of the merchant, the sedentary *négotiant* who dominated the business and usually the government of port cities, who dealt in a variety of import/export lines of trade with overseas correspondents, and who settled accounts by means of an internationally accepted set of protocols governing the use of bills of exchange. Merchants traded in bulk and operated as sole traders, in partnerships, and often in a mixture of arrangements to reduce risk. As collectivities, Irish 'merchant communities' ranged from less than a dozen international traders in Sligo or

Galway to around 500 in the case of late eighteenth-century Dublin (a size comparable at that point with Bordeaux and about a sixth that of London). They were overwhelmingly male and culturally diverse: in the great Dutch commercial diaspora of the early to mid seventeenth century and the Huguenot religious diaspora a generation later, Cork, Dublin, Limerick and Waterford had attracted small numbers of 'foreign' Protestant and often transient merchants, but the infusion of newcomers, even from England, became much less pronounced after 1700. Thereafter no Irish merchant community was as strongly 'foreign' or cosmopolitan as eighteenth-century Bordeaux, Cádiz or London. Most Irish merchants had regional if not local origins; they drew their strength and much of their custom from social and family networks within their respective hinterlands. The costs of entry were not high, for the fixed capital required to operate as a wholesale merchant was modest (the fit-out of offices, cellars and warehouses near the quays, and shares in a ship or two) and access to credit – vital in an era when cash flows were unpredictable, debt settlement often painfully slow, and losses on the high seas not unusual – rested on reputation and family networks, not on a huge initial investment. Trust and the necessary technical know-how were hard-won assets needed by every merchant, and these were acquired and shaped in an urban environment.[2]

That said, the growth of the Irish economy in this period was based almost entirely on what was happening in the countryside, on the growth of agricultural output and the spread of rural industry. Cities acted as the central marketplaces, the home both of specialist processors who added value to rural produce destined for export and of the import/export traders who maintained an international network of correspondents. But merchants had limited agency; they were entirely dependent on the capacity of rural producers to respond to market demand, and they in turn had to adapt to external shocks, whether the closure of markets because of wartime embargo or regulatory changes, or the interruption of maritime trade caused by enemy privateering. Some cities also became centres of consumption, and as a consequence city businesses supplied a vast and growing range of goods and services for the social classes that enjoyed the profits from trade (in the form of income drawn from land rents), most notably the Irish gentry who for two centuries flocked to the winter delights of Dublin. But those who serviced the new consumer appetites were also at the mercy of sudden changes of economic sentiment.

Berkeley was on more contentious ground by implying that Catholic merchants had a pre-eminent position in this wholesale trade. After the enormous setbacks of the seventeenth century, such a claim seems at first sight outlandish. The true picture was much more complex and depended on the particular place, the period, and the line of trade. But first, the economic context.

UNEVEN DEVELOPMENTS

State revenue receipts from customs and inland excise, which exist from the 1680s, provide a barometer of Irish economic trends throughout the eighteenth century. From the 1680s to the 1740s they point to a pattern of short-term oscillation rather than sustained economic growth. Sharp setbacks were of course a feature of all pre-industrial economies involved in international exchange: severe weather at home or abroad, external market changes, the outbreak of international war or a specifically financial crisis, any of these could precipitate sudden reversals in economic activity and a wave of bankruptcies. Despite the exceptional dislocation of the Williamite war in parts of the country, economic recovery was quite strong in the 1690s, but thereafter the country was adversely affected by several very severe weather-induced crises (in 1708–10, 1727–29, and 1739–41), by warfare on the high seas (with privateering hitting maritime trade in the 1690s, early 1700s and early 1740s), by external financial crises (notably the South Sea Bubble in 1720–21), and by local credit crises. The first of the latter came with the collapse of Burton's Bank in Dublin in 1733, which sparked a short recession.

Customs returns also point to some growth spurts in foreign trade and, by implication, in economic activity, notably at the turn of the century and in the years after the Peace of Utrecht (1713). And although the momentum was on each occasion dissipated, every expansionary cycle left a legacy. Thus the stuttering character of the economy in early decades of the century that is suggested by customs returns masks huge structural changes occurring under the surface: the intensification of regional agricultural specialization, the extension and proliferation of the network of livestock fairs, and the seemingly unstoppable concentration of commercial activity on Dublin and Cork. And while Anglo-Irish trade was temporarily less important than in the past or the future, English capital was increasingly financing much of Ireland's long-distance trade and supplying a greater share of both shipping and marine insurance.[3]

Berkeley had deprecated the huge growth of livestock farming in the southern counties. But this was a long-term process that reflected the underlying movement of relative prices away from cereals. The intensification of grassland farming had been the dominant feature of rural economic change in southern Ireland since the 1620s, with the end product increasingly destined for Continental and Atlantic markets. Wool had been the principal traded commodity for much of the seventeenth century but that was in decline, and beef and butter, salted and barrelled for distant markets, had expanded from small beginnings in the Restoration era to become the great export staples. The commercial beef trade (which included the valuable by-products of hides and tallow) was generally more valuable than dairying, and in the 1720s and 1730s it enjoyed particularly rapid growth, helped by buoyant French colonial demand. Growth in beef exports continued at a more sedate rate up until the 1770s, after which time it fell back and was eclipsed by the trade in pig-meat. Butter exports grew inexorably over the whole century, although the way the product was processed changed as tropical markets gave way to British domestic demand in later decades.[4]

There was a very different trajectory of economic development in Ulster: its staple exports had not been particularly distinctive in the seventeenth century – although butter, salmon and timber had featured strongly – but the catalyst for drastic change came in the 1690s with linen. In little over a generation an export trade in fine cloth, manufactured in the towns and villages of the Lagan valley, grew from a small exotic activity to become the staple product of the whole northern province, its momentum continuing through the otherwise depressed 1730s. White linen exports from Ireland averaged around 7.5 million yards per annum by the 1740s, roughly three times the level in the 1710s, and linen yarn exports nearly doubled over the same period.[5]

The 1740s were in many respects the economic nadir: eight years of warfare during the decade, coinciding with several harvest disasters. Nevertheless naval contracting filled the pockets of Munster merchants and this was again the case during the Seven Years War (1756–63), which was broadly positive for graziers and provisions dealers, bad for consumers. High food prices, bank failures (in 1759–60) and speculative demand for land during the war triggered novel episodes of social protest in both town and countryside. The early 1770s saw another very sharp recession and the worst setback for linen exports in a generation, and this affected incomes and land values across the whole country. Recovery had hardly set in before the shock of the American War of Independence (1776–83), a time of mixed economic fortune. International market dislocation, a financial crisis in London and harvest failure at home produced one of the sharpest downturns in half a century in 1778/79. However, despite further severe economic difficulties at the end of war (exacerbated once again by repeated harvest failure), the economy bounced back quickly and entered a fifteen-year 'goldilocks' period between 1783 and 1797, a time of highly visible and apparently benign structural change in manufacturing, infrastructure and urban development. By this stage Britain had replaced Continental and Atlantic markets as the principal source of demand for Irish agriculture, and cereal-based exports began to loom large from the 1770s. These shifts helped reverse the concentration of trade and economic activity on the largest cities – Dublin and Cork – that had been so evident in the century up to 1750, and also challenged the status of seaport merchants.[6]

ECLIPSE AND ASCENDANCY

Berkeley's 'keys of the kingdom', the cities of the south and the west, may have shared a deep common history, but their economies from the mid seventeenth century diverged quite markedly and the dividends earned from international trade were very unevenly distributed, with Cork as the long-distance winner and Galway the clearest loser. Despite the traumatic events of the 1650s, Galway's small band of merchant families had continued to trade with France and directly with the Caribbean, using the archaic practice of one family member in a shared overseas venture travelling on board as 'supercargo', often with full discretion as to how goods (and ships) might be sold or exchanged, all the while gaining personal experience of disparate markets. But by 1700 war and the changing scale and character of Atlantic commerce brought the super-cargo system to an end, even in Galway, and a number of Galwaymen became permanent residents in the French Atlantic ports, from where they maintained close links with kindred in the Caribbean, London and Dublin (who were often on the move themselves). Galway's international network of traders was certainly not unique but was distinctive in that it was late to take shape (compared to Waterford), evolving at a time when home was a small port in relative decline, and its Connacht hinterland was being poached by Dublin suppliers.

Louis Cullen has argued that the key to understanding this great mercantile diaspora was the unusual survival in Co. Galway of a substantial Catholic gentry (beneficiaries of the 1691 articles of surrender): a career in a trading house overseas was an attractive option for younger sons of such families when the openings available to their Protestant peers (such as the law, the army or the Established Church) were denied. Galway's multinational trading network, dominated by the names of the old 'tribal' families, may explain the precocious emergence of banking in the town, where Lynch's private bank was operating from the 1730s. And in mid-century Dublin there was a distinctive Galway group of merchants, almost all Catholic, who among other things controlled a major share of the wine trade, helped not a little by the presence of six Galway firms operating close to the Quai des Chartrons in Bordeaux. But Galway's own quays remained fairly quiet until late in the century.[7]

Cork by contrast sprang into new life in the 1650s, its mainly Protestant merchant community seizing the opportunities to engage in the provisions trades and act as commission agents for wealthy principals in England and Holland, while venturing on their own account to Spain, Portugal and the Caribbean. Indeed, 17 ships were built for the city's merchants in the first seven years after the Restoration which, boasted the Earl of Orrery, 'is more than [the rest of] all Ireland has done', and a Revenue Commissioners' memorandum in 1683 observed that although 'merchants generally throughout the kingdom drive a peddling trade upon credit, having not stocks of their own . . . in Cork . . . they are substantial rich men'. Dissenters, in particular Quakers, were already prominent, many with close family links to Bristol, but a few Old English houses also benefited from the city's take-off as a major Atlantic port: Ignatius Goold, the most prominent of them, was able to commit to a huge dowry of £2,000 on the marriage of one of his daughters in 1685.[8]

Despite the shock for the new order of the Jacobite takeover in Cork and then the near total destruction of the city's substantial suburbs in Marlborough's siege, reconstruction was surprisingly rapid, with building activity by 1694 reported to be 'more considerable than in all the rest of the cities and towns in Ireland put together'. Meanwhile the big pre-war merchants led an impressively strong recovery of the city's trade. They were joined by new faces, including a small but energetic group of Huguenot traders (and the community later supplied at least five of Cork's eighteenth-century mayors). Over the next two decades of warfare the city benefited from official English naval contracting and, more importantly, from ready access to naval protection against the pervasive threat of French (and French-based Jacobite) privateers, an advantage that its old rivals, Kinsale and Youghal, lacked.[9]

By the 1670s, Cork merchants had perfected the processing of salted beef for sale in southern Europe and the Caribbean. Imported expertise had played a key role in fashioning what became Cork's premium product on international markets for a century or more. In the early days some of the biggest merchants had invested in cattle production as well: Alderman George Crofts claimed in 1692 that before the war he possessed livestock in north Cork and Kerry worth over £5,000. Processing trades were at first dominated by immigrant families, but that gradually changed in the early eighteenth century. An increasing number of 'new' Catholic families made their first fortune in the slaughter-yards of the north suburbs before diversifying, in a few cases becoming wealthy export merchants in their own right like the Moylan clan, whose family members settled in ports in southern Europe and North America.

Cork continued to control the beef trade in all its parts, evident in the profusion of tallow-chandlers, skinners and tanners, each commodity with a distinctive overseas market. And within Munster the city became the unchallenged centre of the butter export trade as well. Here once again it was the introduction of English and Dutch practices in the seventeenth century that laid the basis for what became one of the staples of the eighteenth. Maintaining a consistent quality in the produce despatched for consumption in tropical heat was even more demanding than in the case of beef, and protecting the reputation of a merchant's brand overseas required a close oversight of city butter buyers, coopers and packers. Wool, woollen cloth and yarn exports were also a major element in the rise of Cork, and for a few years in the early eighteenth century these were actually more valuable than beef and butter combined. However, the value added to wool within the city was far less than for beef or butter.[10]

Ship tonnage invoiced in Cork Harbour at the beginning of the century far exceeded that for Limerick, Waterford and Galway combined (see Table 3.1). Cork held the dominant position within Munster, and although it was beginning to weaken from the 1780s, invoiced tonnage was still nearly twice that of the other four ports combined in the last quarter of the century. However, for most of the century only about 20 per cent of the ships dropping anchor in Cork Harbour were Irish-owned. This was because most provisions trading was conducted on a commission basis, with orders reaching Cork from all directions ranging from large London merchant houses to substantial slave-owning planters in the British Caribbean.

In the late seventeenth century around three-quarters of the vessels sailing from English ports to the Caribbean stopped off either in Cork Harbour or Dublin to lade provisions, and the strategic role of Cork as larder of the British

Figure 5 The Exchange, Cork, occupied an awkward site at the intersection of Main St and Castle St and was completed in 1710; the design was a grander version of a fairly standard market-house template, with the council rooms of the Corporation on the first floor and the ground floor left open for trade and business behind the arcading.

slave islands still held true on the eve of the American Revolution. At that time Richard Hare (*c.* 1719–94), youngest son of a Presbyterian merchant and son-in-law of a cooper, was probably the wealthiest merchant in the city, yet he too was primarily a commission merchant, owning no ships and venturing little on his own account. In the course of twelve months he communicated with 265 correspondents, four-fifths of whom were outside Ireland and the majority in England or Scotland.[11]

However those of Hare's contemporaries who specialized in trade with southern Europe (principally Bordeaux and Lisbon) were trading on their

Table 3.1

Ship Tonnage Invoiced (excluding coastal vessels) at Galway, Limerick, Cork and Waterford: 1701–1800

25-year averages (1701–25 = 100)

	1701–25	*1726–50*	*1751–75*	*1776–1800*
Galway	100	98	107	199
Limerick	100	141	220	419
Cork	100	157	230	366
Waterford	100	158	290	610

Absolute tonnage values for 1701–25: Galway, 1,577; Limerick, 2,629; Cork, 26,436; Waterford, 6,282.
Coastal shipping was not included in the Customs enumeration.
Source: TNA, CUST/15.

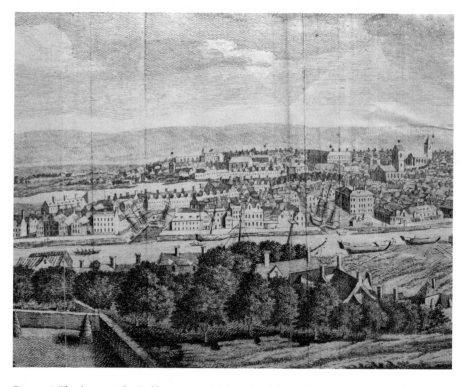

Figure 6 The 'new city': Cork's commercial heartland by mid-century was now located on reclaimed land downstream of the old walled town.

own account, usually sharing ship space with many others. Ships were getting bigger and probably more efficient: average ship tonnage invoiced at Cork roughly doubled between the first and last quarters of the century. Most of the city's 140 merchants in 1795 relied on one of the city's six ship brokers, on the six 'constant traders' that sailed regularly between Cork and Bristol, or on other independent shipowners. But a minority of merchants still continued to invest in shipping, evidenced by the relatively large number of Cork vessels licensed to engage in privateering during the century. But the profits of war were principally derived from official contracts with the British navy or army, or from covert private orders that originated from French naval sources. Several of the century's largest mercantile fortunes seem to have been based on astute wartime deal-making.[12]

Cork's exports exceeded those of Dublin, but its imports were far more modest. The impact of the English Navigation Acts (1663, 1671 and 1685) had a direct bearing on patterns of importation: in rare moments in the late seventeenth century when the English prohibition on direct importation of 'enumerated goods' from the American colonies to Ireland had lapsed, tobacco and sugar imports coming into Cork from across the Atlantic soared, and indeed at one point a sugar refinery was opened which supplied all Munster 'and even Dublin with great part'. But after 1685 Cork lost out on the chance to become a great tobacco entrepot (like Glasgow), and when 'free trade' in colonial goods was finally conceded by London in 1780 it was far too late to make a difference. However, in the meantime Cork's natural advantages more than offset the opportunity lost. Its superb harbour, adjacent to the sea routes used by English and northern European traders entering the Atlantic, and its location as outlet for a grass-rich hinterland meant that it could supply durable and sought-after foodstuffs in high volume and at competitive prices, and could therefore reap powerful economies of scale.[13]

Most of Cork's Anglican merchant families lasted in business for no more than two generations, with family heirs directed to the professions and to rural respectability (see Plate 8). Indeed, a retreat to broad acres was perhaps more evident here than in other Irish cities, as the less than salubrious state of the city and the delights of the Harbour and its surrounds removed many from an everyday presence in the city, although they still retained a major stake in town. Kinship links with the minor gentry of the wider county were notably strong and mutually beneficial. This was of course much less true with merchants of dissenting or Catholic background. Some Dissenters did buy land on a large scale (like Richard Hare), but most did not. And among Catholics the old tradition of intermarriage between well-to-do merchants in Cork, Waterford, Limerick and overseas remained a dominant pattern, reinforcing advantageous kinship networks, although Cork's Catholic diaspora was less numerous than that of other Munster cities. In the case of the six daughters of David Rochford, a Cork Catholic trader with a Limerick landed background, two were married to Irishmen resident in Spain, one to a resident in Nantes, two to Catholic merchants in Waterford, and only one locally. A similar pattern of commercial alliances through marriage continued among the Quaker families in the city, sustaining multiple links between Cork, Waterford and the other centres of Quaker strength within the province.[14]

ADAPTATION AND SPECIALIZATION

Limerick had its Quakers too, but the leading merchants on Shannonside throughout the eighteenth century were predominantly Catholic. The city had been developing something of a cosmopolitan character in the previous century with strong Dutch influence. At least three of its mayors between 1669 and 1679 were of Dutch or French extraction and one, the rumbustious Dutchman William Yorke, served on three occasions; he built the Exchange immediately beside the cathedral and contributed to the casting of the latter's great 'bells and chimes'. Dutch influence had faded by the time of the Williamite sieges, and the post-1691 city made a slow and fitful recovery. Thereafter it attracted few expatriate traders, its strength being more as a great regional centre, a magnet for the wealthy graziers, sheep-masters and gentry of its fertile hinterland, evidenced by the variety of crafts and shops. Its first bank, Maunsells (established in 1789) reflected this upper-class milieu.[15]

Activity in the port was slow to grow (see Table 3.1), but business links with Cork were close and land carriage between the two cities was unusually busy. Limerick city may indeed have benefited more from Cork's pre-eminence than its modest export performance suggests. Thus when beef was running scarce in Cork, supplies were on occasion hurried southwards overland. Limerick's reported share of Irish beef and butter exports peaked quite late and declined sharply in the last quarter of the century, but other commodities – pork and cereals – more than compensated. Shipping based at the port was much smaller than in Cork or Waterford, with an overall tonnage of less than 1,000 registered in 1776, but there was a sharp increase in local shipping from the 1780s.[16] However there had always been a handful of ocean-going vessels, and several Limerick families became major traders in France and the Caribbean, venturing afar if not always owning ocean-going vessels. But a Limerick-owned vessel, the *Prosperity*, is recorded as sailing the Middle Passage into Barbados with some ninety-two slaves in 1718. There are recurring references to men of Limerick origin participating in both the British and French slave trades, a pattern perhaps traceable to the purchase by Limerick's David Creagh of a plantation in Barbados in 1706 and later investments, also by Creagh, in Jamaica. The last act in that story was the notorious attempt in 1784, in the heady days after 'free trade', to raise funds in Limerick to outfit no less than six slaving vessels. It flopped.[17]

The small knot of Limerick merchants who traded overseas were mostly Catholic, some with old roots in the city (the Creaghs, Arthurs and Stacpooles), others marrying into these families (the Roches from north Cork, the Kellys from the Midlands). And when ship tonnage began to pick up from the 1750s, the same families dominated the scene, led by the ubiquitous Roches. Until that time the old Merchant's Quay had been a bottleneck for shipping, although a consortium of Protestant merchants had reclaimed what became Mardyke Quay on the Abbey River in the 1710s. But from the 1760s the riverside began to be transformed, with Stephen and Philip Roche and Patrick Arthur leading the way with investments in quays and stores, maltings and cooperages. The same Limerick families achieved greater notice in the world outside in the final decades of the century when, as we shall see, they played a decisive role in the most ambitious urban development initiative outside Dublin. They were also swept up in the turbulent politics of the 1790s, with dramatically contrasting outcomes.[18]

Waterford's eighteenth-century revival began earlier, helped by the city's intimate links with the near Continent. Trade with Spain and France was locally organized and financed, and was conducted on locally owned vessels. It was greatly facilitated by the ongoing migration of Waterford traders to Flemish, French, and Spanish destinations, notably to Ostend, Saint-Malo, Nantes, Cádiz, Malaga and Tenerife, a pattern of movement that was older, larger and more enduring than elsewhere in Ireland. It predated the Cromwellian expulsions, although the 1650s stand out as a time of unprecedented exodus of merchants and their families, most of whom never returned. But, as Talbott has argued, the extensive commercial network that was in place on the Continent by 1700 was not primarily created by politics nor constrained by it: there was after all a particularly powerful group of Waterford-born merchants in eighteenth-century London, and there was a continuity of movement of Catholic youth from Waterford to Europe stretching far into the eighteenth century and operating as a form of chain migration, with nephews and young cousins being sent out as apprentices and *commis* to trading houses in familiar destinations. In Cádiz, possessing the largest Waterford colony anywhere on the Continent, a census of 1773 revealed that the great majority of the 243 adults whose origin was Ireland were themselves Irish-born, both the fully-fledged merchants trading to the Americas, and their clerks and young assistants. Over a third of the 680 'Irish' wills recorded in eighteenth-century Cádiz were of persons of Waterford origin and, unlike the Galway diaspora, there was a great spread of surnames (44), many of which barely register in the civic record at home. In no sense then were these religious refugees.[19]

Even in the first decade of the eighteenth century, a few of Waterford's Catholic families secured greater concessions from the Corporation than was the case anywhere else in Ireland including, remarkably, civic freedom – but without the franchise – which was given to a handful of Catholics each year, starting in the 1710s. Whether this leniency arose from the depressed state of the city in the first decades of the century or reflected the greater leverage of Waterford's Catholic merchants, thanks to well-endowed kith and kin overseas, is unclear. But the family names of the new Catholic freemen suggest that they came from outside the old civic elite; indeed some of the successful Catholic firms that emerged during the century had very modest beginnings, graduating from ship captaincy into wholesale trade. Later explanations that Waterford's Protestant citizenry were simply more tolerant have not been proven.[20]

At the centre of the city's revival was the Newfoundland trade: from the 1670s Waterford had been the stop-off point for English West Country vessels sailing to the great cod fishery, supplying foodstuffs and labour in a trade that expanded greatly in the eighteenth century. Gradually, Waterford merchants and Waterford mariners became directly involved in the fishery and the colony itself. By the 1770s, beyond butter and pork, candles and beef, the city was supplying huge quantities of bread and beer, clothing and leather footwear to the sixty or more English vessels preparing each spring to make the crossing to the Cod Banks. The trade in servants, temporary and permanent, was also big business by then: almost 5,000 young men (and a few women) were going out from Waterford each year. In subsequent decades small numbers of local vessels and local merchants began to venture across the Atlantic as well and make their mark in Newfoundland. Eventually at least ten Waterford firms had close trading relationships with family connections based in St John's and neighbouring stations.[21]

Waterford nevertheless took a very long time to mount a challenge to Cork in the provisions trade. Its involvement with the Caribbean and the mainland colonies never amounted to much. One factor, perhaps more relevant at the beginning of the century, was that despite the excellence of its capacious quays, in wartime the Waterford estuary was far less secure than were Cork's approaches. And for English vessels sailing into Atlantic waters, Waterford had no locational advantages over Cork, where the safety and capacity of the lower harbour were unrivalled. A more specific issue was inland access: the movement of livestock into Waterford from much of its hinterland (south Kilkenny and Wexford) was impeded by the breadth and depth of the river and by the absence of a bridge below Carrick-on-Suir, Inistioge or Graiguenamanagh on any of the three rivers, as was recognized in 1770:

> In driving those useful and beneficial creatures to our markets, just at the door thereof through which they are to enter, behold! there is a full stop made: they must be battered and drove into a ferryboat, fretting and wasting themselves, while they are bound down with rings and ropes to secure them. The young well-fed beast will not comply to this usage, but often plunges out into the tide, and after a long drift way up stream or down stream as the current answers, the fatigued creature is with much difficulty got to land. What relief then can there be, for what is so prejudicial to the trader, but a BRIDGE.[22]

Two decades later a fund of £30,000 was raised (mostly by private subscription, some by parliamentary grant) to buy out the owner of the ferry and underwrite the costs of constructing a great timber bridge. This was completed in 1794 under the Bostonian Lemuel Cox's direction, and it had considerable impact on the city's capacity as a commercial centre. The precedent was the great Foyle bridge in Derry, built three years earlier by the same engineer. However, Waterford's potential to become a processing and manufacturing hub was still constrained by water: the River Suir was tidal and deep and nearby tributaries were inadequate for water-powered industry. But there was no such problem on the Suir further upstream as the remarkable growth in flour milling in the city's hinterland (notably around Clonmel) demonstrated.[23]

By then the revival of the English market for Irish foodstuffs was well and truly established, following the lifting, in 1759, of the English import ban on Irish cattle and salted provisions. Waterford merchants were notably successful in developing markets in London and in lesser southern and western English ports for their butter and bacon, flour and tallow, much of it sourced in the rich hinterland that had previously supplied Cork. Some commodities, notably pork and bacon, that had first been developed for the Newfoundland trade were now adapted for the English consumer. In this re-orientation of trade towards England, Waterford was of course better placed than Cork, and a group of merchants relatively new to the city, predominantly Quakers drawn from the south Midlands, dominated this sector well into the nineteenth century. Courtney & Ridgeway, the largest such firm, has been studied by Cullen: the firm shipped some 1,294 tons of butter in the single year from June 1791 to May 1792, representing about a third of the city's butter exports at the time; they purchased the butter unsalted from upstream dealers in the hinterland, processed it and sold it mostly on commission to 108 English buyers (many of them inland). Unlike commission merchants of old, they also provided the shipping to convey the butter to English ports. Even the product was different from the heavily salted butter that Cork merchants had been supplying to tropical markets for a hundred years.[24]

Bristol connections with Waterford always loomed large, and there was a two-way movement of apprenticeships and young traders of all denominations. But Waterford's Quaker firms, most of whom had only gravitated towards the city in the mid eighteenth century, came from within Ireland – from Tipperary and the south Midlands – and were the largest firms in the city by the end of the century; as John Mannion has observed, they were 'by far the most durable of Waterford's merchant community'. Anglican and Presbyterian merchants had featured strongly in the mainland American and Caribbean trade, but their longevity was less. In all, about half of the 120-odd merchant houses identified by Mannion as involved in foreign trade in the decade 1766–75 were Catholic, but only a minority of the 120 were shipowners. The ship-owing minority and the sea captains they employed were predominantly Catholic, and it was from the ranks of men who knew their rigging that new generations of venturers emerged. But one indication of enduring Protestant dominance was the composition of the new bridge commissioners: most of the thirteen members were townsmen, and all but one of them were Protestant. In the same month that the bridge's foundations were laid, Waterford's first multi-denominational private bank, Hayden & Rivers, formed by a Kilkenny Protestant and a leading Catholic merchant fifteen years earlier in 1778, entered bankruptcy (see Plate 9).[25]

INLAND HUB

Eighteenth-century Ireland was unusual in that all but one of its cities were on the coast. Pre-industrial port cities have in general tended to be more cosmopolitan than inland cities and more at the mercy of the external world than was the case with deeply rooted regional capitals, where smaller enterprises were protected from competition by the high costs of overland transport. Was this true of Kilkenny, the only inland city in Ireland, and did its merchant community differ from those in the ports?[26]

Like most of the ports, but unlike many smaller inland towns in the south, Kilkenny's population grew quite strongly throughout the eighteenth century, probably at around 1.0 per cent a year between 1731 and the final years of the century, by which time it was close to 15,000; then came a period of higher growth (nearer 2 per cent a year) in the lead-up to the 1821 census.[27] From the first Duke of Ormond's time, Kilkenny had a strong workshop economy based on textiles, principally involved in the production of medium and coarse woollens for the Irish market. Kilkenny's great fairs drew cloth buyers from Dublin and beyond, and the city became almost a national hub for the sale of coarse woollen cloth, much of it manufactured in the towns and countryside further south.

Thanks in part to the patronage of the Dublin Society in the 1740s, the city's workshops came to specialize in the manufacture of worsted blankets, and this became the staple manufacture of Kilkenny up until the 1820s; at least 10 per cent of the city's population in 1800 were directly dependent on the blanket industry, and Irishtown, the cathedral parish of St Canice's where most of the manufacturers lived, contained nearly half the city's population in the late eighteenth century. But blankets alone do not explain Kilkenny's dynamism. The key was the growth of Dublin. Despite its distance from the capital (over 125 kilometres) and the absence of inland navigation, the naturally fertile tillage country south and east of Kilkenny city became a breadbasket for Dublin from the late seventeenth century, and large quantities of wheat were carted overland at around the same time that anthracite coal from north Kilkenny (mined on the Castlecomer plateau) began to be carried along the same roads to the capital. Thus in the first half of the eighteenth century, a time of very uncertain external markets for Irish produce, the Kilkenny region's farmers could count on the regularity of Dublin demand and they benefited accordingly. It helped that Kilkenny was on the principal road from Dublin to Waterford and Cork, and the opening in the early 1730s of direct turnpike links with the capital to the north-east and Clonmel to the south-west reinforced its position as a transport and communications hub. From early in the century its service industries – notably its inns – reflected this; it was the only significant inland centre of wholesale brewing in the country, and from 1767 it became home to one of the earliest and most influential provincial newspapers, *Finn's Leinster Journal*.[28]

Kilkenny's civic leaders were for the most part drawn from 'new' families, the descendants of Cromwellian settlers who had acquired urban property in the 1650s and who then consolidated their position during the long decline of Ormond power. They were almost entirely Anglican, and unlike the Munster cities there were few Dissenters and almost no Quakers here (despite the large clusters in neighbouring south Tipperary and Queen's County). Kilkenny Corporation itself was almost entirely controlled by rival factions of county gentry, and they took little interest in municipal affairs until the 1780s although, in a most unusual concession to the Catholic majority, the Corporation removed the distinction between freemen and residents in 1741, allowing the latter the same privileges to trade duty-free in the city's markets as were enjoyed by freemen. The first trade directory for the city (1788) suggests a well-developed regional centre evolving slowly, with a few specialist trades and the retail dominance of 'grocers'. The business names are overwhelmingly Catholic. Only a small handful of traders described themselves as 'merchants', suggesting the absence of speculative wholesalers engaging in bulk transactions over long distance. No trading family rose to great wealth in the city during the century and, tellingly, no private bank was established until 1800. Rather, it was a city populated by a multitude of small workshops, busy warehouses, and inns. There were about 30 professionals in 1788, with lawyers the most numerous (see Plate 10).[29]

Yet there was scope for innovators: William Colles (1702–70), second son of an immigrant surgeon and twice mayor of the city, is credited with single-handedly commercializing the extraction of the black marble that was quarried south of the city, and pioneering new ways of handling, cutting and

Figure 7 High St, Kilkenny, was dominated by the great fourteenth-century market cross until this was removed in 1771 to open up the street.

polishing the stone by water power. Colles was both an inventor and entrepreneur, sending the keenly priced 'chimney-pieces, tables and other marble furniture' to Dublin (where he opened a warehouse in the 1730s), and to Bristol and Liverpool. His marble water pipes were offered to Dublin and taken up in Cork. And like many contemporaries he tried his hand at cultivating flax and developing a handicraft linen industry (less successfully); he built one of the earliest multi-storied flour mills a short distance out of town at Abbeyvale in 1762 to supply the Dublin market. This was the first of a great string of bolting mills constructed during the next thirty years along the Nore, all focused on Dublin sales. He rebuilt bridges, barracks and the city's very impressive town hall, the Tholsel, and was the champion of plans to build a canal southwards to Thomastown. Small flat-bottomed cots made the journey down the Nore, but Colles had a much greater ambition to construct a commercial link to the sea. Yet despite considerable investment of parliamentary grants, the waterway was only partially completed by his death and it never became operational.[30]

4

NORTHERN TURN

Kilkenny and Belfast, two communities of similar size in 1700 with populations somewhat over 4,000, had each been shaped by a great aristocratic dynasty, the Ormonds in Kilkenny, the Donegalls in Belfast. The power of both families was drastically diminished in the early eighteenth century through a mixture of debt, strategic political miscalculation and the failure of healthy heirs. Despite this there was a strong element of continuity in Kilkenny: it retained its status as an inland regional capital with an old urban fabric, a Catholic business community and a weak Protestant presence. But Belfast underwent great change: it was much more of a colonial town (in every sense) than Kilkenny, an international trading hub dominated by a wholesale merchant community that was overwhelmingly Presbyterian.

That community was, and would remain, small and intimate. Eighteenth-century Belfast never had more than forty to sixty general merchants trading overseas at any time, although by 1800 they were joined by growing numbers of specialist importers of consumer goods. From the 1660s it had built up a lively maritime trade (see Table 4.1), but the physical transformation of the town really only began a century later. Its population roughly doubled between the 1690s and 1757, when it was put at 8,549; unlike the southern cities it did not become a great migrant destination until the growth spurt at the end of the century. Despite the ease of navigation in Belfast Lough, the town lay too far north to attract British or European vessels destined for southern Europe, nor was it optimally placed as a transatlantic stopover. Therefore most of the shipping at Belfast was locally owned and Belfast merchants were obliged to be venturers at sea themselves.[1]

In Jean Agnew's study of thirty-two Belfast merchant families active in the second half of the seventeenth century, the two most successful and long-lived

Table 4.1

Ship Tonnage Invoiced (excluding coastal vessels) at Belfast, Derry, Sligo, Drogheda
and Dublin: 1701–1800

25-year averages (1701–25 = 100)

	1701–25	1726–50	1751–75	1776–1800
Belfast	100	132	180	548
Derry	100	146	317	490
Sligo	100	142	304	466
Drogheda	100	126	237	615
Dublin	100	158	257	345

Absolute tonnage values for 1701–25: Belfast, 8,123; Derry, 2,408; Sligo, 734; Drogheda, 3,611; Dublin, 69,933.
Source: TNA, CUST/15.

were from Galloway, George Macartney of Auchinleck, and 'Black' George
Macartney of Urr (*c.* 1630–1702); they were religious conformists, but nearly
three-quarters of their fellow traders were Presbyterian and, like them, Scottish-
born or of recent Scottish vintage. More than half of Agnew's group of merchants
owned or part-owned trading vessels. By the 1680s some sixty-seven ships were
attached to the port, some admittedly very small, by which time the town was
clearly a place of burgeoning trade. Agnew's thirty-two families inter-married
and developed wide social networks; about a quarter of them had family or business links with Dublin (Black George had six regular correspondents in the
capital), and from the 1690s traders of Belfast origin were appearing in London,
Rotterdam, Bordeaux and Barbados, sourcing raw materials and luxury and
exotic goods for the home market. Nevertheless, as in Cork, the restrictions on
trade with the American colonies resulting from the Restoration Navigation
Acts were heartily resented, and the 1705 concession allowing the direct export
of linens to the English colonies was seen by Isaac Macartney as a welcome relief
for 'poor Ireland'.[2]

For a long time after the take-off of the linen industry, Belfast handled only
a small share of cloth exports, but it quickly established itself as an entry point
for the raw materials, notably flaxseed and potash (for bleaching). From the
1730s flaxseed sourced in the Middle Colonies (specifically Connecticut and
New York) was Belfast's principal transatlantic trade in what became a complex
web of long-distance venturing, with linen, beef and other provisions being
sent out to the slave islands, and linen and passengers to the Middle Colonies;
flaxseed, rum and flour, sugar and tobacco came east on the return journey,
either directly or via British ports of convenience. Almost all the prominent

merchant houses in the town seem to have had a passing involvement in trade with the Caribbean. In 1792, shortly before the trade was eclipsed by war, nearly two-fifths of Belfast's beef and pork exports were going to the islands, despatched in the course of the year on 25 ships (see Plate 11).[3]

The Belfast merchant community of this era has been characterized by Norman Gamble as 'cohesive but hierarchical', and what distinguished it from the southern cities was its adaptability and freedom from institutional constraint. The Corporation had a marginal role in the life of the town, although still controlled by the Earls of Donegall, with the office-holders drawn from an Anglican rump. But after Belfast Castle was destroyed in a fire in 1708 the Donegall family never resided in the town again until 1799. Tellingly the Castle grounds, despite their centrality, remained an empty space. Other big landowners of the region were rarely in evidence either, and there was no trade guild and almost no local involvement in parliamentary contests (the constituency being a closed borough). Local energies were therefore not diverted into Dublin-style political gamesmanship. Even the fissiparous tendencies of the Presbyterian Church, so evident in rural Ulster, impacted relatively little on the town's solidarity.[4]

So, left largely to itself, Belfast served its increasingly wealthy and commercialized hinterland very effectively. Business partnerships, at wholesale and retail level, were more prevalent than in the southern cities, and this presumably reflected Scottish practice (even though the Irish courts gave far less legal protection to partnerships until the Anonymous Partnerships Act of 1782). From the late seventeenth century, maritime ventures originating in the town were normally funded by two to eight partners brought together in a charter-party contract that lasted until the return of the vessel from overseas, and ownership of the vessel itself was shared in more permanent contracts. There was nothing unusual in such arrangements – it was one of the principal ways of raising both working and fixed capital – but partnering seems to have endured longer than elsewhere and the number of shareholders (notably in ship contracts) to have increased. By 1807 in the town's first trade directory nearly a fifth of all the entries related to partnerships of one kind or another – a far higher proportion than in southern directories. This multiplicity of long- and short-term non-family partnerships was a form of communal risk-sharing, and its prevalence may have helped cushion the impact of business failure and external shock and have contributed to the pervasive local belief in the town's 'good character . . . justly obtained for integrity and exactness'.[5]

One of the more remarkable if untypical partnerships was that between Thomas Gregg (1718–96) and Waddell Cunningham (1729–97), at a time when Gregg was a major Belfast merchant and Cunningham a young Belfast emigrant in New York. In just a few years in the city, Cunningham had graduated from being a store-owner in a side street to a shareholder in at least seven ships engaged in long-distance trade. Thomas Truxes has documented how this trans-atlantic partnership, principally involving the export of Irish linen and the importation of flaxseed, grain and flour, began in 1756: Gregg was the senior partner with superior financial muscle, Cunningham the pugnacious deal-maker, and they were involved in a range of Irish-American–Caribbean ventures, some of them clearly illegal in time of war. It was both highly profitable and, albeit with various modifications, long lasting, being dissolved only in 1775. But a decade earlier Cunningham had returned to Belfast, leaving members of the consortium to trade in continental America and to invest in land and slave plan-tations (in Dominica). The two gained notice and notoriety at home, Gregg as leading financier in the Lagan Navigation, Cunningham as promoter of a string of industrial ventures, and both of them as controversial investors in rural leases on the ample Donegall estates in Antrim (culminating in the torching of Cunningham's Belfast home in 1771 by displaced tenants). But neither they nor their peers chose to invest heavily in rural freehold purchases, and while there was a long tradition of mercantile investment in urban property speculation, neither Gregg nor Cunningham was tempted to play such a long game.[6]

They were however involved in a remarkable set of actions at the end of the American War that boosted Belfast's great leap forward in the 1780s.[7] The most public initiative was the decision to establish a huge white-linen hall that would rival that in Dublin (and one that was simultaneously being planned for Newry); this was funded locally and was brought into service within two years (1784–1785) on a 5-acre site provided by the Earl of Donegall. The formation of a Chamber of Commerce in 1783 provided the platform for exploiting this initiative. In preparation for the opening of the Hall, the organizing committee was involved in creating a 'discount office', a novel type of publicly sanctioned private bank designed to facilitate the processing of bills of exchange, and in establishing a fund to coordinate and expand the number of 'constant traders' sailing between Belfast and London. None of these initiatives as originally conceived was entirely successful, least of all the Chamber of Commerce itself, but the efficient operation of the discount office and the enhanced transport links with London were reflected in the marked expansion of Belfast's linen

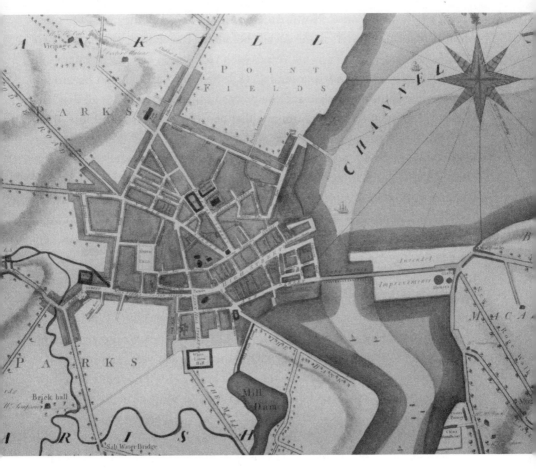

Figure 8 Belfast's late eighteenth-century great leap forward captured on paper for the first time: James Willliamson's elegant *Map of the town and environs of Belfast* (1791).

exports on the eve of the cotton boom. But one initiative that did not take off was Cunningham's attempt in 1784 to raise funds for a great slaving vessel to exploit the African market and purchase slaves for the plantations, where several Belfast merchants now held extensive stakes. As was the case of the failed slaving project in Limerick, Cunningham's bravado found no public support.[8]

DERRY'S CHALLENGE

Cunningham and the Gregg family had made much of their money in another form of human traffic: the transportation of indentured servants and other passengers from Belfast to North America. In a busy field, they were the most prominent local venturers in the decade before the Revolution, sending out two or three large passenger-carrying vessels each year. When organized emigration to the Americas had started around 1718 it had been a small and hazardous business, the ships diminutive and the profits limited. By the 1770s all that had changed. But the merchant community that benefited most from the growth of the passenger trade was that of Derry. From the beginning, the Presbyterian districts of the north-west had shown a heightened propensity to emigrate, although it was only from the 1740s that the movement became regular, closely complementing the reverse flow of flaxseed from the Middle Colonies in which Derry's merchants also invested, making the best of both opportunities. Given Derry's remote location, a high proportion of the shipping was locally owned (some 67 sea-going vessels in 1767, compared to 'about 50' in Belfast), and the trade was largely conducted on local Derry account, although there were close business links with kin and co-religionists in Philadelphia's merchant community, including some Derry investment in American-based vessels. When Arthur Young visited Derry in 1776 he was informed that 'over the previous eighteen or twenty years' 2,400 persons had departed the city each year, and indeed the number was probably higher in the depressed early 1770s. Emigrants were now accommodated on ships that were up to ten times the tonnage of the pioneering vessels of 1718.[9]

On the strength of the American trade, Derry moved from being something of a backwater in the 1720s to a wealthy port by 1770, drawing its human cargoes from a wide swathe of west Ulster and, in reverse, distributing the flood of flaxseed across half the province. The other element in its prosperity was linen yarn, almost all of it exported on the 'yarn ships' to Liverpool. This trade had grown from almost nothing in 1700 to be worth, at its peak in the 1760s, over £100,000 per annum (straining the capacity of small Ship Quay, despite improvement grants received from the Irish Parliament). This yarn trade to south Lancashire stands comparison with the huge flow of worsted yarn from Waterford and Cork that was despatched to East Anglia, in both instances a semi-processed product destined for English looms that gave thousands of marginalized rural households a ready income – until advances in English mill technology almost completely undermined both trades in the 1790s.[10]

Derry however remained a prosperous trading town, the rural linen industry in its hinterland expanding and its business community becoming more diverse. Throughout the century it enjoyed the patronage of powerful politicians and

Revenue Commissioners – notably William Conolly in the early decades, John Beresford after 1770 (his country home was not far away in Ballykelly). Thus Derry's traders were well looked after: in 1761 one Philadelphia merchant wrote knowingly to his Sligo correspondent about the favoured position of Derry arising from 'the influence of the merch[an]ts there over the [Revenue] officers'. And it is undeniable that having the same Revenue Collector, Hugh Hill (a kinsman of Beresford) in office for thirty-two years (1763–95), during which time he was mayor and a long-standing MP for the city, was doubly advantageous for the small business community around him. There was also the Earl of Bristol (1730–1803), Derry's singularly energetic Church of Ireland bishop: he championed the city's interests and supported the Corporation in its near twenty-year struggle to secure statutory powers to bridge the Foyle (against strong political opposition from the Earl of Abercorn and the Strabane merchants among others). When finally given the go-ahead in 1789, the Corporation commissioned Lemuel Cox to install the first of his great wooden bridges.[11]

Derry's passenger trade had fully recovered by then, but at that stage it was mainly operated by American-owned vessels, 'all beautifully neat to catch customers', and they were no longer indentured servants. Derry had much the largest share of this trade, which reached an all-time peak just after the turn of the century and prior to the imposition of controls and regulations in 1803 (by which time there were fearsome tales of overcrowding). Derry's history of venturing far afield continued into the nineteenth century, with increased linen exports, notably to new Caribbean destinations. But only one Croesus emerged on the Foyle: James Alexander (1730–1802), younger son and brother of Derry merchants and sugar refiners, who in a short period serving as an officer in the East India Company made a proverbial fortune and returned to the city in the early 1770s. 'Nabob Alexander' built locally and bought land in nearby Inishowen, then ploughed £96,400 into purchasing the Caledon estate in south Tyrone in 1776. The same year he became an MP for the city and was a willing patron of local merchants while helping to launch one of the most successful business partnerships in Cork (which later became Beamish & Crawford). But his own focus was on Dublin Castle and a peerage, which he finally secured in 1790.[12]

COLLATERAL BENEFITS

Sligo, despite its vast hinterland, was one of the slowest port communities to register the eighteenth-century upturn. At mid century, brick and slate were still a rarity in the town. Its merchants and shopkeepers were a religious mix and only a handful of them traded at sea: six of the nine merchants present in 1749 were Protestant, and four of these had Catholic servants in their household. Local demand from the large garrison and a cluster of nearby resident gentry brought money to the town, but the big change came from the 1750s as demand for grain and cattle from the linen districts in Ulster had a transformative effect, and linen yarn in large quantities was transported overland for shipment from Derry or Drogheda. Edward Corkran, then head of the most successful Catholic business in Sligo, was trading with Philadelphia in the 1760s, where at least two of his fellow townsmen were based. 'Much more flourishing than Galway' was Daniel Beaufort's judgment of the town in 1788, and 'no party divisions much obstruct its improvement'. Andrew Maiben, a Sligo merchant and linen bleacher for more than thirty years, reckoned in 1790 that the growth of linen manufacturing in and around the town over that time 'will amaze you', what with a ten-fold growth in the number of webs brought to market since the 1750s. But with a measure of prosperity came controversy: where should public markets in the growing town be located? In 1785 'the majority of the mercantile inhabitants' appealed to Charles O'Hara, one of the county's MPs, to halt the actions of the sovereign and his clique of burgesses in their plans to close the traditional marketplace, and to 'lay open the enormity of the measure and do justice to an injured people', an elegant transmission of political discourse from the national to the intensely local.[13]

Sligo was a western beneficiary of the North's linen economy, the impact late in coming but important: in the 1780s at least one Belfast firm was a sleeping partner in a Sligo trading enterprise. Drogheda on the southern boundary was also a beneficiary, and there the impact of linen on the urban economy was a much older story. Like other ancient secondary ports along Ireland's east coast – Wexford, Dundalk and Newry – most of Drogheda's trading was restricted to the Irish Sea, its merchants few in number. Admittedly, Newry briefly broke out of this group in the third quarter of the century and for a time a group of ambitious firms based there built up extensive American trade and posed a real challenge to Belfast, exploiting the town's proximity to the heartland of the fine linen manufacture and the relative security of anchorages on Carlingford Lough.

In Drogheda's case, located near the mouth of the Boyne, larger shipping had major difficulties reaching its quays, and there was limited secure anchorage downstream. Thus while there was some North American trading with several merchants importing flaxseed and rum, the town was far better placed to expand its cross-channel trade, in particular with the rising town of Liverpool. Since the sixteenth century Drogheda merchants had shipped linen yarn to Lancashire, and in the Restoration era yarn was second only to wool in its exports. In the 1680s Pippard and other long-established Catholic merchants were trading to Saint-Malo, Cádiz and the Canaries, but most of the town's trade was already with Liverpool. And with the exceptional growth on Merseyside at the end of the seventeenth century Drogheda's other associations faded, and the export of linen yarn and cereals became the safe and profitable business of the town. The supply hinterland for yarn was huge, but after mid century Derry merchants had managed to capture most of this export business. The fundamentals for Drogheda were food exports – oats and oatmeal, wheat and later flour, drawn from its wealthy Boyne valley hinterland, and despatched on small vessels to Scotland and the north-west of England.

By the late 1780s Drogheda had become the largest grain market in the country, the conduit for a huge movement of flour and oats to feed humans and horses in Lancashire and Clydeside's industrializing towns. Good years for the traders when grain prices were high were bad years for consumers, and Drogheda, like Cork and Waterford, was the scene of food riots directed at exporters and at the ships on the quay. The town features prominently in James Kelly's history of Irish food rioting: between 1729 and 1817 there was major trouble, sometimes violence, on at least eleven occasions, which put a brake on trade in the hungry years. Meanwhile Drogheda had its own distinctive industrialization, with a huge growth of linen weaving in and around the town itself, producing a cheap-quality cloth for the Liverpool market, some of it destined for slave clothing. At the end of the century new firms and predominantly Catholic ones emerged on the strength of this linen boom.[14]

Drogheda was more than an old trading community. For much of the century both the Anglican and Catholic archbishops of Armagh resided intermittently in the town, and this helped strengthen it as a place of resort. One of its natives, Henry Singleton (1682–1759), after representing the town in Parliament for many years (as had his father), achieved high judicial office in 1740, but he remained a very active patron of the town, maintaining a great house in St Laurence Street until his death. And a small knot of Protestant families who controlled the Corporation and its valuable land-bank retained an involvement in trade and residence in town over a surprisingly long period, notably the Hardmans, merchants from the 1680s until Edward Hardman (1741–1814) retired in about 1809. The town's wealthiest merchant, he was handling some £20,000 a year in grain sales in the late 1780s and was also a substantial wine importer. In later life he sat as one of the town's MPs for eight years, the confidant of John Foster (1740–1828) – a major Louth land-owner and for a quarter of a century one of the most influential figures in Parliament and in Dublin Castle. Foster was Speaker of the Commons for sixteen years and was the most energetic public champion of projects for Irish economic development, not least the linen industry. Yet even with Foster as a powerful patron of the town and with the presence of old money, investment to improve the quays and maritime access to the port was hesitant, and only had real momentum from 1797 when the powers of the Harbour Board, created in 1790, were considerably strengthened.[15]

DUBLIN AND THE NORTH

The 30 miles of toll road between Drogheda and Dublin was probably the busiest carriageway in eighteenth-century Ireland. It was the route between east Ulster and the capital, and most of the whitened linen coming south will have come this way. One of the first Irish stage-coach services linked Drogheda and Dublin from the 1730s (Belfast and Dublin did not have a mail-coach service until 1789). On the approaches to the capital city, the landscape was by then dotted with villas owned by men of northern background, notably Violet Hill, Samuel Dick's 'spacious mansion' at Raheny, 'a place where there are plentiful signs of what the metal gold can perform'. Dick (d. 1802) was perhaps the city's most successful linen draper turned financier, a major investor in the East India Company and the Bank of Ireland, sleeping partner in a brewery and a promoter of the Commercial Buildings in Dame St., which opened in 1799 and provided a home for the fledgling Irish Stock Exchange.[16]

In its ascent to become a premier European city, Dublin owed not a little to the linen trade, to the wider prosperity of the northern province, and to the many northerners who chose to settle in Dublin. Indeed the contribution of people with strong Ulster associations in the physical shaping of the city is striking – from 'Black' George Macartney's business partner, Humphrey Jervis, who became Dublin's first property developer in the Restoration period, Charles Campbell, who played a decisive role in the development of the Drogheda estate before Luke Gardiner got his hands on it, William Conolly and Archbishop William King, who between them transformed the public architecture of the early Georgian city, to the Earl of Charlemont, John Beresford and Francis Johnston, whose combined impact on the look of the city late in the century and beyond was, as we shall see, immense. But the North's impact on Dublin's economy was broader than that, and most of it started and ended with linen, the handling and export of which in the 'short eighteenth century' was the principal export of the city.[17]

This was first evident in Restoration Dublin, with a cluster of Ulster merchants already present in the 1670s. A critical step-up came in 1696 with the removal of English customs duties on Irish linen (at a time when tariffs on rival continental linens were being raised). This handed Irish producers a strategic advantage on the English market and opened the way for linen to become the great industrial success story of the next century. Dublin was central in that success: it became the unrivalled national marketplace for whitened linen in the 1690s and held that position until the 1780s, during which time annual exports from the port rose from less than half a million yards to nearly 22 million by the 1790s. This ascendancy found physical expression in the Linen Hall, constructed during the 1720s on a green-field site on the northern edge of the city by the Linen Board, a parliamentary body established in 1711 to promote and regulate the trade. In place of haggling in the small inns along Church St and Pill Lane, northern drapers now flocked to the vast quadrangular trading hall, eventually containing over 280 small rooms (see Plate 12).

The thousands of webs of plain white linen traded there were mainly destined for export, to Chester, London and the colonies beyond. This success story was choreographed in Dublin, not because of the Linen Board or statutory interventions, but because it was Dublin finance and Dublin merchants that funded the growth of Irish linen. The practice grew up for the Dublin dealers to give seasonal credit to Ulster bleachers, allowing them in turn to make cash purchases in the brown linen markets, and this facility endured for most of the eighteenth century, giving Dublin substantial leverage over the Ulster economy. That said, most of those Dublin dealers were themselves of northern Presbyterian or Quaker background, and they maintained strong personal connections with the North. Their concerns were located on a small sector of the city's north side, and the Capel St Presbyterian congregation was for many the focus of their social world.[18]

THE PEOPLE OF BUSINESS

There were other types of specialist trader within Dublin's wholesale commerce whose focus was primarily the home market, notably the grain and flour factors who were increasingly operating outside the confines of public markets and a few of them, like William Colville (1737–1820), another northerner, became major business figures in the city. The salesmasters of Smithfield, brokers who handled the sale of upwards of 30,000 cattle and hundreds of thousands of lamb and sheep annually (all destined for local consumption) were also pivotal in the credit structure of the cattle trade across the Midlands and the east of the country. Yet another trade was represented by the multitude of woollen cloth dealers, associated particularly with Francis St, lying just outside the old walls but inside the city boundary. By the 1750s dealers in cloth (including much of the blankets and stuffs manufactured in Kilkenny) outnumbered all other traders on the street.

Francis St was not a fashionable thoroughfare, but a busy one. Set back on its east side was the largest Catholic church in the city, St Nicholas, which had by default become the Catholic archbishop's principal church. Like all Catholic places of worship it had uncertain legal status; however in 1737 it was saved from legal expropriation by a 'discoverer', thanks to the pre-emptive ingenuity of several Catholic laymen. The religious make-up of the street was typical of the wider city: roughly balanced. One of the long-established Catholic traders was William Toole, variously described as a grocer and a merchant. Among his apprentices in the 1750s was Edward Byrne (1739/40–1804), son of a substantial farmer based close to the border between Dublin and Kildare. During Byrne's apprenticeship, Toole and his brother Dennis, their sister and one of Dennis's daughters all conformed to the Church of Ireland over a twelve-month period in 1759–60. Toole pressured his apprentice Byrne to do the same.[19]

With religious affiliation so deeply enmeshed with identity, conformity was a public act that carried multiple meanings. In Irish cities the principal reason for such an action was to protect property from adverse discovery (where title to a property may have been compromised by the anti-Catholic legislation of 1704 and 1709), or to avoid the legal penalties associated with mixed (Protestant/Catholic) marriage. A large family conversion was therefore highly unusual, and events in the Toole family suggest an evangelical dimension. Byrne not only refused to follow his master in a change of religion but he attempted to dissuade one of Toole's relatives (a daughter or niece) from changing. This row escalated into a legal dispute between apprentice and master, drawing in other Catholic traders on both sides. Byrne eventually won in the courts, by which time he had moved swiftly to become an independent trader: in the 1760s he was listed as a grocer at three nearby addresses, and was then involved with several other Catholic traders in a 'sugar house' near Grafton St. By 1771 he had become a 'sugar baker and distiller' in Mullinahack (off Thomas St) in partnership with John Byrne, presumably a kinsman. Later nicknamed by his political associates as 'The vintner', Byrne was both a wine merchant and a large-scale sugar refiner; he rose to become the city's largest sugar importer from England and Scotland. And the import of sugar, which maintained a remarkable 3.5 per cent growth rate across the whole century, gave ample dividends to those who could scale up their operations.

Byrne's success was all the more remarkable since the wine trade and sugar refining had for a century been bastions of Protestant dominance. In the 1780s he diversified both sectorally (into textile printing) and geographically (investing in sugar bakeries in Cork and Newry), and by 1792 he was generally regarded as the wealthiest merchant in Dublin. A private, astute and energetic trader, he left little trace of his ascent to great wealth, and even after he became a national public figure in 1792 as president of the Catholic Committee he remained more than a little mysterious to contemporaries. By that time he was living in style in a new terraced house in North Great George's St, had a country house in Bray, and landed property in the counties of Dublin, Louth, Tipperary and Down (ear-marked for different members of his large family). Unlike many of his associates he avoided contamination with radical politics after 1795 and remained an active trader operating from a cramped back street within the old city until his death in 1804. It was claimed then that his 'property is almost incalculable, and there are few London merchants who possess more'. Three sons (and a son-in-law in Bordeaux) were also merchants, but they all faded into landed respectability.[20]

In 1761, around the time that Edward Byrne was ending his fraught apprenticeship, a lobby group describing itself as the Committee of Merchants was established in Dublin, 'a voluntary society, composed indiscriminately of all merchants . . . the mere objects of which were the defence of trade against any illegal imposition, and the solicitation of such laws as might prove beneficial to it'. This innocuous-sounding manifesto disguised its significance: while some of those involved were senior members of Dublin Corporation, the new committee distanced itself from 'corporate bodies', constituting itself on 'liberal principles . . . no regard being had in it to any difference of party or opinion, but merely to consideration in trade or capacity, and [an] active disposition to be useful'. This was indeed something new, and 'liberal principles' was code for a membership that would be religiously mixed. Around seven of the twenty-one merchants were Protestant Dissenters and four were Catholic. The inclusion of Catholic merchants such as Anthony Dermott of Usher's Quay and Michael Cosgrave of Abbey St, was a political risk, but it indicates where the impetus for the initiative lay. And while between a fifth and a quarter of the city's merchants were by that stage Catholic, their combined trading assets were almost certainly more modest. The only 'popish' private bank in the eighteenth-century city, that of Dillon & Ferrall, had failed in 1754.[21]

Despite its size, Dublin's merchant community did not dominate eighteenth-century Ireland: there was no 'city' lobby in the Irish parliament. In each generation there had been a few firms that had been trading for two or more generations, but most merchant houses were first-generation businesses, operating without complex partnerships and doing much of their business on the account of overseas traders, their profit coming from a commission charged on the purchase or sale of an agreed stock of goods. Very few of the commercial high-flyers seem to have been city natives, although in the eighteenth century nearly all were Irish-born. But the distinct status of being a wholesale merchant was universally recognized; most of those active in the early eighteenth century were freemen of the Guild of Merchants. Yet neither that guild nor the Corporation acted in the name of the merchant body. There were two reasons for this – the complete exclusion of Catholic traders from full guild membership from 1692, and the progressive exclusion of Presbyterian, Baptist and Quaker merchants after the Test Act of 1704. The number of Catholic merchants involved in overseas trade was by that time quite small, but the number of non-conformist traders had mushroomed: Joseph Damer and Humphrey Jervis had been leading merchants in Restoration Dublin, and they were still around to see their Presbyterian co-religionist Thomas Bell become lord mayor in 1702/3 – and to see him surrender his place as city treasurer and alderman a year later, following his refusal to take the new sacramental test. Benjamin Burton, banker, Dissenter and lord mayor in 1706/7, was similarly disbarred in 1709.[22]

There were perhaps 150 merchants in the city at that time. Listed in the first city directory in 1751 are some 238, and by the 1790s there were over 500, by which time there was an inner core who were officially recognized as wholesalers trading in bulk: they were allowed the 'five and ten' discount on import duties by the Revenue Commissioners, a concession granted to 289 firms by the end of the century. Within this large group were some specialists, but the

Figure 9 Built during the worst of times in 1704/5, Thomas Burgh's Dublin Custom House was increased in height during construction, a measure of the city's commercial primacy and of the importance of the Revenue Commissioners, who were based there.

age of narrow specialization lay in the future. A shrinking minority of the 289 were shipowners or shareholders of a vessel, and it was only those venturing to southern Europe, the Caribbean and the American colonies who maintained a direct interest in shipping. Small firms, with one or two principals, a string of apprentices and a few book-keepers, were the norm, many with a short business life and a vulnerability to the huge vagaries of uncertain markets, unrecoverable debts, fraud and uninsured losses. Daniel Geale, nephew of a former city treasurer and lord mayor, was one of the bigger firms: he traded as a general merchant on Bachelor's Walk, enjoying a net profit from trade of £671 per annum between 1783 and 1785 and over £1,100 per annum between 1786 and 1790, then three leaner years before the return of war brought higher profits in 1794.[23]

NATIONAL MARKETPLACE

The growth of merchant numbers was roughly paralleled by the growth of Dublin's international trade. The total tonnage of vessels from overseas discharging at Dublin's quays in the 1740s was rather more than double that of the 1700s, a growth rate of just under 2 per cent a year. This was probably ahead of population growth in the city and came at a time when many other Irish ports were in the doldrums. War and the Restoration Navigation Acts that had prohibited direct Irish importation of tobacco and sugar from the English colonies had a disproportionate impact on smaller ports, and only Dublin and Cork increased their share of these lucrative but regulated trades. In the capital's case, the focus was on the importation of higher-value goods (ranging from fashion fabrics, wines, tea and tobacco to industrial raw materials like silk thread, hardwood and unrefined sugar), and it was this import-led commerce that gave Dublin such an ascendancy in shipping activity. Most of the high-value imports were now coming from London or on the much shorter journey from the west-coast ports – Glasgow, Liverpool, Chester and Bristol – and in addition there was the huge coal trade from Whitehaven and the Ayrshire ports that was also focused on Dublin and its domestic needs.[24]

The first step towards such commercial dominance had been Dublin's rise as undisputed centre of internal Irish communication: in the 1660s a rudimentary postal service had been established linking a network of post-houses in the main towns, with a post office in Dublin's High St operating as national hub. Also in the late seventeenth century and over quite a short period the city achieved a near-monopoly within Ireland in the provision of wholesale financial services, specifically offering a market in bills of exchange 'on London', the means whereby funds (such as rents) could be remitted to England and beyond, and external commercial debts and credits settled. Restoration goldsmith-moneylenders and speculative merchants like Abel Ram, Thomas Hackett and Joseph Damer had been the key proto-bankers in the early days, but this kind of trade was becoming archaic by 1700, their place being taken by specialist bill dealers, namely 'bankers' in a narrower sense. And although there were separate bill trades between Cork and London, the Dublin–London axis grew ever stronger. With at times as many as eight banking businesses in Dublin regularly creating and dealing in bills of exchange, provincial traders and the out-of-town estate agents employed by absentee landowners saw the capital (via its nexus with London) as by far the most reliable, and usually the cheapest, place in Ireland to negotiate the transfer of internal Irish, Anglo-Irish and foreign debts and credits. The turbulent and often depressed economic conditions of the early eighteenth century helped cement Dublin's financial status, and to be 'as safe as Ben Burton' became the conventional compliment in trade - until his bank collapsed in 1733.[25] By then the principal Dublin banks, operating from fixed premises, were issuing their own promissory notes when discounting bills of exchange. Indeed the huge growth of paper money issued against the credit of a small number of apparently powerful individuals appalled the likes of Bishop Berkeley and Jonathan Swift. And it did not help in their estimation of banks and banking that nearly all the Dublin money-dealers were outside the Established Church; they were Presbyterian, Baptist or Quaker (see Plate 13).[26]

Banks were concerned with the short-term, with the movement of monies and the provision of credit through discounting. Longer-term concerns relating to the investment of personal assets, the transfer of property and the creation of family trusts were primarily the business of the chamber lawyers, the attorneys and public notaries. And although every county town, with their municipal courts and manorial jurisdictions, gave business to local 'gownsmen', Dublin was pre-eminent in the number and sophistication of its army of attorneys, public notaries and solicitors – over 600 by the 1760s and over 1,300 by the 1790s. By then, Cork had sixty-two resident practitioners 'to conduct and manage suits at law . . . of very great consequence, particularly relative to trade', and Limerick fifteen, but at assizes time, brigades of Dublin attorneys trailed into the county towns behind the judges and the barristers. And it seems that Dublin attorneys often had one or two partners or agents in provincial towns to stir up business. As Barnard has shown, the profession offered the talented few an opportunity for remarkable upward social mobility from an initially low-cost apprenticeship (William Conolly was one of the first attorneys to demonstrate this), and ample pickings for the majority, whether attached to one of the Four Courts, to municipal courts, to manorial courts or to one of the prerogative (diocesan) courts. Professional regulation of attorneys only began in the 1780s, but long before this, their role in facilitating both the enforcement of property rights and the criminal law was central: they made the system work. From the 1690s it had become an overwhelmingly, but not exclusively, Protestant profession, with Catholic attorneys restricted to chamber business as notaries – conveyancing and drafting settlements, wills and judgment bonds. But that too could be highly lucrative: the (largely undocumented) involvement of many attorneys as professional intermediaries in arranging mortgages and placing large personal loans was probably their most profitable and valued activity.[27]

NEW DIRECTIONS

Within a few years of its establishment, the Dublin Committee of Merchants had launched a plan for an architectually distinguished merchant exchange, something worthier of Dublin's scale and wealth than the congested ground floor of the ageing Tholsel, the pokey dealing rooms in Crampton Court behind the Custom House, or the neighbouring coffee houses where so much informal business was transacted. The Committee advertised its plans in November 1765; within weeks the Guild of Merchants began a rival move, with the same end in view. Parliament eventually gave financial support for the scheme but only after imposing a compromise: the site was to be assigned to trustees made up of representatives drawn from both the Committee and the Corporation, and they were to assume responsibility for financing, design and construction of a new exchange. Predictably, it was the Committee men who did most of the work.

The site was a challenging one: on rising ground beside the Poddle, it was at the intersection of two vistas, eastwards from Castle Street, southwards from Capel and the new Parliament Street. The Trustees' plan was to build on a scale that would proclaim the centrality of commerce in the city, even if the resulting edifice overshadowed the Castle. It was part funded by parliamentary grant but more came from a series of lotteries. The resulting structure with its white Portland stone, soaring Corinthian columns and stunning interior was (unusually for Dublin) admired from the very beginning. The high quality of construction and its neo-classical finish in stone and stucco contributed to its lasting impact.[28]

It was a very powerful piece of architecture on a most sensitive site. Yet in several respects the great project belied the truth: the vastness of the rotunda assembly-room implied the existence of a community of wealthy merchants engaged in international deal-making face-to-face, as had been the case in the great bourses of early modern Europe. However, the character of wholesale trade was changing, and by the time the Exchange opened its doors, the attraction of a great trading room for dealing in international bills of exchange was fast diminishing. Dublin's maritime commerce was becoming more standardized, more exclusively Anglo-Irish in character, and the supporting financial services more specialized as the city's role in handling Anglo-Irish commercial settlements became even more pronounced.[29]

By the mid 1780s there were only about five ship movements per day in the port (not including coasting and fishing boats), and although there was still some regular long-established direct trade, chiefly with Rotterdam, Bordeaux, Cadiz, Philadelphia and the Caribbean, most vessels were trading with Liverpool London, Chester, Whitehaven or Glasgow. The number of timber boats from Norway and the Baltic may have been increasing (as were timber merchants), but that related directly to the city's physical growth. In the Admiralty enumeration of Irish shipping (including coasters) carried out in 1776, 55 ships were registered as based in Dublin (with an average tonnage of 103 and an average crew of 13.4 men), the fleet constituting around a third of the fairly modest total registered Irish tonnage. But with fifteen 'constant traders' taking freight and sailing regularly either to Chester or London and with four ship-brokerage firms offering their services, clearly the one-time link between merchants and ship-owning was now dissolving (see Plate 14).[30]

Expectations that the Exchange would firmly anchor Dublin's wholesale business district to that quarter of the town were also dashed: the issue was the location of a new custom house. The battle went back to the early 1750s and at that stage the controversy had been over whether a new bridge should be built 1 kilometre downstream below Essex Bridge to link the newly fashionable neighbourhoods that were being developed on each side of the river. Luke Gardiner, office-holder and developer, had tried and failed in his efforts to secure such a bridge, stirring up huge opposition from both wholesale merchants and retailers in the old city, who were appalled at the prospect of such a drastic shift of commercial activity downstream: 'no trading port in Europe can be instanced that the gentry get between the traders and the sea . . .', and they secured sufficient support within Parliament to halt the idea.[31]

But in the 1770s those who supported the plan for such a bridge focused on the need for a new site for an enlarged custom house, which if granted would remove a key argument against the new bridge. The planned closure of the old Custom House on Essex Quay threatened to collapse a crucial social habitat: the zone of coffee houses, still the principal venue for social intercourse for merchants and professionals, which were nearly all located in the immediate vicinity of the existing Custom House, as were many of the best taverns and the Smock Alley theatre. A decision in favour of relocating the

Custom House eastwards was eventually made in 1781, but it had to be decided by the Treasury in London, not the government in Dublin. The doleful warnings of those who had fought to retain the Custom House in Essex St and to keep the river unbridged below that point turned out, after some delay, to be quite accurate.[32]

The great Exchange survived, but despite the lofty intentions of the original committee, the merchant community was riven by disunity in the decades ahead; religion and the new political climate of reform sharpened old cleavages. When the Bank of Ireland was established in 1782, perhaps a tenth of its 228 subscribers were Catholic; Dissenters were more strongly represented. But Quaker and Catholic merchants were debarred from becoming directors. The barrier on Quakers was overturned by the Court of Directors in 1784, but a parallel resolution to admit Catholics led to a tied vote, and the chair voted against it. The first Court of Directors was composed of 13 city merchants and 4 private bankers, all but 2 of whom were Anglican. In contrast, when the Committee of Merchants reconstituted itself as a Chamber of Commerce in 1783 its membership was initially large and diverse: it had some 250 members (and no retailers apart from wine merchants), and Dissenter and Catholic merchants were again prominently involved. However, in the divisive political climate of the later 1780s, the more conservatively minded merchants and those with strong links to Government withdrew from the body, notably those who inhabited the social world of the Huguenot La Touches.

The Chamber expired through lack of support in 1791. The agitation for Catholic political relief was deepening divisions. Tellingly, when the great Roman Catholic Relief Act of 1793 opened up the possibility of civic freedom for Catholic traders, Edward Byrne was the first of thirty-three to be proposed for membership of the Dublin Guild of Merchants; it took two attempts before a grudging majority in the guild admitted eleven from the list, including Byrne, but when his and other names went forward for freedom of the city (usually an automatic consequence of receiving guild membership), all but one were rejected by the aldermen of the Corporation. The one exception was Valentine O'Connor (1744–1814). The last of the great merchant shipowners in the city, his nomination was sent down for approval by the lower house, the Common Council, to complete the process, but two-thirds present rejected it and there the matter rested.[33]

O'Connor's family had come from Galway via the Isle of Man to Dublin in the 1760s and they had some knowledge of quasi-legal as well as conventional lines of international trade; they were among four Dublin firms to receive letters of marque allowing them to engage in privateering during the American War, and were the only Dublin house to become involved in privateering against French vessels in the 1790s. Around 1800 Valentine and Malachy O'Connor, and Valentine junior owned altogether nine vessels that were engaged in trade between Dublin and the Caribbean (importing cotton, sugar and rum), at a time when the total of Atlantic vessels belonging to Dublin firms was said to be twenty-five; the combined tonnage of the O'Connor ships amounted to precisely half that of the 'Atlantic' total for the city. Valentine was one of the Catholic merchants who had invested in the Bank of Ireland in 1782 and had then been debarred from becoming a director, an exclusion from insider knowledge which Catholic traders felt was putting them at a severe commercial disadvantage.[34]

But an older handicap no longer existed: prior to the first Catholic Relief Act of 1778 Catholic traders had enjoyed very limited opportunity to invest in urban real estate; any leasehold property which they acquired on terms longer than 31 years was open to discovery and confiscation. For their Protestant peers however, building up a mixed portfolio of urban property held on long lease terms had been a common if not universal practice. A few men of business engaged in speculative development on a grand scale, such as Humphrey Jervis and, a generation later, Joseph Leeson the brewer. Most famously there was Luke Gardiner senior who, it was rumoured, began as a wine merchant. But the fact that dozens of minor Protestant traders were doing the same thing suggests how alluring urban property investment was as a means of protecting wealth and ensuring its transmission to preferred heirs. Quaker merchants, clothiers and tanners in late seventeenth- and early eighteenth-century Dublin were particularly active investors and house-builders, notably in and close to the Meath Liberty, with portfolios of a dozen up to fifty houses being rented out; and the northside tallow chandler Joseph Rathborne, who held leases for fifteen properties from nine ground landlords at his death in 1738, was hardly exceptional among Anglican traders.

The inability of Catholic traders to diversify into long-term urban real estate was a major disadvantage. Perhaps for a few wealthy Catholics, moving funds abroad was the only option when they retired from trade, but William Stevens's claim that before 1778 'every Catholic who acquired [personal] property in Ireland, concluded his labours by establishing his family in a foreign country' was a fantasy, and his estimates of the large amounts of capital supposedly repatriated after 1778 are implausible; apart from the case of the draper-cum-banker

Nicholas Lawless there is no direct evidence of such expatriation (and subsequent repatriation) of wealth. Rather, the relative longevity of many Catholic merchant houses, in Dublin and elsewhere, points to the more mundane possibility that before 1778 accumulated capital was kept within trade and in movable urban assets. Admittedly there were some cases of Catholic emigrés who having made fortunes abroad brought funds home in the final years of the century, and Stevens was undoubtedly correct in claiming that after 1778, 'numbers of middling Catholics who had idle money[,] so soon as they could take satisfactory leases[,] ran into house building . . .', both in Dublin and the southern cities. But Catholic money poured into productive projects too: the principal investor in what was the largest industrial enterprise in Dublin in the 1790s, the textile printworks in Ballsbridge, was one Edward Byrne, a silent partner with inner-city neighbour and co-religionist, James Duffy.[35]

WORKSHOP, WAREHOUSE AND THE PRIMACY OF DUBLIN

Duffy and Byrne's great textile-printing enterprise on the Dodder at Ballsbridge, probably the largest of eight such plants surrounding Dublin in 1800, promised a new economic era, the marshalling of capital to exploit waterpower on a novel scale. Over a thousand hands were employed on the site and the standardized end-product, printed calico based partly or wholly on cotton, supplied the Irish market for furnishing and clothing fabrics. Protected by wartime tariffs, this new type of enterprise enjoyed high but precarious profits and was vulnerable to sudden changes in consumer spending power. In some respects it was an old story writ large – a textile enterprise supplying the national market, enjoying close links with city wholesalers and cloth warehouses. But where once employment had been overwhelmingly male, skilled, workshop-based, and regulated by custom and the rules of apprenticeship, now mechanization (initially of cotton spinning and printing) was undermining the old order. In Ballsbridge, as in other such ventures, some, perhaps most, of the workforce was female and very young, the required skills rudimentary, the earnings low and the conditions of employment entirely unregulated. And as things turned out these enterprises, in Dublin at least, were to have a limited future: they were less the harbingers of a new industrial age than the final chapter in that old story, of Dublin as national warehouse and national workshop.[1]

NATIONAL WORKSHOP

In the sixteenth century, Waterford had been the country's principal port of entry for fine cloth, metal goods and all the new-fangled luxuries circulating in Tudor England, but after the end of the Nine Years War Dublin seized that role and emerged as the national warehouse for imports. It was already being taken for granted in 1611 when Robert Cogan, a crown official comparing customs returns of the various ports, noted of Dublin that 'the state [i.e. government] of the whole kingdom is continually resident here, and the four [law] terms are kept here, all the kingdom resorts hither, by which means the trade is far greater than [in] any other port . . .' That was, however, more prediction than plain truth: Dublin's contribution to customs revenue between 1615 and 1619 (when collection arrangements were still highly anomalous) was still below 20 per cent of the national total; the share doubled to 41 per cent in the years 1634 to 1640, a level that was maintained in the Restoration period. It rose further in the 1690s, and in the following quarter century averaged around 55 per cent. Dublin held that dominant position until the 1780s.

This was of course no measure of the relative volume of trade being handled in the port nor indeed of its market value, but it did reflect the movement of duty-bearing commodities, and it was precisely these, the wines and the luxury clothes, the spices and finely crafted wares, that congested Dublin's first custom house. The very strong showing of Dublin's customs receipts from the 1630s is a measure of the city's success in cornering the wholesale market in high-value imports: thus Richard Stone, a wealthy city grocer, was listing debtors in at least nineteen counties outside Dublin at the commencement of the 1641 rebellion, many of them west of the Shannon. And the capital was also becoming the venue for wealthy consumers to come, admire and acquire a growing diversity of luxury goods. Dublin's long ascendancy happened at a time when demand for such goods in all their bewildering diversity continued to grow, thanks initially to the conspiciuous consumption of the new land-owning class.[2]

Being the principal high-value warehouse in the country brought about Dublin's transition to being the national *workshop* for luxury and quality goods – not the only such location, but the dominant one for more than a century. This was a gradual process, first evident in Wentworth's Dublin in the 1630s and more clearly visible in the 1660s and 1670s with the very rapid development of the Meath Liberty as the great artisan quarter of the city. The late seventeenth century was also the time when the number of guilds in the city greatly expanded (from fifteen in 1641 to twenty-four in 1700); only one more was established after 1700. Guild membership in Dublin expanded rapidly in the second half of the seventeenth century and more sedately up to the mid eighteenth century. Certainly no other Irish city had such a vigorous guild history: in the west and northern ports there were simply no guilds; in the

Figure 10 *The fortunate farrier*: the Lottery in Dublin was not slow to publicize an artisanal windfall, as in the scene here depicting the moment good news arrived in the farrier's workshop; it suggests that the recipients were well-dressed young men and women going about their business.

southern cities the old 'retail' guilds (the bakers, butchers, smiths, carpenters, with some new additions) were important in the later seventeenth century but mutated after 1700, some into Protestant fraternities that retained a formal but fairly passive involvement in municipal government (as in Drogheda and Cork), others losing their customary status altogether and becoming little more than benefit societies. Only in Limerick did the guilds retain a strong identity and bear comparison with Dublin.[3]

It is tempting to see the efflorescence of the Dublin guilds as no more than one element of the mid seventeenth-century Protestant 'capture' of the city, embodying rules and practices designed to marginalize or entirely exclude Catholic craftsmen from the privileges of civic freedom and trade protection. This was certainly part of the story, first with the total civic exclusion of Catholic artisans in the Cromwellian years, then with an inconsistent state policy during the Restoration: Catholic access to craft and civic freedom was permitted in the 1660s, opposed in the 1670s, and then in the mid 1680s, during James II's reign, came a short-lived policy reversal. After 1691 the Protestant character of guilds was once again reinforced and there were attempts (both in Dublin and in Cork) to deprive all Catholic freemen of their civic status, but small numbers of long-established freemen of the old religion were tolerated in some guilds. From that time it seems that all guilds attempted to license Catholic craftsmen as quarter-brothers: this followed London precedent and was first evident in the 1660s, later becoming standard in Dublin, Cork, Limerick and Waterford. Quarterage conceded the existence of non-free craftsmen but required them to pay a modest quarterly fee, licensing them to practise their craft and exempting them from the tolls and charges required of strangers. But, critically, it meant that the civic and social privileges of guild freedom were denied (apart from the quarter-day feasts held in some guilds), and there were restrictions on their right to take on apprentices. Some quarter-brothers were Protestant who, for whatever reason, delayed taking the necessary oaths, but the great majority were Catholic. The loss of guild records makes it difficult to assess just how far quarterage was enforced or what limited benefits it may have conferred on those who paid it. But it was standard practice up to the 1750s. By that time the ratio of freemen to quarter-brothers within many Dublin guilds was beginning to tilt in favour of the latter. Dissenter and Quaker tradesmen were however fully represented, forming about 17 per cent of all registered freemen in 1749; in the large Weavers Guild they approached parity with Anglicans.

In Cork city there was a history of muffled Catholic opposition to quarterage from as early as 1717, but this only emerged as a public issue in the late 1750s when a group of 'popish tradesmen' mounted a series of court challenges; they were supported in this by the newly established Catholic Committee in the capital. Then, in reaction to the repeated failure of the courts to uphold quarterage, the Dublin guilds and their parliamentary friends began a long battle in 1765 to secure statutory confirmation of their right as ancient corporations to license unfree fellow traders. It was a sign of how the world was changing that despite repeated attempts over thirteen years they failed to secure legislation to copper-fasten their privileges, and the failure to secure political support from government precipitated the collapse of the quarterage system. The guilds, of course, continued as political players up until 1840 and the transformation of municipal government, but from the 1760s they were portrayed by their opponents as no more than Protestant monopolies, and by the readers of Adam Smith as parasitical rent-seekers fulfilling little or no vocational role in the trades that they claimed to represent.[4]

However true such a portrayal of the guilds may have been in the era of reform, this masked their earlier economic importance. In fact, the renaissance of Dublin's guilds in the seventeenth century was not just a *symptom* of industrial development and physical growth but also an enabling factor in the city's rapid development as a manufacturing hub. Quite apart from the generic benefits of all such institutions (as championed by Stephan Epstein in his celebrated rehabilitation of European guilds as a critical element in the long-run growth of the European economy), they had a particular role in post-Cromwellian Dublin. The protections and privileges that they offered helped to attract, acclimatize and retain skilled craftsmen from England, France and further afield at a formative stage in Dublin's industrial history, and they provided an effective means to regulate quality (especially in the luxury crafts and building trades), to establish and maintain the reputation of Dublin goods as measured against imported equivalents, and to diffuse technical skills at a time of rapid growth (through the oversight of apprentices).[5]

The identity of the new guilds in Dublin is suggestive: three were textile-related, the Sheermen (1660), the Feltmakers (1667) and the Hosiers (1688); two in the leather trades, the Curriers (1670) and the Tanners (1688); two in construction, the Bricklayers (1670) and the Joiners (1700); two related to food and drink, the Coopers (1666) and the Brewers (1696); and St Luke's Guild (1670) which represented cutlers, painters, paper-stainers and stationers, was soon dominated by the city's printers. The older guilds, increasingly controlled by producers and wholesalers rather than retailers, remained somewhat larger than the new creations. They were foremost in civic ceremonies and maintained the city's six guild halls. These were clustered in the old city and were lent to the lesser guilds for formal meetings, dinners and, from the 1740s, election hustings. Together the twenty-five 'corporations' had a combined membership of perhaps 2,000 in the 1680s (nearly all men), and around 3,000 (exclusively male) in the 1750s. As freemen of the capital city they were an elite group and, unlike most of their provincial peers, they had a strong say in its governance, a power that was actually enhanced after the Dublin Reform Act of 1760. As far as we can tell, trade regulation and quality control remained the foremost concerns of most guilds until that time. The ancient triennial 'riding of the franchises', the great parade around the city boundaries by mayor, aldermen and all the trade guilds counting 'about fifty [men] to every corporation' with their floats and pagentry, had been held even in Cromwellian times, and it was a great moment in the civic calendar up to the 1760s, a spectacle that drew visitors from far outside the city. But it was abandoned in 1785, ostensibly because of violent behaviour at the sham battle on the boundary between the city and the Liberties. Its demise symbolized the retreat of the guilds from the street and from a public role in the life of the city, but it also reflected a new distrust felt by many masters towards the ranks of wayward journeymen.[6]

As the symbolic power of the guilds was weakening, some crafts were graduating to higher things: the largest group of medical practitioners in Dublin, the apothecaries, had been a discontented section within the old Barber-Surgeons Guild until they received their own charter in 1747. But they did not oversee the craft with much care and gave out freedom to non-practitioners, while many *bona fide* practitioners were unfree and unregulated, despite being 'the gate-keepers of the consultative process'. Commanding much lower fees than physicians, apothecaries diagnosed and dispensed as well as compounding their remedies. The big change came with legislation in 1791 establishing an Apothecaries Hall, a licensing and self-regulating body that elevated the medical foot-soldiers to professional status and ignored their religious affiliation. Their former guild brothers, the surgeons, underwent an even greater transformation with the establishment in 1784 of a chartered College of Surgeons in Dublin with training and licensing as well as regulatory powers. The professionalization of surgeons reflected both the rapid growth in the number of unfree (mainly Catholic) practitioners since mid century and the desire of the state, particularly with the approach of war, to raise the supply and competence of body-repairers.[7]

FAVOURED PLACES

The particular catalyst for Dublin's emergence as Ireland's centre of manufacturing in the seventeenth century had been the growth of the apparatus of government and the associated arrival in the city of large numbers of upper-class families. Whether as visitors or as residents, these families felt obliged to spend lavishly on clothing and hospitality, both to impress their peers and to promote their family's prospects. A similar albeit more sumptuous process was observable in baroque court cities across early modern Europe, from Copenhagen to Naples. Even the short-lived extravagance of Wentworth's viceregal court in the 1630s demonstrated how this could have direct economic impact in Dublin, evident in the sharp rise in goldsmiths, saddlers and mercers and the overall surge in the number of freemen (226 were added in 1638 alone). And many seasons in Restoration Dublin were marked by a 'great concourse' to the city when the demands on milliners and coachmakers reached new heights.

The presence of the viceroy in Dublin Castle was one factor making for a busy winter, but the legal calendar became the strongest determinant of upper-class movements and, in addition, the long uncertainty over the Cromwellian land settlement kept provincial landowners (and ex-landowners) pinned down in Dublin for months and years. The growth in court business at that time was palpable: Barnard has calculated that the number of fines levied annually in one of the high courts, the Court of Common Pleas, doubled between 1661–70 and 1681–85, and that the earnings of leading Restoration barristers were on par with the higher gentry and probably ahead of all merchants. Busy courts attracted litigants from the four provinces, and the legal fortunes earned by top barristers were spent at least partly in and around the capital. Meanwhile, viceregal sponsorship of public building created an added demand for specialist craftsmen, notably the major extensions within Dublin Castle during the Duke of Ormond's last term in office and – his favourite project – the building of the Royal Hospital at Kilmainham in the 1670s and 1680s. The Knight of Glin and James Peill have suggested that the quite outstanding carving and sculpture by the Tabary brothers in decorating both the interiors and exteriors at Kilmainham mark 'the foundation of high-style Irish wood carving', their influence still evident a generation later in, for instance, the superb carvings in St Michan's church.[8]

The Tabarys were French and Huguenot. The supposedly huge influence of their co-religionists on the rise of Dublin crafts has been overstated but their impact was perceptible. There had been a trickle of Huguenot traders taking advantage of Restoration inducements to 'foreign' Protestants to come and avail themselves of fast-track civic freedom, but most Huguenot craftsmen and their families only reached Dublin (or other Irish destinations) in the 1680s and 1690s, often via a less than friendly sojourn in London. Many of them sought patronage and custom from the wealthy Huguenot military veterans who settled in the city during the 1690s. It was entirely fortuitous that this was a time of rapidly growing demand from the upper ranks of society at large for silks and time-pieces, jewellery, glassware, tapestry and decorative pieces in gold and silver.[9]

The Huguenots did not pioneer any of the luxury crafts, but they were the vectors of new designs and forms. The belief that they launched Dublin's silk industry and that most Huguenots were silk weavers is a complete myth, reflecting perhaps the singular ascent of the La Touche dynasty: David Digues La Touche (1671–1745), a young veteran of the Boyne, began as a silk and cambric manufacturer, based advantageously in Castle St. He was also agent for fellow aristocratic emigrés, handling their pensions and remittances from the homeland. In a long and remarkably successful career he diversified into banking and, later, became the largest property speculator on the south side of the city; his younger son continued in silk and overseas trade, while the senior line consolidated the family's banking business. Such a move from workshop to wholesale trade and/or the professions over two generations was fairly typical among Dublin Huguenots; between 1692 and 1745 only about a fifth of those for whom occupational data exist were associated with luxury crafts, textiles or apparel. But there are well-attested Huguenot asssociations with gold- and silvermaking: 22 per cent of all masters of the Goldsmiths Guild in 1706 were Huguenot, and Cunningham has identified altogether 128 co-religionists associated with the guild between 1690 and 1750. However, the first generation of Huguenot craftsmen may have been quite small dealers, shop-keepers or mere journeymen to judge by their modest showing in the guild's assay records.[10]

The sitting of the Irish Parliament was a high point for seventeenth-century Dublin traders and tavern-owners, its impact probably greatest in the 1660s (after which it did not sit for more than two decades). There were three parliamentary sittings in the 1690s, and then from 1703 a pattern of bi-annual meetings began. From 1715 sessions tended to run for a little less than six months during every second winter. From the 1770s the sessions lasted longer and from 1785 Parliament became an annual event. College Green was never more active than in the 1790s, its final decade, when sittings ranged from two to nine months. The only indication of the direct economic impact arising from the presence of the 350 to 400 parliamentary families in Dublin comes from the last days of the institution when the case for parliamentary union was being furiously debated; one of the more measured estimates claimed that each MP who attended Parliament spent (with his family) on average over £1,400 a year in the city. Their departure, it was confidently claimed, would ruin the 'coach-makers, cabinet makers, woollen drapers [and] haberdashers . . . who live by the consumption of people of fortune'. To this could be added the thousands employed in domestic and personal service for upper-class households, the physicians and accoucheurs, the perfumers and the jewellers, the tutors and the courtesans.[11]

The anti-union doomsayers overstated their case, but nevertheless the cumulative effects for Dublin of hosting Parliament had been enormous. Quite apart from the recurring benefit to the capital's retail trade and the strikingly privileged position enjoyed by Dublin in the allocation of parliamentary grants for infrastructure and welfare institutions, Parliament made a series of grants that directly affected manufacturing in the capital. We have already encountered the Trustees of the Linen Manufacture, the Linen Board, and their decision in 1721 to copper-fasten Dublin's role in handling linen exports by building a great cloth hall. The Board also acquired what eventually became the Byrne & Duffy site in Ballsbridge where the first linen-printing yard started *c.* 1727, and this was the first of more than a dozen printing yards that operated along the rivers ouside the city. These businesses were nurtured by the Board and met with mixed success, their patterned cloth being produced almost exclusively for local sale.[12]

Support from the Board and, later, directly from Parliament, was part of a wider policy of import substitution. Several yards were notably successful and innovative, technically and commercially. However parliamentary support for industrial initiatives was scrappy and fairly random, and was really only of importance from the 1750s. Dublin supplicants outnumbered all others, but the common denominator was the promotion of Irish manufacturing and the reduction of dependence on English, Dutch and French imports. The 'Dublin Society for promoting husbandry and the useful arts in Ireland', established quietly in 1731, had initially a rural focus, but from the 1740s it too had an industrial role. The prevailing belief among the founding group was that the importation of foreign luxuries was intrinsically damaging to the country; four decades later a Dublin Society report was still maintaining that 'in proportion to the increase of our importations, so is the increase of the number of our poor, by consuming in luxury the wealth of the rich, and diminishing the employment of the poor'. The Society became best known for its suite of premia (or prizes) that were offered annually to promote an eclectic range of craft innovations (in 1762, for example, non-agricultural prizes were advertised for carpet making, tobacco pipe manufacture, scraping in mezzotint, paper made from rags, and 'toys made of bones'). The Society, always good at generating publicity, secured its first parliamentary grant in 1740; this was greatly increased in 1764 when, with a budget of £8,000, it was given responsibility to promote

Figure 11 This image of 'the distressed manufacturer' was an unusually rapid commentary on the depressed state of handicraft textile trades in Dublin during the harsh downturn of 1792/3, suggesting a respectable but penniless weaving family, their loom idle, receiving charity from an upper-class donor.

twelve categories of manufacturing. The Society allocated almost half that sum to bounties for textiles, specifically the manufacture of silk and the printing of linen, principally to applicants in and around Dublin. The most tangible outcome was the establishment that year of a silk warehouse in the newly opened Parliament St, in collaboration with the Weavers Guild and overseen by upper-class women. Following its success and with continuing parliamentary subvention, the Society opened a superfine woollen warehouse nearby in 1773. These market-distorting initiatives lasted for two decades and offered a striking example of parliamentary support for the city economy; they found little echo in the provinces.[13]

The justification for such intervention was that 'high-end' textile manufactures (other than linen) were in trouble. That trouble was the rise in imports from England from the 1760s. Aside from domestic service, high- and medium-quality cloth-making was the largest employment sector in Dublin for over a century, and this was reflected in the fact that most of the silks and broadcloth worn across Ireland up to the 1770s were woven, dyed and finished in the neighbourhood of Dublin. The import of fine cloths was always important, but in the case of silk the value of raw materials imported up to the 1760s normally exceeded the declared value of incoming finished cloth.

The noise of the loom and the smell of the dye-yard were therefore as embedded in the life of Dublin's Liberties as mashtuns and the smell of hops would be for later generations. The archetypal 'common man' whom Swift chose to ventriloquize in 1724 in his political campaign against the hated 'Wood's Halfpence' was of course the 'Drapier' (he sometimes referred to him as a 'weaver'). And in Swift's first polemic in 1720 on the state of the economy the suffering manufacturers whom he defended were clothworkers. When, in 1721 his neighbour, Archbishop Edward Synge, exhorted the public to respond to the devastating effects of the South Sea Bubble on employment in the Liberties, his focus was also on the plight of the weavers. But for that generation of artisans their real problem was the violent swings in income; certainly Swift's dystopian view of the state of the poor in his locality was shaped during the bad years, but his attention was drawn elsewhere when times were good.[14]

Textiles remained very vulnerable to short-term shifts in the wider economy, though in no sense was this a declining sector. Long-term trends in key imported raw materials for the silk and woollen trades confirm this: between the 1680s and the 1770s, indigo, madder and alum imports all peaked in the 1760s, at which time there were well over 10,000 men and women directly engaged in textile-related employment in Dublin. Roughly a quarter of the 4,500 traders listed in later eighteenth-century trade directories were involved in the making or marketing of cloth, whether as master manufacturers, dyers, wholesale dealers handling one or more cloth types, cloth importers, or else involved in the clothing trade (ranging from breeches-makers to hatters). And these were all employers.[15]

But there was a gradual change in the character of textile manufacturing: the great majority of the 250-odd freemen in the Weavers Guild in the 1720s were self-employed and were not tied to selling their output to a single buyer. But the number of apprentices that masters took in began to grow after mid century, the size of workshops increased, and many apprentices never became masters (or even quarter-brothers), remaining in limbo as journeymen, some of whom not even serving a full apprenticeship. In addition there were sharpening differences of wealth within the ranks of master. But across textile manufacturing the various branches evolved differently: groups of masterless linen weavers were evident in the city long before this was the case in the finer branches of silk. By the 1760s a number of processes in woollen manufacture were being executed by young women, whether as wool combers or light weavers, and this intrusion stirred up male journeymen who had served their apprenticeship to protest, harass and eventually exclude women from the loom. Why was this occurring specifically in the 1760s? Technical changes affecting the weight of equipment may have been part of it, as were changes in fashion. But the growing challenge from cheaper and/or superior imported English cloth was the principal factor undermining customary workshop practices.[16]

The catalyst for the Dublin Society's intervention into marketing was a major incident that occurred in 1763: rumours had circulated that Cottingham & King, the largest mercers in the city, were about to import Lyon silk in bulk and to abandon their thirty to forty local suppliers in the Liberties. A black flag was hung above the Weavers Hall in the Coombe and there was prolonged rioting in Dame St outside their shop; later, some 500 journeymen and apprentices sabotaged the workshops of eleven indigenous suppliers of the hated wholesalers. In the wake of this, Cottingham & King abandoned business and the Weavers Guild approached the Dublin Society to establish a not-for-profit retail warehouse to display city-made silks.

The quantity of manufactured silks imported into the country (and principally into Dublin) in 1763/4 was the highest of the century, but this was not the whole story: two years previously the imports of raw and semi-processed silk thread had also soared to an all-time peak (60 per cent above the official value of finished silk imports in 1763/4). This suggests that Irish demand for silk cloth had grown very sharply around 1760 and that wholesalers had responded first by expanding orders to local producers (thus the jump in raw silk), then a year or two later (at the end of the Seven Years War when trade with France was open again) they turned to sourcing additional supplies abroad, much to the chagrin of weavers who had temporarily been enjoying rising earnings.[17]

HIGHER ARTS

The Dublin Society's eclectic range of 'industrial' prizes reflected the views of its earliest members and supporters, notably their mentor George Berkeley. He had been unusual in suggesting an intimate link between promotion of 'the arts' and the public good, and it was one of his recurring themes in *The Querist*: 'whether human industry can produce, from such cheap materials, a manufacture of so great value by any other art as those of sculpture and painting?' This line of thinking led to the Society establishing three schools of drawing and design, beginning with their take-over of Robert West's private drawing school in 1750. Fortunate in the calibre and drive of the principal instructors, the Society's Schools of Architectural, Ornament and Figure Drawing functioned as a highly successful training academy in the plastic arts, and had no obvious parallel in Ireland or Britain. In the first twenty-five years the Schools admitted over a thousand students, many it seems city-based apprentices whose education was largely or completely subsidized by the Society. Deploying French models, practices and materials, the Schools profoundly influenced the standards of draughtsmanship and design for several generations of carvers and engravers, cabinet makers and coachbuilders, and arguably had a much greater impact on the applied arts and architectural ornament than had the Huguenots at the beginning of the century.[18]

Even those who worked in gold and silver benefited. The (incomplete) assay records of the Dublin Goldsmiths Guild examined by Alison FitzGerald provide a unique insight into one sector of the workshop economy over the course of the century: in the seven years from 1706 to 1712, an annual average of 45,327 ounces of silver objects were submitted to the assay master; volumes were rising at that stage, and in the four-year period from 1726 to 1730 they reached an average of 62,436 ounces per annum. Activity was lower over the next two decades, then rose fitfully in the third quarter of the century. Only one late eighteenth-century assay return, that for 1788, survives in full, by which time the total assayed stood at 80,784 ounces, broken down into over 200 types of silver object that had been submitted by 49 silversmiths. These included over 24,000 buckles and nearly 40,000 spoons. Revenue returns of duty paid on gold and silver (introduced in 1731) suggest a loose correlation between retail sales and fluctuations in the wider economy. However, business in the second half of the century may have been even more buoyant than the figures suggest, as neoclassical designs displaced rococo (thereby reducing hallmarked weights), and cheaper silver-plated goods became more common. But the market for full-silver buckles and spoons, sugar dishes and body ornaments now extended far beyond the upper-class clientele of 1700. It is striking that almost half of the Dublin Quaker wills for the years 1690 to 1760 include references to silverware, confirmation that even the Quakers, supposedly the least ostentatious of Dublin's bourgeoisie, regularly accumulated precious chattels.[19]

According to the guild's admission books, 715 youths were apprenticed to 230 masters in the Goldsmiths Guild in the course of the eighteenth century; a minority of these masters were not metal smiths but jewellers, watch and clock-makers, and lapidaries. Dublin was the unchallenged centre for these and other high-value crafts, but it was not alone: at the time of the general re-launching of the guilds in Cromwellian Cork one of the new creations was a guild of gold-smiths, and between 1656 and 1750 around fifty gold and silversmiths were active there, a surprisingly large number for a provincial centre. New entrants doubled in the quarter century after 1750 (to thirty-three), and fresh names appeared at the same rate during the final quarter of the century. The Cork guild seems to have then quietly faded out of the picture, perhaps because no assay office was established there. In Limerick (where silversmiths effectively domi-nated the Smiths Guild) about twenty names associated with the trade have been identified for the century up to 1750, and then a jump in new entrants similar to that in Cork in the third quarter of the century, with a levelling off in the final quarter. Ten silversmiths were active in eighteenth-century Waterford, and other centres supported no more than one or two practitioners at any one time. But even in Cork and Limerick silversmiths were increasingly importing much of their wares from Dublin or from England and they were no longer executing larger commissions involving casting or chasing.[20]

In the related but less prestigious watch and clock-making trades, it was a rather different story: timepieces in the seventeenth century were expensive and novel, and four-fifths of the craftsmen recorded by William Stuart as active across the ten Irish urban centres in the second half of the seventeenth century were based in Dublin. Perhaps a concern with time came a little earlier to the capital city, but as prices fell and more modest timepieces became available, the numbers recorded in provincial centres rose, first in Cork and then more generally. In the last quarter of the eighteenth century, Stuart records 217 watchmakers, clock-makers and allied craft workers active across the ten centres: Belfast, which had no tradition of luxury manufacturing, had no less than 33 individuals associated with the craft by that time. By contrast, Sligo and Galway had none, Waterford and Kilkenny two each, Derry four, Limerick five, with only Cork ahead of Belfast with thirty-seven.[21]

Recent checklists of cabinet makers, upholsterers, glaziers and looking-glass manufacturers, carvers and gilders active during the eighteenth century point to broadly similar conclusions: the absolute dominance of Dublin, but some quite strong provincial growth after 1750. In the manufacture of decorated wall-paper and wall-hangings, the fashion for 'India paper' and Chinese patterns developed slowly, but by the 1750s there were Irish imitations and a group of Dublin workshops built up a national market; indeed, one of their number seems to have introduced new-style wallpaper manufacture to colonial America, another to Bordeaux. Fine ceramic manufacture represented a short-lived but more ambitious case of a very large Dublin initiative. In the early 1750s, the well-connected Henry Delamain, a wholesale importer of 'china and tea', took over a delftware manufactory on Dublin's North Strand and greatly expanded it with heavy Dublin Society and later parliamentary support. His 'World's End' delftware was highly successful for a few years and exports began, but with his early death and then that of his widow, the enterprise slumped and was gone by 1771. Less ambitious fine ceramic potteries in Limerick and Belfast enjoyed moderate success, but nothing approached the quality of Delamain's delicate work.

With fine cabinet-making the skills were more dispersed, in Belfast, Cork, Limerick and Waterford (in that order), but even in the last years of the century there were almost three times as many cabinet makers in Dublin than in the other nine centres combined. Dublin workshops continued to supply wealthy clients across the country, but provincial cabinet makers presumably continued to make all their own furniture. However, their connections with the fount of fashion remained important: Nicholas Underwood, moving from Dublin to begin business as a cabinet maker in Sligo in 1752, claimed that he was able to produce at least sixteen types of furniture from his imported stock of mahogany, oak and walnut, and 'as convenient in their several kinds and as well furnished as may be found in London or Dublin, which he will sell at Dublin prices . . .' Similarly a Limerick cabinet maker and upholsterer, Richard Clarke, advertising his new business in 1780, made a virtue of the fact that he had 'a number of years experience in Dublin and London', that his parlour and drawing-room chairs would be 'stuffed with the best Dublin curled hair', and that amidst much else he had a stock of 'Dublin paper hangings, [and] English counterpanes'.[22]

LUXURIES AND NECESSITIES

For provincial traders specialising in lighter and more portable products (such as perfumers, haberdashers, woollen drapers or wigmakers), announcements of new stock 'just arrived from Dublin', or even better 'from London', were standard fare in newspaper advertisements, but the balance between what they sourced outside and what they manufactured themselves was never clear. In Dublin the separation of retailing from processing and manufacturing had begun much earlier: fixed retail premises – shops – were selling durable goods in small quantities in sixteenth-century Dublin, 'openly displayed, no barrier of glass separating the merchant's goods from the customer', but at that time street markets, regulated or unregulated, were far more important. Thomas Denton, a visitor to the city in the 1680s, was struck by the array of specialist markets running along Thomas St: turf and Kilkenny coal at the west end, then hay and vegetables, leather, shoe and milk stalls, with vendors in nearby streets selling lace, linen and stockings. There may have been no shops on that side of the city as yet.[23]

In a reconstruction of retailing in mid eighteenth-century Amsterdam, Clé Lesger has revealed a clear spatial pattern: 'convenience shops' scattered across the whole city, but shops selling textiles and consumer durables concentrated, often in clusters, in the city centre and along the main axes leading to municipal markets. The greatest contrast was between bakers, located in every neighbourhood, and silk mercers who were highly concentrated in one or two locations – and yet no Amsterdam city or guild regulation had ordained such a well-defined pattern. There was a broadly similar story in Dublin: a multiplicity of 'convenience' shops or covered stands scattered widely, and then at specific locations small clusters of dealers trading in durable or more expensive commodities. Thus the fifty-three bakers named in the *Dublin Directory* of 1768 were located in thirty-seven different streets, whereas the twenty-two silk and stuff mercers were limited to just three, and in fairly close proximity (Dame, Parliament and Francis Streets). Again, there were no public controls affecting these choices of location.[24]

But one can make a further distinction between the types of retailer, based on customer profile, which was first evident in Dublin. All the new shops in Parliament St and Dame St and an older generation of shops in Castle St and Essex St sought to attract high-status custom, whether local or visiting, and they became increasingly specialized. High officers of state and parliament were invited to sample the exotic furs in Dennis Callaghan's establishment in Eustace St – ermine from Siberia, squirrel fur from Hudson Bay, musquash skins from Acadia. All such purveyors claimed great discernment in what they offered, and from the 1720s they were regularly advertising their wares in the newspapers. They were likely to have both the resources and the inclination to import a substantial proportion of their stock, even when similar goods might be locally manufactured. These 'capital shops' were the first to follow seventeenth-century London and Paris in the use of glass windows and in the introduction of browsing space and display-cases inside the shop. However, despite the early appearance of a colonnaded walkway in Essex St (built probably in the 1670s in front of nine, presumably retailing houses), for a long time shop frontages were not incorporated into eighteenth-century speculative building. Window glass was expensive and vulnerable, although its large-scale manufacture in Dublin from around 1760 reduced costs and improved availability.

However in Parliament St, the first initiative of the Wide Streets Commissioners in the 1760s, the presence of shops was assumed, and in the 1780s discreet shopping units became an integral element in their principal street plans, to materialize on the ground a decade later. By then, judging from Malton's *Views* of the city (drawn *c.* 1791), the bow-fronted shop window was becoming common in prestigious locations, appearing in three of the seven engravings that included commercial premises. One of these windows (on the street-front beside Powerscourt House in South William St) advertised the contents of a 'stuff warehouse', and many other shops by then were branding themselves as 'warehouses', specializing for example in tea, china, earthenware, 'Manchester goods' and 'Venice glass'. The use of the term implied that they stocked only the finished article, that no processing was involved, and that they imported their stock from afar for ready payment. Thus Wade & Marshall, owners of The Earl Macartney Indiaman Tea Warehouse in Dame St boasted in 1797 about how they had 'received from the last [East] India sales . . . from

Table 5.1

Capital Shops in Four Cities in Ireland and England: 1788–1795

	Dublin (1794)	Cork (1795)	Limerick (1788)	Bristol (1793)
Booksellers	58	3	4	11
Coachmakers	29	5	4	4
Clock/watchmakers	60	16	4	32
Glass/china/ earthenware shops	71	30	8	23
Gold/silversmiths	35	10	5	12
Jewellers	33	2	1	3
Mercers	17	4	3	6
Opticians	5	1	-	2
Perfumers	30	8	-	10
Toymen	10	3	1	3
Upholsterers	32	3	2	5

Sources: Wilson's *Dublin Directory*, 1794; *Cork Directory*, 1795; Lucas, *General Directory*, 1788; William Mathews's *New Bristol Directory for 1793/4* (Bristol, [1794]).

London a fresh supply of teas, sugars, spices . . .'. A few of the early 'warehouses' made less exotic claims, serving as the salesrooms for local proto-factories.[25]

Directory-based comparisons of the number of capital shops (Table 5.1) provide a tantalizing sense of Dublin's position as a prestigious market place, whether compared with an old regional capital in England or with Cork and Limerick: Bristol, historically a much wealthier city than Dublin, had perhaps a third of Dublin's population in the 1790s, and a comparison with Dublin suggests that the two cities had – in per capita terms – a similar profile. Dublin had a higher number of booksellers, coachmakers, jewellers and upholsterers per capita, while Bristol capped Dublin in watch and clockmakers. The totals for Cork compared to Bristol (by then the two cities had very similar populations) also suggest broadly similar results in most retail categories, but with vendors of books and timepieces underrepresented in Cork, while glass and earthenware shops are overrepresented.

The Limerick totals (for a city less than half the size of Cork or Bristol) suggest a rather older pattern of high-income consumption: no perfumers or opticians, only four watch and clockmakers, but more booksellers than Cork and almost as many coachmakers. However, Dublin was clearly in a league apart in the density of its up-market premises. These provided a spectacle for

1. Micro-city on the marsh: Cork, *c.* 1601.

2. Gabriele Ricciardelli, *A view of Drogheda from Millmount, c.* 1752.

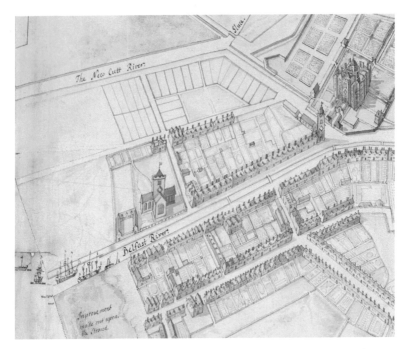

3. A detail from Thomas Phillips's plan of Belfast in 1685, with the proprietorial landmarks – the parish church, the market-house and the Castle – giving no clue as to the Presbyterian character of the town itself.

4. Hugh Douglas Hamilton, *A tinker, c.* 1760: one of more than sixty images of the capital's street life drawn by a recent pupil of the Dublin Society's School of Drawing.

5. Single-storey cabins in Shandon suburbs: detail from John Butts, *View of the city of Cork from Audley Place, c.* 1760.

6. Thatch without the walls, brick within: George Petrie, *Saint Laurence's Gate, Drogheda*, 1819.

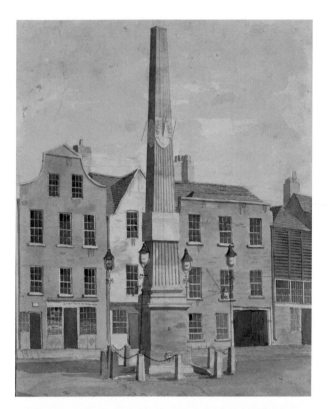

7. One of the ten ornate public fountains built in Dublin *c.* 1790, some of them the result of aristocratic benefaction: George Petrie, *The fountain, James Street, Dublin, c.* 1810.

8. Few young Cork merchants could afford to have their portraits painted by Giuseppe F.L. Marchi, protégé of Sir Joshua Reynolds, but the sitter here in 1773, assumed to be William Jameson, was among the wealthiest: both his father and father-in-law had been aldermen and long-established city merchants, and the Jamesons remained a prominent force in the city's wholesale business for a generation.

9. Celebrating the father's cathedral: *East view of the city of Waterford* (1795), by Thomas Sautelle Roberts, second son of architect Thomas Roberts.

10. Painted shortly after John Rocque's *Survey of the city of Kilkenny* (1758), Thomas Mitchell's *Panorama of Kilkenny* (1760), taken from the south-east in early morning light, captures a sense of the wooded environs of the city and the monumentality of the Castle (L) and the Cathedral (R, in the distance): an urban landscape that gives little hint of the modern.

11. The children of Margaret and Thomas Bateson, the former Antrim-born, the latter from Lancashire. Wine merchant, Caribbean trader, ship-owner, sugar baker and banker, Thomas was a central figure in Belfast's maritime trade for more than half a century until his death in 1791. His wealth was evident in the family's suburban villa in Orangefield, the location for Strickland Lowry's 1762 study of the Bateson children, complete with cues as to their accomplishments – whether in handling the harpsichord or the globe – and the scene is backed by local topographical views.

12. William Hincks's *Perspective view of the Linen Hall in Dublin* (1783) was the final engraving in a set of twelve which documented the various processes in the handicraft linen industry, from rural flax garden to the wholesale market on Dublin's northside where bales of white linen were traded for export.

13. Son of a Dublin linen draper, Joseph Fade became one of the city's most successful private bankers with large premises in Thomas St, a large northside residence, Furry Park House, beside Dublin Bay (shown here in the background), and a portfolio of properties in town and country. Unlike some of his Quaker co-religionists he was not afraid to display his wealth. The bank, inherited by nephews after his death in 1748, failed spectacularly six years later.

14. Timber ship-building became quite important late in the eighteenth century in Cork and Belfast, but in Dublin – for all the volume of business in the port – it was limited to several small yards, such as that of John Clements on the east bank of the Dodder near the mouth. J.H. Campbell's *View of the shipyard at Ringsend* (1814) looks past Clements's yard, westwards across the slobland, and through the masts of shipping berthed in the new Grand Canal Dock towards the encroaching city.

15. Most of Thomas Malton's twenty-five views of Dublin (drawn in 1791) were of modern streetscapes or of recently constructed public buildings. The only street views within the once-walled city were of Thomas St and, as here, of the crumbling Tholsel and adjacent buildings, including a section of High St.

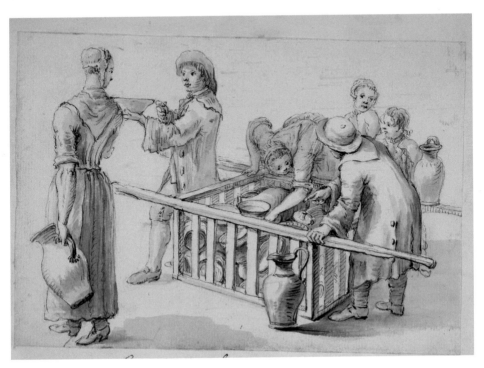

16. Cheap goods for young buyers: Hugh Douglas Hamilton, *Coarse earthen ware*, c. 1760.

17. A frequent visitor to Ireland and possibly Irish-born, John Nixon was an accomplished caricaturist with an eye for the picaresque. It has been suggested that the smoky and Spartan candle-lit tavern, with its drunken harpist and pair of fiddlers (one of them African) surrounded by a cast of disreputable revellers, could only be Irish and that it was probably in Dublin *c.* 1790, but this must remain speculative.

18. A 'fine modern building' complete with gallery, St Patrick's Catholic parish church was built before 1746 *inside* the western walls of Waterford city, eloquent testimony of the presence of Catholic money in the city and of a degree of local religious tolerance.

19. Chichester strikes back: Roger Mulholland's St Anne's church (1774/76) was entirely funded by the fifth Earl of Donegall and became the parish church for Belfast's Anglicans.

visitors both from the country and afar like Mirza Abu Taleb Khan, the Indian traveller who visited Ireland on his way to London in 1799:

> Many of the best streets are entirely occupied by shops; these have all large glazed windows, in which the articles are exhibited to attract purchasers. They also have over the doors a plank painted black, on which is inscribed, in gold letters, the name and profession of the owner. These shops are at night brilliantly lighted up, and have a handsome effect. In them is to be found whatever is curious or valuable in the world. My attention was particularly attracted by the jewellers' and milliners' repositories; nor were the fruiterers or pastry cooks' shops without their attractions. I generally spent an hour . . . in some of these places.

The sheer number of fashionable Dublin shops and their window displays struck the Saxon visitor Karl Küttner in 1784, a consequence he assumed of the extravagance of the wealthy, but he was impressed by the shop assistants: predominantly female, clean, and fashionably dressed.[26]

Quite distinct from the capital shops on Dublin's east side were 'the country shops'. These were clustered near wholesale markets and depended primarily on discounted wholesale business with out-of-town dealers and provincial merchants, but also made retail sales to carters and farmers. Old streets – High St, Francis St, Meath St, and Thomas St south of the Liffey, and Church St, Capel St and Pill Lane (near the markets and the Linen Hall) – remained prime locations for the country trade (see Plate 15). Thus three-quarters of Dublin's ironmongers were clustered in these streets at the time Henry Jackson began his remarkable career in the late 1760s; over the next three decades he built a nationwide business in Pill Lane and Church St, eventually diversifying into steam- and water-powered iron-founding (in Ringsend and Clonskeagh respectively). But a political radical of stern resolve, he risked all to become one of the pillars of the revolutionary movement in the 1790s. After lengthy imprisonment in 1798–99, he took his entrepreneurial skills to Pennsylvania.[27]

For 'country shops', credit terms and price were all important and sensitivity to changing London fashion less pressing. Probably a higher proportion of stock, at least in textiles, was sourced locally than was the case in the capital shops, although one of the earliest riots directed against a cloth importer occurred in High St when the house of a draper, Richard Eustace, was ransacked in 1734 and a weaver killed. There were around two dozen drapers on that street, several of whom grew to great wealth, most famously Robert Lawless. But for less bulky objects than cloth most lower-class households resorted to the street pedlars and chapmen. Almost none of the profusion of cheap street goods documented by Hugh Douglas Hamilton in his 'Cries of Dublin' in 1760 – brooms and brogues, rushes and mats – had any pretensions to fashion or design, except perhaps the hardware, earthenware, old clothes and second-hand wigs, some of which may have been 'populuxe' copies of the fine goods that had previously been on display in capital shops (see Plate 16).[28]

In Cork, the contrast between 'capital' and 'country' shops may not have been as pronounced, for the city lacked a captive market of gentry or professional consumers. But the distinction still applied and it had a religious edge, with the capital shops, such as they were, overwhelmingly located in the island parishes, notably in Castle and Paul Streets, and mainly Protestant owned; the country-dependent shops were located mainly in the north and south suburbs and increasingly Catholic. In a bitter attack in 1737, an anonymous pamphleteer lampooned the 'upstart beggars' setting up shop along the street near the butter market on Cork's north side:

> Pray is it not a very uncomfortable sight for any Protestant shopkeeper of this city to behold thatch and sky-light edified into cant-windows and slat[e]; wherein a flat-footed Milesian [i.e. Irishman] shall have the impudence to have his table graced with a chaplain and pinch'd diaper; and . . . [to] raise himself from thongs and lank hair to pumps and a periwig . . . They buy as dear, retail cheaper, live better and grow richer than other, fair dealers in this city.

The Mallow Lane/Shandon St district, attracting vast numbers of small butter-producers every summer where they did business with private buyers, may have been unusual in its retail development, but the shopkeepers in every city who specialized in trade with the country, whether grocers, drapers or ironmongers, developed a different set of skills and strategies from those who catered for the wealthy client.[29]

For the everyday needs of most citizens, shops of any kind were secondary to the public markets. Colin Smith has argued that in London at the end of the eighteenth century as much as 40 to 50 per cent of all retail food purchases were still being made in one of 24 public retail markets, apart from the direct purchases from hawkers and informal street traders. In Irish cities, public markets, whether established by patent, statute or city ordinance, were also a crucial element in food distribution. In eighteenth-century Dublin there were up to ten wholesale markets operating several times a week (handling cattle, hay, grain, linen, fish, butter, bacon, eggs, potatoes, vegetables and fruit), and about ten retail markets selling principally meat and vegetables that were open daily. It was estimated in 1817 that there were 360 stalls distributed between these retail markets, with the northside Ormond market, close to the slaughtering yards around Smithfield, much the busiest. Potatoes and fish were almost certainly the principal commodities sold in these markets, but the basic staple of nearly all townspeople – bread, in some shape or form – was either purchased daily from the retail baker, or produced at home (on the griddle pan or in the oven) from flour or from meal purchased from meal-mongers or in the public markets. We get only a fleeting sense of the importance of hawkers and specialist street traders thanks to Hamilton's remarkable portfolio of drawings: some of his studies are of sedentary stall-holders (selling eggs, fish, tripe, black and white 'pudding', hot peas, greens, whey, apples, vegetables, cake and gingerbread), but many of his subjects were carrying their wares through the Dublin streets, whether for instant consumption (oranges and lemons, hot pies, oysters), or for food preparation at home (milk, butter, butter-milk and herbs).[30]

In Limerick, there were up to seven meat markets operating at some point during the eighteenth century; two are recorded in Cork, and elsewhere usually only single meat and fish markets. While their respective corporations authorized or were responsible for most of these markets, policing them rested with the toll-gatherers who leased the right to collect the tolls, usually for a year at a time. In a few of the more prestigious markets, individual stalls were leased out on terms of up to seven years.[31]

Dublin and Cork Corporations were more heavily involved in market management than elsewhere, especially of their grain markets, monitoring adulteration, false weights and a host of other potential malpractices. Well-managed markets were a major source of income for corporations and an insurance against trouble when food prices were high. This was probably best demonstrated in Cork, where there was a tradition of market intervention from the 1690s, possibly because of the constricted nature of the urban site and the social tensions that came with rapid growth. By the 1750s the wholesale grain, butter, fish and cattle markets had been rehoused or expanded several times since the Williamite war, and there were retail markets for meat (three), milk (three), potatoes, poultry and eggs. The Corporation at that time was determined to chase traders, particularly those vending cheap cloth, 'gartering, and . . . small wares' off the public street and into the formal markets. Later in the century, the policy was to reduce the number of secondary markets and bring business to the new retail market hub constructed in the late 1780s beside Grand Parade. The meat market there became the 'English Market', an accolade previously attached to the only meat market operating within the old walled city, where individual stallholders had enjoyed extended leases from the Corporation and where, even in the 1770s, attempts had been made to restrict lease-holding to Protestant butchers only. The background was the eclipse of Protestant control of the huge slaughtering industry in the northern suburbs and a concern to keep the most prestigious retail end of the trade in 'respectable' hands, but the plan was reversed almost immediately.[32]

THE BUSINESS OF DRINK

The most common of the 'common shops' were places for the sale and consumption of alcohol, without food or allied comforts. Despite the state's attempts to load taxation on all forms of alcohol, much of the 'low' trade in drink existed on the edge of the law. Thus the many drinking dens in the back lanes and cellars of the big cities have left almost no historical record. However, the types of beverage consumed are better known: in the seventeenth century home-brewed ale was the principal stimulant, nearly all of it produced close to the point of sale, but wines from France, Spain and the Canaries were the alcohol of choice for those who could afford them. In the eighteenth century, imported spirits, chiefly brandy and later rum, challenged older preferences, and new-style English ales and porter were increasingly popular in Dublin and Cork. Changes in tariffs and excise levels from the 1770s radically altered these consumption patterns, bringing about a great decline of rum from the Americas, a near-total eclipse of brandy imports, and an increase in heavier beers, both imported and locally produced. Then, beginning in the 1790s, came a transformation in the size and output of breweries and distilleries in Dublin, Cork and Belfast, and this huge growth in local output ended the importation of beer and spirits, although it did not prevent the rise of a vigorous black market in illicitly distilled whiskey emanating from remote districts in the northern half of the country. Wine retreated slowly from its central position – and slowest among high-income consumers.[33]

Petty suggested in 1672 that there were 1,180 alehouses in Dublin, and Rutty claimed that almost a century later there were no less than 2,000 alehouses and 1,200 brandy shops in addition to some 300 taverns in the mid-century city. Such figures imply that rough single-room premises may have been the norm. The licensing of alehouse keepers had been introduced in 1634, most of whom presumably brewed their own product, but by the 1670s there were some ninety-one 'public brew-houses' in Dublin and a new brewers guild. A few, like Joseph Leeson (1660–1741) and the Sweetman clan, made a small fortune in commercial brewing, but most 'common brewers' oversaw very small operations. It was only with a battery of new legislation in the 1790s that the retail drinks sector began to be closely regulated: public houses in Cork, Dublin, Limerick and Waterford were loaded with the heaviest license duty and by 1793 a total of 504 licences had been issued for Dublin city and county. Three decades later *Pigot's Directory* listed an almost identical number of 'vintners, spirit dealers, and porter and punch houses' in the city and inner suburbs, and a further thirty inns and taverns (see Plate 17). The true number of tippling houses and dram shops in the capital may indeed have been much greater, but the relative importance of these unlicensed premises in terms of sales and visibility was probably quite limited. Estimates for Cork (500 alehouses and taverns in 1806) and for Limerick (240 dram shops in 1790) are also substantially higher than the licensed premises listed in Pigot in 1824 (201 in Cork and 86 in Limerick), but the missing 'shebeens' probably commanded only a small share of the overall sale of alcohol.[34]

The wine business was a different matter: it was always something of a hybrid, involving merchants and wholesale importers who generally sold by the cask to private buyers, to inns, taverns and institutions, but also to retail grocers and vintners. Around half of the legally declared French wines entering Ireland in the 1680s were landed in Dublin, and that share grew noticeably in the early eighteenth century. At the peak of the trade in the 1760s Dublin handled almost three-quarters of the business; Cork merchants, who had handled a third of Irish wine imports in the 1680s, handled only a seventh in the 1760s. And only in Dublin did a corps of 'wine merchants' emerge to form a wealthy sub-section of the merchant community: there were forty listed in 1768, and sixty-nine a quarter century later, most of whom traded close to the quays. But by 1794 fewer than half (thirty-two) were recognized by the Custom House as bona fide wholesale importers and about three-quarters of this select group were Protestant, as indeed was much of their private out-of-town custom.

Presbyterians were over-represented among the top wine merchants, which cannot have been unconnected to the strong presence of Ulster-born and Scottish merchants in the western French ports since the 1680s, some of whose families sojourned in Dublin. Huguenot merchants also insinuated themselves into the wine trade in the early eighteenth century, but never dominated it. However, it has been discovered that they invested very heavily in Dublin taverns and alehouses in the first half of the century, with Huguenot ownership or leaseholds of no fewer than thirty-five premises, seven of these held by one family. Even David La Touche had four, all in Dame St, and nearly all the others lay south of the river where their co-religionists' numbers were greatest.[35]

A few of the Dublin wine merchants operated on a grand scale, holding large stocks in their vaults and offering *premier cru* wines from named vineyards, targeting gentry consumers in the four provinces. But none compared with George Boyd of Abbey St: at mid century he was head of the Dublin branch of a family that had been trading in Bordeaux since the 1680s, his brother Jacques head of the Bordeaux house. Boyd was supplier of wines for Dublin Castle in 1760 and an indication of the family's wealth was the size of his daughter's dowry in 1776 (£20,000) on her marriage to the future second Earl of Carhampton. But, as Kelly has argued, the market for wine and other expensive alcohol had by that time moved far beyond the upper classes, evident in the constant appeal to householders that wines and spirits could now be purchased in convenient quantities, and by the rise of well-stocked grocers.[36]

The brandy trade was a late developer, only featuring from the 1730s, and was most popular when rum was scarce and local grain distilling was halted by bad harvests. Although sourced in the same region in south-west France as the bulk of wine imported to Ireland, it was traded in a rather different fashion. At the French end, several Irish-born merchants played a critical role as buyers and shippers, and the trade had a distinctly Catholic character. In his study of the early brandy industry, Cullen has illuminated the unlikely career of Laurence Saule (born *c*. 1700), who for many years had traded at The Golden Key in Dublin's Fishamble St. Describing himself variously as a grocer and a wine merchant, in 1740 he was advertising 'in large or small quantities' teas and coffee, 'old brandy, choice rum, Bordeaux vinegar and orange shrub, esteem'd by judges to be very extraordinary', Irish cider and whisky, sugars and 'chocolate of his own manufacturing, at 3s the pound, with the name SAULE . . . impress'd thereon'. The brand-conscious Saule was in fact an importing wholesaler, handling spirits and exotic groceries, a mix that was not remarkable in itself, but he was evidently more adventurous than most. He was one of the small coterie of wealthy Catholic merchants in the capital at mid century, many of them living in close proximity, but somehow he became embroiled in the bitter dispute beween Toole and Byrne in 1759, sheltering Toole's daughter (or niece) after she had refused to follow her father into the Church of Ireland. That cause célèbre led to his prosecution, a bitter experience which prompted him (several years later) 'to sell out and to expatriate' from what he saw as 'this place of bondage', and go to France, 'begin the world anew', and try his hand as a brandy dealer and shipper. Based in Charente from the end of the Seven Years War and trading with considerable assets, 'my Lord Saul' built up a remarkably successful brandy exporting business in a few years, principally with Dublin itself, where by 1767 he had fifty correspondents (and seventeen outside the capital). He died suddenly the following year, but not before the entrepreneurial skills of the old Fishamble St grocer had been amply demonstrated on a much larger stage.[37]

6
TOGETHER AND APART

Lord Chancellor Bowes, hearing the case in 1759 against Laurence Saule for sheltering Miss Toole, was reputed to have uttered sentiments that echoed down through Irish history, that 'the law of the land did not suppose any such thing as an Irish papist to exist'. The technical issue was it seems whether or not Irish Catholics could plead that they were members of a distinct corporate entity; Bowes was denying the formal existence of such a body, or the possibility of formal membership of such an entity, not the rights of access to common-law protection enjoyed by all the king's subjects. It underlined the contrast between the non-existent legal status of the Catholic Church and the exclusive constitutional position of the established Church of Ireland, replete with its well-defined rights and privileges, its clerical orders and its vast real estate. Bowes's comment implied a legal chasm between the Catholic Church and all other corporate institutions – whether dissenting Churches, guilds, municipal corporations, colleges, or voluntary bodies, chartered and statutory. Some of these enjoyed a very visible existence, and nearly all had a legal status and the financial resources to ensure their reproducibility.[1]

THE OLD RELIGION

The eighteenth-century Catholic Church enjoyed none of those resources. It was frequently riven by internal dissent yet, despite the hopes of the Cromwellian social engineers in the 1650s and the intermittently repressive climate that existed up to the mid 1740s, it continued to function both in Dublin and the southern cities. But deprived of the patronage of a sympathetic gentry the Church as an organization was drastically weakened after the Jacobite defeat. Recovery was first evident in the 1720s, a result of the continuing supply of young clergy (trained in the Irish colleges on the Continent) and the willingness of lay people to support them financially. Until the 1720s bishops and those in the mendicant religious orders who had chosen to ignore the banishment act of 1697 kept a very low profile, and for another generation they continued to operate with great caution: Archbishop Byrne of Dublin (1706–23) went into hiding on at least four occasions and was twice imprisoned (briefly); two of the Catholic bishops of Cork between 1698 and 1725 were, between them, detained in gaol for some nine years. A supposed political link with Jacobite conspiracy was the rationale in such cases. Several friars and other religious in these cities were also imprisoned for lengthy periods without trial – and without evidence of political involvement. However, members of the male religious orders became increasingly visible from around 1720, often in bitter competition with the parish clergy for fees and funds from the faithful. They had a notably strong presence in Galway (the Augustinians were living within the old town walls by 1731, and there were two other orders residing just outside), and in Kilkenny, where the Dominicans were firmly re-established and the Franciscans lived almost on the doorstep of the Church of Ireland cathedral. In the east and south of the country the number of priests and friars based in cities and large urban centres was far higher than in the countryside: Drogheda, for instance, had more clergy in 1744 than had the rest of Co. Louth. And as early as 1731 Protestant authorities in Dublin were estimating that there were up into 117 regular and secular priests regularly officiating in the city (including 40 to 50 in the Cook St, Bridge St and Back Lane area alone), implying a large increase in a single decade. By contrast, in Sligo town in 1766 there were only two priests, one fresh from Rome and the other 'advanced in years'.[2]

The clearest evidence of Catholic organizational recovery was physical: after the Williamite victory many post-Reformation Catholic chapels had been closed or even destroyed, and only private chapels in well-to-do households remained in regular use. But a tentative process of reconstruction was under way in Dublin before 1714, and by the late 1720s churches were reappearing within, or on the edge of, all the southern cities, the largest of them serving as parish churches. These were built and fitted out from voluntary contributions. None of the new structures displayed external architectural features except in Cork city, and nearly all were adapted warehouses or barns, removed from public view down lanes and alleyways. Yet they were not secret venues. Indeed, the location of many was published in the 1750s in John Rocque's maps of Cork, Kilkenny, and Dublin, where seventeen chapels in the city were identified by a cross (four of them owned by mendicant orders, four convent chapels). But the punctilious Rocque did manage to overlook two other mendicant chapels in the capital.

The emerging pattern of church building reflected ancient parish boundaries and the pre-Reformation location of monasteries and friaries. In Dublin, Kilkenny and Galway this led to a cluster of chapels within or adjacent to what had been the circuit of the walls; in Waterford, where there had been four chapels inside the walls before 1690, Catholic townsmen struggled in 1701 to hold onto their single new-built premises within the perimeter, assuring the Corporation that two of the congregation 'are appointed every Sabbath day at the door of the chapel to keep them [the country men] out, so few or none of them do now come in [to the city], but do tarry abroad in the little cabin house chapel made for themselves', a rare hint that urban Catholics (at least in Waterford) still felt they were culturally distinct from their rural co-religionists, who should be cordoned off at a distance. They succeeded in their appeal, the first of many local victories (see Plate 18).

However, in Cork, Limerick and Drogheda, the earliest eighteenth-century parish 'mass houses' were all outside the walls or where walls had been. In Cork's south suburbs 'a long cabin that will contain about 400 persons' was built in the 1690s and then replaced by a slated chapel in the 1720s, while on the north side in Shandon a new site was chosen in 1730 for a replacement chapel 'on a fine eminence, [built] in a large and sumptuous manner'; it overlooked the 'island' parishes where more modest friaries were beginning to appear. For many in Cork the four smaller chapels of the religious orders became the focus of loyalty, and when suspicions arose in 1774 that Bishop Butler was trying to close them 'and unite their members to the two parish chapels', it caused huge controversy and an appeal was sent by 'about a hundred' Cork laymen to Pope Clement, urging him to halt the threatened slight on 'this extensive city, the second Dublin, to which Waterford is but a village'. No more was heard of that plan. In Limerick the first chapel to re-open inside the old city was built in Englishtown by Dominicans in 1730, to be quickly followed by the Franciscans almost next door.[3]

After the Hanoverian succession, apart from a few moments of panic (notably during the early stages of the Jacobite invasion threat in 1743/4), local authorities did not interfere in the regular celebration of Mass in any of the southern cities. But there was severe under-capacity, at least in the Dublin churches, where the maximum that any could hold was estimated to be 500.

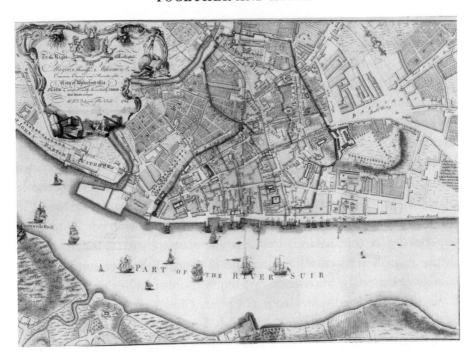

Figure 12 Most of Waterford's citizens still lived within the line of the old walls when William Richards and Bernard Scalé published their *Plan of the city and suburbs of Waterford city* in 1764. They made no attempt to disguise the centrality of Catholic places of worship, notably the 'Great Chapell' close to the County Courthouse, the Playhouse and the Quay.

Despite the installation of galleries, overcrowding led to a series of injuries and fatal accidents, both there and in Cork. However, Thomas Brennan, a Jesuit reporting back to Rome in 1747, was delighted to find that in Dublin 'we now begin to have vespers sung and sermons preached in the afternoon'. And in 1761 a full programme of Sunday services in the Dominican chapel in Bridge St began with 7 a.m. Mass and a sermon in Irish, and finished with a sermon and the rosary in the evening. There and elsewhere sacristies, confessionals, altars, pulpits and pews 'for the better sort', tabernacles, paintings and other decorative features were becoming quite common in well-supported urban churches; in Dublin's Townsend St chapel the altarpiece, a copy of Rubens' *Descent from the Cross*, was set within an exceptional chinoiserie frame that may have been carved locally.[4]

This was a far cry from the situation in the northern centres: Catholic numbers were so small in both Belfast and Derry until the second half of the

123

century that it is hardly surprising that there was no Catholic place of worship in Belfast until *c.* 1769, or in Derry until 1788. And chapel-building in their respective hinterlands also began much later than elsewhere. By contrast, in the south of Ireland the collective resort to sacramental rites at regular times and locations, the emergence of a few gifted preachers with a 'homely manner', the knowledge that it was all to some degree a collective act of defiance, helped to ingrain a sense of religious community. Yet the intensity of Catholic religious practice, even in the capital, may be doubted: in 1761, the Rome-trained Father James Lyons was shocked at the uneven level of religious observance there, and in 1776 Archbishop Carpenter worried that 'many [Catholics] in this city . . . have not yet seriously thought of their conversion nor are resolved to partake of the spiritual treasures . . . so abundantly offered to them'. Sermons in the English vernacular had long been standard, but lay confraternities (usually promoted by the religious orders) were only now beginning to spread. Collective religious displays such as Corpus Christi processions that might encroach on the street were unheard of before 1790, no priest or friar wore clerical garb in public before then, and no bell was rung except at the altar until after 1800. The rituals surrounding baptism, marriage and death seem to have been largely contained within the home, or at least conducted outside the chapel. And all public burial grounds in the cities were attached to the Church of Ireland parish churches and were tightly controlled, meaning that the clergy of other denominations were denied the right to pray at the grave.[5]

KNOCKING AT THE DOOR

1759 was a critical year in the creation of a new Catholic politics, urban and lay in character. It began with the sensational defeat of Cork Corporation's attempt to enforce quarterage after John Meskell and the other 'popish tradesmen' had used the Court of King's Bench to challenge the powers of the mayor, who was obliged to pay a hefty fine. Coming at a time of war and rumours of French invasion, the suit was hugely controversial. It came in the wake of elaborate attempts within Parliament to introduce fresh legislation intended to moderate but copper-fasten the penal restrictions on Catholic clergy. At this time a small Catholic ginger group began to collaborate: a medical doctor, John Curry, a Dublin merchant, Anthony Dermott, and *rarae aves*, two minor Catholic landowners, Thomas Wyse from the environs of Waterford city and Charles O'Conor from Roscommon. They were a formidable quartet: Curry had a huge city practice, Dermott was probably then the wealthiest Catholic merchant in Dublin; Wyse a pioneering lead miner and manufacturer of metal goods in Waterford city; and O'Conor, a widower and active farmer who was spending half his year 'in our capital city where I mix with men of all descriptions', because 'it is *there* in truth that I made my acquaintance[s], having but little knowledge of the gentry of my own countries . . .'.

Between them they managed to persuade 307 Catholic Dubliners – merchants, but predominantly specialist traders and professionals – to put their name to an address of loyalty to the Lord Lieutenant, the Duke of Bedford, in December 1759, triggering similar addresses from Cork, Waterford and Limerick and attracting a further 273 signatories. There were discreet precedents for Catholic addresses to the Crown in 1727 and 1739; as on those earlier occasions it was a highly controversial move and opposed by the Catholic bishops and by most clergy, on both political and theological grounds. And, as before, it had almost no political effect. But the 1759 addresses were novel in three ways: they were explicitly urban in origin; appearing over several weeks in the midst of war, they were a public act with all the signatories' names appearing in the official *Dublin Gazette*; and they were received with conspicuous courtesy by the government of the day. The Dublin address was handled with particular civility by John Ponsonby, Speaker of the Commons and leader of the newly ascendant faction in Parliament, and thereby the principal manager (or 'under-taker') of Irish government business. Ponsonby, and particularly the Duke of Bedford, had their own (tactical) reasons for a markedly less abrasive attitude towards Catholics at that time, but for the signatories to the addresses it was a potentially dangerous declaration of membership of a legally unrecognized body.

The loyalist addresses from Munster were more obsequious than that from Dublin; indeed the Cork Catholics touched on the imminent possibility of invasion, the French acting on 'the imaginary hope of assistance here from the former attachments of our deluded predecessors'. But the Dublin address spoke, albeit obliquely, about the 'restraints of the many Penal Laws against them' and how they were anxious that ways might be found to strengthen Catholics' friendship towards the state. O'Conor was delighted that the Dublin address had 'touched on the bondage you are under with great delicacy of sentiment'. However, a year later, when six hundred of 'the most considerable Catholics of the kingdom' signed an address of loyalty on the accession of George III, they had retreated into voicing uniformly milder sentiments.[6]

THE CHURCH ESTABLISHED

'The city seemed to every one at a distance to be in one entire flame, guns incessantly firing and all the bells ringing.' It was 1 July 1740 (OS), the fiftieth anniversary of the Battle of the Boyne: for some thirty hours Dublin skies were lit up by bonfires and illuminations. Flags were flown from the steeples of the Church of Ireland churches of St Michan's on the north side and old St Catherine's in the south-west, right beside the Meath Liberty where 'the inhabitants' had reportedly adorned their doors and windows with flowers, specifically orange lilies, for the great day. Who organized all this? Unlike later extravagant celebrations of William and the glorious memory, this effusion seems to have been locally inspired and to have focused on the two largest Anglican parish churches in the western half of the city. The attention was not, it seems, on the equestrian statue of William III in Dame St close to the Parliament house, which subsequently became the site for elaborate civic and governmental celebration of the king's birthday and, much later, a microcosm of sectarian hostilities. The Church of Ireland, despite its somewhat compromised role in 1690, was now fifty years later quite demonstrably the Church of the establishment and its premier cathedral, Christ Church in Dublin, surrounded by 'grubby hinterlands', was the site for the most solemn and colourful state ceremonies in the kingdom. The Church's archbishops were active members of the Privy Council, and several (Agar, Boulter, King and Stone) became key figures in the permanent government of the country. All bishops were spiritual peers and sat in the Irish House of Lords, and nearly all maintained Dublin houses, in addition to which several of the wealthier bishops built (or rebuilt) palaces – in Cork, Derry, Kilkenny, Limerick and, most spectacularly, the great pile in Waterford which cut through the city walls to dominate the new mall at the east end of town. The scale of these episcopal palaces reflected the very sizeable rental incomes from diocesan estates that accrued to bishops while in office, and the expectation was that the great houses would be purchased by their successors.[7]

In the capital the number of functioning parishes of the Church of Ireland grew from ten in 1660 to nineteen by 1810, and they attracted for the most part an enviable supply of well-educated incumbents: in the 1790s there were at least sixty clergy formally attached to the city's cathedrals and churches. As for buildings, seventeen Church of Ireland parish churches were built in Dublin between the 1660s and 1800s (three of which were re-built again during the period). Several of those erected in new parishes attracted direct support from urban estate developers (including the Presbyterian, Humphrey Jervis), but most city churches were built through fundraising, parish cess and once-off crown or parliamentary grants (and not, as in the nineteenth century, from the well-resourced Board of First Fruits). Some of Dublin's inner-city churches were as modest as their Catholic counterparts, others towered over the neighbourhood as in the case of St Michan's, rebuilt in the 1680s and modified a generation later, which, its minister believed, could hold a congregation of 4,100. Dublin's two medieval cathedrals, Christ Church and the much larger St Patrick's, were not rebuilt at this time, although shortly after Dean Swift's death the latter finally got its steeple. But even then, several of the new parish churches built on higher ground cut the skyline more effectively. The last of the great inner-city churches, St George's (1802–06), became a soaring landmark on the northern approaches.[8]

Further north, Drogheda's great medieval church, St Peter's, was only partially rebuilt after the Cromwellian firestorm in 1649, but almost exactly a century later the church was demolished and in its stead a fine replacement with a Palladian facade by local builder Hugh Darley became a new landmark above the town, complete with a superb interior. Sligo's new parish church, designed by Richard Castle c. 1740, was also 'a stately building', albeit erected on a less imposing site. Derry's defining building remained St Columb's, the plantation-era cathedral that was enhanced by the Earl Bishop in the 1770s with a remarkable (but short-lived) spire; a nearby chapel-of-ease within the walls was added around this time. Belfast's most eye-catching building at that point was the parish church of St Anne's, erected between 1774 and 1776 on a new site in Donegall St with seats for nearly a thousand worshippers; it was funded entirely by the fifth Earl of Donegall, an unsubtle gesture signalling the re-assertion of the family's primacy in what had once been their fiefdom (see Plate 19).

But these symbols of Anglican primacy in the north were misleading: Drogheda was becoming an increasingly Catholic town, and Derry's new money was predominantly Presbyterian (even if the local gentry and professionals were mainly Church of Ireland). In Belfast the reality was starker: despite St Anne's physical prominence, it was still an overwhelmingly Presbyterian town – from the Exchange to the poor-house.[9]

In the southern cities there was a real contrast in Anglican church building activity between Galway, Kilkenny and Limerick, where patched-up medieval churches met the needs of the Church of Ireland, and Cork and Waterford, where in each case a medieval cathedral was demolished and rebuilt. Peter

Browne, long-serving Tory bishop of Cork (1710–35), was unusual in his drive to consolidate the Church of Ireland presence, both architecturally and pastorally, in the mushrooming city. Even before the new cathedral was built he oversaw the demolition and reconstruction of four parish churches in the city and suburbs, securing a temporary coal tax from the Corporation to augment public subscriptions, and he was able to execute this work fairly quickly. The rebuilt Christ Church, beside South Main St, was the largest, accommodating a congregation of 3,000.

The old cathedral had long been in a dangerous condition but, as with the other Cork churches, growing congregations rather than damage from the siege explain the great rebuilding. The enduring legacy of this building spurt was the eccentric and utterly distinctive parish church of St Anne's Shandon, the most emblematic building surviving from eighteenth-century Cork, equipped (from 1752) with its eight bells that still promise 'when us you ring we'll sweetly sing'. Browne's modest cathedral was completed shortly after his death and was itself fated to be demolished in the 1860s. Over the rest of the eighteenth century, only one other Anglican church in Cork was rebuilt (St Peter's in North Main St during the 1780s).[10]

In Waterford, the demolition of its fine but decayed Gothic cathedral had been under discussion in the 1730s when two Anglican parish churches, St Patrick's and St Olaf's, were completely rebuilt. But the cathedral had to wait until the mid 1770s. Bishop Chenevix gave the reconstruction project to a local builder and architect John Roberts, who took nearly twenty years to complete the challenge, but against the odds he produced, in Mark Girouard's judgement, 'the finest eighteenth-century ecclesiastical building in Ireland'. What was, of course, even more remarkable was that in 1792 the octogenarian Roberts was given the commission to extend and rebuild the Catholic 'Big Chapel', thereby creating a cathedral 'warm, luscious and Mediterranean' to rival his cool and neoclassical design for the Church of Ireland. We will revisit that strange conjuncture later.[11]

DISSENT

Until mid century the Church of Ireland had the unquestioning loyalty of the great majority of Protestants in the southern cities. In Dublin it catered for the needs of the powerful at prayer in the fine pews of the new eastside churches of St Werburgh's, St Peter's, St Thomas's and St Mary's, but also for the teeming

Protestant population of the Liberties that filled St Luke's in the Coombe and St Catherine's on Thomas St. On the north side, the garrison marched to Sunday service in one of several parish churches. But there was a slow exodus of low-status Church of Ireland families to other denominations, underway well before mid century; in the 1731 Popery returns the mayor of Cork claimed that the priests of the city were active, 'some of the unthinking weak [Protestant] people being frequently perverted by their persuasions, they being extraordinarily industrious in making converts, and many families are ruined by the clandestine marriages celebrated by them', and there were similar warnings in Limerick and Dublin and a pervasive fear that 'couple beggars' were facilitating such matches. This probably overstates the incidence of mixed marriage in artisan circles, but where it did occur and the mother was Catholic (as was usually the case), the children were most likely raised as Catholics.

A more visible challenge to the Church of Ireland in artisan districts came with the arrival of a string of Methodist preachers, and they had an immediate impact in Dublin: John Wesley returned to the country to preach twenty-one times in forty-two years, always coming to Dublin and helping to lay the foundations there for a wider evangelical resurgence at the end of the century. A large Methodist preaching hall was opened in the city *c.* 1750, appropriately within sight of St Patrick's Cathedral, for the formal breach with Anglicanism lay in the future. The movement also gained considerable traction in the southern cities (but not in Belfast, Galway or Kilkenny). Its signal success in the capital was critical in preparing for its later expansion, mainly into rural districts where Anglicanism had deep roots.[12]

If Dublin was the crucible for Irish Methodism, and if the revival of institutional Irish Catholicism also germinated there and in the southern cities, what of the largest group of Protestant dissenters, the Presbyterians? At first sight, that seems an Ulster story, their troubled history closely aligned to developments in Scotland, their ministry very largely Scottish educated, and the ethnic identification of their laity with the Scottish homeland slow to weaken. But Presbyterians, pre-eminent politically in Dublin at the end of the Commonwealth regime, remained a powerful constituent in the southern cities, and particularly in Dublin itself. By the early eighteenth century – a time of intense theological dispute and fragmentation among Irish Presbyterians – there was a complex three-way movement of ideas between Dublin, Ulster and Scotland. At that stage there were no less than six congregations active in the capital, while Derry had only one and Belfast two, until a new one was established in 1722.[13]

That was 'Third Belfast', located beside the two existing congregations in Rosemary St, and established as a direct result of the tensions within the Synod of Ulster over the status of the Westminster Confession and its uncompromising Calvinistic tenets; its chief sponsor was a Belfast merchant, Samuel Smith. However a 'polite reading group' of young ministers, physicians and elders, later known as the Belfast Society, had been meeting in the town since 1705 to explore and interrogate scripture in the light of natural philosophy. The key figure was John Abernethy, a Presbyterian 'blue blood' all of whose siblings had been child fatalities in the siege of Derry. Championing the centrality of personal judgment in religious belief and action and asserting the capacity of the rational individual to be a competent truth seeker, Abernethy became the most prominent of the 'New Light' group of ministers. They affiliated together as the autonomous Synod of Antrim in 1725, and were formally excommunicated from the Synod of Ulster the following year. New Light beliefs and practices took root and endured for the rest of the century and beyond, associated (perhaps too readily) with Belfast and its immediate hinterland, and with Presbyterians of greater wealth and education. The 'Old Light' stronghold of Third Belfast, despite its initial wealthy backers, sold its pews to shoemakers and weavers, maltsters and a great cross-section of the town's lesser traders. By the 1770s there were five large churches in town, three New Light and two Old Light, each commanding strong associational loyalty and, whatever the prestige of many of their ministers, each of them was managed by elders drawn from well-to-do business and professional families.

Dublin, however, had been vital in the emergence of the reformist tendency in Presbyterianism: observers from the capital had tried to mediate at meetings of the Synod of Ulster and identify theological compromises in the early 1720s, and after the split two Dublin congregations had raised funds to support New Light ministers (although support for the Old Light position was also strong in at least two other Dublin congregations). Abernethy himself found the capital city a salubrious sanctuary when he moved there in 1730 to minister to the wealthy New Light congregation in Wood St. That congregation was unusual in supporting a Presbyterian academy in the northern suburbs which prepared students destined for the Scottish universities. One of its teachers took the same path himself: Francis Hutcheson, whose later fame in Scotland

Figure 13 The oldest Presbyterian congregation in Dublin was associated with Wood St on the south side, but the meeting moved north and established the Great Strand St chapel near Ormond Quay in 1764. Supported by many of the wealthiest and most prominent Presbyterian families in the city, several of its ministers gained international celebrity for their writings, and most Presbyterians involved in reform and radical politics were also members here.

and far beyond rested on the philosophical ideas that he first developed in Dublin during the 1720s with his Wood St friends.[14]

Presbyterian congregations existed in every urban centre except Kilkenny; in Galway they faded out early, in Drogheda late in the century (although revived later). Southern Presbyterianism was always somewhat different from that in the North: the earliest congregations had English Puritan or English Presbyterian origins, and thus denominational distinctions – with the Baptists, Huguenot Non-Conformists and other dissenting congregations with an English ancestry – were less pronounced. And their internal doctrinal divisions did not prevent the clustering of meeting houses in Dublin, notably in the Mary's Abbey neighbourhood of the Jervis estate where Old Light, New Light and later the Seceders co-existed in close proximity. All dissenters were united by a common resentment of the 1704 Test Act that had drastically diminished their involvement in municipal government in Belfast and Derry and was only partly offset by the Toleration Act of 1719. That said, the latter concession provided a legal basis for dissenter religious activity and for protecting church property. Thus the first truly substantial Presbyterian meeting houses in Dublin and Cork date from the following decade; the largest, in Eustace St, near Dublin's Custom House, was built by a congregation from the old city moving up in the world, and it was strongly New Light in sympathy. As Michael Brown has suggested, Dublin Presbyterianism was an unusual amalgam, a mix of the conventicle and the kirk, its leaders serving the interests of their own people but lacking a strong conversionist impulse, and eirenic in their response to disputes in Ulster. Over-represented within the merchant and wholesale business sector, Presbyterians permeated the wider society in unexpected ways.

John O'Keeffe recalled that the finest picture collection in mid-century Dublin had been that of Robert Stewart, an elder in Great Strand St congregation – but he was a landowner too, and was the future Marquess of Londonderry. Of greater local significance was the display of Presbyterian political muscle after the entry of one of their own, James Dunn, into a closely fought city by-election in 1758, when he sought to become the first Presbyterian Member of Parliament to represent Dublin in a century. His victory marked a breakthrough in the decade-long assault by the lesser guilds on the oligarchic powers of the aldermen, but it also established publicly the association between Protestant dissent and the cause of political reform.[15]

On a more modest scale, Huguenots in Dublin and Cork mirrored some of these tendencies: a history of enervating disputes and splits, yet a high visibility in civil society. They were also present in the congested spaces of Mary's Abbey where there was a Huguenot congregation for many years (which maintained an Anglican liturgy but rejected the authority of the archbishop). However, some two-thirds of Dublin's Huguenots were fully non-conformist (although not the more prominent families) and they supported two 'temples', one on each side of the Liffey. The Society of Friends offered a strong contrast: no other dissenting group was as self-disciplined in the home, as visually distinctive in public, or as commercially resourceful as the Quakers. Again, as with most southern Presbyterians and Baptists, their family origins were overwhelmingly New English, mainly as migrants of the 1650s, and Dublin and Cork had the strongest clusters. In the early years they had two meeting houses in the capital and one in Cork (with a smaller presence in Waterford and Limerick). Quakers could tell a richer tale of communal oppression by church and state during the Restoration era than other dissenters, and this legacy reinforced their sense of a righteous people wronged. While communal discipline was a defining charac-teristic in all dissenting denominations, with the Quakers it remained far more rigorous and intrusive. The high level of endogamy and mutual support and their formal commitment to probity, personal modesty and material restraint gave them a potent advantage as a trustworthy social network with whom to do business. And usually when a Quaker business failed or a member married out, the consequence was suspension or expulsion from the Society.[16]

THE PARISH

The parish vestry of the Established Church, as conceived in another place at another time, had the responsibility to police the godly community, but in an Irish context the vestry became an immediate, and at times oppressive, local authority governing the whole community. From Elizabethan times parish vestries in Dublin had had a series of civic responsibilities thrust upon them (beginning with fire-fighting), and in the early seventeenth century this had been extended to scavenging, road maintenance and poor relief, but the evidence suggests very haphazard implementation. Poor relief meant little more than the distribution of alms and pensions from parish funds and church collections, and it was usually confined to conformists. However in the late 1720s St Michan's in Dublin was supporting forty-three 'needy' parishioners, probably not all conformists, and many parishes in Dublin and Cork were by then licensing ('badging') their indigenous beggars to differentiate local hard cases from the ever-present vagrants.

Parish officers gained an expanded role in tax collection from the 1660s with the introduction of 'minister's money', a valuation-based tax in lieu of tithe, and they were required to collect this together with parish cess (for the upkeep, possibly the reconstruction, of the parish church) plus a growing list of city taxes. As a consequence most of the (unpaid) administrative energies of the elected churchwardens and sidesmen were devoted to the endless intricacies of applotment and collection, and election to such offices was increasingly unpopular. For some, the experience was perhaps 'a nursery in civic duties', but for most involved the only consolation was that of gaining a uniquely fine-grained knowledge of who was living where in their own neighbourhood. The administrative burden on city vestries was increased during the century with the development of various night-lighting initiatives, following the legislation in 1719 and 1729 requiring parishes in the five largest cities to organize public lighting themselves or to raise the necessary cess for their respective corporations to deliver the service. But the decision by Parliament in 1721 to give Dublin parishes the primary responsibility for policing, thereby transferring the city's recently established night-watch system from the municipality to the parish, created the heaviest burden, even if it was a back-handed recognition of the relative effectiveness of vestry governance. The arrangement lasted, against the odds, for more than sixty years and was extended to Waterford in the 1780s, just when it was about to be phased out in the capital.[17]

Elsewhere, Church of Ireland parishes, rich and poor, functioned as the basic unit of local government, controlled by and answerable to municipal authority, and with even fewer statutory powers than in the principal cities. Where the preponderance of Catholics was greatest – as in Kilkenny and Galway – the parish vestry as an institution seems to have had very little agency beyond organizing tax collection and maintaining the parish church and graveyard. But even there the vestry was not an exclusively Anglican male preserve, for despite the 1704 Test Act non-conformists had no compunction about attending the Easter vestries that made annual budgetary decisions, and Catholic householders began to attend in the final decades of the century. Long before that in Dublin parishes, the somewhat feeble watch system was recruiting large numbers of (paid) watchmen and (unpaid) constables, some of whom were evidently Catholic. The parish vestry was not an entirely male preserve: Church of Ireland women attended from time to time, but they were never elected to parish office, other than to act as nurses for the abandoned infants that were left to be rescued by parish authorities.[18]

GENDER, RELIGION AND OPPORTUNITY

The masculinity of eighteenth-century public life from vestry room to council chamber may be somewhat exaggerated in the historical record. But as in almost all *ancien régime* societies, law and custom reinforced patriarchy, even in the cities, and the wealth-creating activities of wives, widows and unmarried women were taken for granted in public discourse and were rarely a matter of comment until late in the century. But by the time that trade directories for Dublin and the Munster cities began to appear, women were listed in up to a tenth of all commercial entries; many of these were widows managing the family business until a male heir came of age, or were acting in partnership with the male heir or heirs. Over 70 per cent of all women listed in the Dublin trade directories between 1766 and 1800 disappeared in less than five years (although they may often have remained as substantial partners in a family business). However some women developed small businesses independently, principally in the retail sectors of food and clothing, whether as grocers, retail linen drapers, haberdashers or milliners, and these were sectors witnessing strong growth in the late eighteenth century. Some married couples operated separate retail businesses from the same address. However, the odds against women surviving as principals in trade were high: they had to manage often wayward male apprentices, and may have had greater difficulties sourcing credit or legal redress. No woman in trade or the crafts enjoyed the benefits of full civic or guild freedom, and only a few registered as 'quarter-brothers'. Apprenticeship contracts for girls in those sectors such as millinery where women were well represented did exist, but these arrangements were unregulated.[19]

Urban women were however catching up in one important respect: literacy. The hard evidence is very late, dating from the next century: the 1841 census returns on literacy, as calculated for each age cohort. An examination of the reading and writing skills of relatively elderly citizens in 1841 gives some insight into gender and literacy in the second half of the eighteenth century (keeping in mind the obvious caveats as noted below in Table 6.1). The contrast here between the cities and towns for which data are available is quite striking. As was the case across pre-industrial Europe, female illiteracy was everywhere

Table 6.1
Urban Illiteracy Levels of Males and Females of School-going Age: 1761–70 and 1791–1800 (%)

	Males 1761–1770	Females 1761–1770	Males 1791–1800	Females 1791–1800
Derry	n.a.	n.a.	n.a.	n.a.
Sligo	n.a.	n.a.	n.a.	n.a.
Galway	46	76	45	70
Limerick	27	64	28	58
Cork	33	55	30	51
Waterford	28	62	29	51
Kilkenny	36	70	31	58
Dublin	19	43	18	33
Drogheda	50	82	36	60
Belfast	13	27	15	24

Sources: Census of Ireland, 1841, p. xxxvi.

Note: The school-going cohort related to those aged 5 to 14 in the decades specified who were unable to read or write. Changes in urban boundaries, migration fields and class-specific mortality rates during subsequent decades will have affected this profile derived from the 1841 census returns, and the numbers in the older cohort are very small for Galway and Drogheda in particular. The 1841 enumerators' schedules for these cities and towns do not survive.

much higher than for males, with the urban gap greatest in the south and west, least in Belfast and Dublin. A narrowing of the differential came about very slowly, but by 1800 was well under way in Dublin and (from a much lower base) in Waterford. Belfast was already showing an exceptionally low level of female illiteracy in the 1760s, but this is somewhat deceptive: around 53 per cent of the females recorded as literate (then and in the 1790s) were able to *read only*, whereas in Dublin and the south women with *full* literacy outnumbered those limited to reading only, in both the 1760s and 1790s. Of course we can assume that there was no simple binary division, rather a broad spectrum from near illiteracy, perhaps a halting ability to decipher the letters of the alphabet on a sign-board in the street, to full literacy and an everyday engagement with letter-writing and the habit of voluminous reading.

This somewhat archaic pattern of semi-literacy in Belfast is also present throughout its east Ulster hinterland. It has been explained by reference to the Presbyterian emphasis on intensive scripture reading and the early development of Sunday school for all adults, meaning that reading skills were a prerequisite to full participation in religious life, even for the 'unlettered'. The relative decline from the 1780s in the demographic predominance of Presbyterianism in Belfast (as the town rapidly expanded) may explain the limited change in both female and male scores there. But perhaps the most striking feature is the relatively high *male* literacy levels already present in the 1760s, with only modest further improvement by 1800. This would suggest that there were established systems of elementary tuition already in place by mid century, and that these more or less kept pace with urban growth in the late eighteenth century, despite heavy immigration from less literate districts. But it is Dublin's qualitatively higher literacy score, already evident in the 1760s generation, that really stands out. If the semi-literates are excluded, Dublin's literacy levels were higher even than those for Belfast, with 74 per cent of males and 42 per cent of females in the capital in the 1760s able to both read and write, compared to 67 and 34 per cent for Belfast (the 1790s tell a similar story: 72 and 47 per cent in Dublin, 66 and 36 per cent in Belfast). By comparison full literacy in the three Munster cities in the 1760s ranged between 61 and 65 per cent for males and 22 and 33 per cent for women, and in the 1790s between 61 and 62 per cent for men, 26 and 33 per cent for women, with Kilkenny, Galway, and Drogheda far behind. How can Dublin's more advanced literacy be accounted for?[20]

Several processes were at work here. One related to Dublin's status as a capital city. Seventeenth-century London (and probably other early-modern capital cities) had higher literacy levels than provincial cities, a reflection of a larger and more sophisticated service sector, a higher level of paper transactions in everyday commerce, and a distinct political culture: in Civil War London the printing press was precociously important, both in broadening religious belief and in unharnessing political debate, and despite later controls this was never quite forgotten. For the much smaller world of seventeenth-century Dublin, Barnard has supplied one telling piece of evidence: the growing capacity of those acting as sureties for debtors in the city's Tholsel court to sign their names: signers rose from about two-thirds of the sureties in 1652–53 to around 80 per cent in the 1690s, and while these were by definition men of at least modest means they included Catholic retailers and craftsmen, with only butchers and bakers, gardeners and hawkers unable to sign their names. We have no evidence on female literacy in Williamite Dublin, but we can presume that a majority of adult males were now literate, its now stronger Protestant character reinforcing that tendency. But what is unexpected is that eighteenth-century Dublin as it grew and became a more Catholic city seems to have maintained (by Irish standards) fairly high literacy levels, particularly for men: 84 per cent of those registering as quarter-brothers in the Weavers Guild between 1747 and 1760, nearly all of whom were presumably Catholic, were able to sign their names.[21]

SCHOOL

The capital's advanced literacy raises the obvious question of educational access. There were of course many paths to literacy, and the correlation between school attendance and literacy levels in early nineteenth-century Ireland has been shown to be much weaker than might be expected. But although the impact of schooling on literacy in eighteenth-century cities cannot be measured with any precision, it is likely that Dublin's relatively high literacy score was to some degree a function of its educational infrastructure. At the time of the 1791 parliamentary inquiry into Irish education, nearly three-fifths of the functioning parishes of the Church of Ireland across the country were flouting the law by failing to operate a parish school, but every Church of Ireland parish in Dublin operated at least one free school, supported by endowments, voluntary contributions or charity sermons (and usually a combination); some of these supported boarders and most catered for both boys and girls. Charity schools had sprouted in Dublin in the 1690s and grown in number and capacity, but they were small, educating at any time around 500 poor Protestant children in all, with the largest and best endowed in the eastern half of the city. For the children of poorer freemen there was the attractive alternative of the Corporation's 'blue-coat' school in Blackhall Place, the well-endowed King's Hospital, from which there were prospects of far better apprenticeships than for those coming from a charity school. In addition, Parliament supported a number of larger educational initiatives that were also Protestant in design, notably the ostensibly proselytizing Charter Schools, a national project that impacted relatively little on the cities, the Hibernian Marine School for the children of seamen, and the Hibernian Military School in the Phoenix Park, both of which did cause a local stir, the former in the riverside world of St Mark's, the latter in the neighbourhood of the Royal Barracks. The Military School had been set up as a philanthropic response to the number of distressed children of soldiers present in the city at the end of the Seven Years War (orphaned, or left unsupported by those serving outside the country), and it became the largest purely educational establishment in the kingdom, with 260 on its books in 1791 and over 500 by 1816. For such a large institution, its very positive health record suggests a rare instance of enlightened governance, and it stood in marked contrast to the schooling provided by the Foundling Hospital.[22]

Meanwhile, despite the ban on Catholic schoolteachers in the penal legislation of 1695 and 1709, at least fifty-two 'popish' schoolteachers were active in ten of Dublin's parishes in 1731 and all but two of these 'garret schools' were located in the western half of the city. Some of the teachers were friars and clergy, but most were lay and at least a dozen of them women. Sixty years later the number of Catholic schoolteachers was still quite low (sixty was the estimate by Protestant clergy for the 1791 enquiry), but pupil numbers were rising sharply: around 2,000 by then, and slightly more than double that figure was given in a private survey of 1816 (after the emergence of a number of larger enterprises run by the religious orders). But unlike the Protestant parish pupils, the great majority of Catholics were paying for their tuition. The 1791 inquiry, the first to map out what a national system of parish schools might look like, advocated a radical extension of the (free) parish schools to embrace the whole population:

> The children of Roman Catholics and Protestants should be admitted indiscriminately into the [parish] schools, and ... the clergy of each

persuasion should attend for the purpose of instructing the children belonging to their respective communions in the principles of religion; a mode practised, as we are informed, with great success in the school of Saint Andrew's, Dublin, and of Saint Peter's, Drogheda.

Whatever became of those liberal experiments, mixed free-schooling was developed in Dublin on a more expansive scale at the behest of a group of Quakers in the 1790s (notably the Dublin Free School in the Liberties), and in the following generation a number of ostensibly non-denominational enterprises flourished, albeit briefly. However, the confessional character of primary education was already deeply rooted. Even in the case of the children of Catholics serving in Crown forces during the Napoleonic Wars, the Protestant character of the Hibernian Military School was regarded as unacceptable and a Catholic equivalent, the General Asylum, was established as an alternative in 1812.

But what was common across the denominations was a great expansion of female education from mid century. The most famous pioneer in Dublin was the milliner Teresa Mullally: she started a charitable day-school in 1766 with a strong religious inflection; in 1789 it became the first convent free-school in Dublin. And in the same markets district of the city, a predominantly female confraternity supported a team of ninety-six women teachers (presumably working as catechists) at the end of the century; it was shortly afterwards taken over by the local priest. By 1816 over half of all pupils registered in public schools in Dublin were girls and, in a more rigorous survey a decade later, Dublin had the highest female participation rates in education across the whole country, with precisely half of the school-aged cohort enrolled (against 62 per cent for boys); Waterford and Cork cities were not far behind.[23]

Similar developments in Cork were also shaped by a female pioneer, the French-educated Nano Nagle, who came from one of the region's few patrician Catholic families. She started a moral crusade in the Cork suburbs by opening, close to family property, a charity school for poor children in the South parish around 1755. Adapting the model of the *petites écoles* with which she was familiar in Paris, she oversaw the education of some 200 children within a year; for the girls reading and catechesis preceded a training in practical skills, whereas boys were then taught 'to write and cypher'. Within a decade she was managing seven charity schools across city and suburbs, five of them for girls, and she remained involved both in religious teaching and in fund raising for

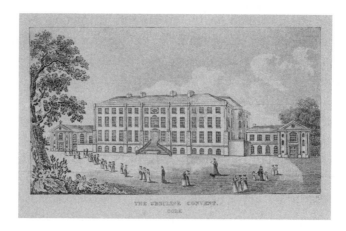

Figure 14 Established in Cork by Nano Nagle in 1771, the Ursuline order remained French in ethos, and it was highly successful in attracting the patronage of the city's Catholic bourgeoisie. The convent and boarding school migrated to these much larger premises near Blackrock in 1825, settling in the remodelled house of a former business family.

nearly thirty years. Utterly averse to publicity, she had a fraught relationship with Francis Moylan, future Catholic bishop of Cork, and against his wishes she established a new religious congregation in 1775 (later becoming the Presentation Sisters) that would continue to provide education for the poor, not (as Moylan planned) an enclosed community like the Ursulines (introduced, with her help, to the city in 1771).

The Ursulines developed a successful academy for Cork's well-to-do daughters, but Nagle's vision was wider. Papal recognition of her proposed congregation took a quarter of a century to secure, and for a while after her death in 1784 the initiative was in trouble. Perhaps coincidentally, a number of Protestant merchants and professionals launched plans for free Sunday schools in the city in 1789, with an elementary curriculum, limited religious instruction and no dogmatic teaching. There was some Catholic support for this idea at the beginning, and over 700 children 'of all persuasions' were enrolled when the 'Sunday and Daily School' opened on Hammond's Marsh in 1791. But later that year Bishop Moylan (who now lauded Nagle's achievement) organized a rival fund-raising committee, the Committee of the Roman Catholic Poor Schools, belatedly championing Catholic elementary education in the city. When the Sunday and Daily School trustees changed tack and introduced Anglican religious instruction into the curriculum in 1797, some 300 Catholic children were

withdrawn on the orders, it seems, of the Catholic clergy. This far more assertive approach rescued the Nagle schools, expanded the number of free schools
for boys, and visibly tightened the Catholic Church's hold on education in the
city by the time Nagle's Presentation Order was formally recognized by Rome
in 1802.[24]

The children of bourgeois and upper-class families were of course not sent
to elementary parish schools or to other charitable enterprises. Home tutoring
was the normal preparation for those destined for an endowed classical school
or for one of the private post-elementary academies that proliferated in the
second half of the century, first in the capital, then in the provincial cities. Such
enterprises were concerned with preparing boys for a profession, for college
entry or for a higher trade. Academies for young teenage girls (where many
of the schools boarded their charges) also began to appear from mid century
and, as Enlightenment ideas on female education began to seep in, courses in
domestic management, French and the social graces were supplemented by the
teaching of history and geography.

Clergy of all denominations were frequently involved, principally tutoring
their own flock: Jonathan Swift's confidant, Thomas Sheridan, ran a prestigious school in Dublin's Capel St for a quarter of a century, regularly preparing
half a dozen or more students for Trinity College each year but few if any of
them came from outside the Established Church. Hutcheson's academy in
Drumcondra Lane (later Dorset St) was resolutely Presbyterian, and the Jesuit
John Austin, who had received childhood encouragement from Swift, ran a
highly regarded Latin school beside Laurence Saul's warehouse in Cook St,
which prepared many prospective seminarians, and expanded to take boarders
in 1770. But the Reverend Thomas Hincks's famous academy in Cork, which
opened in 1791 offering exposure to 'a greater variety of subjects than ...
usual', both practical and scientific, was also distinctive in appealing far beyond
his Presbyterian congregation.

Kilkenny was perhaps the earliest provincial city to rebuild a network of
Catholic schools – there were reportedly a dozen teachers active there in 1731
– and Limerick cannot have been far behind. But in Cork an 'exhaustingly
dynamic' young Church of Ireland cleric, Henry Maule, launched his pet
project, the 'Green Coat School' in 1716 – amidst great civic ceremony. He was
an excellent publicist and fund-raiser and his 'little body of young Christians'
in Shandon grew to eighty, half of them girls, who were

... now formed into proper classes suitable to their years and capacities ... and as some of them had been taught to read before in the small English schools in the parish, where the children of poor Protestants and Papists are taught gratis by the bounty of private benefactors ... so these children were the more capable of learning.

The school in the north suburbs was located in the only part of the city where Catholic schoolteachers had returned in force (six were present in 1731), so the mixing of the faiths 'in the small English schools' set up something of a contest. By the time Maule left Cork in 1732 there was an impressive network

Figure 15 Examination certificate from the Mercantile Academy, North Strand, Dublin issued to Denis [*recte* Denys] Scully (aged *c.* 13, of Kilfeacle. Co. Tipperary), 24 May 1786.

for the daughters (and sometimes the widows) of wealthy Catholics in Galway, Drogheda and Dublin. The two most important communities, the Dominicans and the Poor Clares, moved from the town of Galway in the 1710s to the markets district of Dublin. Enclosed bastions of patrician women, they were quietly allowed to thrive.[30]

CROSSING BOUNDARIES

In this urban landscape of confessional division, there were rule-breakers. Some of the more bookish clergy of rival denominations jousted enthusiastically in print (famously Cornelius Nary and Archbishop Synge in the 1720s and 1730s), and more rarely in public spaces. A few Protestant 'sermon-tasters' were occasionally drawn to witness the Catholic star performers in Dublin chapels or to attend charity sermons there, and in the early 1780s during the heyday of the politically charged Irish Volunteer movement there was a series of very public visits to local Catholic chapels in Cork, Dublin and Belfast by various corps of what was of course a predominantly Protestant militia. These were gestures of broad-church patriotism, but the traffic was one way and the fashion did not last.[31]

A taste for fine music was perhaps a more powerful solvent. The high reputation of the choir sisters in the enclosed Dominican and Poor Clare convents in Dublin attracted discreet Protestant admiration, and fashionable musical societies in several cities included Catholic members: the Dublin Charitable Music Society, the group responsible for the New Music Hall in Fishamble St (1741), was for its time strikingly mixed, both religiously and socially, as later was the Anacreontic Society. And at least some of the native-born professional musicians employed in Dublin theatres were Catholic, not to mention the very many French and Italian musicians who tarried awhile, perhaps even 'ruled' Dublin music, creating the possibility for the cross-fertilization of styles and genres. Among the latter was the Neapolitan Tommaso Giordani (c. 1733–1806), a dominant figure on the city's music scene as composer, teacher (of John Field among others), theatre owner and Rotunda conductor. The high point of a rather rackety career came in May 1789 when his setting of the *Te deum* was performed by choir and band in the Catholic St Nicholas's Church in Francis St to mark the recovery to health of George III. As the choir performed, three Catholic prelates occupied the sanctuary in front of a congregation of half a dozen peers and up to 3,000 worshippers.

That was exceptional, for the public performance of music, whether in theatre, assembly rooms, city churches or the two cathedrals, remained part of what was an essentially Protestant public sphere, and in Dublin strong upper-class patronage of concerts maintained this pattern until late in the century. Unlike theatre, which was broadly commercial (but with many 'benefit nights'), musical performances were nearly always intended to raise funds for specific charitable purposes; some of these were denominational, but most (like the concerts to empty the debtors' prisons) were not. By far the most important venues in Dublin for musical performance were the Rotunda gardens, the manicured space adjacent to the Lying-in Hospital, and indoors in the great Rotunda room built immediately beside them; the concerts there provided an abundant income for the maternity hospital. Huge and doubtless religiously mixed audiences supported the more than 2,400 concerts staged between 1749 and 1784, but the patrician music committee, the 'gentlemen of approved taste', chose the repertoire and took pains to maintain the social cachet of the venue. Their offerings were modelled on London musical fashion and they hired expensive international talent, as always mixing fashion and philanthropy. But they did employ up to twenty local musicians, and Irish 'airs' (notably 'Eileen Aroon') often featured as the 'after acts' to Handel or Haydn. But demand fell away in the 1780s. Military bands became more popular and they were much cheaper to hire; upper-class musical activity was retreating into domestic spaces where 'the amateur practice of music in small groups' remained at the centre of private sociability.[32]

REPOSING

If there was limited enough togetherness in civic life, in death there was rather less distinction. Since the enforcement of the Reformation, the state Church had enjoyed exclusive control over the many urban graveyards that were attached to nearly all parish churches. However, burial grounds attached to the pre-Reformation religious houses that had been sold off with the rest of the monastic real estate in the sixteenth century were generally lost to public use, with the exception in Dublin of the Knights Hospitallers graveyard in Kilmainham. Some dissenters chose to have their own sacred space: non-conforming Huguenots in Dublin, Waterford and Cork, similarly the Quakers who had dedicated plots in Dublin and the Munster cities. But Presbyterians of all tendencies buried their dead in Anglican-controlled parish graveyards: in

Belfast they maintained a preference for the old Shankill churchyard over the Corporation ground attached to the Chapel of the Ford (later St George's), and a few of the wealthiest Presbyterian families were buried in mausolea in the fashionable precincts of Knockbreda church overlooking the town (see Plate 20).

But for Catholic citizenry the rituals surrounding death and interment, both Tridentine and popular, carried particular significance, yet religious obsequies had to stop outside the churchyard. In Dublin this meant one of three possibilities: burial in a city graveyard for a fee; burial in the old consecrated ground in Kilmainham; or burial in a country graveyard, possibly one no longer attached to an active Anglican church. The majority of Catholic families accepted the first option (to which they were legally entitled if they paid minister's money), but they gravitated towards three of the eighteen parish burial grounds in the city. These were among the most venerable: St Michan's on the northside, St Kevin's on the south and, busiest of all, the large graveyard of St James's on the western edge of the city, where Catholic archbishops and society courtesans were all laid to rest. It was indeed a ready source of parish income. However, 'Bully's Acre' in Kilmainham, an even larger space associated with the Knights Hospitallers, became the preferred destination for poorer citizens, incurring very little – and at times no – burial charge. Sean Murphy has suggested that 'many hundreds of thousands' of Dubliners may have been interred in Bully's Acre during the centuries that it remained in use up to the 1830s. However, those who died in detention or in welfare institutions were usually buried in unconsecrated ground: some 550 skeletons have been excavated from within the grounds of 'new Newgate', the city gaol opened in 1780.[33]

In the city of Cork every parish had a graveyard, but Catholics buried their dead either in old St Mary's Shandon or in St John's on Cove Lane, cemeteries that were disconnected from functioning Anglican churches and were possibly not policed with the same diligence as newer churchyards. It was not until Theobald Mathew purchased the city's Botanic Gardens in 1828 and created St Joseph's, a new-style garden cemetery, that the Catholic citizenry had adequate space for formal obsequies. In Limerick, Waterford and Kilkenny the established church graveyards within the old walls continued to accommodate Catholic and Anglican burials, and in the case of St Mary's Cathedral in Limerick a formal documentary account of Catholic as well as church interments was kept, creating for many the only evidence of a life lived. By contrast, Belfast Catholics had to bury their dead a mile out of town in Friar's Bush, which they used long before the site was tidied up and re-consecrated in 1829.

Derry Catholics had the old churchyard outside the walls; it was in use decades before the first Long Tower chapel was opened there in 1788.[34]

The inscribed gravestone, once a rarity in city cemeteries and confined to the box-tombs or recumbent stones commemorating those of high status, began to be erected by the families of minor traders and master craftsmen, both in Dublin and provincial city graveyards. In the 1980s, a survey of the 239 eighteenth-century memorials in St James's graveyard in Dublin showed that more than 82 per cent dated from the last four decades, suggesting a new willingness and financial capacity after mid century to purchase a grave plot and to memorialize the dead. Nearby, on every 25 July, St James's Day, one of the great carnivalesque fairs was still held on the street, despite official disapproval voiced since the sixteenth century. The event extended into the churchyard where it became the custom on that day

> for the relations and friends of those buried in St James's churchyard to dress up the graves with flowers, cut paper, scripture phrases, garlands, chaplets and a number of pretty and pious devices, where those affectionate mementoes remained until displaced by fresh ones the next year . . . everybody went to see it.

There is no suggestion that this was an exclusively Catholic or Protestant act of remembrance.[35]

7
PROJECTS AND PROJECTIONS

Siege warfare caused huge physical damage in four of our ten urban centres during the seventeenth century – in Drogheda, Limerick, Sligo and the suburbs of Cork – but no Irish city saw devastation comparable with that in London after the Great Fire of 1666, or in Lisbon after the devastating earthquake and fires of 1755. The centre of the Portuguese capital was radically altered in the following decades and an unrelenting gridiron street plan was imposed which entirely disregarded old patterns. In London the outcome was very different for, despite paper schemes outlining a new configuration of streets, the old layout was re-created in brick, and the intricacies of pre-fire property rights were faithfully respected. This contrast reflected different political systems, with no equivalent of Portugal's Marquis de Pombal willing or able to force a redesign of the street system of Restoration London.

ORMOND'S LEGACY

In Irish cities, those who held power rarely spoke with one voice and for the most part they simply reacted to the challenges of prolonged urban growth. Very rarely was there a single agency with the power or incentive to engage in urban planning. However, there were a few moments of strategic redirection. The most obvious case was in Restoration Dublin where the actions of the first Duke of Ormond had a radical impact on the city, coming at a time when property rights were still in flux and forfeited lands in the process of re-allocation. It is unclear just how much Ormond, despite his years of exile in Continental cities, had educated his eye to the finer details of baroque urban planning, but some of those around him did have such interests. In his two periods as a Restoration viceroy spanning the years 1662 to 1684 he was associated with a number of decisions that had profound consequences for the Irish capital. He was personally committed to the creation of the vast deer park on the edge of the city, incorporating what had once been the demesne of the Kilmainham priory, and through a vigorous programme of land acquisition on Crown account and drastic budget overspending he supervised the creation of the Phoenix Park, containing more than 700 hectares and 7 miles of walling as it began to take its modern shape around 1670. It permanently closed off the possibility of urban development on the hilly expanses north-west of the city. A decade later and immediately south of the Park, construction of the vast military hospital at Kilmainham got underway: this was also entirely Ormond's project and the campus with its generous grounds modified the later expansion of the city westwards. No subsequent viceroy had either the financial freedom or the political will to engage in such grand schemes, and land prices in and around the capital would never be so low.

Ormond was also concerned with viceregal accommodation – in the Park, at Chapelizod and within the ramshackle Dublin Castle. Together with his son and deputy the Earl of Arran, he toyed with the idea late in life of securing royal support for the disposal of the Castle altogether and of building a palace elsewhere, and he also explored the possibility of acquiring land on the Castle's perimeter, demolishing the curtain walls, and making 'four fair streets into the Castle'. A huge fire in April 1684 destroyed Ormond's, and all earlier seventeenth-century accretions to the Castle, and the old cavalier was out of office a few months later. But in 1711 his grandson, the second duke, pondered 'rebuilding the Castle . . . and pulling down the houses on Cork Hill to enlarge the passage up to it', but his stay was too short. No successor took an interest in the appearance of the Castle and its environs before the 1730s, and very few of them afterwards.

The first duke may also have been instrumental in acquiring Chichester House, the eastside mansion close to the College, to accommodate Parliament when it sat, and although the building was palpably inadequate for the enlarged gatherings after 1700 the site became invested with great symbolic meaning, even before Edward Lovett Pearce's Palladian tour de force replaced Chichester's Jacobean home. Ormond's influence also lived on in two other respects: in the 1680s he helped establish the principle that the banks of the Liffey should become open thoroughfares and clear of buildings, and that the fronts of riverside houses should face the river 'for the greater beauty and ornament to the city . . .' And although it took until the early nineteenth century for all obstacles along the course of the river to be demolished, allowing free movement of east/ west traffic through the city, there was a certain inevitability from Ormond's time that this would eventually come about. Secondly the duke and, more particularly, the duchess, by their love of conspicuous pageantry, lavish entertainment and the patronage of theatre consolidated a court culture in Dublin that enticed the top tier of the landed classes to come to the city and build. That, in turn, created the demand to which the first speculative developers responded: Francis Aungier on an 8-hectare portfolio of land south of the Castle, Humphrey Jervis north of the river, the former a relative and intimate of the first duke, the latter a risk-taking merchant who won Ormond's support against his many city opponents. Both imposed their new street plans on a much older monastic palimpsest, and Jervis recycled the very stonework from the ruins of St Mary's Abbey to help wall-in the river and create what became Ormond Quay.[1]

Neither in Dublin nor in the provincial cities did municipal authorities play a strategic role in the physical development of their cities. Dublin and Drogheda had extensive corporate land, and all cities on the coast had established rights over land reclaimed from sea or river. But from the early years of the Restoration, when all municipalities were financially stricken, there was a very powerful incentive to lease out corporate property on long leases and in large blocs, with few restrictions or controls. The classic case was in Dublin where the Corporation decided in 1663 to privatize a large part of two great public spaces on opposite sides of the city, Oxmantown Green and St Stephen's Green, and building plots were allocated by lottery to freemen on long or perpetuity leases. Oxmantown, lying close to the river and west of Smithfield on the north-west of the city, was at first the preferred site for upper-class houses, but the government's decision c. 1699 to locate a huge barracks complex next door diminished its attractions, whereas the appeal of the huge 'waste ground' beyond the south-east of the city grew over time, and although it took a century to be completed, St Stephen's Green eventually became a fully developed square, more fashionable in the eighteenth century than in the seventeenth. Initial leases specified house dimensions and materials, but the sanctions were light, and it was the leaseholders and their assigns who over time determined street alignment, building height and the subdivision of plots, not the Corporation.[2]

Eight of the first fifteen houses on St Stephen's Green were owned by Francis Brewster, merchant and land speculator of obscure origin, who teamed up with a London alderman, William Hawkins, to lease the southern foreshore of the Liffey from the College and the Corporation; they engaged in speculative reclamation work around Lazer's Hill, creating a small street network (including the future Townsend St). Brewster, lord mayor in 1674–75, commissioned Andrew Yarranton, an Englishman with recent expertise in inland navigation and a close knowledge of Dutch canal technology, to draft a plan for the radical reorganization of Dublin's port involving reclamation of the marshlands towards Ringsend, the re-routing of both the Poddle and the Dodder rivers, new downstream bridges, and a relocated custom house. But given the fire-storm that Jervis's more modest innovations generated a few years later (moving the principal public markets northwards across the river to Smithfield, and creating two new river crossings), the Yarranton plan had absolutely no chance of implementation. It reflected the exuberant free-thinking of newly monied speculators in Restoration Dublin rather than a search for practical solutions to the very real problems of congestion on the river and of silting along the inner approaches to the port.[3]

GARDINER'S SCHEMES

Dublin Corporation secured parliamentary legislation in 1707 to establish a Ballast Office which was given responsibility for 'cleansing' and deepening the channel into the harbour and up to the Custom House, and for providing better protection for shipping in the Bay outside. It became the first development agency in any Irish city, and in the early years it built new quays to protect the principal channel and an artificial bank running eastwards from Ringsend across the sandy approaches. The bank became a timber palisade, and then (beginning in 1748) a masonry wall, the Great South Wall. Its construction spanned more than seventy years (1715–90) and experienced many setbacks both human and natural, massive borrowings, and the deployment of a substantial labour force (some of it convict). But the end result was a remarkable public work stretching out to the Poolbeg Lighthouse; it reduced shipping losses, improved (somewhat) the tidal scouring of the bar beyond the harbour, and maintained the navigability of the inner channel. A century later in 1817, the American Andrew Bigelow marvelled at the end result:

> The greatest work which we have yet seen here [in Dublin], and the most stupendous of its kind perhaps in the world, is the mole . . . an immense wall, composed of huge masses of stone strongly riveted and

cemented, has been built into the open bay ... nearly three miles in length ... A work of this kind is sufficient to illustrate the public spirit and persevering enterprise of the citizens of this great metropolis.[4]

Two of the initial members of the Ballast Office were Humphrey Jervis and Sir John Rogerson (c. 1648–1724). Both were successful merchants before they invested heavily in land, in Rogerson's case both in rural Leinster and around Dublin. Lord mayor in 1693/4, he was more adroit politically than Jervis, but like Jervis he took a strategic approach to urban development, specifically in exploiting a huge area of slobland downstream from the city that had previously been used as saltpans. He took a short lease of this in 1699 and in 1713 secured a long-term interest in the best portion, some 115 hectares of riverside ground. The lease bound him to an expensive programme of drainage and the building of some 1,165 metres of quay frontage (his friends in the Ballast Office marked out the precise line in the sand along which the quay walls were to be built). A financial return from this quayside development was slow to materialize, but his heirs reaped a rich reward once the estate began to attract commercial and industrial tenants later in the century.[5]

This was a southside story, but from time to time the Corporation was also attracted by the possibility of reclaiming the hard sands lying north-east of the city between the Liffey channel and the road to Clontarf, intersected by the Tolka river. The area was first surveyed in 1682 and allocated by lot to members of the city assembly; the scheme was mismanaged and abandoned for a generation. The new Ballast Office launched an even larger scheme in 1717: the 210 hectares of the 'North Lotts' were now divided up into 266 plots in a rectilinear pattern, and once again were allocated by lot; the Corporation undertook to build an outer seawall, quays and 'all the streets ... [to] be walled foundation high'. Proprietors were obliged to build up their lots from rocks and sand purchased from the Ballast Office. Progress was very slow in the early years and the northern half of the project was quietly abandoned by the 1740s. However, backed by new legislation in 1728 and a parliamentary grant, the land south of the Tolka was secured from the sea by the mid 1730s. Many abandoned lots were however forfeited. Luke Gardiner (c. 1677–1755), the first secretary of the Ballast Office, was tempted to become involved, building up a portfolio of twenty-two such lots. They were not developed during his lifetime, but when the Custom House eventually came downstream the real potential of the district began to be revealed.[6]

Gardiner was a man who was good with figures, loved the proximity of power and was always discreet. His family origins may have been in Kilkenny city but his early patrons were close to Dublin Castle and his responsibilities, informal then official, were connected to Revenue Commissioners' administration. In 1712 he had acquired the lease of a block of south-bank property lying to the west of Rogerson's holdings; it formed a large segment of the future George's Quay. Dealing there with carpenters and shipwrights as tenants turned out to be Gardiner's apprenticeship before he emerged to become the most formidable property developer in the eighteenth-century city. Marrying well and favoured at different times by the Duke of Bolton, William Conolly and Archbishop Boulter, Gardiner managed to thrive in bad times and in good. He became the Register of the Barracks Board in 1718, and this proved a major stepping-stone towards a pivotal role in government treasury management. It is typical of the man that beyond a taste for theatre, tantalizingly little is known of his personal life or the details of his private finances. He was probably never as wealthy as the public believed, but through guile and good intelligence he managed to benefit from the misfortune of others. His career as a developer was nevertheless plain to see: how over twenty years he created a compact property portfolio on the north side of the city, culminating in the expenditure of around £44,000 to achieve complete control of the Earl of Drogheda's estate by 1730; how he moved slowly in developing the portfolio once he had secured clear title; and how he cut hard bargains with speculative builders and, in some cases, employed builders directly himself.

Henrietta St was his boldest project. The street was laid out on rising ground beyond the Linen Hall, with plans for two sets of palatial brick mansions to face each other. These materialized fitfully between 1730 and *c.* 1750, some of them funded by Gardiner himself. Then when he was quite elderly Gardiner launched an even more ambitious initiative: the redevelopment of a 320-metre section of Drogheda St east of the Jervis estate, massively widening it and utterly changing its character. This was re-named Sackville St to honour the then viceroy's family (and changing again, in a later age, to O'Connell St), it was laid out to accommodate some forty-four houses, residents being offered the alluring prospect of a central mall for promenading. The area formed part of a new parish, St Thomas's, which was created in 1749, presumably at Gardiner's instigation; a fine Palladian Anglican church was subsequently built a block eastwards in Marlborough St, and this became the final resting place for the Gardiner family.

Several elements of Gardiner's remarkable career stand out, notably his financial resilience: promoted to become Deputy Vice-Treasurer of Ireland and Receiver-General in 1725, he enjoyed unfettered personal access to idle balances in the Treasury, and held these offices of state until his death some thirty years later, displaying until his final years an unusual degree of administrative competence. Access to public credit gave him a critical advantage in his accumulation of mortgages and freehold property across the city – from the Liberties to the partially reclaimed marshlands of the North Lotts – but his principal achievement was to re-assemble the old St Mary's Abbey estate in a series of complex transactions between 1714 and 1730. His pattern of acquisitions suggests that at some point he devised a master plan for the development of the whole north-east quarter of the city and acted accordingly (although there is no explicit evidence for this). Where the inspiration for Sackville St came from remains unknown.

The new street took two decades to be built, some of it by his successor in office Nathaniel Clements, and the final five houses were erected by George Darley, the leading stonemason in the city. At first sight the precinct appears to have been intended as a private upper-class oasis, its houses set in common alignment with deep rear gardens and generous stables, close but not too close to the river and the northside markets. But it seems that Gardiner intended that Sackville St should eventually be brought down to the river (cutting through property he did not own), be linked via a new bridge to the south side of the city and College Green, and thereby also become a magisterial boulevard linking the northern approaches to the parliamentary centre of town. Gardiner failed to get that bridge in his lifetime: as we have seen (in Chapter 4), the proposal attracted bitter criticism from city interests and was halted in Parliament on no less than five occasions, thanks to broad support for the Corporation's robust opposition (and to the government's temporary loss of control over parliamentary business). It was perhaps also a reflection of Gardiner's now diminishing influence. The bridge was not built until the ascendancy of his grandson in the 1790s, when the fully widened street was extended down to the river. But 'Gardiner's bridge' was only constructed after the great battle over the future of the Custom House had finally been resolved.[7]

Old Gardiner was in several respects an innovator: unlike other developers he preferred to remain owner in fee and not to sell off, or fine off, house sites; his rents were high but his leases were set for very long terms, and he seems to have skirted round the penal laws for some of his (few) Catholic tenants. His willingness to demolish existing buildings (as in Henrietta St) and to redevelop brown-field sites as well as green-field sections of his estate was unusual, and his capacity and willingness to fund and build for some of his prime tenants was probably without precedent; he shared this practice with Clements, who built at least four of the Henrietta St houses. Gardiner consorted with the best architects available: Pearce was heavily involved in Henrietta St, and Richard Castle, the busiest architect in town before his sudden death in 1751, has been linked to no less than five houses in Sackville St; and Clements himself was something of an architectural enthusiast. But Gardiner did not seek to achieve uniformity in any of his developments. Even in Henrietta St most of the houses differed markedly in scale and design, although they all respected the line of the street.[8]

REARRANGING THE CAPITAL

The mid forties to the mid sixties were seminal years in the physical evolution of the capital city. If there was a single catalyst, it was the sharp upturn in the economy, for although there were shuddering credit crises in 1754/55 and 1759 following the run of bank failures, the growth in rentier income and of public tax receipts created a continuously benign environment for urban investment. But there was also something fortuitous in the way several discrete projects clustered in these years. Thus, close by Pearce's parliament building, Trinity College's monumental cut-stone entrance building was raised up in the 1750s (thanks entirely to parliamentary largesse), creating the enclosed public space of College Green and an unexpectedly powerful centre-point for the city. At the same time, to the south-east, on the city margins, the truly palatial town house of James FitzGerald, nineteenth Earl of Kildare, became 'live' in 1753 when it was first occupied by the family who had ambitions to make it rival Dublin Castle as the hub of Dublin fashionable society.[9]

Beyond the great house lay the expansive prospect of Dublin Bay – and the polluting brickworks, the orchards and the green fields of the oldest private estate near the city, that of the FitzWilliams of Merrion. The mottled appearance of the district was about to change. Despite a testy relationship between the representatives of the FitzGeralds and the FitzWilliams, the completion of Kildare House (soon to become Leinster House) greatly enhanced the attractions of the district to the south-east. Its imposing monumentality led directly to plans for an adjoining residential square on FitzWilliam land.

Jonathan Barker, a professional surveyor, produced an ambitious blueprint for Merrion Square in 1762, but only one side of this square was built during the next decade. The estate was curiously tentative in settling on a final ground-plan, and it took over fifty years for all ninety-two sites in the square to be converted into terraced houses (see Plate 21). Unlike the Gardiner story, developments on this estate were only loosely choreographed (the sixth and seventh Viscounts FitzWilliam were generally absentee and poorly connected politically), and the 'scheme for building the square' rested with junior relatives and diligent agents; they worked closely with builder-speculators and others in the trade, all of whom were sensitive to the fluctuating demands for substantial houses. Nevertheless, the square became the real epicentre of fashion by the end of the century, and its final orientation and appendages permanently affected the configuration of the south-east quarter of the city.[10]

Around the time the first plans for Merrion Square were being mooted, Luke Gardiner was finding tenants for a new street (Cavendish St) which had been staked out on rising ground north of Sackville St. The first residents could enjoy the adjacent amenity of the 'New Gardens', a resort for the fashionable by day and by night that had opened in 1749, and so popular was Cavendish St (later Row) that a similar development to the west of the Gardens was being planned at the time of Gardiner's death in 1755. On the higher ground north of the Gardens – not Gardiner property – a double site was then chosen by the Earl of Charlemont for a new town house. He was the most architecturally literate aristocrat of his generation, a patron of Sir William Chambers whom he commissioned in 1762 to design a stone-fronted *palazzo* that was intended to become a treasure house for his library, pictures and statuary. That, in turn, was the catalyst for the rapid development of adjacent sites along Palace Row, thus creating as if by design yet another residential square in the city.[11]

Meanwhile, to reduce traffic congestion, Parliament passed legislation in 1763 for a 'circular road' (it was in fact oval) to link the four toll-roads and twelve other routes converging on Dublin. It was to be located outside the areas then witnessing residential development, and several amending statutes were needed before the 10-kilometre circuit could be completed over the next three decades. The oval route, chosen almost casually, may not have had much impact on traffic flows, but it did become the marker defining the limits of the enlarged city. It influenced the route taken a generation later by the Grand Canal along the southern fringes, and on the north side it provided something of a boundary line for high-status residential development on the Gardiner estate. Between them, these two arcs created a lozenge-shaped boundary encompassing the city. When an internal threat to the regime emerged once again in the 1790s, they were quickly co-opted for military defence.[12]

If these various initiatives were occurring at around the same time fortuitously, other developments in the heart of the city were clearly interrelated and not mere happenchance. We return to the great controversy stirred up by Gardiner and his allies at the end of the 1740s when they pushed for a new downstream bridge. One of the many outcomes of that fracas was, as we have seen, the construction of the spectacular Exchange on nearby Cork Hill in the 1770s. But the immediate consequences in the 1750s we have yet to encounter: firstly, the complete reconstruction of the city's notorious pinch-point, Essex Bridge, by a gifted bricklayer turned engineer and architect, George Semple (c. 1700–82). He had been the protégé of the archbishop of Dublin, and had designed and built the spire for St Patrick's Cathedral. He tendered for the new project by studying Westminster Bridge (on site) and the Pont Royale in Paris (in print), and he became not only the architect and clerk of works for the bridge but also originator of a radical plan for the redevelopment of the neighbourhood south of the river.

The key proposal was for a new street to run from the bridge to a modest square that would be created immediately north-east of the Castle; Semple was later to claim that it was only after studying the environs of the Pont Royale that he had had the idea of a new street to complement his plans for the bridge, its width to be precisely that of the bridge, but as John Montague has recently revealed, the creation in London of a 'new grand street' running north off Westminster Bridge through an older street system provided Semple with more immediate inspiration. He attracted high-level support, possibly as a riposte to Gardiner's friends who were still pressing for the downstream bridge. At any rate, Semple's plan was finally published in 1757 and adopted that year by Dublin Corporation. They in turn secured support from the Speaker John Ponsonby, and this led to a parliamentary grant for the project and the establishment of the Wide Streets Commissioners (to include the Speaker). Their remit was to plan the route of the new avenue from river to Castle, to acquire the land required, and to issue leases to builders who would be bound to execute their house designs. But the lowly Semple fades from the story, apparently because of ill-health.[13]

The result was Dublin's first publicly funded wide street, Parliament St, which was completed within a decade. At the prescribed 51 feet in width, it was narrower than several private developments of the previous generation, notably Dawson and Molesworth Streets on the city's south side, but unlike them it was a wholly commercial development from the beginning: the proposed buildings were to be terraced, tall and narrow, two bays wide and four-storeys over street-level shops, with the frontages brick and in perfect alignment. The builders, including Philip Crampton, lord mayor in 1758/9, sought to attract 'trading people of the genteelest occupations and largest fortunes', and the builders and tenants did well by the project, for 'capital' shops were soon clustering along the street. But the fact that Crampton, a former bookseller turned merchant with a reputation for 'griping avarice', had been one of the original Wide Streets Commissioners *ex officio*, set the precedent for business practices that would later appear to be corrupt.[14]

THE SPECULATIVE TURN

Parliament St was an unadorned corridor of brick, but even in the upper-class terraces now appearing further east the extensive use of cut stone was the exception; only public buildings and the dozen or so great *hôtels* displayed the stone-cutter's art. Locally manufactured brick was otherwise the universal building material in Dublin. Christine Casey, observing the 'relentless minimalism' of the vast majority of brick houses built in this era – so plain when compared to fashionable new housing in English cities – has suggested that this reflects not so much an Irish taste for understatement in their urban facades but rather the predominantly speculative character of most building projects. Final owners may have had quite specific preferences as to interior finish, but accepted without question the prevailing conventions as to the external presentation, even with very large townhouses, in the interests of economy. And in the final decades of the century, even internal decoration and fittings were often pre-selected by builder-developers before the sale of a house.[15]

This points to the centrality of speculative building, carried on as a piece-meal, small-scale activity, and to the likelihood that the majority of houses built for bourgeois families were the result of temporary business ventures initiated by modest developers (brickmakers, stonecutters, stuccodores and particularly carpenters) who contracted out elements of the building process to masters in other complementary trades. Small developers often held a bloc lease from the ground landlord and sold on divisions of their holding as buildings were completed. But since Jervis's first development of the north side there was sometimes an intervening tier between estate owners and artisan builders: middlemen developers, whether merchants or professionals from outside the building trades who leased large blocks of ground which they then subdivided, marking out the proposed house frontages and plot dimensions, and securing basic services; they also provided credit to a master builder, possibly mortgaging their leasehold interest and using the proceeds to lubricate development. Such practices were of course very close to what had first become standard in Restoration London.

Some of the small house builders became wealthy and some ended up in the debtors' prison, whether because of fraud, mismanagement or bad timing. Swift maintained that 'one half' of the many small building craftsmen around him were 'infallibly undone', their shells of houses regularly gobbled up by the greedy few with ready money. Swift's pessimism reflected the particular hardships of the 1720s for, as Brendan Twomey has suggested, taking the longer view, upwards of a hundred new houses must have been completed in Dublin every year, most of them by small builders working 'for clients of middle station'.

The intense vagaries of the building trade probably account for the emergence of a few prominent dynasties of craftsmen builders. George Semple was a member of one such family: four other Semples appear in early Dublin directories as stuccodores, bricklayers or stonecutters. And a few other names keep recurring in public building accounts: three generations of the Darley family, dominant in the supply of building stone to the city, dabbled in speculative building; two generations of the Balls, carpenters and timber merchants, similarly appear as occasional speculative builders; and the Wills, father and son carpenters, the latter trading under his father's name while he translated and glossed the first four books of Vitruvius in his spare time. Arthur Gibney has noted of such craftsmen that 'their freedom to choose their own standards of workmanship ... their broad theoretical knowledge, and ... their social mobility among the merchant community' stood in marked contrast with later times. And it is striking that nearly all the big names in Dublin construction up until the 1780s appear to have been Anglican and of English ancestry.[16]

IMPROVING WATERFORD

The classical streets and squares of Dublin were therefore the work of many classes over many years: the Crown, the office-holding elite, the landed gentry, the Corporation, private estate owners, petty developers, artisan builders, all had a share in shaping the eighteenth-century city. In the provincial cities there were fewer elements involved, less innovation in the process of building, and much less evidence of grand strategies. Large merchants played the central role in urban development, both in their private capacity and through their role in municipal government where (except in Belfast) they were the dominant voice. Quaker merchants were notably active in Waterford and Cork – as they were in Dublin's Meath Liberty – preparing, designing and developing sites, and less frequently involved in the actual building of houses. It is striking that in Kilkenny, the one city where there were no export merchants (and no dominant proprietor after the fall of the house of Ormond), there was no large-scale re-working of urban space, so that even in the 1830s the judgment was that 'the streets are very irregular' even though 'the city has an air of venerable magnificence'.[17]

The impact of property investment in Waterford was slow to show. Its commercial expansion came, as we have seen, later than in Dublin or Cork, and it lacked the huge artisan suburbs that were such a feature in other southern cities. The topography of Waterford port was also distinct: the ample depth and breadth of the Suir offered exceptional berthage and, unique for an Irish port in the eighteenth century, this led to physical expansion both upstream and downstream of the old walled city. The swift demolition of the quay walls at the beginning of the century and the construction of an Exchange and Custom House side by side on the waterfront helped maintain and stabilize the city's historic centre of gravity until the 1790s. Then the opening of the great bridge to the Kilkenny side of the river nudged commercial development upstream.

The price to be paid for this was intense congestion in the old intra-mural streets, with even fashionable ones like Lady Lane too narrow for coaches. Ian Lumley has suggested that, compared with eighteenth-century Cork or Limerick, Waterford failed to engage in large-scale street planning, and certainly its Wide Streets Commissioners, established in 1784, only began to tackle a few pinch-points in the 1790s. Up to then it had been the building enthusiasms of successive Church of Ireland bishops that most affected the townscape. But the Corporation was responsible for the new Exchange in 1715, and marked out several new streets in the 1720s upstream of the walls (including George's St). They also oversaw the many extensions of the line of quays: by the 1770s this was nearly a mile long. But although no external landed family had a major stake in the city's development, it seems that it was the politically inspired largesse of the Mason family, at differing stages MPs for city and for county, that funded the Corporation's activism in the first quarter of the century. By contrast, the parliamentary leviathans, the Beresfords and the Ponsonbys, although never far away, had less tangible influence.

At Waterford's east end there was the Mall. It was created in the 1730s out of Miller's Marsh and a tidal pool, and lay just beyond the old city walls. Later it became the city's most striking urban improvement. Initially the Corporation had laid it out as a tree-lined promenade and a bowling green. Major residential development only began in the 1780s when the Corporation auctioned off building lots and facilitated the construction of a theatre and public assembly rooms by a private consortium, 'the most elegant suite of rooms in the kingdom'. By the end of the century several sets of four- and five-storey brick houses adorned the Mall, while further east, overlooking the river, a similarly striking development, Adelphi Terrace, appeared (see Plate 22). However, despite the city's Napoleonic prosperity, the Mall ran out of steam; as one observer lamented in 1813, 'if only it were finished (which is very far from the case) it would be very respectable'. Most of the new housing elsewhere in the city avoided brick, which was of poor quality locally, and instead used stratified shale, faced with rendering.

The Quaker Penroses, the city's principal timber merchants, were heavily involved in the development of the Mall, and they built Adelphi Terrace and much else in the city. Other Quakers (including the Strangmans) spread some of their commercial wealth into urban property too, and Catholic names begin to appear as speculative builders in the 1780s (notably among developers of the Mall). Members of the dozen-odd Anglican dynasties controlling the Corporation and its land were also active developers over several generations. Two of the largest beneficiaries of corporate leases helped to adorn the city through their private enthusiasms: Samuel Barker, merchant and long-running city MP, created a much-admired Dutch-style water garden on rising ground behind his town house in the 1740s; and William Morris, merchant and developer, commissioned a great townhouse on King St in the 1780s that, despite the pokiness of the site, was on a scale and of a standard of neoclassical finish that would have caused a stir even in Dublin. John Roberts (1712–96) may have been its designer and builder. He was certainly responsible for five public buildings in Waterford city including, as we have seen, two cathedrals, plus the theatre and Assembly Rooms, the House of Industry and the Infirmary, and he completed the bishop's palace that dominated the Mall. Apart from the great Dublin-based architects, no eighteenth-century Irish architect could match Roberts's impact on his own backyard.[18]

It is quite surprising that the works for which Roberts is celebrated were only carried out when he was past middle age, although he had been an experienced builder and timber importer in his earlier years. He lived to a great age, his reputation and popularity undiminished. His capacity to respond to his diverse clients' tastes was remarkable, and this was nowhere better demonstrated than in the contrasting styles and finish of the two cathedrals. Yet apart from some years spent in London as a young man, it seems he spent all his life in the Waterford region. Admittedly it was no architectural backwater: both James Gandon and James Wyatt were also working on commissions in the region in the 1780s (the former designing the new courthouse and gaol, the latter improving the Marquess of Waterford's Curraghmore House). Yet the sophistication of Roberts's work suggests deep reading and a sharp eye, but how far he influenced either the Corporation or the developers in their choices has gone unrecorded.[19]

EXTENDING CORK

No landed proprietor built up a major stake in Cork city either, and although property ownership was concentrated into much fewer (and newer) hands following the 1660s' land settlement, these were principally merchants' hands. Land use within the old walls intensified, even as the walls crumbled. Rocque's map of Cork (1759) identified more than sixty commercial laneways running east or west off Main St in a double-comb pattern. Most of the lanes were medieval in origin, but by Rocque's time they bore the names of the post-Cromwellian merchant families who had presumably been active in their recent development. The focal point of the city was still the intersection of Main St and Castle St where the Corporation built the very substantial Exchange between 1708 and 1710 (see Figure 5). This junction remained an active trading point as the Corporation's own council chamber and offices remained immediately adjacent to the ever-busy Exchange, unlike Dublin where bookshops, coffee-shops and respectable taverns were clustered round the Essex Quay Custom House rather than the Tholsel.

There was relentless suburban growth north and south of the Lee that went largely unregulated, and the Corporation seems to have exerted little influence over the process. But it was a different story on the valley floor where close to the old walls there were about a dozen mudbanks that were habitually flooded at spring tide. The Corporation's charter gave it ownership over these marshes, but as in Dublin the revenues or resources to reclaim such land were lacking. Thus from the 1670s leases were issued to wealthier freemen on long terms, both to the west and east of the city. They and their descendants slowly developed these marshes, but with the perennial risk of flooding and much cheaper green-field sites around the suburbs it was not for the faint-hearted. From the 1690s (and thus much earlier than in Waterford) Quaker merchants were prominent in reclamation and development (these included the Pikes, Hamans and Fenns).[20]

The low ground immediately to the east of North Gate was drained and developed first, with new quays and a custom house facing the North Channel completed in the 1680s. That channel became the preferred line of access for shipping, although most ocean-going vessels discharged 11 kilometres downstream at Cove (modern Cobh) or at Passage, with shallow-draught lighters shuttling goods between these anchorages and the city. After the siege the marshes to the west of the city were drained and partially developed in a flurry of activity. As channels were gradually eliminated it became a high-status area, helped by the creation of the lengthy Mardyke Walk in 1719 (a private initiative), by the great houses on Bachelor's Quay and Fenn's Quay, and in the mid 1760s by the construction of Davis Ducart's monumental mayoralty house in Henry St, much the largest official residence for a provincial city mayor. Meanwhile the push eastwards from the Custom House began in earnest in the 1690s: William Dunscombe (1660–1720), only son of a Restoration merchant, acquired a series of near-perpetuity leases and slowly began to turn them to account. He was probably responsible for determining the basic pattern of development south of the middle channel (on what was long known as Dunscombe's Marsh) where he laid out a set of narrow streets, running north and south across the new thoroughfare of George's St (so named c. 1715, now Oliver Plunkett St).

The move eastwards was an incremental process, with the Corporation overseeing the alignment and upkeep of new quay walls and protecting the rights of way, but playing no role in the provision of infrastructure in the new east side (such as paving or drainage). However, the city Grand Jury, heavily aldermanic in its make-up and with fuller tax-raising powers, was used to fund such improvements. But in general it was the sub-tenants of the early-bird lessees who were the risk-takers in the development process, employing masons and carpenters to turn the marshland into narrow but bustling streets. The only broad spaces within the 'new city' (as cartographer Joseph Connor called it in 1774) were the quays facing the middle channel and the tree-lined mall that looked southwards across a shallow artificial channel (cut *c.* 1670) towards Morrison's Island. When the Corporation eventually filled in or culverted these waterways, three great wide streets were created: the Grand Parade, 'too wide for a street and too narrow for a square' (*c.* 1780), Patrick St, 'broad yet winding' as it followed the course of the middle channel (drained *c.* 1783), and the South Mall (culverted only in 1801).[21]

Bridges across Cork's various channels were generally small and uncontroversial, but there was an echo of Dublin's battles in the long-running resistance to the proposal for a new crossing of the North Channel below the Custom House. An application to Parliament in 1763 sought support for such a bridge, but it provoked strident opposition both within and outside the Corporation (two dissenting aldermen pleading the 'prodigious' growth of the city and the dangerous congestion, especially along Mallow Lane, that a new bridge would relieve). It was more than two decades later and after the filling in of the Patrick St channel that the push for a new bridge at its northern end resumed. Despite public meetings called by those with a stake in the north suburbs, who feared business would migrate eastwards, the project went ahead. The architect was Michael Shanahan, the much-travelled protégé of the Earl Bishop, who was completely familiar with classical concepts of bridge design. But that did not take account of the vagaries of the Lee valley: the new bridge was badly damaged in the great flood of 1789. It was repaired and finally opened later that year. A private venture, the bridge generated large toll revenues for decades and greatly accelerated the development of the north-east suburbs (see Plate 23).[22]

Cork did not receive the level of parliamentary investment lavished on Dublin. But unlike other provincial centres it had powerful political leverage: in peacetime the city was far too important as a source of public revenue for its concerns to be ignored by Dublin Castle, and in wartime its staple commodities (naval provisions) had huge logistical value, a point that registered even in London. Cork was never short of powerful advocates close to the heart of the Irish government, the Boyles and the Brodricks providing a vital link in the first half of the century, and from 1760 until his death in 1794 there was the chameleon figure of John Hely Hutchinson, one of the city's MPs. He did not reside locally but was its most effective lobbyist in Dublin and key to the city securing parliamentary grants for a range of infrastructural improvements over two decades. These included bridge building (over the South Channel) and dredging the approaches to the city's quays, but the principal capital project was a navigation mole. The rationale, as in Dublin Bay, was that a new 'tracking' wall would help maintain the deepened channel and aid navigation in the tight approaches to the city, thereby encouraging ship captains to bypass Cove and come directly to the city quays. It offered the prospect of faster despatch for those merchants shipping food to the growing English market.

The Irish Parliament gave at least five grants to improve the Lee navigation, and there was a sharp rise in the number of large vessels reaching the city during the 1770s thanks to the tracking wall. But despite the construction of some 2,000 metres, the project was still incomplete in 1800 and in poor repair. However the new wall prompted the Corporation to initiate plans for an entire new urban quarter in 1780, to be laid out south of the wall on reclaimed ground with a 'great street' (far wider than George's St) to run the length of the development, and with ten intersecting side streets and a small square at the centre. Whether the initiative was a response to the creation of Newtown Pery in Limerick, or just a revenue-generating initiative to help complete the wall, remains unknown. The plan was still 'in contemplation' half a century later (and almost a hundred years later much of it became the city racecourse).[23]

Unconnected with this but around the same time, a short-lived group, the Cork Society for Arts and Sciences, engaged in some blue-sky thinking and commissioned a local architect, Daniel Murphy, to produce a city map that would include a series of proposals for new streets and bridges. Published in 1789, some of his suggestions were modest and were indeed later realized, but one radical proposal was to drive a new street from Fenn's Quay in the west of the city through the old walled area to terminate at the Custom House which, Murphy claimed, would make 'a delightful street and add much to the beauty and health of the city'. He also advocated demolition west of North Main St, allowing 'the new church St Peter's to stand in the centre as St Mary's [in] Dublin, and St Mary's Le Strand [in] London'. There was no high-level patronage for any such action, and Cork Corporation had neither the appetite nor the finances to engage in compulsory purchase of ground leased out on century-long terms. Nothing more was heard of the Society's schemes. Visitors of the time were struck by Cork's 'want of uniformity and regularity', its cluttered quays, and by the relative absence of brick compared to Dublin: 'the

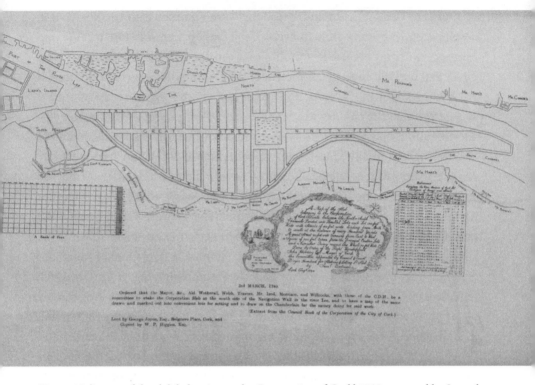

Figure 16 'A map of the slob belonging to the Corporation of Cork', 1780, surveyed by Samuel Andrews, Engineer of the Navigation Wall.

houses are almost universally weather-slated, which gives them a very heavy and dull appearance'. But that reflected the redstone rubble in general use for construction, not an aversion to brick.

What focused local minds more was the city's old vulnerability: flooding, usually when spring tides and exceptional rainfall coincided. The great flood of January 1789 was the worst of the century and inundated every street across the central parishes, testing the resolve of developers. Nevertheless construction on the newly fashionable South Mall adjacent to the South Channel continued, and this was closely linked to the development of Morrison's Island nearby. By 1800 this quarter had become the preferred address of many of the city's wealthier merchants and professionals. It is noticeable however that the principal entrance to many of the South Mall houses was made on the first storey above the street, prudently keeping the basement above ground.

And there was a shadowy Wide Streets Commission in Cork too: established almost as an afterthought in one of the omnibus Cork improvement acts in 1765, Hely Hutchinson and Ponsonby were nominated to the board. But, despite acquiring some of the powers of the Dublin Commission, it came into existence with no recurring funding and did little beyond widening Castle Street in the 1790s. But a generation later the Commission was reconstituted in 1822 with borrowing powers, so it then had the resources to drive a great avenue through the old city westwards (Great George's, now Washington, St), and to build a new artery (the Western Road). The vista eastwards down old George's St was finally closed with the building of a chaste Custom House, completed in 1818, strategically placed where the two channels of the Lee come together. Immediately to the north of this was the site for yet another round of reclamation and quayside development: Penrose Quay became the new epicentre of the port during the French wars and attracted some of the largest merchant houses. Cooper Penrose (1736–1815), a Quaker merchant who had learnt the timber trade in Waterford before moving to Cork in 1763, remained one of the largest timber importers in the city while investing heavily in property in the 1780s. By the time of his death nearly half of his rental income came from urban tenants, many in the new north-east quarter and beneficiaries of Shanahan's bridge. He was possibly the last of the Quaker merchants to shape the city, but his patronage of the arts and conspicuous life style led to his disownment from the Society of Friends, and that was many years before he had built his 'five rooms for statuary' and a 'very remarkable picture gallery' on the sylvan heights overlooking the river.[24]

TRANSFORMING LIMERICK

'A classic piece of Enlightenment town planning, comparable in ambition and execution, if not in scale, to the New Town in Edinburgh or the Teresienstadt in Trieste': Eamon O'Flaherty's verdict on Limerick's Newtown Pery sets the bar high. South Priors Land, once part of the extensive Franciscan property stretching south-westwards from the walled city, had been in the possession of the Sexton family since the monastic dissolution, and this property was the setting for a remarkable green-field development on the scale of the Gardiner estate in Dublin. However, it had a different time frame: the plan was only hatched in the 1760s and primary development continued at an uneven pace for nearly eighty years.[25]

Least dynamic of the Munster cities since the Williamite war, Limerick in 1750 was still largely contained within its two sets of walls, its principal streets dominated by archaic stone-built houses. The Corporation for decades had been the cockpit for bitter factional disputes, and when two-thirds of the corporation estate fell out of lease in 1747–48, old ways of doing business among aldermanic friends still prevailed. But the strengthening economy was felt in Limerick in the following years, and the first speculative development in the city got underway during the 1750s with the creation of John's Square: a set of eight elegant stone-fronted townhouses that were attractively laid out opposite an Anglican parish church on the southern edge of Irishtown. The two principals involved financed and directed construction, and the first residents were gentry families from the region. It was symptomatic of the changed climate that, shortly afterwards, the demolition of the great walls of the city began in earnest.

One of the developers involved in John's Square was Edmond Sexton Pery (1712–1806), MP and heir to the Sexton estate. Like John Hely Hutchinson in Cork, he was a politically ambitious lawyer, building up support among the merchants of his city. And he also tapped the budgetary surplus in the Treasury to secure parliamentary funds for local infrastructural improvement: he claimed credit for obtaining £27,000 in grants to extend the city's quays and to open a canal that would give Limerick navigable access to Lough Derg and the middle Shannon. The involvement of the two men in these pork-barrel projects happened early in their careers and they largely disengaged from such concerns after 1780 (although Limerick's canal project dragged on fitfully for decades). But both men maintained a reputation for being notoriously 'watchful jobbers', both reached high office (Hely Hutchinson as Prime Sergeant, Pery as Speaker of the Commons), and both died very wealthy.

But there were two obvious differences: Hely Hutchinson never involved himself in municipal matters, and he had little or no property in Cork city, whereas Pery in the early years was immersed in local politics, championing various improvement schemes, notably the city water supply, and was the heir to the hugely valuable Sexton estate that adjoined the eastern and southern bounds of the city. The lavish parliamentary grants that he secured had mixed results, but he handled his successes in a way that avoided public opprobrium. And it helped that he could convince outsiders like Arthur Young in 1776 that he alone had remade the city.[26]

The idea for a new town outside the walls and beyond the reach of the Corporation was hatched in the mid 1760s, at the time when new quays were being completed (notably George's and Charlotte Quays along the Abbey river)

Figure 17 By the time W.H. Bartlett sketched the Limerick Custom House (with George's Quay in the background) around 1830, substantial quay development had occurred downstream, while to the south and east Newtown Pery was almost complete.

and as plans for a new custom house were being thrashed out. Pery was centrally involved in both, expanding the brief (and the budget) for the Custom House and securing the services of the brilliant but perverse Davis Ducart in 1765; the end result, a seeming Palladian villa overlooking the Shannon, was perhaps the finest public building in eighteenth-century Munster.

At the same time, Pery commissioned Ducart to draw up a plan for the development of that part of his suburban property that lay to the south of the Custom House. The plan does not survive, but a map of the whole city was drawn in 1769 by Christopher Colles, Ducart's clerk of works at the Custom House, and this included an eye-catching plan of 'New Town Pery', a gridiron of some forty-five development blocks created by four streets running southwards and intersected by eight streets of equal width, running at right angles at regular but not identical intervals. The new town would nearly double the size of the existing city (see Plate 24).

The proposed development ran almost parallel to the east bank of the Shannon, but otherwise it displayed a relentless disregard for topography or earlier land use; it was not aligned to old city streets nor to the new Custom House. Pery himself would have been entirely familiar with Sackville Mall in Dublin and the early plans for Merrion Square, but the intention here was for something entirely different: the speculative development of a dense street system to attract professional and high-status private tenants, the gridiron effect to be relieved by three small squares. If the template as set out in Colles's map did originate with Ducart, a man of shadowy origins but apparently from Piedmont, then it seems plausible that his inspiration came from the city of Turin, a classic example of an organic gridiron street plan, framed within its formidable ramparts.[27]

The line of Newtown Pery's principal street (named George's St of course) was settled before 1770, but the project was very slow to be realized, reflecting the long view and comfortable finances of the Pery family. In the 1770s and 1780s most speculative development was on land leased from the Corporation along the Abbey river or adjacent to the Custom House, areas that had been transformed by parliamentary largesse in the sixties and which were not on the Pery estate. Limerick's merchants and traders were still overwhelmingly based in the old city. The first merchant builders to exploit the new possibilities were Patrick Arthur and his son Francis, leading timber importers and the embodiment of Catholic old money. Their triangular bloc, part commercial, part residential, was not shown on Colles's map, but it became the border between Limerick past and Limerick future. Beyond it, sites near the river were initially prized for their fine prospects: the future Honan's Quay site was promoted in 1769 solely for the great view: 'the most elegant town residence in the kingdom, or perhaps in the world, cannot boast such rural beauty or so fine a landscape, and the variety is daily increasing'. Despite such boosterism the site was destined to become a great grain warehouse.

Newtown Pery became a built reality during the Napoleonic Wars, its austere brick terraces, four storeys over basement, drawing bourgeois Limerick to decamp southwards. In the speculative rush, there was no sign of the small squares envisaged in the original plan. However, in the 1830s Pery Square with its private gardens was laid out at the southern end of the estate, an unintended tribute to the original vision for the estate. Catholic families who had been noticeably prominent in the early years (the Roches, Honans and Arthurs) were less so after 1800, whereas Quaker and Anglican traders (the Marks,

Fishers, Harveys, Hills and Russells) became major players both in quayside construction and later residential development. The grant in 1808 of strong local government powers to commissioners in the new town (officially the parish of St Michael) ended any residual power the Corporation might have asserted over the Pery estate, and emphasized the growing distance between the affluent and salubrious world of wide streets south of the Abbey river and the increasingly congested and degraded lanes and alleys of the old city.[28]

WEAKER ECHOES

Elsewhere there was no great scheme of urban improvement undertaken between the 1690s and the 1820s, only modest interventions by corporations (as in Drogheda and Derry) and by ground landlords (as in Galway and Belfast). Drogheda Corporation with its great land bank certainly had the opportunity to develop its quays and land access, and it was active in addressing 'nuisances', removing bottlenecks and investing in other minor improvements. The town was embellished by several very fine replacement public buildings during the century, notably St Peter's on the hill (completed in 1752), the Mayoralty House (1769) – more an assembly house than the mayor's private space – and the Tholsel (1770), all buildings associated with the Darley family who skilfully exploited the town's topography in each building. Drogheda gradually lost its gentry and archepiscopal patrons and became a great textile centre and conduit for cross-channel business, so the priority by the end of the century was to remedy the congested quays and access to the port. The creation of Merchants Quay and the construction of an elegant corn market building during the 1790s temporarily relieved pressure, but the inherited streetscape remained largely intact.[29]

In Derry's case, eighteenth-century development outside the small confines of the walled city was unplanned, and Cox's new bridge across the Foyle (completed in 1791) had noticeably less impact on street development than in Waterford where his second bridge was opened a few years later. But extensive foreland reclamation continued throughout the century outside the walled city, helped no doubt by modest injections of parliamentary bounty in the 1760s. The ground landlord of the city itself was the London-based Irish Society, which played an entirely reactive role until the nineteenth century, and immediately *outside* the walls much of the property was church land, entirely in the gift of the Church of Ireland bishop. And although it was a very wealthy diocese and several eighteenth-century occupants of the see took a lively interest in the city's improvement, notably the long-serving Earl Bishop, this did not add up to very much beyond lobbying the Irish Society to cooperate in plans for a bridge. The unendowed Corporation was in a particularly weak position to initiate change, had it so wished, so it mortgaged future toll income in order to fund Cox's great wooden bridge. Thereafter bridge maintenance proved to be a constant drag on the Corporation's resources, and this led to its eventual bankruptcy in 1831.

But by then the linear extensions of the city, particularly its new brick terraces along the reclaimed north shore, were physically quite impressive, now that the 'ancient prejudice that to reside without the walls was not respectable' had gone and 'mud cabins have been gradually superseded by comfortable houses'.[30]

It was a little different in post-Napoleonic Galway where its first historian, James Hardiman, lamented in 1820, 'the shamefully neglected state of the streets' with most of the housing stock still 'old' stone buildings. But change had begun: Merchants Road as it became known was laid out *c.* 1779 outside the walls and close to the shore, and the town's remaining walls were demolished shortly after 1800; several landholders on the perimeter invested in reclamation and quay construction. Dominick St across the river stood out as distinctly modern and uniform, while the Erasmus Smith estate just outside the line of the walls was one example of schematic street replanning, albeit on a small scale. The estate fell out of lease in 1785 and new ones were issued after a re-drawing of the 6-acre estate, now branded as 'Newtown Smith'.[31]

Sligo's building stock was younger, but the streets were 'irregularly formed, which detracts much from its internal appearance', and the approaches to the town were strikingly awkward. From the 1760s the town was dominated, politically and economically, by the nearby Wynnes of Hazelwood, but their investment in the town was very limited. Local improvement acts of 1800 and 1803 established mechanisms for large-scale intervention, but to little effect. It was only decades later with the vast public works programme during the Great Famine that strategic change came to the town: two elegant and entirely new approach roads from north and south were built in 1847–48.[32]

Belfast had also suffered from weak local government. After the passing of the Test Act (1704) and the exclusion of Presbyterian aldermen, the Corporation had neither power nor local standing, and the town remained an unambiguously proprietorial borough until the early nineteenth century. Control over its physical development would in normal circumstances have resided with the agents of the ground landlord, but from 1706 until 1761 the Donegall estate was in the restrictive hands of various trustees (the result of minorities and the mental incapacity of the fourth earl). For most of that time no leases for the lengthy terms that builders and speculative developers expected were issued; disputes among trustees and guardians only worsened the impasse. As a consequence, the town's physical growth was stunted, its buildings not reflecting what was happening in the counting house. But Belfast was not dormant: old burgage plots in the heart of the town were progressively subdivided and, as in central Cork, lanes, rows and entries proliferated, filled with retail and craft subtenants. Isaac Macartney (c. 1670–1738), son of 'Black George' and for a time the town's wealthiest merchant, built two major quays (one of which accommodated the new Custom House of 1720), and he planned a small residential development consisting of four blocks around a small central square beside the river. Perhaps because of his own financial eclipse, little of this was built.

All changed with the fifth earl of Donegall. He signed off on some 200 new leases in the late 1760s that incentivized development and included covenants controlling height and building materials. Not surprisingly, this was the catalyst for a spurt in building activity in the following decade: by 1769 James Young, the leading brickmaker, claimed to be producing a million bricks a year. Donegall went on to out-spend any other Irish urban landlord (helped by having an Irish rental income of around £48,000 in later life). He stayed largely outside Irish politics, was entirely non-resident, and did not seek parliamentary support for any of Belfast's infrastructural improvements (although parliamentary grants were received for the construction of the Lagan navigation between Belfast and Lisburn). The impact of Donegall's spending on new institutions was greatly amplified by a willing flow of public subscriptions (£17,550 was raised in local subscriptions for the White Linen Hall), and by the capacity of leading merchants to work together, notably in running the new Ballast Board (established in 1785).

It is estimated that Donegall invested over £30,000 in the town's public infrastructure over three decades, financing the building of the very imposing Anglican parish church of St Anne's (1774–76), the nearby Exchange and Assembly Rooms (1769–76), and the meat market (1792), as well as handing over a large site for the town's poor-house (in 1774) and Belfast Castle's one-time gardens for the new Linen Hall (in 1784–85). The estate also laid out an axial avenue from the Hall across Castle Meadows towards the town centre, the aim being to attract top-tier tenants: Linen Hall St (later Donegall Place), with its uniform but austere frontages, was an early success, and this led to the building of large private houses around much of the perimeter of the Linen Hall, which became Donegall Square in the early years of the new century. Donegall also invested up to £60,000 in the Lagan Navigation to complete the link between Belfast and Lough Neagh; this was operational in 1793, an event invested with huge import, but the dividend both for the estate and the town proved very disappointing. Yet Donegall paid almost no attention to Belfast's quays, which even in the 1790s were barely able to cope with the town's burgeoning maritime trade.[33]

If the fifth earl was a distant guiding hand, the man on the ground building – and in some cases designing – his commissions was Roger Mulholland (1740–1818). Although trained as a carpenter, he attended the Dublin Society Drawing School and worked on a succession of Donegall's projects, probably including the Linen Hall, while operating his two timber yards. Shortly after completing St Anne's church he was commissioned by the First Belfast Presbyterian congregation to rebuild their church nearby; completed in 1783, this was to be his masterpiece. The irony is that the striking interior design, a perfect ellipsis, was the choice not of Mulholland but of the elders of the church; but like Roberts in Waterford he had a rare ability to interpret his clients' tastes and the superb woodwork was indeed his hallmark.

Mulholland was also the largest house-builder in town, developing sites on the northern edge close to the new parish church, in Linen Hall St, and in other premier locations, being involved in at least 160 brick houses altogether. Hugh Dunlop, another carpenter, and John Brown, one of the town's wealthiest merchants, were engaged in the 1780s in speculative construction of a different kind, the rush to provide small houses for textile artisans, notably in the new markets area in the north-west quarter. This was a novelty for Ireland, or was at least the first such initiative in a large urban setting; the houses were intended to be let to cotton weavers.

Something similar occurred across the Lagan in the fledgling suburb of Ballymacarret, part of the large Pottinger estate. This had changed hands in 1779 when Barry Yelverton, the 'patriot' MP who, with Donegall's support, sat for Carrickfergus, became the surprise purchaser. He left politics in 1784 to become a senior judge and about this time began to plan a new town for Ballymacarret, marking out the streets and giving incentives to prospective builders. He oversaw an extensive reclamation programme, but did this without securing the blessing of his erstwhile patron. Donegall asserted ancient rights over the river and its tidal edge, began legal proceedings, and eventually ordered (from afar) pre-emptive action, using his canal diggers to move in by night and destroy the Ballymacarret embankment. His *force majeure* caused a sensation, but it led Yelverton, who had no other stake in the province, to sell the property to Donegall in 1787 (at a modest profit). Ballymacarret went on to become Belfast's first distinctly industrial district, a zone of smoke (with its glass, vitriol and iron works) and of handloom industry, but it was no planned town. Insofar as there was schematic development, it was in the brown-field sites east and south of the Linen Hall where large blocks were leased out by the fifth earl's son in the early nineteenth century on very attractive terms. This reflected not proprietorial vision but the latter's extreme financial distress, and their disposal formed a part of the comprehensive dissolution of the Chichester inheritance, all occurring within a single generation.[34]

BERESFORD'S LEGACY

Dublin's eighteenth-century transformation dazzled the provincial cities. From mayoral houses to Wide Streets Commissions, urban parks to public statuary, innovations in the capital shaped urban ambitions around the country, most of which went unrealized. However comparison could nurture envy and resentment at the way public money was directed so disproportionately towards Dublin-based projects. Of course, most provincial MPs were part-time Dublin residents and had therefore an interest in the amenities of the capital city, so anti-Dublin sentiment was slow to show. It was only in 1799 when the closure of the Irish Parliament became a looming possibility that this became explicit among the provincial champions of the Union proposal.[35]

The quite unprecedented cluster of 'metropolitan improvements' undertaken during the 1780s and 1790s highlighted Dublin's special status in the grand scheme of things. These improvements combined six interlocking elements. The first, the Custom House project, dated from 1781 when the thirty-year war over the site for a replacement building was concluded (in secrecy). Political opposition, both in Dublin and in London, to moving the Customs and Revenue establishment 1 kilometre downstream had eventually been overcome through administrative subterfuge and a political trade-off in Whitehall. There was no architectural competition, and the commission to construct the building on reclaimed ground was given to a well-connected English architect new to the country, James Gandon. His design of what amounted to a vast riverside palace for the Revenue Commissioners was mired in controversy all the way to completion (costing over £200,000 and coming in vastly over budget). But it was a challenging site and Gandon's design was hugely demanding, with its four immense facades and slender dome. But he created for Dublin its finest neoclassical public building (see Plate 25).

A second element was the parliamentary 'capture' of the Ballast Board and of the governance of the river and its quays in 1784. This takeover of a heavily indebted municipal department allowed the government to override city opposition to a downstream river crossing, and the construction of the much anticipated Carlisle Bridge finally got underway as the Custom House was being completed in 1791. Maritime access to the quays above the new bridge was halted at that point and with remarkably little controversy.[36]

The third element was the Wide Streets Commission, largely inactive since the 1760s, which came back to life in 1782. The revival was no accident, for the composition of the board was drastically altered, its statutory powers strengthened, and the proceeds from a city coal tax allocated on a permanent basis. The original Commissioners in the 1750s had helped to halt old Luke Gardiner's ambitions to draw the epicentre of the city downstream. Now in the 1780s the tables were turned: the revival of the Commission was in the first instance part of a Castle strategy to ease the transfer of the Custom House and related businesses downstream. And it was the implied logic of Gardiner's street plans (creating the Mall and Cavendish Row) that now shaped and informed the Commissioners' ambitions. Chief among these were the re-design and extension of Abbey St eastwards; the extension of Sackville St at full width down to the river; and, in preparation for the new bridge, an avenue of equal magnificence to run towards College Green that would become, in Casey's words, 'a *coup de theatre* which created a dynamic baroque termination' looking southwards. Some older plans of the Commission, notably the widening of Dame St, were incorporated into this, and the inclusion of ground-floor shops in the planned terraces, even in the designs for Lower Sackville St, was seen as a startling intrusion in some quarters. However, the concept was developed, with quite a time-lag, in Cork's Patrick St (see Plate 26).

The following fifteen years up to 1797 saw the partial realization of this 'noble' plan for Dublin, a time when new street lines were agreed, properties compulsorily purchased, building designs debated, and sites auctioned to prospective builders. The scope of the Commission was enlarged in 1790 when it became a requirement that all plans by private landowners for new streets or for the widening of existing streets were to be laid before the Commissioners.

It remained a voluntary body of parliamentarians with only a handful of professional staff, but the overall costs incurred (nearly £700,000 in the quarter century beginning 1782) far exceeded coal tax revenues; once again it was the huge grants from Parliament that sustained these plans for upwards of a decade.[37]

A fourth element related to the Four Courts and the long overdue replacement of the miserable court building crouched in the shadow of Christ Church Cathedral. A site on College Green close to Parliament and the Post Office was widely favoured, but instead the choice in 1784 was for Inns Quay, far upstream and close to the city markets. It was another deeply unpopular decision, at least with the lawyers. Gandon got the commission and designed a remarkable domed pantheon with its airy courtrooms and great public hall, which was not fully completed until 1802. Its location, apart from visually enhancing the river, strengthened the urgency for improved access along the western quays, thereby realizing Ormond's old vision.[38]

Meanwhile on the Gardiner estate, the fifth element, extraordinary things were happening: Luke Gardiner's eldest grandson, also a Luke (1745–98), had a more informed interest in architecture and the arts than his namesake, and enjoyed a higher public and political profile. He was one of the new Wide Streets Commissioners, and had (to put it mildly) a powerful vested interest in their programme of improvements. As the Custom House took shape he laid a new street, Gardiner St, running some 1,200 metres northwards onto higher ground, and astride that elevated section of the street he laid a new square, Mountjoy, which in the early plans was more architecturally sophisticated than anything the city had seen. Smaller landowners responded, most notably Nicholas Archdall on whose estate North Great George's St was developed, its fine neoclassical terraces being built and completed between 1780 and 1795, while the FitzWilliam estate, discreet as ever, began to submit new street plans for the Commission's approval. By the 1790s Gardiner's ambitions stretched beyond Gardiner St as he harboured plans for two facing crescents creating a small oval, to be known as the Royal Circus, close to the North Circular Road. However this development was never more than a ghostly presence on early nineteenth-century Dublin maps.[39]

The final element was the penetration of the canals into the city. As in the provinces, the chimera of inland waterway construction had teased minds in the capital since the early years of the century. Parliamentary funds to give Dublin navigable access to Kilkenny coal and to the Shannon heartland had been forthcoming since the 1730s, but until the 1760s there was little to show for it. However the engineering problems west of the city were overcome following the involvement first of the Corporation, then of a joint-stock company, and in 1779 the Grand Canal began a modest freight service from Co. Kildare to a harbour on the western side of town off James St (and, more importantly, it was immediately used to supplement the city's water supply). The commercial value of the canal grew appreciably in the 1780s as the network was enlarged and living conditions, even for the poorest citizens, were positively affected – by the fall in the price of cheap fuel (turf), and by the more ready disposal of 'night soil' from lanes and middens. However, the impact on the wider city only came in the 1790s with the building of a 5-kilometre extension from west of James St sweeping around the southern perimeter of the city and terminating at a huge dock that was excavated east of the Rogerson estate. The new city section of the Grand Canal carried little enough business considering the scale of the investment, but the 'wide street of water' lined by elm trees became a new boundary line. In the revised design for new wide streets south of Carlisle Bridge, a second avenue was marked out, D'Olier St, that would run from the new centre of the city south-eastwards towards the great canal dock. On the north side, the rival canal project, the Royal Canal, only got under way in the 1790s, the intention being to bring to Dublin the mineral riches of Co. Leitrim. That too was a chimera, but the canal was extended all the way down to the mudbanks east of the Custom House, its physical impact on northside development not at all comparable with that of the Grand Canal.[40]

These 'metropolitan improvements' were therefore a mixture of initiatives undertaken during years of urban prosperity and fiscal optimism. And while the brief viceroyalty of the charismatic Duke of Rutland (1784–87) coincided with the first wave of investment, he was no Ormond, and the decision to name the three terraces that had grown up around the Lying-in Hospital as Rutland Square was mere flattery. But within the machinery of government in the 1780s and 1790s there were several key office-holding politicians who were defined by their loyalty to the imperial government in London but whose base was Ireland and whose perspectives were entirely shaped by that – John Foster (the patron of Drogheda), John Fitzgibbon (1740–1804), Attorney-General and later Lord Chancellor who kept a close eye on Limerick city, and John Beresford (1740–1806), brother of the Marquess of Waterford. Beresford enjoyed a parliamentary career that spanned nearly five decades, but it was as a Revenue

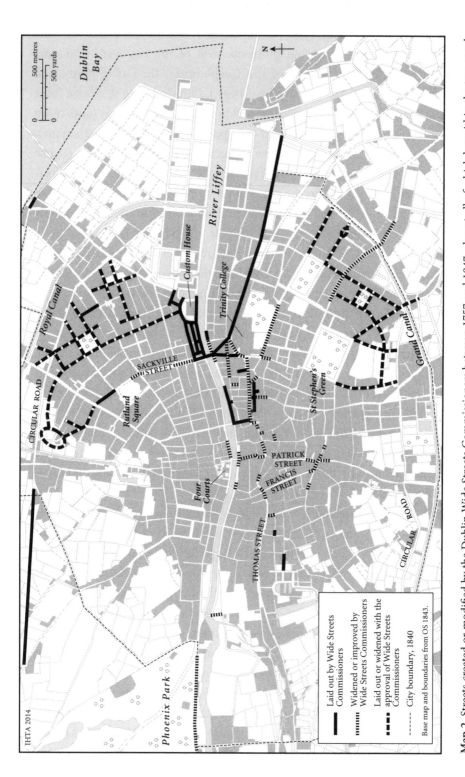

Map 2 Streets created or modified by the Dublin Wide Streets Commissioners between 1757 and 1847, almost all of which lay within the two canals [Rob Goodbody, ed. *Irish Historic Towns Atlas: Dublin, III, 1756-1847* (Dublin, 2014), Fig. 3]

Figure 18 Closing the eastward vista along Molesworth St, one of the earliest private wide streets in the capital, was Leinster House; it was much the largest centre of upper-class sociability in Dublin, but the FitzGerald family was never entirely comfortable there. The house performed a very different role after 1815 when it passed from aristocratic ownership to the well-resourced Dublin Society.

Commissioner that he wielded great power and influence. From the early 1770s he had pushed for a new custom house in Dublin, and he painfully negotiated the deal in 1781 that secured Whitehall support for the new site, in the process helping to win over one member of the British cabinet, Welbore Ellis, who happened to own a large underdeveloped property in Oxmantown on the north-west side of Dublin. It was Ellis who had held a veto over any move of the custom house for many years, but the proposal to make Inns Quay, not far from Ellis's concerns, the site for the new Four Courts won him over. Beresford's hand is evident in most of the metropolitan improvements – in the refashioning of the Wide Streets Commission and the Ballast Board, in securing parliament funds for the major schemes, and in backing and protecting Gandon in his boundless plans. There were of course other parliamentarians who were enthusiastically involved as Commissioners in matters that concerned Beresford less, not least the scheme to open up and re-order the facades of the parliament house, the design of the Four Courts, or the aesthetics of the Grand Canal extension. But Beresford's single-minded energy and strategic grasp gave crucial momentum to the improvements programme whatever the expense, all of which suggests his record stands comparison with the first Duke of Ormond.[41]

Things however went badly wrong for the Wide Streets Commissioners from the time of the economic downturn in 1792 and the coming of war. The cost of acquiring property for demolition was proving far higher than estimated (values were determined by a jury system), and the appetite of developers was proving weaker than expected. The bidding process was flawed, and Beresford's political opponents accused him of corrupt practices in relation to the bidding. The bloc between Eden Quay and Abbey St became the focus for a succession of parliamentary inquiries. Nothing was proved against Beresford, and his summary dismissal from office by the incoming and reform-minded viceroy Earl Fitzwilliam in January 1795 was taken as an insult to his honour (excessive use of official patronage was the ostensible reason). Fitzwilliam's early recall to London was at least partly over Beresford's humiliation, and he was restored to office within weeks by his successor, on the orders of Prime Minister William Pitt. But Beresford still found reason to challenge Fitzwilliam to a duel later in 1795 (over references to his 'much imputed' corruption), and some months afterwards he lashed out in the Commons at his parliamentary opponents:

> He confessed . . . that he was a member [of the Wide Streets Commission], perhaps too an active member of that board, so far as related to the New Bridge and New Custom House; but the House would do him the kindness to recollect that it was the earnest desire of nineteen-twentieths of the Members of both Houses of Parliament that he become one; that several persons had before undertaken the same object and failed; and that, perhaps, but for his particular exertions, nothing would have been done in comparison to what had been done.[42]

But there were few defenders outside government of the improvement programme, and the prevailing belief among most citizens seems to have been that the Commissioners had enriched themselves at the public's expense. In an ever more polarized environment, this was perhaps to be expected. The fact that Beresford's brother had his townhouse in Marlborough St, a short distance from the Custom House, and that his brother-in-law (by his second marriage) was none other than Luke Gardiner Jr made it appear entirely credible that the improvements programme was no more than 'a great job' for those involved. But Beresford's motivation is hard to pin down: he was, like many of the Commissioners, a collector of fine art, and in picking Gandon he identified the man for the job – an outstanding architect who could work wonders on a difficult site. Beresford was undoubtedly vain and saw in the Custom House a monument to his own achievements as a servant of the state. He became the butt of opposition politicians and of the radical press, a reactionary who consistently opposed Catholic relief and Irish parliamentary reform. Yet he had perhaps a wider vision, for the Custom House's superb sculptures are a celebration of Irish potential, of its great rivers and of its foreign trade spanning four continents – while Hibernia and Britannia embrace. There is a sense that Beresford in this and in the broader programme of metropolitan improvements was urgently seeking to make Dublin a neoclassical showpiece, a capital worthy of the kingdom that was his home.[43]

8
FOOD FOR THOUGHT

Prior to the construction of Gandon's Custom House, the great library of Trinity College was the largest building visible to mariners entering Dublin port. Set some distance back from the south quays, it appeared to be a great warehouse rising out of the marshes, one of a growing cluster of buildings inside the university. As with Gandon's Custom House, the building attracted much controversy in Parliament before being funded. The crowning achievement of a prolific architect, the Surveyor General Thomas Burgh (1670–1730), it also went far over budget, being much larger than was currently required (see Plate 27).

The library's severe rusticated exterior was immediately imposing, but contemporaries were more struck by the timbered interior and vast single chamber. It was certainly an ambitious building, its scale reflecting the vision of the Archbishop King (an avid bookman with a personal library of over 7,000 titles) and the architect's desire to build on a grand scale. There were many delays, but on completion in 1732 (after Burgh's death) it stood 'as much a symbol as an instrument of civility', a visible demonstration of the vastness of the world of print and the primacy of the book. The library's collections consisted almost entirely of scholarly works published throughout the world, some of them purchased locally, many of them benefactions (although a large proportion of the College's 20,000 volumes had to be rebound before being set on the pristine hardwood shelves, a task that kept Joseph Leathley, a Dame St bookseller, and his binder busy for more than a decade).[1]

The library served what was a small but well-endowed university which lay adjacent to the most prestigious urban spaces in the capital city, and had its own marshy campus of nearly 20 hectares. In the first half of the century student numbers rarely approached 500 and its recruitment field was now almost entirely restricted to Ireland. Close on half of its students came from homes outside the province of Leinster; most students were from land-owning families, but a fifth were sons of Church of Ireland clergy and indeed almost all the Church's ministers were Trinity graduates. However, by the 1730s the College was far more than a seminary for the Established Church. Most of the country's barristers were alumni, and law and natural philosophy were studied within the capacious library building. An astronomical observatory operated for a while on the top floor and, just as the library was being completed, a small Doric temple was under construction in a nearby garden; it was to house the university press.

The library was however no powerhouse of new learning: undergraduates were denied access, and its users then were few. Furthermore there were exceptionally few publications by fellows of the College in the following half century, and it is a moot point whether any of the great minds associated with eighteenth-century Dublin – Swift, Hutcheson, Burke or Berkeley himself – darkened its doors. Despite an anatomy house and a physic garden not far away, the training of physicians was almost entirely neglected until after 1800.[2]

The building was nonetheless a powerful statement of future intent. The other Dublin library of that era, the gift of Archbishop Marsh, was located beside St Patrick's Cathedral 'for public use, where all might have free access', and it was (and remains) a remarkable time capsule of the early eighteenth-century concerns of Marsh, a cleric with strong interests in the New Science, and of a Huguenot physician, scholar and bibliophile, the much-travelled Élie Bouhéreau, its first librarian. But it too remained a quiet place.

DUBLIN'S BOOK TRADE

To find local evidence of the impact of the Enlightenment we must look elsewhere. If the College press was not unduly busy, this was not the case outside: Dublin by 1730 had become a major centre of publishing in the English-speaking world, much smaller than London but ahead of both Edinburgh and Bristol, and licensing controls were now relaxed. From an annual total of 52 published titles appearing in Dublin in the 1680s, the figure had more than quadrupled by the 1720s with 226 titles a year, a level that was maintained until the final two decades of the century, when again it rose sharply. A small proportion of these titles were only issued after pre-publication subscriptions had been raised: for example, of the 109 such titles that were published in Dublin in the 1740s, 39 related to literature (ancient or modern), 24 to history and biography, 15 to religion and philosophy, and 13 to medicine or science. Two-thirds of these publications were original titles, the rest reprints, mainly of London originals. The subscription titles were highly diverse and the print runs short, but they were a prestigious segment of what was a highly eclectic mix of publications.

Men of the cloth associated with Trinity College were among the small coterie of regular subscribers to new book proposals, and indeed in the first half of the century clergy of all denominations, but principally the Church of Ireland, were the group most inclined to build personal libraries, well ahead of other professionals; merchants as a group were far behind, and large-scale gentry investment in books was only evident from mid century. Even in 1770 John Murray, a visiting London bookseller, made a jaundiced assessment of the market, finding Dublin 'not a reading but a hard-drinking city'.

There were nevertheless over sixty booksellers in the capital by the 1730s, and lively auctions where private libraries were dispersed became a regular event. Most booksellers combined the importation and retail sale of books with occasional publishing, and in some cases with the business of printing. But even with diversification it was a precarious business. In Mary Pollard's remarkable reconstruction of the personnel of the Dublin book trade, close to 10 per cent of all those involved during the eighteenth century experienced prison at some point in their career, whether on charges of libel (or worse) or for debt. Most of those who died wealthy had diversified into paper-milling, property speculation or been involved in the Lottery. And even some of the most adventurous book traders failed to be rewarded financially: John Smith (c. 1700–71) was probably the leading importer of books directly from Holland and France for 'near forty years', and at his shop on Blind Quay (The Philosophers' Heads), works on architecture, gardening and household management shared space with the Whig classics, Enlightenment philosophy and the writings of his friend Francis Hutcheson. But in 1758 falling sales of 'foreign books' and heavy debts forced him out of business: some of his stock was sold to the College, the remainder in 4,683 lots was auctioned off – disastrously.[3]

Smith and his contemporaries had played a critical role in introducing some of the canonical writers of the French Enlightenment to Irish readers, both by sourcing foreign-language imports and by reprinting English translations at rates cheaper than London. And as Máire Kennedy has shown, the

Figure 19 'A view of a print shop': William Allen's premises in Dame St, Dublin, was probably the best-known print and map shop in the city for nearly half a century (relocating along the street once), but it can rarely have attracted such a large crowd.

strong presence of Huguenots in Dublin accelerated the reception of French Enlightenment ideas within Ireland, whether as booksellers importing French-language works from Continental co-religionists, as willing translators, or as a retail market for such texts. Most remarkable was Jean Pierre Droz (d.1751), a Dublin Huguenot minister, bookseller and publisher of the quarterly *A Literary Journal* (1744–49), which gave abstracts in translation of new French publications, and included his own glosses on them. In all, 279 texts associated with the French Enlightenment were published in Ireland during the century in Graham Gargett's estimate, the overwhelming majority in translation. Voltaire of course led the way. A generation after Droz, the 'ghost of Croesus', Luke White (*c.* 1740–1824), dominated the Continental trade, sourcing the latest through his Swiss suppliers in Neuchâtel, and for some years he issued an annual book catalogue. He rose to enormous wealth with estates in five counties, and he engaged in a series of very costly electoral contests. His fortune came in part from two advantageous marriages and some highly astute financial speculation, but the ongoing demand in Dublin for French literature which he serviced so well may also have helped.[4]

Back in the 1720s, Jonathan Swift's polemical interventions into public affairs had created a new currency for the political pamphlet, perhaps even giving birth to a 'literary public sphere'. About a hundred pamphlets and broadsides relating to the Wood's Halfpence controversy, most of them anonymous, were rushed through production during the crisis and were instantly hawked on the street. This level of print warfare had no precedent in Dublin – and it was never forgotten. In the same decade, the number of Dublin news-sheets and newspapers – a phenomenon almost non-existent in 1700 – reached critical mass. However, the inclusion of local content touching on political controversy only really began in the 1740s when turmoil inside the Corporation, stirred up by Charles Lucas, flooded the presses and affected newsprint permanently. The unusual success of the *Freeman's Journal*, launched in 1763, was evidence of how things were changing. Published by a group of nine reform-minded professionals and merchants, all of them sympathetic to Lucas and his politics, it had an avowedly political purpose: to strengthen the 'patriot' opposition in Parliament and to inform its readers on pressing matters touching state and city. But, echoing Lucas, it was entirely unsympathetic towards Catholic relief.[5]

Most newspaper titles faded quickly, but there were rarely less than eight titles competing each week for readers within Dublin, and as the postal service improved the country market was exploited to the full: publication schedules were tied to the arrival of the Holyhead packet and news from London (that only became a daily service from 1768), and to the days in the week when the Dublin mail was despatched to provincial post towns. One of the most successful and long-lived papers was the *Dublin Journal*, launched in 1725 by a young Dublin printer George Faulkner (*c.* 1703–75), which soon had a circulation approaching 2,000, thanks principally to its abundant crop of advertisements for property, print and fashionable consumer goods (see Plate 28).

Faulkner's greater fame rested on his dealings with Swift: he became in effect the dean's literary agent as well as his co-publisher in later years. Faulkner was however unusual: no Dublin publisher/printer later in the century collaborated with an Irish author of international repute. Burke, Goldsmith, the Sheridans, Edgeworth and the many others with ambitious pens engaged entirely with London publishers, even before they took up residence there. Richard Sher has contrasted the pattern in Edinburgh with that in Dublin: the total imprints published in the two cities over the course of the century were very similar, but Edinburgh publisher/printers developed a close and supportive relationship with many of the great names of the Scottish Enlightenment, while also collaborating with key London publishers and drawing down financial support from that quarter. Some Dublin publishers developed quite close London connections, but the relationship between the two cities was for the most part competitive, and for one good reason: from the time of its passing in 1709, the British copyright act did not extend to Ireland, and from 1739 Irish printed editions of British published books could not be legally imported across the Irish Sea to Britain.

For a commercially minded author, Dublin was no place to begin unless their intended market was entirely Irish. However, the other side of the coin was that works published in London could be reprinted in Dublin without permission or royalty charge, and on that basis a great reprint business grew up from early on in the century. London publishers from mid century became fixated on the rascally behaviour of Dublin printers, exporting cheap-format, shoddy versions of the latest in fiction or philosophy to England or Scotland, and they lobbied to change the law, but the dimensions of the supposed 'pirate' trade were greatly exaggerated. Dublin editions of fashionable authors were indeed quick to appear and usually in a cheaper format, and publishers' overheads were lower. But their market was overwhelmingly Irish, not British, until American sales began to be important from 1780. The cheaper Dublin reprints significantly widened the market for the canonical works of the Scottish Enlightenment (as for other genres of reprints), and this may have had a decisive effect on reception and readership in the late eighteenth century, both inside and outside Ireland, particularly in America.[6]

-<+--+>-

Engagement in the world of print formed a political apprenticeship for John Curry and Charles O'Conor, the pioneers of the new Catholic politics as they first sought to map out a post-Jacobite dispensation for Catholics in a Hanoverian world. In their early writing they campaigned anonymously – for a radical re-interpretation of the 'black legend' of the 1641 massacres, for an oath of allegiance that would not be repugnant to Catholic sensibilities, and for some modest reform of the statutes restricting Catholics lending money. But they courted trouble: when O'Conor's *Case of the Roman Catholics of Ireland*, first published in Dublin in 1755, was re-issued in Cork later that year, the local edition was seized by order of the mayor. Curry, O'Conor and their Dublin printers were indeed very cautious in declaring authorship of their early works. However, there was no other instance of censorship after mid century. Indeed there was no single authority to police print, and the only weapons of control were very blunt. Thus when Lucas, who had begun to attack the city's aldermen in the early 1740s, switched in 1748 to inflammatory criticisms of the government itself, it was Parliament that prosecuted him and precipitated his exile. However four years later, at the time of the Money Bill crisis, when prolonged parliamentary faction-fighting spilled out beyond College Green, there was an unprecedented wave of unrestrained political pamphleteering. That experience gave printers and authors a new sense of impunity. One facet of this greater freedom of the press was to allow the likes of O'Conor to publish with growing confidence.[7]

Even before the first political essays began to appear, there had been a noticeable growth in Catholic religious printing (both devotional and catechetical). Imported missals and other Catholic material had been regularly impounded in the early years of the century, but from the 1720s Catholic literature of all kinds was openly imported, much of it standard French and English works, and this was now being reprinted in cheaper formats, both for a clerical and a lay readership, and invariably in the English, not the Irish language. A case in point, and one of the most successful reprints, was a work by Richard Challoner, the prolific and long-lived Vicar-General of London whose accessible spiritual manuals sold strongly for decades; his *Morality of the Bible* (London, 1762, reprinted Dublin, 1765) was a simplified and cheap anthology of the Douai Bible. The Dublin publisher managed to secure no less than 780 subscribers, fewer than 5 per cent of whom were clergy but fewer than 3 per cent were women. The rest were for the most part non-elite subscribers, including over eighty 'merchants' or booksellers; a few had addresses in Cork, Kilkenny, Limerick and Waterford, but the great majority were near neighbours of the publisher and bookseller Philip Bowes of Church St, or of his Cook St printer James Byrn. The subscribers included coopers and tobacconists, hardware merchants and grocers; several were booksellers who opted to take from 25 to 200 copies. All presumably were Catholic.[8]

The Dublin book trade reached its apogee between the 1760s and 1790s, both in terms of business sophistication and scale of operations, despite the fact that imports, mainly from London, were stronger than ever. By the standards of wider Dublin business, it was collaborative 'and surprisingly orderly', despite political and religious differences within the trade. The publication of collaborative catalogues 'of books in all languages, arts and sciences, that have been printed in Ireland, and published in Dublin, from the year 1700', which appeared five times between 1774 and 1791 is the most eloquent evidence of that collaboration. And copying London practice, many booksellers had widened their activities to include a lending service: K.A. Manley has identified at least twenty-one such 'circulating libraries' in Dublin before 1800, the importance of which in widening readership was immense but is unquantifiable. The largest of these libraries in the 1780s, that of Thomas Jackson, reportedly had a stock of 'above 10,000' volumes. Some of the larger bookshops also provided comfortable reading (and meeting) spaces on site.[9]

PRINT IN THE PROVINCES

By the early 1790s there were just over fifty booksellers and just under fifty printers known to be trading in Dublin, and the annual number of imprints was close to 550. By contrast, specialist booksellers outside the capital were, as we have seen (Table 5.1), quite rare before 1800, and they relied on Dublin for most of their stock. They were more likely to be stockists of patent medicines, lottery tickets, fancy goods and much else than were the Dublin booksellers. The number of printers at work in the provincial cities is more difficult to determine; the great bulk of their business was ephemeral – legal and administrative forms, handbills, stationery, templates, all of this a symptom of an ever more literate society.

Bookseller/publishers were becoming more common in the last quarter of the century and, as in the other 'luxury' trades, skills learnt in the big city were carried to the provinces. The number of recorded titles printed in the nine centres outside Dublin over the whole century was less than a tenth of those for Dublin itself (the dominance of London within the English book trade was probably even more extreme). But the imbalance was narrowing as provincial demand grew for cheaper books and pamphlets, reflecting rising aggregate literacy and the willingness of grocers and petty dealers, chapmen and lottery keepers to market print products. Books became a regular part of the great portfolio of consumer goods carted from the 'country shops' in Thomas St and High St, and they were usually paid for in ready money. But bigger traders helped: many of the provincial subscribers ordering multiple copies of Dublin-produced books, presumably for re-sale, were categorized as 'merchants', not as booksellers.

Critical to the growth of provincial print culture was the spread of news-papers: from early in the century a few merchants and professionals in each city were subscribing to London and Dublin papers, and many more read them in the Exchange or the tavern. But the coming of a local press with local advertising marked a step change: all ten urban centres had regular newspa-pers by the 1770s. These usually took the form of four large folio pages carrying recycled news from Dublin, London, Paris and beyond twice a week, with very little original copy apart from the advertisements (which were as always the main source of a publisher's revenue). One or two papers in Cork and Belfast were by then selling a thousand copies an issue; elsewhere print runs were much lower, at a time when, according to Robert Munter's calculations, upwards of 40,000 newspapers a week were being printed in Dublin.[10]

The regional differences are however striking (Table 8.1). The presses in Sligo and Galway were it seems only involved in newspaper production and jobbing work, while the output of most southern cities was entirely eclipsed by that in Cork. But it is the strength of book and pamphlet production in Belfast that is most striking (by comparison, Derry's showing was paltry). This points to a distinct print culture in east Ulster, reflecting the demographic dominance of a literate Presbyterian laity and a religious culture that gave primacy to the reading of scripture and theology. Belfast's printers thrived on this and indeed on the disputatious character of Ulster Presbyterianism. However, secular titles became more prominent later in the century, with the proliferation of works relating to education and moral improvement. 'Lighter' reading – fiction and poetry – was even slower to develop. But the hinterland of Belfast had the highest density of reading clubs by the 1790s.[11]

The first newspapers in Limerick and Cork appeared in the 1710s, but these were short-lived and did not circulate widely. Continuous newspaper publica-tion in Limerick dates from 1739 (*Welch's Limerick Journal*) and the first provincial trade directory appeared there in 1769. The latter initiative was the work of the ever-resourceful John Ferrar, who found time to write the city's

Table 8.1
Provincial Imprints, Newspapers, Circulating Libraries, and Booksellers: 1701–1824

	Total recorded titles printed 1701–1800	Total newspaper titles 1701–1800 and date of first publication	Circulating libraries 1762–1824	Booksellers/ stationers 1824
Derry	28	1 [1772]	5	4
Sligo	3	1 [1752]	1	2
Galway	9	3 [1754]	5	4
Limerick	118	6 [1716]	6	9
Cork	727	(19) [1716]	14	18
Waterford	84	(5) [1729]	1	5
Kilkenny	57	1 [1766]	2	2
Drogheda	33	2 [c.1770]	4	2
Belfast	803	5 [1737]	14	14

Sources: See Appendix 6.

history and establish what became the city's principal paper (the *Limerick Chronicle*). Yet, despite his efforts the city had a weaker market for print than its southern neighbour. Cork's strength – in imprints, in the number of newspapers, in circulating libraries, and later in booksellers – indicates both a distinctive local market and regional cultural leadership. Regular newspaper production only began in 1753 (with the *Corke Journal*) but the city had already developed a lively print culture; taking the century as a whole, Cork printers produced more original titles and far more poetry and miscellaneous literary work than anywhere else outside Dublin. William Flyn's long career there as bookseller, publisher and printer touched all bases: his *Hibernian Chronicle* (from 1769) copied the *Freeman's Journal* in including original essays and local commentary from the very beginning, and it was greatly helped by the editorial (and possibly financial) support of Henry Sheares (1728–75), a minor Cork landowner, banker, freemason, bibliophile, philanthropist and, briefly, MP. The fact that Flyn was Catholic and Sheares Church of Ireland was further evidence that print culture at this time was breaking, not raising, barriers.[12]

PRESS FREEDOM AND ITS LIMITS

From the time of Queen Anne's reign those in power had complained about the improprieties of the press and its use as a dangerous tool in the hands of opposition factions, yet it was only in the politically charged 1780s and 1790s that interference and manipulation of the print media by Dublin Castle became a constant threat, affecting Dublin printers in particular. Even the early 'library societies' (Belfast in 1788, Dublin in 1791 and Cork in 1792) that were at first sight were an entirely innocent cultural phenomenon became objects of official suspicion simply because they were strongly supported by political reformers (the unusually artisan character of the original Belfast society made it doubly suspicious). But the areas of public contention in the 1790s were not new-style libraries or urban reading clubs, but opposition newspapers and cheap political ephemera. Francophile papers, notably the *Cork Gazette* and the *Northern Star* in Belfast, trod a fine line: they were profoundly hostile towards government yet, despite legal attack, they survived through most of the 1790s, with the *Star* claiming regular sales of over 4,000, spread across Ulster. However, in May 1797

> a party of the Monaghan Militia attacked the *Star* office ... gutted it, threw out the money from the window, destroyed all the books, types, papers etc. – by which a property of many thousands may be lost. No magistrates – no officer ...

The *Cork Gazette* was closed down in less dramatic fashion four months later. The baton was then taken up by *The Press* in Dublin, which in the winter of 1797/8 claimed a print-run of 6,000, its readers waiting outside the printers on publication night in 'a revelry of sedition' to get their hands on each new issue. It continued to appear after the printer, John Stockdale, was imprisoned in March 1798, but it too ceased after soldiers entered Stockdale's Abbey St house and destroyed his 'types and printing implements'.[13]

The radical newspapers of the 1790s were for the educated and disaffected, but a more profound democratization of print was underway in urban Ireland, a process that shocked authority because of the speed at which it was happening. For, beyond pay-to-read newsprint, there was a great outflow of subversive print matter, heavily subsidized by the radical societies in Dublin and Belfast, some of it indeed distributed without charge. Subsidized print products had of course a long history since the Incorporated Society had first produced religious reading materials for the semi-literate. From mid century there had also been a gathering flood of chapbooks and ballad sheets, religious woodcuts ('eye catechisms') and caricatures costing between a farthing and a penny entering general circulation, emanating chiefly from Dublin, Cork, Limerick and Belfast. Crudely produced picture books, some of them celebrating the daring-do of Irish highwaymen and of heroic rapparees who had been worsted in the seventeenth-century land settlement were mixed with more generic folktales, classical and chivalric histories, sensational stories and natural wonders. From small beginnings this poorly documented trade seems to have grown exponentially in the last quarter of the century. It was conducted almost entirely in the English language. Despite the palpable bilingualism of the street and the marketplace in southern and western cities, printers could find no commercial incentive to invest in Irish typeface or even to produce hybrid material, the few exceptions being modest works of devotion and meditation that post-date 1800.

Thus when United Irish societies in Belfast and Dublin in the 1790s turned to the provinces and the countryside to mobilize popular support, one of their strategies was the production in English of cheap or free versions of revolutionary texts and on an unprecedented scale, most notably Thomas Paine's *Rights of Man*. The sudden potency of the printing-press profoundly frightened Government and its supporters, although the impact of this political literature outside the towns was almost certainly exaggerated, and in the rural world subversive ballad sheets and political song-books may indeed have had far more impact. The slow-moving but eventually robust response by the state and the Protestant Churches to subversive print was the subsidized production of educational, moral and religious tracts, many from the pen of Hannah More, which were aimed at a mass readership. This 'battle for hearts and minds' was to dominate the first quarter of the next century; it was spearheaded by Dublin-based Protestant educational charities (notably the Kildare Place and the Cheap Book Societies) as the battle moved from being principally an urban contest into the village and the countryside.[14]

FINDING THE READER

One of the first Dublin printers of Paine's inflammatory pamphlet was James Moore. His principal preoccupation at that time was rather different: the production of an Irish edition of the recently published third edition of the *Encyclopaedia Britannica*. Copies of Diderot and d'Alembert's *Encyclopédie* and of earlier editions of the *Encyclopaedia* were well known to wealthy Irish book buyers, but this Irish reprint was touted as 'the most expensive and spirited' publication project when announced in 1790. The eighteenth and final volume in the main series appeared in 1797; the set included 542 original copperplate engravings and much other original matter; two supplementary volumes, as in the third Edinburgh edition, were published in 1801. It was the biggest commercial undertaking of an Irish publisher during the century. Moore was a young, ambitious and well-connected College Green bookseller and lottery-keeper; he is associated with over 600 imprints (nearly all reprints) between 1786 and 1802, but in this case he bore the risk singly as 'printer, publisher and sole proprietor'. He secured 1,201 subscribers, 70 per cent of whom were peers or esquires, and fewer than 10 per cent gave provincial addresses. All but 2 per cent were male.

Moore's wider career is revealing: he was a Catholic, but even after the relief act of 1793 he had no involvement in St Luke's, the printers' guild. He was an early and active member of the Society of United Irishmen, and a proposer of Paine for honorary membership. He collaborated extensively with the most established Catholic publisher in the city, Patrick Byrne of Grafton St, but he kept out of the political limelight more successfully than Byrne. He published Mary Wollstonecraft's *Vindication of the Rights of Women* in the only Irish edition (in 1793) and some of her later work, as well as her husband William Godwin's *The Enquirer* (in 1797). But he also reprinted many conservative writers (including Burke), which may have helped him mask his radical sympathies and to escape attention in 1798. However, he was centrally involved in the paper war against the government's proposals for parliamentary union in 1799, publishing two newspapers and nearly fifty pamphlets, not without some profit to his business. But a year after the Union was in place, he closed his business, auctioned his stock, and died in middle age a year later.

As a Catholic publisher/printer, Moore was one of a long line of successful innovators, particularly in newsprint, running from James Hoey, Faulkner's one-time partner in the *Dublin Journal*, Eugene Swiney and William Flyn, proprietors of two of the principal Cork newspapers, and Edmund Finn who, together with his wife Catherine, made a regional success of the *Leinster Journal* in Kilkenny. They were all discreet as to their religious affiliation, but when Cork Corporation suppressed the local edition of O'Conor's *Case of the Roman-Catholics* the action was immediately presented (in Dublin) as an outrage 'in a land of liberty'. In fact, compared with many other branches of enterprise, printing and bookselling became quite religiously mixed, and cross-denominational business collaboration was not unusual in the second half of the century, although there was something of a special *esprit de corps* among Dublin's Catholic booksellers. But Flyn in Cork was remarkable in the diversity of his religious patronage (although by being strongly involved in the

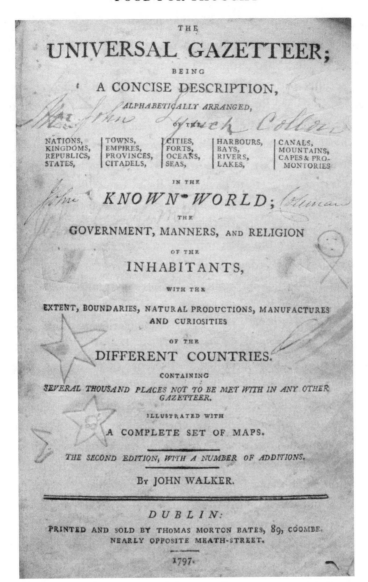

Figure 20 Title page of the Dublin edition of John Walker's *Universal gazetteer* (1797), 'printed and sold by Thomas Morton Bates, 89 Coombe', where he was based for at least twenty-five years and was one of very few printers or booksellers in the Meath Liberty, where he remained in business until 1814.

push for Catholic relief in the early 1790s that may have worn thin). Only in the North was the print trade in exclusively Protestant hands.[15]

Publisher/printers also employed women and catered increasingly for women as serious readers. Whether James Moore, Wollstonecraft's publisher, had a particular regard for his team of women sewers in the bookbindery is unknown, but the involvement of women in all aspects of the book trade is striking. The many newly widowed who managed to keep their husband's printing business active are well known, helped perhaps by the fact that most print shops in this era seem to have made heavy use of female labour, skilled and unskilled. The celebrated instances of female involvement – from Swift's favourite proofreader Constantia Grierson, to Catherine Finn, who over three decades extended the circulation and reputation of the *Leinster Journal* – hint at the decisive but unrecorded role of women.

Subscription lists offer some clue as to the growth of female readership in and beyond urban boundaries. In Kennedy's sample of Irish book-subscription lists between 1738 and 1796, 14.2 per cent of the names are those of women; in a much smaller sub-group of subscribers to *female* authors, the figure rises to 30 per cent. From small beginnings the presence of women on subscription lists was a rising trend, notably in the fields of poetry, drama, fiction, household management, and educational and conduct literature. The success of the monthly periodical business, starting with London-published journals in the 1740s and Dublin titles from the 1760s, was a clear symptom of the widening world of reading: by the end of the century roughly a quarter of the known subscribers to Dublin magazines had provincial addresses. Most of these were of course men, but several short-lived periodicals made a particular pitch for female subscribers. And *Walker's Hibernian Magazine* (1771–1805), by far the most successful of the Dublin magazines, enjoyed a countrywide distribution and was always gender sensitive, publishing many pieces on female education and displaying a sympathetic interest in Wollstonecraft. It is likely that the key group here was the cohort of bourgeois women who had benefited from the marked expansion of female boarding schools and academies, evident in Dublin and the larger cities after mid century, and that they formed the bulk of the avid readers who patronized booksellers later in the century. It was presumably the same cohort who sought and achieved public visibility within the Volunteer movement during the American War and an opportunity to display 'patriot femininity'. A more modest sign of changing times was the success of Anna Milliken, a teacher in one of Cork's schools for girls, who had four novels published by local bookseller/printers between 1792 and 1804. Educational in intent, they were a decided commercial success.[16]

Thus, in the final decades of the century leading bookseller/publishers were producing more original work than ever before: in the well-studied case of John Chambers of Abbey St, Dublin, who traded between 1775 and 1798, two-thirds of the sixty-five books he published were originals, one-third reprints, and in addition he was an active jobbing printer and a stationer. But then everything, at least in Dublin, went wrong. The imposition of paper duties in 1795, the wartime harassment of the opposition press, and the complicity of key figures (including Chambers) in revolutionary politics, led to imprisonment and exile, and drastically affected the whole sector. Finally, and most critically, came the extension in 1801 of British copyright to Ireland in the wake of parliamentary union. Book imports from Britain to Dublin (at official valuation) quadrupled over the next 15 years and the city's book trade was changed beyond recognition, entirely shedding its prestigious character. The most innovative and enterprising members retired from the trade or re-established themselves in America. After a spell in prison, Chambers was lucky to end his days as a stationer on Wall St, New York.[17]

Yet it is striking that after 1800, with the great contraction of Dublin book publishing, the number of booksellers increased, library societies sprouted in all urban centres, and circulating libraries in provincial centres became far more common. The infrastructure of reading was being transformed as the cost of print began to fall and aggregate demand grow. But Dublin's dominance in the supply of books was broken and provincial booksellers now dealt directly with London: by 1815 around two-fifths of Irish book imports were coming straight to the provincial ports. Only in the supply of newsprint, educational texts and devotional literature were Dublin presses still dominant. They could content themselves that it was precisely that kind of literature that the newly literate masses outside the cities would be most likely to read.[18]

9
ORDER AND DISORDER

Thomas Burgh's greatest building project in Dublin was the Royal Barracks, constructed between 1704 and 1708 on a large site west of Oxmantown Green that had been purchased from the second Duke of Ormond. Arranged around four courtyards, the great limestone terraces became a dominant landmark at the city's west end, forbiddingly austere as they had been deliberately left without 'mere ornament'. The complex initially housed some 1,500 men, but by the 1760s that had risen to around 4,000.

The creation within a capital city of such a vast military establishment had no obvious European parallel. But the decision to build on such a scale was not a defensive measure as such, rather a consequence of the agreement by the (all Protestant) Irish Parliament in 1697 to house and maintain on Irish soil the bulk of the English standing army during peacetime. This was part of a post-war political trade-off, with whatever economic and security benefits this might bring to Ireland being a secondary consideration. At the beginning of the century the officer corps of the Irish-based regiments was largely British and the non-commissioned ranks even more so, making the Royal Barracks in some respects an alien enclave. And even though that changed from the 1740s with greater recruitment within Ireland, it still remained an ostensibly Protestant army, its officer corps with strong gentry links.

Burgh's Barracks was one of over a hundred such facilities established across the country between 1697 and 1704. Most were very modest; only those constructed in the cities and at the naval port of Kinsale were substantial structures. The earliest designated complexes were in Limerick (completed in 1694), Cork and Waterford, located inside or adjacent to existing urban fortresses. By 1710, two-fifths of barracks capacity in Ireland were within the ten urban

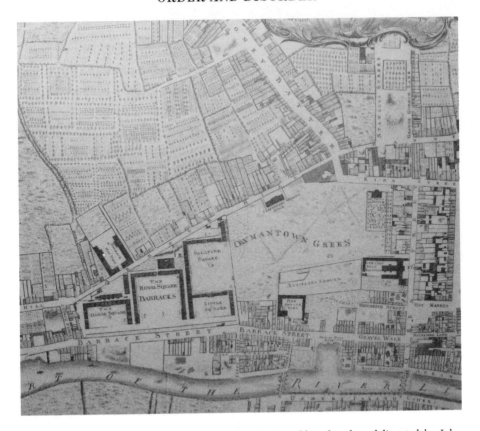

Figure 21 The Royal Barracks and the Oxmantown neighbourhood as delineated by John Rocque (1756).

centres; by 1752 the proportion was slightly over half, with a strong bias towards the larger cities. Major barracks were only built in Derry and Belfast in the 1730s, by which time Dublin accommodated at least a third of the army resident in Ireland. A small proportion of these, perhaps 300, were deployed on garrison duty, principally as the Main Guard protecting the Castle and, at times, patrolling outside Newgate gaol.

The Royal Barracks created its own ecosystem in the Smithfield area. It transformed demand for food and fodder, drink and prostitutes, and for 'respectable' taverns to serve the officers, but the area as a whole gained an unsavoury reputation. The South Parish in Cork was similarly shaped by the military presence, reinforcing its status as the poorest part of the city. By contrast much of the modest prosperity of early eighteenth-century Sligo was attributed to the large cavalry barracks and the spending power of the soldiery there.[1]

AIDING THE CIVIL POWER

But what was the logic behind the increased concentration of the military in the cities? The original deployment c. 1700 seems to have been to strike a balance, on the one hand a recognition that control of the port cities and their provisions stocks would be critical in any future war and that in peacetime the logistics of provisioning and of troop movements into and out of the country made them the locations of choice. But against that, recent experience of sustained French privateering on the high seas and the persistence of Jacobite banditry in several parts of the country favoured a policy of troop dispersal. It was only with peace after 1713 that the case for dispersal weakened and city garrisons grew in size. And, although it was not articulated explicitly, the permanent presence of military manpower, albeit in largely open residential barracks, helped make the case for continuing the gradual process of urban de-fortification. Moreover, in time of war or Jacobite threat (as in 1715), the Irish government believed that it was essential to contain a large part of the military establishment within 'Dublin, Cork, Waterford, Limerick and Galway for the security of Protestant inhabitants', even at the expense of their deployment elsewhere. The absence of funding for a properly constituted (Protestant) militia in the cities strengthened that argument; only in Dublin and Cork was the array of local militia a regular feature in wartime.[2]

This very substantial military presence achieved an additional importance: 'to aid the civil power'. Inherited systems for maintaining public order were heavily shaped by English law and practice, and they depended on unpaid communal service – by aldermen serving as justices of the peace and by parish-appointed constables and overseers, with the employment of unarmed watchmen as enforcers on the street. The watch systems in Dublin (parish-regulated) and in the southern cities (controlled by their corporations) were reformed and adapted at several points between 1715 and the 1780s, but the system was ill-suited to eighteenth-century conditions for two reasons: from 1704, municipal and parish office-holding was restricted to members of the Church of Ireland, and only Dublin and Cork had a sufficient pool of Anglicans on whom to draw; secondly, the self-policing model was ill-equipped to respond to the massive growth of urban populations, to the expansion of marginalized social groups, or to the social tensions increasingly evident later in the century. Inter-personal violence and property theft became an issue of recurring concern from mid century, and the growing resort to capital punishment for property crime, notably in Dublin, was a sign that the legal framework protecting property and deterring crime was coming under severe strain. In the seven years from 1780 to 1786 there were an unprecedented 116 public executions in Dublin city and county, 103 of which related to theft, burglary or fraud (and at least as many were sentenced to transportation). But that was perhaps an extreme case of a cyclical pattern, for property crime in the cities surged in years of high food prices and economic difficulty, notably in the early 1740s and the mid 1760s as well as in the early 1780s. But the thirty-three public hangings in 1785 outside Dublin's gaols probably broke all peacetime records.[3]

THE URBAN RIOT

Riots were however unusual, and where they occurred they were generally contained without loss of life. The first Irish Riot Act was only slipped onto the statute book in 1771, dealing specifically with Cork, and another for Dublin in 1780. Therefore, was the general absence of large-scale trouble on the streets a consequence of the army presence? Parish constables and city aldermen (acting as justices of the peace) were ill-equipped to challenge disorderly crowds, but in fact crowds were rarely disorderly, swarming principally for recreation (at carnivals, fairs and patterns, or to watch football and wrestling contests), for upper-class funerals or choreographed public celebrations (the opening of the assizes, a mayoral inauguration, news of British military victory, the monarch's birthday and, in Dublin, the formal state events around Parliament, the Castle and Christ Church Cathedral). The greatest Dublin crowds gathered at the Palmerstown and Donnybrook fairs, the former some miles west of the city, the latter on the southern outskirts, and both in August. An ancient horse and livestock fair, Donnybrook broadened out during the century to become a vast site for carnival and sport, bull-baiting and wagers, drinking, pimping and brawling; one Sunday in 1790 it was claimed that upwards of 50,000 people were in attendance, returning to the city 'like intoxicated savages'.

Magistrates regularly intervened to halt proceedings there, forcibly demolishing tents and booths at the end of the week's excesses. But, as Séamus Ó Maitiú has argued, from the late eighteenth century Donnybrook was becoming less participatory and more commercialized, dominated by exotic acts, travelling theatre troupes, and freak-shows, and it was also better policed, thus still attracting upper-class patronage long after other sites of popular recreation were shunned.[4]

203

Figure 22 Donnybrook fair, where 'all the ancient rites of bagpiping, fiddling, drunkenness, debauchery and riot [are observed], to the great edification of servants, apprentices and the lower orders...' (*FJ*, 29 August 1793).

There were however three collective threats to urban order: faction fights, scarcity riots and artisan protests. All were new to the eighteenth century.

The Sunday faction fights in Dublin between the Liberty Boys and the Ormond Boys, first noticed in the 1730s and recurring for some forty years, took place at city junctions and bridges, at seasonal fairs and on suburban open spaces, and they involved young male tradesmen – for the most part (Protestant) textile workers from the south side and (Catholic) butchers' boys from the markets and shambles on the north side, with the area around St Patrick's cathedral being another seedbed. Indeed, clashes between different trades within the Liberties were not unknown.

Violence in these clashes was against the person rather than against property, but parish constables were entirely unable to control the larger skirmishes, and the army was repeatedly called out. But was this no more than recreational excess? Timothy Watt has suggested that these territorial factions could also transmit communal anger against unjust or corrupt law officers, gaolers or constables, and that their origin in Dublin lay in the near collapse of the parish police system in the 1720s. The principal gaoler in the city, John Hawkins, had developed something akin to a protection racket and was acting with complete impunity. They were not however politicized in any way, nor did religion as such inflame factional rivalries, although it has been suggested that the surge in attacks on soldiers before and at times during the American Revolution, particularly by the city's butchers, was politically motivated.

Faction fights were not exclusive to Dublin: in Cork from the 1720s the butchers of Fair Lane and the weavers of the northern suburb of Blackpool met at pre-ordained venues, notably on the days leading up to the greatest celebratory moment in the calendar, May Day, fighting with a ferocity to match the Dublin exchanges and involving on occasion 'females ... armed plentifully with stones, and the male combatants ... with tomahawks'. In Limerick there was a long history of factional sparring between Englishtown residents and those on the south side of the city but, as in Dublin, the gangs occasionally collaborated, acting together at times of communal grievance against petty figures of authority or against transgressive activities in their midst. This was demonstrated most spectacularly in the capital with the recurrence of collective looting and destruction of city brothels.[5]

However, soaring food prices were the most powerful trigger for potentially destructive collective action. Food rioting may have been less common than urban faction fighting, but its impact on property was much greater: James Kelly has found no instance of a riot before the winter of 1709/10, but that thereafter scarcity protests recurred in almost every year of high grain prices. A wave of such protests, usually but not exclusively confined to the cities, took place at least once in every decade when severe deficits in local grain or potato supplies coincided with strong overseas demand. The first eruption was in 1709 following *le grand hiver* and return of famine to France: this drove up Irish (and European) grain prices, raised urban mortality levels, and in March forced the Irish government to prohibit grain exports. The following autumn rumours circulated in Cork that at least three merchants had stocks of corn for export, and this led to trouble in December: 'several papers were dispersed in this city privately, to and from persons concerned with the mob . . . . to meet in arms' in order to pull down the houses of the three offending aldermen. That led the mayor to arrest and imprison two of the organizers, but some nights later,

> a great number of people arose in a very violent and riotous manner, assembled on the East Marsh of Cork, and unanimously ran, armed with guns, swords, staves and other dangerous weapons through the city, still crying out for others to assist them, and swore they would pull down the city gaol (in which these two persons were committed) . . . .

According to press reports, the mayor ordered a drum-beat, and thirty 'gentlemen' with swords drawn faced the crowd, protected the gaol and made several arrests. The Irish Privy Council's response was simply to reiterate the export ban and to warn merchants against engrossing. This novel act of urban protest appears to have involved *literate* participants who had ready access to firearms, and the reaction of both government and corporation was almost tolerant. Professional soldiers were not it seems involved, and there is the strong likelihood that the participants were largely Protestant; the repertoire of protest that they employed was borrowed from England, as similar protests against grain exports had occurred in Bristol the previous May, and more widely during the previous decade.[6]

Then, in the late 1720s, severe food shortages across Ulster had a knock-on effect on southern markets: consumers in the southern port cities, witnessing sharply rising food prices, sought to interrupt the coastal trade drawing oats and meal to the linen districts of the North. The mayor of Cork, Hugh Millerd, himself a leading merchant, refused to impose an export embargo in March 1729, whereupon his house – and several others – was 'torn down in pieces' by a crowd of several hundred 'with clubs and other instruments'. In the weeks following, other less spectacular incidents were reported from Drogheda, Dublin, Limerick, Waterford and several smaller Munster towns, and there is the first evidence that *taxation populaire*, the communally sanctioned re-selling of captured food at a 'fair' price which was well-established in France and England, was becoming commonplace. Later, during the worst food crisis of the century in 1740–41, there is evidence of riots in six of our urban centres (including Galway, Sligo and Belfast), a widening of the targets, and the suggestion of more sophisticated modes of protest. Shippers, bakers, millers and carriers were now at risk, and the participants included skilled artisans, notably weavers and coopers. In the violent protests in Dublin in May 1740, bakers' shops were attacked, ships were boarded on the quays, and suburban mills searched for meal, with it seems several fatalities.

A pattern of consumer behaviour was now firmly set: direct action and the intimidation of suppliers in the years of high food prices became normalized, and although there was often extensive physical destruction of property and the seizure of food for re-sale, there was also an element of negotiation between municipal authorities and riot leaders, whether because of the weakness of the mayor and sheriffs, latent sympathy for the protestors, or a mixture of both. Thus, for the rest of the century, attacks on the premises of exporters and middlemen handling grain, flour, meal and potatoes became a recurring feature in the cities and towns of east Leinster (including Kilkenny) and south Munster, giving plebeian consumers a degree of agency and constraining the freedom of would-be exporters to exploit overseas opportunity.[7]

The official response to that first protest in 1709 – a trade embargo and an armed posse of 'gentlemen' – was palpably inadequate, so that with the return of food protests in 1729 civic authorities now turned to the military: Cork led the way, and the large-scale deployment of troops had predictably bloody consequences ('three or four' fatalities and dozens injured). A few weeks later Waterford Corporation was preparing for a similar call-out (although that proved unnecessary), but in April 1741 when a crowd of artisans in nearby Carrick-on-Suir attempted to prevent grain boats moving down the Suir to Waterford, military intervention led to five deaths. The call for military aid was already seen as a municipal measure of last resort, reflecting badly on city authorities, but sometimes a brief show of military force, as in Kilkenny in June 1765 after days of protests, could settle things immediately. It is striking that in Belfast in the late summer of 1756, where direct action by 'weavers and other tradesmen' menaced leading merchants and gave 'the mob' control of the meal market for several weeks, army aid was requested but was not deployed. Four months later the market house was attacked and emptied of its reserves, whereupon the town sovereign moved immediately to set up 'an association for suppressing riots': 200 armed citizens, not the military, were organized to guard the embattled market house.

In later bad harvest years – 1765–66, 1783–84 and the early 1790s – the repertoire of protest broadened: crowds were larger, the range of commodities attacked greater, the involvement of women somewhat more visible, and the resort to violence against the person more common. In and around Dublin and Limerick, the canal as the artery for the movement of food became a fresh zone of conflict, and there was a particularly violent episode beside the new waterway at Limerick's Lock Mills in May 1772: the mayor called for military support to protect the flour-mill and this led to three civilian deaths. In response, protestors laid the corpses in front of the house of the mill-owner, and the mayor's effigy was carried through the streets, 'a speech in one hand, and a rod in the other, with a rope about his neck, held by a chimneysweep as hangman' – angry street theatre that would have been understood far outside Ireland. The army again intervened and the death toll doubled. That shocking set of incidents seems to have weakened the temptation to call out the military to calm the markets; they were now seen as 'a dangerous remedy'.[8]

However, as in all pre-industrial cities, other ways of deflecting trouble in the markets were constantly being tested and adapted: the ancient responsibilities of mayors and sheriffs to police food markets to prevent hoarding, false weights and measures, food adulteration, or profiteering, were often lazily interpreted, but the few mayors who took great pains to enforce market regulations were acclaimed. In Dublin, the logic behind building an enormous new corn market in 1725–26, set awkwardly in the middle of Thomas St, was to help police such regulations; it forced the city into debt, but the underlying motives were food security and a peaceful city. A substantial corn market was built in Cork in 1739, both for retail and wholesale, and there the upper storey was designated as a public granary; it was indeed used as such the following year when the Corporation engaged in extensive meal and flour purchases from individual merchants (a policy also pursued at that time in Waterford). This however proved financially costly and open to corruption, and in 1766 an alternative Cork scheme, a publicly subscribed fund to buy in grain and sell below cost, was led by Hely Hutchinson. Calls for public subscriptions to provide emergency food aid had been tried in various ways since 1729 (in Cork, Dublin and Drogheda), encouraged initially by Swift's nemesis Archbishop Boulter, and this was pursued far more energetically in 1740–41 in response to the extreme food shortage. It was more than paternalistic grandstanding, for the fears of the wealthy as to what empty markets might mean, in terms both of public order and public health, were well-founded, as was hinted at by Dominic Farrell, a Waterford merchant, in April 1757:

Our mob took about 40 tons [of oatmeal?] that was several miles near this city and retailed it out in our market . . . they vow vengeance against any man that would attempt shipping corn or meal from this [city], and really I don't find any quantity in this neighbourhood so that we dread much a scarce summer; the merchants of this city made a subscription of £1,500 which we intended to lay up in meal and sell to the poor dwellers of town at prime cost but we cannot get any to buy . . .

The most important preventative measure following the 1756–57 crisis was the creation by Parliament of a permanent fund to subsidize the transport of Irish grain and flour from any county outside Co. Dublin to the city's markets: this 'inland bounty' scheme, eliminating carriage costs at a stroke, transformed the supply lines of food coming to Dublin and ended the partial dependence of the city on overseas supplies. The bounty came to be seen as another unfair privilege enjoyed by the capital city, but it remained in place for forty years and meant that until the 1790s there was remarkably little agitation over basic food supplies within the capital at least (see Plate 29).[9]

ARTISANAL PROTEST

If consumers were sometimes moved to protest, so too were producers. Industrial protest – in the sense of collective action by producers taken against their masters, other traders or workers, or even against consumers – was first recorded at the beginning of the eighteenth century when, in 1711, the London press reported that four to five thousand Dublin weavers had gone through the city destroying imported printed linens and calicoes found in shops and on the bodies of the female citizenry. As the Irish Privy Council issued no proclamation in the wake of the story, the reports were clearly exaggerated but they were not implausible. The heated and ongoing controversy in London over the ill-effects of imported East India textiles on the English superfine textile industry (culminating in the 'calico crisis' disturbances of 1719) had an echo in Ireland, not least because of the already very well established traffic of skilled textile operatives between London and Dublin (the two-way movement of Huguenot families was only one part of this).[10]

It was rare for tensions within the workshop to boil over onto the street. Yet there is abundant evidence of journeymen within a number of the crafts organizing to oppose the trade practices of their masters, and of masters using the common law against journeyman 'combinations', even when these were ostensibly 'friendly societies' providing mutual aid to their members. Until mid century such societies were largely a Dublin phenomenon. One or two had particularly deep roots there: journeymen tailors in the 1670s were being legally harassed for organizing a friendly club outside their guild.

But there was a sudden growth in such clubs and in industrial disputes during the 1720s, by which time some nineteen journeyman societies were believed to exist in Dublin. Most, it seems, were related to the unstable textile and clothing sector: terms and rates of employment and the exclusion of apprentices who had served their time outside the city ('colts') were the principal issues, and presumably those involved were for the most part Protestant at that time. In one notorious incident in August 1728, the sheriffs failed to break up a group of 'several hundred' young tailors ('apprentices etc.') who were kidnapping and parading migrant 'colts' from the country on long poles through the city 'with music going before them', days after a colt in another trade had been killed. Over 100 soldiers from the Barracks were called in before arrests could be made. In the following year Edward Lovett Pearce shepherded through Parliament an Irish Combination Act outlawing all such journeymen societies, the first of many statutes that failed to curtail the growth of journeymen organizations. But Pearce's involvement is intriguing: he was at the time overseeing the greatest building project in Dublin, the new parliament building, and was presumably encountering the added industrial leverage of building craftsmen when working together on such a large project (Gandon was to experience very similar pressures during the building of the Custom House).[11]

Journeyman clubs, increasingly common in English towns and cities, were also present outside Dublin, notably in Limerick and Kilkenny, where they were effective in controlling apprenticeship numbers and in protecting real wage levels. But it was the clubs in the capital that appear to have been far more active and pervasive. They eventually incorporated all branches of textile work, printing, baking, carpentry and the other building trades (whether organized in guilds or not), and after mid century many, perhaps most, clubs had a committee structure, kept regular records, issued membership cards, kept a regular 'house of call' (a public house), and some were beginning to employ oaths of secrecy.

Thus, when a far more punitive ban on combinations than that of 1729/30 was under debate in Parliament in 1780, there was a remarkable, albeit momentary, display by the journeymen clubs in Dublin: a crowd of 'journeymen artificers to the amount of several thousand' met in the Phoenix Park in June and planned to process to College Green to present a petition to the Privy Council against the bill, but the mayor 'supported with 1,000 citizens in arms' sent a message to the Park that a group of no more than six would be allowed into the city to present their petition. The assembly dispersed without incident. The speeches and petition have gone unrecorded, but their evident ability to coordinate on such a scale and to maintain a peaceful demeanour throughout the event was a matter of comment, not least because the parade came only days after news arrived of the devastating Gordon Riots in London. It set the precedent for at least one further mass meeting in 1792 of journeymen 'principally in the building line': again a general combination bill, again an assemblage in the Park, but on this occasion parading en masse to the House of Lords to petition against the bill. Legal counsel subsequently represented the journeymen, and Fitzgibbon, the Lord Chancellor, was won over: the bill was quite unexpectedly thrown out.

By the 1790s there was almost endemic low-intensity industrial conflict in Dublin, notably in the Meath Liberty, which revolved around the familiar issues of piece rates, the exclusion of colts and controls on apprenticeship. Almost all of the disputes were in the textile and clothing trades, and for the first time resistance to the introduction of labour-saving machinery (particularly in silk manufacture) was an additional strand of protest. During the 1780s a concerted attempt had been made by several leading politicians, notably John Foster, to encourage the owners of more capital-intensive textile enterprises – new-style cotton spinners and print-yard proprietors in particular – to locate or re-locate at least 10 miles outside the city, away from the supposed scourge of combinations, drunkenness and disorder.[12]

THE FIRST POLICE

The 1780 combination legislation came in the middle of the American War when Anglo-Irish relations were in some turmoil. The security vacuum caused by depletion of regular troops stationed in Ireland to fight in America was the principal reason behind the Volunteer movement in Ireland, what was in many respects a Protestant citizens' militia, independent of and at times hostile towards the Irish government. For some five years the Volunteer movement absorbed and energized the urban bourgeoisie as much as it did the minor gentry of rural Ireland, and it attracted financial support from leading Catholic merchants in the southern cities.

The Volunteer reviews, whether on the Mardyke in Cork or in St Stephen's Green, were theatrical spectacles without precedent. But in terms of security, Volunteer corps played a crucial role in mobilizing against the Dublin

211

journeymen in June 1780 and in enforcing the Combination Act thereafter, creating an unusual degree of industrial calm for several years. It was only after the war and the sharp recession of 1783–84 that trouble returned, and by that time the Volunteers were a greatly diminished force. With very high unemployment affecting most branches of textiles and a misplaced expectation that the Irish Parliament was about to raise import tariffs on cheap English cloth, the spring and summer of 1784 were something of a perfect storm in the artisan districts of Dublin. Extra-parliamentary political protests melded into a wave of industrial violence to enforce another non-importation campaign, and violent action was taken against cloth importers and master manufacturers accused of flouting customary apprenticeship practices.

The presence of firearms and of demobbed soldiery did not help. For some weeks a military company was posted on sentry duty in the Meath Liberty. Government and Parliament were much exercised at this point by rowdy protests in College Green: large numbers of unemployed textile workers from the Liberties harassed MPs who did not support protective tariffs, and on 5 April the Commons gallery was temporarily occupied, a mock speaker elected, and sanguinary resolutions passed. Similar invasions of Parliament had occurred in 1759, in response to rumours of an imminent parliamentary union, and early in 1771, in opposition to the Townshend government's policies. Military support was required on each occasion to protect parliamentarians and overawe the protesters, but this time the anger seemed deeper.

The main consequence of the security crisis in 1784 was a radical innovation for Dublin: a professional police force. The plan was hatched by Attorney General John Fitzgibbon and was a version of what had been envisaged for London but rejected by Westminster in 1785. A uniformed armed Dublin police force was established amidst huge political controversy in 1786; it was answerable to government but funded by the citizenry, and possessed legal powers far beyond those of the old parish constables and watchmen. And while the 1786 force was drastically modified in 1795 as a political sop to the parliamentary opposition, and was strengthened again in 1799, the template of 1786 was epoch-changing. The Dublin constabulary may have struggled to manage the revived industrial conflict of the early 1790s and have played no direct part in meeting revolutionary subversion after 1795, but in visibly patrolling the streets by day and night and by enforcing the by-laws of the city, the uniformed force imposed a new order on the everyday conduct of the capital's 'lower orders', at least in theory (see Plate 30).[13]

10
THE SHUTTING OF THE GATES

The 1790s were a decade like no other. The collapse of the *ancien régime* in France at first excited, then divided the urban world. Where the American crisis in the 1770s had drawn opposing elements in Irish cities together in support of Volunteering and the public articulation of Irish grievances, the French Revolution opened up cleavages and profoundly sharpened social and religious divisions. In December 1779 the exuberant public celebrations that followed the major commercial concessions ('free trade'), extracted from London at a time of imperial weakness, had been a moment of unqualified civic unity, but there was no equivalent moment in the 1790s.

The process of polarization began when events in France were subject to the very different interpretations of Edmund Burke and Tom Paine, and their arguments were extensively reproduced in the Irish print media. But it was the impending Anglo-French hostilities, followed by the drive towards total war in 1793, which greatly hastened the process, given the covert government influence over a string of newspaper titles (initially in the capital and then in at least four provincial centres), the curbs on public assembly, and a degradation of the rule of law that ultimately led to the red summer of 1798: a United Irish-led insurrection, a French landing in Connacht, and the eruption of sectarian violence. Urban Ireland was profoundly affected by the blood-letting in the countryside that year, and it carried a large measure of political responsibility for what happened, for the champions of political reform and the architects of revolution had been almost entirely city folk. Even though the fighting was contained within half a dozen counties, and both rebellion and invasion were defeated within weeks, the events of that year became very deeply imprinted on urban society.

Space for the development of political ideas hostile to the status quo had been consolidating, at least in Dublin, since Swift's unfettered attacks on government in the 1720s, and had been permanently widened by Lucas's use of the printing press and guild-hall hustings in the 1740s. But Lucas's appeal was to disenchanted Protestant freemen. The politicization of those denied civic freedom and without a parliamentary vote, plebeian Catholics, only began a generation later, stirred up by the patriot discourses of more radical Volunteer corps (notably those in Dublin, Cork, Belfast and Derry), and by the general expectation in the early 1780s that political reform, whatever that might mean, was imminent. The *Belfast News Letter* had educated its readers in American ideas over the years, providing remarkably full coverage of American political debate before the Revolution, and American ideas permeated southwards; indeed one army officer in Cork city claimed in September 1775 that 'the lower class [of Catholics] . . . are, to a man, attached to the Americans, and say plainly the Irish ought to follow their example . . .' But for bourgeois Catholics the American crisis brought the prospect of orderly political relief a little nearer.

Some could not wait: the young Mathew Carey, a Dublin baker's son, was unusual in his imprudent willingness to articulate in print the enormity of Catholic grievances. In his *Urgent necessity of an immediate repeal of the whole penal code candidly considered* (partially printed in 1781 but never published), he argued for an inclusive patriotism and asserted that Catholics were being denied 'the inalienable rights of human nature', and prefaced this by repudiating the conventional genocidal view of the 1641 rebellion ('I glory in the war of 1641'). Whatever many may have felt privately, Carey was out of step with the emollient tone of public discourse, and he was despatched in great haste to France by his disapproving family. But when he returned to enjoy brief celebrity – and notoriety – in 1783 as a newspaper editor, he careered into trouble again. His violent criticism of Dublin Castle, of the English connection and of local political heavyweights ended with his flight to America in disguise in 1784.[1]

FROM STAGE TO STREET

Carey's outspokenness was a taste of the future. Public sentiment in the heyday of Volunteering had been relatively benign, quite unlike the polarization of debate in the 1790s. The history of local theatre provides some insight as to how far political attitudes shifted. For most of the century the bill of fare in Dublin's two, sometimes three, theatres had been modelled closely (but not slavishly) on London fashion, and that repertoire was in turn brought to the southern cities in summertime when the capital's theatres fell quiet. Political controversy occasionally disturbed theatre in the capital, as in 1712 when Tory and Whig supporters had assailed each other in the Smock Alley theatre and, more spectacularly in 1754, at the time of the Money Bill dispute: one evening in March the theatre audience turned on Smock Alley's manager, the younger Thomas Sheridan, the largely male audience believing that he had become a mouthpiece for an unpopular government, as evidenced by his attempt to halt the recitation of a partisan prologue. The theatre was pulled apart and its fittings destroyed in six hours of uninterrupted mayhem.

In the following years, parliamentary controversy regularly coloured Dublin theatre, often in allegory and during the entr'acte, and Castle patronage became much weaker. There was a growing sense that audiences were now more heterogeneous and that upper-class cultural dominance was being eroded. However, playhouses in the provincial cities were much smaller and more intimate places (although Cork's third theatre, built in 1760, had an 'immensely large' stage), and the tradition of socially mixed audiences distributed between gallery, pit and boxes, which had always been a feature of Dublin theatres, was less evident. These were precarious ventures for all concerned, but the excitement surrounding Volunteering in the late 1770s brought new material and new audiences, 'with strongly Irish colouration', so that the usual stock of Shakespeare and Bickerstaffe, Cibber and Garrick was varied with far more topical fare. And as the veteran Garrick observed of Cork in 1778, 'every gentleman of the place wears uniform, and is under military discipline', and the militarization of the repertoire followed. 'The Volunteers' and 'Free trade' featured briefly as entr'actes on the Cork stage. In Dublin the actor-manager of Smock Alley, Thomas Ryder, managed to combine free-trade celebrations with his campaign to defeat plans to take theatre regulation out of the lord mayor's hands: he erected great illuminated transparencies in the windows of his Temple Bar house declaring 'Ireland's prosperity, a free trade' beside 'The theatre of Dublin free while the public please and mine be the lot to please the public'. The Corporation supported him and the proposal was withdrawn. The most popular figure then based at Smock Alley was John O'Keeffe, actor and playwright, whose success, Christopher Morash has suggested, lay in the prolific output of gentle comedies that were 'parables of reconciliation, heavily laced with Irish music and displays of landscape', in which he made 'challenging ideas palatable to a wide audience by encasing them in unobjectionably conventional forms'.[2]

The proposal to transfer the power of licensing Dublin theatre to the government was revived in 1785–86 and passed into law, the principal beneficiary being

Richard Daly, Galway actor turned manager; for some years he was sole owner of the two Dublin theatres, as well as those in Limerick, Cork, Waterford and Newry. Daly's near-monopoly gave provincial audiences longer seasons and perhaps the sight of more celebrities, but he was a figure of opprobrium in Dublin, pilloried as the creature of the Castle, and with good reason. It had begun in the tumultuous summer of 1784 when the new viceroy, the Duke of Rutland, was humiliated by parts of the Smock Alley audience during a command performance; at the same time around the corner the refurbished Fishamble St theatre was becoming an increasingly political venue favoured by the government's opponents. The move to tighten theatre regulation played to Daly's advantage, allowing him to get exclusive control over all Dublin theatres for some years, and he played a safe hand. What Lady Morgan later characterized as her father's 'national theatre' in Fishamble St ended its brief history in 1785.[3]

Events in France in 1789 quickly resonated on the Irish stage. In September the Cork theatre mounted *The Triumph of Liberty, or, The Destruction of the Bastille*, an entertainment involving elaborate scenic backdrops. Some weeks later rival stage spectacles, *Gallic Freedom* and *Bastille: The Triumph of Liberty* were drawing audiences in Dublin. But the excitement wore off and, despite huge newspaper coverage, public interest in the events in France was slow to manifest itself, and it was only from 1791 that the 14th of July became a day of outdoor theatre in Belfast, Derry and Dublin. The Belfast celebrations at the Linen Hall involved the five old Volunteer corps, with some 350 men in uniform wearing green cockades. Waddell Cunningham was still a power in the land and a Volunteer captain, but the momentum was now with a younger generation, notably woollen draper and son of the manse Samuel Neilson (1761–1803); indeed the town's democrats were almost all from a Presbyterian background (unlike their Dublin confidant Wolfe Tone, with an Anglican father and a Catholic mother). The choreography for the next year's Bastille Day was even more elaborate, with banners depicting Washington and Mirabeau amidst the many images that were taken in parade across town, street theatre that involved 'at least 20,000 persons'.

The previous autumn Neilson had played a central role in the establishment of a quasi-masonic political club, Belfast's first United Irish Society, and shortly afterwards he chaired the group that launched the *Northern Star* newspaper ('the public will be our guide – the public good our end'). Neilson was also one of the founders of the Dublin United Irish Society, which from the beginning was more like an open political club on the French model than a masonic lodge. These two versions of democratic fraternity marked the beginnings of radical political organization. Both the Belfast and Dublin societies were initially bourgeois, mainly Protestant, and ostensibly political in their objectives; they were united in repudiating the power of the aristocracy and in seeking a radical reform of Parliament in order to achieve an equality of rights (but not of property). That by definition meant full political partnership with Catholics and a common civic identity. The first generation of radicals in Belfast struggled over the implications of total equality with Catholics, and it was only because of the backroom political skills of Neilson and his circle that a resolution supporting citizenship for all creeds was passed at the Bastille Day rally in 1792.[4]

Parallel with these developments was the revival in Dublin of the Catholic Committee, taking its cue from events outside and the new talk of freedom of religion. There were sharp differences over political strategy among its members, but a resolute group of mainly Dublin merchants engineered a takeover at the end of 1791. They then pushed the issue of Catholic political 'emancipation' into the political foreground. In so doing the Committee engendered a visceral Protestant reaction, which was evident most clearly in Dublin itself and within the chamber of Dublin Corporation. A majority of aldermen and common councillors united in 1792 to become the champions of the Protestant status quo, of – in their words – 'Protestant Ascendancy'.[5]

Theatre provided little balm at such a time of rising civic tension. *Democratic Rage, or, Louis the Unfortunate* was one of the few dramatic successes, the work of William Preston (1750–1807), a Dublin barrister with strongly liberal credentials. First staged in Crow St in June 1793, four months after war with France had commenced, it represented the Jacobin regicides with undiluted hostility; it was performed on a further eight occasions in Dublin as well as in Cork and in the small theatre in Galway. It attracted occasional protests from more radical members of the Dublin audience, but went on to be staged in Boston and Charleston, though not in Belfast. Professional theatre there, despite disapproval from the kirk, had been moderately successful since the 1730s. Unlike the pattern in the southern cities the season was not linked to the holding of the assizes and, although some gentry patronage was involved, the repertoire in Belfast reflected urban more than upper-class tastes. But by the end of 1792, political divisions between moderate reformers and democrats within the town were reflected in the newly built theatre in Arthur St, and 'animosities which have so much prevailed at the theatre this last year' came to a head in May 1793 with the staging of *The Guillotine*, a local author's 'imprudent' work. It attributed part of the blame for the fall of the French monarchy to the king's own inactions: it divided pit and gallery into rival camps, so much so that the play was abandoned on the first night. The elegant new theatre remained closed for fifteen months, and the pit and gallery went their separate ways (see Plate 31).

Theatre managers north and south had to tread cautiously, some (as in Belfast) closing business for upwards of three years between 1796 and 1799, and there were still occasional signs of audience discord in Dublin. But with swollen garrisons, the military character and loyalist colour of audiences became more evident. When Limerick's small theatre re-opened on 1 October 1798, less than a month after the defeat of General Humbert at Ballinamuck, the high point of the evening was the gradual revelation of a great transparency of Humbert's nemesis, Marquess Cornwallis, the painted image supported by the figures of 'Justice and Mercy', while the theatre chorus performed 'See the conquering hero' and 'Rule Britannia'.[6]

UNSHACKLING

Five years previously a delegation from the Catholic Committee had arrived in London, in January 1793, 'making a superb appearance, servants etc.' and been presented to King George, to whom they handed a petition seeking removal of the remaining penal laws. Two of the five delegates were one-time denizens of Francis St, Edward Byrne and John Keogh, whose wealth was now apparent to all, the others minor gentry from Counties Galway and Wexford. The merchants were much older than the gentry and perhaps more focused in their objectives. Indeed, the delegation's secretary, Wolfe Tone, noted in his diary after the trip that 'as for merchants, I begin to see they are no great hands at revolutions'. However, the knot of Catholic merchants around Keogh and Byrne had achieved something almost revolutionary in summoning and organizing during the previous autumn a national assembly of Catholic delegates. The 284 attendees had squeezed into the Tailors Guildhall in Dublin in the early days of December where, with some difficulty, they had drafted a petition to the king enumerating the totality of Catholic grievances. It was signed by over 230 participants. In an inspired move, the delegation of five (plus their secretary) travelled via Belfast, where the still-dominant radicals in the town fêted the party in transit. Then over to London where, with war approaching and the political ground well prepared, the levée in St James was a success. The timing of the trip had been good, Pitt's cabinet was already sympathetic, and the follow-up concessions were substantial, being pushed through the Irish Parliament by a profoundly reluctant executive in the months following.

This removed the religious barriers on the parliamentary franchise, on membership of guilds, corporations, and city and county grand juries, and it restored to Catholics the right to bear arms (subject to a property qualification). An unproblematic loyalty oath was all that was otherwise required. But it was permissive not coercive legislation, and its positive effects were slow to show and uneven in their impact: in most urban parliamentary constituencies Catholics holding freehold leases began to appear on the electoral roll of the parliamentary boroughs where freeholders had the franchise, but admission to

Figure 23 'St. Patrick mounted on the Pope's Bull, appearing to the city sages': the jibe was directed at Dublin Corporation and its policy of 'no admission here' – the outright refusal to offer civic freedom to Catholic merchants (suggested by the modest men standing to the right) in the wake of the 1793 Catholic Relief Act.

city freedom was another matter and was entirely at the discretion of indi-vidual corporations.

However, the removal of the offensive oaths that had excluded Catholics from court business for nearly a century did have real impact and transformed the lower branches of the legal profession within a decade, as former notaries and chamber lawyers were now free to enter court. The legal profession throughout the century had been very heavily concentrated in Dublin, but in the southern cities there was now a striking growth of Catholic attorneys (see Plate 32).

The ending of the firearms ban had more immediate effects: within the year, as the search for new sources of military manpower became urgent, a reconsti-tuted Irish militia was established into which tens of thousands of Catholics were recruited, and they became the reserve army for the defence of the country, a process that was paralleled by intense recruitment into the regular army and navy during the decade. But, like everything in the 1790s, such co-option of Catholic Ireland into the service of the Crown was highly controversial.[7]

'1793/a year rendered sacred/to national prosperity/by the extinction of religious division': thus proclaimed the foundation stone on Waterford's great bridge across the Suir. This certainly reflected the sentiments of Sir John Newport, chairman of the group financing the project, senior partner in the city's main bank, and remarkable as an Eton-educated dissenter, 'with a most ardent love of popularity and distaste of the Church [of Ireland]'. But was there any more substance to such a claim? Waterford was distinctive for the degree of religious toleration that had long been in evidence, and Catholic wealth in the city was deeply rooted and substantial. The grant by the Corporation in 1790 of additional ground for the reconstruction of the principal Catholic church, the future cathedral in Barronstrand St in the heart of the city, was a gesture without parallel, and the bishop's decision to award the commission to design and build what became the largest Catholic church in the country to the Protestant John Roberts reinforced the pervading sense of benign toleration. The perceptive Jacques-Louis de Latocnaye on a visit in 1797 reckoned the city was all in all a remarkably well-ordered place, with 'un amour du bien publique, qui ne serait pas de trop ailleurs'.[8]

Of the 284 delegates who had met in the Tailors Hall, only five were bona fide Waterford merchants or traders. One, the veteran banker Bartholomew Rivers, chaired one of the most critical sessions, but Waterford voices made, it seems, no impact on proceedings. However, the Relief Act had immediate benefits for the local Catholic elite: seven of those chosen to sit on the city's Grand Jury in 1793 were Catholic, and even with the spread of 'disaffection' in Waterford's hinterland, radical politics did not get much traction in the city. With pro-emancipation politicians in the ascendant locally and without a significant Protestant artisanry, Waterford was strikingly unresponsive to the new loyalism being minted within Dublin Corporation. By 1797 it was Carrick-on-Suir upstream with its decaying woollen industry that proved more fertile ground for revolutionary messaging. The arrival early that year of the strong-minded and impolitic Thomas Hussey as Catholic bishop of the diocese threatened to raise the sectarian temperature, but after a few months he left the country for several years. And despite the huge conflagration not far away in Co. Wexford, the city stayed quiet through May and June 1798. There were, it is true, a few who were planning to set off a series of fires across the city in support of the Wexford rebels, but some of those implicated were actually Carrick men.[9]

Waterford's small contingent in the Tailors Hall was probably the largest group of provincial merchants in the Dublin-dominated assembly. Overall, just over half the attendees were Dublin-based. Most of these were merchants, manufacturers or retail traders, and a majority of the remainder were 'country gentlemen'. All delegates sat for a city, town or county, and many of the

Table 10.1

Mercantile and Professional Representation at the Catholic Convention,
Tailors' Guildhall Dublin, December 1792

	Merchants and manufacturers	Professionals
Sligo	1	0
Town of Galway	0	0
Limerick city	3	1
Cork city	2	0
Waterford city	5	0
Kilkenny city	4	0
Dublin city	117	11
Town of Drogheda	2	0
Town of Belfast	0	0
Derry city	1	0

Sources: C.J. Woods, 'The Personnel of the Catholic Convention, 1792–93', and 'Gleanings on the Personnel of the Catholic Convention', in *Archivium Hibernicum*, lvii (2003), 26–76; lxvi (2014), 319–40.

Note: There were in addition two merchants representing Limerick who gave Dublin addresses, and these have not been included here.

Dubliners were representing other counties or towns (reflecting in many cases kin or commercial connections).

The four representing Limerick city were wealthy and very prominent, and they all had been supportive of John Keogh's 'democratic' faction in the Catholic Committee. Francis Arthur, developer and Volunteer enthusiast in 1782–83, chaired a session of the Convention; he remained politically active throughout the decade, and in 1797 he re-established his Volunteers as a yeomanry artillery corps. But becoming involved in the city parliamentary election in 1797 may have been a step too far: he earned the enmity of the local political titan, John Fitzgibbon. Arthur's corps was stood down and he was accused of organizing the United Irish movement within Limerick; court-martialled and heavily fined, he was forced to leave the country. His involvement remains unproven, but another major Limerick employer was a key figure in United Irish planning until his flight to France early in 1798: Richard McCormick, Dublin-based woollen manufacturer, who for many years had been a large employer of Limerick city weavers (and who represented Limerick in the Convention). But the other dynasty of Catholic merchants and developers in Limerick, the Roches, stayed close to Lord Kenmare's faction in 1791 and had little to do with the Catholic Committee after that. They maintained good if discreet relations with Fitzgibbon and with the Catholic bishops, and two younger members of the clan, Stephen and John, moved in Cork in 1800 to open what became the first Catholic-owned bank in that city.[10]

None of Cork's leading Catholic houses had been involved in the Convention, which poses the question: why the political silence? Sectarian tensions, papered over in the halcyon days of Volunteering, had risen sharply within Cork's hinterland during the 1780s with the bitter agitation over tithe payments to the Anglican clergy; this had ignited a sustained counter-attack from clerical apologists. But a more persuasive explanation for Catholic quiescence is that, as in the other southern cities, it lacked the 'guildhall and tavern politics' that for forty years had been so much a feature of local politics in Dublin and a training ground for would-be Catholic politicians. Trade guilds in Cork had had no distinct political role: guild members were city freemen and as such took part en masse in the annual election of the city's sheriffs when the Court of D'Oyer Hundred was convened each June. There were no guild elections as such and no bicameral equivalent of Dublin's Board of Aldermen and Common Council, simply the general court which since the 1730s had been stage-managed by a remarkably successful caucus, 'the Friendly Club'; this controlled the nominations to the shrievalty and to all corporate vacancies. It had the unintended consequence of limiting the scope on the city council for political faction and of leaving the business of parliamentary scheming and election manoeuvring to informal spaces within the city.

Catholic relief never became a public issue in Cork during the 1770s or 1780s, with the leading Protestant firms liberal on the religious question. Even in 1784, when the restoration of the franchise to Catholics became a divisive issue in Dublin, it hardly registered in Cork. The city's bourgeois associational culture, its music societies and its dining clubs, while more Protestant-dominated than in other Munster cities, were not exclusively Protestant, and some at least of the city's seventeen Masonic lodges were heavily Catholic. Nor is there any hint that religion divided the clientele in the city's four coffee houses.[11]

Cross-denominational sociability also took institutional form: the first Committee of Merchants, established in 1769 to reform the Cork butter trade (a remarkably durable and successful organization) involved Catholic and Protestant traders from the beginning, and in the 1770s and 1780s there was a series of public initiatives that boasted about their religiously mixed committees (although all with a Protestant majority): the free Debating Society (1771), the Cork Debtors Society (1774), the Public Dispensary (1788), the Cork Library Society (1792), the Cork Friendly Society (1799) – with the joint patronage of the Catholic and Church of Ireland bishops – and culminating with the Cork Institution in 1803.[12]

So were Cork's Catholic leaders simply too comfortable and conservative to get involved in the new politics? It is not that they were in awe of their Kerry neighbour and Catholic aristocrat, Viscount Kenmare. Only one of the sixty-eight signatories supporting Kenmare in December 1791 was Cork-based (Leinster and Galway names predominate), and the disengagement of Cork Catholics from the Dublin-based Committee was probably much older. None of Dublin's merchant politicians, it seems, had links with Cork apart from Edward Byrne: he had commercial and industrial partnerships in the city, but did not use them to leverage support in the lead-up to the Convention in 1792. Cork city's Catholic leaders were not averse to strong talk, however. Edmund Burke's son Richard was the Committee's London-based secretary, but he fell out with the Dublin leadership; despite this he spent three autumn weeks in Cork that year at a critical moment in the planning of the Convention. There he was fêted with public entertainments, first by the Catholics of city and county, then by the bankers and merchants of the city, and for part of the time he was enjoying the hospitality of Lord Shannon in Castlemartyr. It is likely that he was present at a public meeting when a lengthy and finely drafted declaration in support of total emancipation was passed, far stronger than what emerged from similar meetings in Waterford and Galway. Yet such language would not appear to have raised the local political temperature or forced Cork Corporation into the kind of grandstanding elaboration of the 'Protestant Ascendency' that Dublin Corporation had recently indulged in. The presence of Burke junior and the enormous respect that his father attracted as 'local boy made good' may explain the unanimity at the Cork Catholic meeting and the willingness of a majority of the city's Grand Jury to stay (perhaps unexpectedly) on the side of the Catholics.[13]

RADICALISM CONTAINED

Next year 'emancipation' was duly celebrated in Cork city, although only three Catholic merchants received civic freedom and four were empanelled on the Grand Jury. But when in June 1795 the mayor proposed Edward Byrne's name for freedom of Cork, the mood was quite different: his nomination was overturned in the Court of D'Oyer Hundred by 81 votes to 47. Catholic hopes for that final stage of emancipation, Catholic entry into Parliament, had been raised during the Fitzwilliam viceroyalty earlier in 1795, then dashed utterly with his recall to London. But local political heavyweights wanted no more concessions, and it was later observed that 'the absolute refusal of any further boon to the Catholics has roused the resentments of the quietest spirits . . .'

Denis Driscol's eccentric *Cork Gazette* (1790–97) had meanwhile become the mouthpiece for an assertive anti-clerical radicalism, but the few high-status Corkmen drawn into revolutionary politics were Protestant, notably the francophile MP Arthur O'Connor and the two sons of Henry Sheares. During 1797 the revolutionary movement, organized by a particularly ruthless committee, took root in Cork city and by spring 1798 over a thousand men had been sworn and prepared for military action. But divisions among Cork's United Irishmen and the detention of most of the leaders halted the process. Most Catholics of wealth kept their heads down and concentrated on securing military contracts, while their bishop John Moylan ordered his flock to stop 'bewildering your minds in speculations about government, which you cannot comprehend', and he excoriated the 'atheistical incendiaries' and secret societies, and all that they stood for.[14]

No Catholic priest in a Munster city was implicated in plans for insurrection. However, in Drogheda a well-regarded Augustinian, John Martin, was given the United oath by two Franciscans in 1797, and he became for a time 'the principal man' on the local committee. This was surprisingly rash, given that religious tensions in Drogheda had been simmering there for a decade. That seems to have occurred for several reasons: the expansion of Drogheda's coarse linen industry had created a large but poorly paid industrial workforce on the edge of town and some, perhaps many, of the weaving families had come from the unsettled Ulster borderlands. Secondly (and connected to this), much of Drogheda's hinterland had become the heartland of the Defenders, an oath-bound redresser movement that was viscerally anti-Protestant. Their presence was first felt 'in the town and neighbourhood' in 1788, and in 1792 there was a particular flare-up in Co. Louth and up the Boyne valley, leading to the repeated and harsh deployment of the military, with fatal consequences. In the same year Drogheda Corporation, emboldened by its phalanx of more than 400 Protestant freemen (in what was now an overwhelmingly Catholic town), came out strongly against Catholic relief. Meanwhile, despite the opposition of the mayor, a very substantial Catholic parish church was under construction in West St, the first in a century to be built within the old walls.

Two prominent merchants represented the town at the Catholic Convention, but in 1793 both of them, men 'of the first mercantile consequence' were charged, together with five others, with 'conspiring to incite an insurrection', in effect, with being the puppet-masters of Defenderism. After lengthy imprisonments, their trial in 1794 attracted national attention; all were eventually found innocent. Antipathy towards government and particularly towards Speaker John Foster, who had been personally involved in the campaign against the Louth Defenders, remained intense as Foster was presumed to have been the architect of the Drogheda prosecutions. The United Irish organization was late in coming to the town and, despite the explicit involvement of Catholic clergy, the local cells posed no challenge in 1798, perhaps because, to quote the frank assessment of local landowner, Crown solicitor and spymaster John Pollock, 'papists here who were first among the Defenders were the last among the rebels, because they had been so roughly handled by the Speaker and all the Protestant gentlemen of property'.[15]

Kilkenny city was also quiet in 1798, but the explanation there is entirely different. It had been a centre of support for Kenmare's conservative faction in the Catholic Committee, and no local parliamentary politician had opposed

Catholic relief in 1793 or 1795. No leading figure in the city espoused democratic politics. It helped that there was now a young Ormond back in Kilkenny Castle who was determined to keep the political temperature down. The heir to the highly successful local paper, *Finn's Leinster Journal*, had patronized a small Jacobin club, but in 1796 – through Ormond's intervention – he chose to take financial support from government in return for softening the paper's anti-government tone. At the time when Wexford was in flames over the hills there were claims that a 'revolutionary committee' did indeed exist in the city, dominated by the blanket manufacturers who 'were enlisted in Dublin by . . . a carmaker . . . in Thomas St'. The link with Dublin and with the textile heartland is plausible, but blanket makers were in no sense the elite influencers of Kilkenny.[16]

THE CAPITALS OF TREASON

Belfast had played no part in the Catholic Convention and supplied no representative. But in its aftermath Samuel Neilson expressed his anger that the contribution of Belfast's radicals in preparing the ground for the concessions of 1793 had gone unacknowledged. However, as the Catholic delegation was on its way to London, Chief Secretary Robert Hobart was privately in no doubt that 'the source of all the mischief is the town of Belfast'. The 'mischief' was of course more than just the Catholic Convention but the broad front of political dissent ranging from well-dressed Jacobins and emboldened journeymen to Catholic gentlemen now finding their voice. All had been given oxygen by the propaganda successes of the United Irish societies – in print and on the street – in publicizing the political language of rights and popular sovereignty. At first this was more a Belfast than a Dublin achievement. Why so? Was it that Belfast, far from the seat of government and the anxious eyes of aristocracy and gentry, enjoyed greater freedom to take political risks on the streets and at the printing press than radicals in the capital? Perhaps up to 1792 that was a factor, with four of the capital's newspapers controlled or heavily influenced by the government, but thereafter the suppression of the Volunteers and the recurring legal and military harassment of the *Northern Star* would suggest otherwise. However, the chemistry of Belfast radicalism was different from that of Dublin: the town's democrats nearly all shared a Presbyterian background (and they attracted a remarkably high level of support from Presbyterian ministers within the province). In a sense it was a new town: it had grown very rapidly in the previous two decades in a sustained expansion of wholesale trade and manufacturing that peaked in the early '90s, and both bourgeoisie and artisanry shared in this boom. Thus the extravagant support for the French Revolution, evident in the town up to the outbreak of war, came from a community that was newly affluent but politically marginalized.[17]

By contrast, democratic politics in Dublin was a coalition involving the radical edges of the parliamentary world (a few high-profile gentry and lawyers), the (Protestant) guildhall politicians in the Lucas tradition, now led by Napper Tandy, the Catholic politicians, marshalled by a small coterie of wealthy merchants, joined later in the decade, tentatively, by veterans of the journeyman societies. Dismay at the very negative posture of Dublin Corporation and most Dublin guilds in blackballing Catholics seeking freedom in 1793–94, and collective despair at the prospects for political reform following the collapse of the Fitzwilliam viceroyalty in 1795 formed the backdrop to the radicalization of the reform movement. The United Irish Society's capacity to operate as an open political club in Dublin had ended in mid 1794, by which time many bourgeois supporters had faded from view. But from that point a small group of the old leadership set about to rebuild the organization as a sleeping army, the aim being to lobby the French government for military assistance and to offer the oath-bound mass movement as an asset that would assist the French if they arrived. To this end, elements in the Dublin leadership made tactical alliances with artisan and Jacobin clubs in the city and with rural secret societies (specifically the Defenders) whose political aims and religious exclusivity were sometimes in conflict with United Irish principles. The contribution of the journeyman activists is hard to pin down; their defensive priorities to protect their trade and living standards through collective action found almost no support among bourgeois radicals, but Timothy Murtagh has argued that the culture of the journeyman societies was an excellent preparation for their subsequent collaboration with bourgeois radicals; the traditions of 'community regulation, solidarity, practical democracy and a vibrant ceremonial culture' were, he suggests, refashioned first in the cluster of Jacobin clubs and then, from 1796, in United Irish cells, a phenomenon unique to Dublin.[18]

It has been estimated, using the abundant intelligence gathered by Dublin Castle, that in the open phase of the United Irish Society 44.1 per cent of its Dublin membership had been merchants (with a strong bias towards textiles and the clothing trades), 32 per cent gentlemen and lay professionals, and 22.3 per cent 'artisans' (this figure including independent workshop masters).

By contrast, based on some 727 names, it has been calculated that in the revolutionary phase of the movement between 1795 and 1798 merchant involvement fell by more than half to 20.6 per cent, the gentlemen and lay professionals slumped to 9.5 per cent, and the artisan component rose to 35.6 per cent. The retreat of many bourgeois families, Protestant and Catholic, away from advanced politics after 1794 is hardly a surprise; indeed the commitment in the later 1790s of such a large bourgeois rump to a revolutionary movement predicated on foreign intervention and the establishment of an independent republic is the more remarkable. Some of the former leaders stepped back without repudiating their peers who continued to be involved, but several of those who remained were putting at risk very substantial business fortunes that they had accumulated, men like John Sweetman (1752–1826) the brewer, Richard McCormick the woollen manufacturer, John Chambers the printer, Oliver Bond the woollen draper, and his father-in-law Henry Jackson, the great Church St ironfounder. The latter two, Presbyterians of Ulster birth, were critical in maintaining intimate links between Dublin and the Belfast radicals.

News of the huge French armada of December 1796 which, battered by storms, failed to make a landing in west Cork, strengthened the resolve of the conspirators in 1797 and exposed the limitations of the government's intelligence gathering: in this instance 'small state' government amounted to the indefatigable activities of one key individual, the Under-Secretary Edward Cooke. He had 'spymasters', paid informers and a postal service which he used for the surveillance of known radicals, but the problem lay in interpreting the 300 letters a week that were reaching his desk by 1798. However, as Thomas Bartlett has revealed, Cook eventually got on top of his material and helped neuter the revolutionary challenge. More visible in 1797 was government's hurried defence planning, in particular the expansion of the new volunteer reserve, the Yeomanry. That force echoed in its make-up and composition many of the trappings of the Volunteers except that it was kept under government control, albeit with the capacity to adapt to local sensitivities; social standing as much as religion was used to filter out the politically suspect. By June 1798 there were over 3,000 men in the various Dublin Yeomanry corps, lawyers, revenue officials and merchants predominating, and a quarter were mounted. The great majority were Protestant, but in Cork the Legion corps, under the command of Hely Hutchinson's eldest son, the Earl of Donoughmore, included 'many wealthy Catholics'. The Yeomanry's role in securing and policing the cities through the gathering crisis was to be crucial.[19]

Meanwhile, many thousands were being recruited from the cities into the militia, the regular army and the Royal Navy, and these were now predominantly Catholic. Unofficial recruitment of Irish Catholics (into the Marine, the East India Company army and the Royal Navy) had grown from small beginnings during the Seven Years War – they were openly recruited on the streets of Limerick 'for the first time' in 1759 – to huge dimensions after 1793. It seems that by 1801 around 30 per cent of the British army was Irish, and that the cities were disproportionately well represented in this exodus. Certainly Dublin and Cork were particularly prominent in supplying manpower for the navy: 81 per cent of the huge numbers impressed from Ireland during the American War had been recruited in these cities (over 13,000 men), and in the 1790s, 44 per cent of the volunteer mariners declaring as Irish came via these two centres (the Irish share of volunteers in the 1790s has been estimated at 23 per cent of the total naval intake). Despite a history of violent resistance to the press-gang from the 1740s, the business of large-scale recruitment now proceeded with little urban resistance, although the prospect of deployment overseas in 1795 led to the threat of mutiny in both Dublin and Cork (where in September two regiments took over the Grand Parade for some hours and appealed for civic support in their protest until 'canon placed at every avenue of the city' overawed them). Indebted tradesmen and unemployed textile workers in the towns seem to have formed the bulk of those entering military service in the 1790s, a very similar profile to those who were swept up into radical politics.[20]

⊰⊱⊰⊱

Recruitment into regular Crown service in the heartlands of Ulster radicalism was however low. Curtin's list of 210 Belfast United Irishmen active in the years 1795–98 indicates that merchants there occupied a substantially larger proportion of the revolutionary movement than was the case in Dublin (29 per cent), with slightly fewer gentlemen and lay professionals (8.1 per cent), or artisans (32.4). Such figures can only be suggestive, but they reinforce the impression of greater continuity in the leadership group in Belfast until *force majeure* in 1797 gravely weakened the organization and scattered the leadership. Many of Belfast's most enterprising young business leaders and shipowners had been involved with the United movement since its inception: by 1798 some had been banished, some left Ireland of their own accord for ever, and one, Henry Joy McCracken, cotton manufacturer and commander-in-chief of the United

Irish army of the North, was executed in High St shortly after the failed Co. Antrim rebellion.[21]

In Dublin the revolutionary organization actually grew stronger during 1797, helped by an infusion of exiled Belfast talent, and in the following winter revolutionary 'outreach' from the city encompassed most Leinster counties. In early 1798 it was claimed that there were over 130 United Irish cells within the city, most of them possessing few if any offensive weapons. Dublin Castle's intelligence successes early that year (in particular, the nocturnal arrest of most of the Leinster United Irish leaders in Oliver Bond's house in March), coupled with the delays in the arrival of French help, gravely weakened the revolutionary leadership. Nevertheless, the great insurrection of May 1798, based on a coordinated plan to break the communication lines out of Dublin and to seize key buildings within the capital in preparation for the coming of the French, succeeded briefly in the first aim but not the second. The capital was briefly convulsed, and there was something of a short reign of terror. There was a vicious pursuit of urban suspects, and the very visible signs of violent retribution (floggings in Dublin's Royal Exchange and the corpses of prominent court-martialled rebels displayed on lamp posts) left an enduring memory.

But there was no urban revolt in Dublin – or in any other city (although the United Irish captured and held the town of Wexford). The various revolts in south Leinster and east Ulster were suppressed within weeks at great human cost, achieved in the main by the Irish Militia and Yeomanry. Thus it was civil war, in fact if not in name.

Just under a thousand Dubliners took advantage of an amnesty offered in September 1798 by the new viceroy Lord Cornwallis. Few had firearms or weaponry to hand in, and very few were of sufficient standing to appear in the city directories; many were probably journeymen or apprentices. More than three-quarters of those who surrendered gave addresses to the west of Dublin Castle and south of the Liffey: in the old city or the Meath Liberty. Altogether 53 per cent were in the textile or clothing trades (roughly double their share in the total workforce); other luxury trades were poorly represented, as were the building crafts (at 8 per cent), port workers, and those employed in food preparation. Economic insecurity specific to the textile sector may go some way to explain its over-representation, but the fact that there was such a large number of wealthy woollen drapers and woollen manufacturers in leadership positions within the movement – in Kilkenny, Carrick-on-Suir, Cork, Belfast as well as Dublin – suggests that the association since 1784 of agitation for parliamentary reform

Figure 24 The cartoon commissioned by Watty Cox recalls an incident in Dublin's Bridgefoot St a few days before the outbreak of the 1798 Rebellion in Wexford, when yeomen trashed the Rattigan family home and confiscated 'thousands of papers'; Bridget Rattigan ran a successful timber business nearby with her son Edward, but he was (correctly) suspected of being a major United Irish organizer in the Thomas St area, having attempted to rescue Lord Edward FitzGerald after his arrest.

with strong tariff protection had become particularly attractive for an industry entirely dependent on the home market and vulnerable to English competition. But the long history of journeymen clubs, friendly societies and street politics that had been evolving over fifty years in the religiously hybrid world of the Liberties was also a powerful factor in accounting for the skewed distribution pattern of disaffection within the capital.[22]

CODA

Defender activity and its violent suppression greatly disturbed the hinterlands of both Galway and Sligo from the early 1790s, but neither urban community was directly affected by the political turmoil in the countryside until late in August 1798, when General Humbert's small French army landed on the north Mayo coast. Gaining considerable local support, he captured the county town, Castlebar, then moved eastwards in the direction of the lightly garrisoned Sligo. French victory at nearby Collooney caused 'the utmost consternation' in Sligo itself and Protestant women and children crowded onto shipping in the harbour, often having to purchase deck space. Sligo's garrison beat a retreat northwards, leaving 'three hundred [who] marched round the town in arms and resolved to die in its defence. They were joined by a number of Methodists, singing hymns, who were headed by their preacher ...'. The threat soon passed.[23]

Meanwhile Galway prepared for a visit from Humbert too: the town's Yeomanry was largely Catholic, as were its merchants who 'within an hour' of the news raised funds to allow the garrison commander (Hely Hutchinson's second son), together with the Yeomanry, to make haste towards Mayo. According to Hardiman the town was then left without military protection, 'and the Catholic clergy were indefatigable in their exertions to preserve the public peace ... one of the regulars of St Augustine ... [stood] sentinel on the west bridge, to prevent the entrance of disaffected persons ...' That sounds almost too good to be true.[24]

In Derry there were no clerical sentries and very few Catholic clergy in sight in 1798. Charles Abbot, an incisive English observer, had characterized the politics of the city in 1792 as 'the reverse of Belfast. All here are Government men'. True, the Anglican element was much stronger and the local influence of John Beresford pervasive. But as Breandán Mac Suibhne has shown, the American Revolution had deeply affected the Presbyterian north-west, more

Figure 25 'The key of Connacht': Sligo town looking south.

than a few of its emigrants having gained fame in the war, and there was a 'cordiality to the American cause'. The Volunteer movement in Derry and up the Foyle valley had been remarkably vibrant and it had developed a strongly oppositional tone, helped by the (occasional) presence of its colonel, the maverick Earl Bishop. It was a bracing environment for impressionable youths like Oliver Bond, an apprentice haberdasher in the city before he moved south (see Plate 33).

George Douglas, owner of the *Londonderry Journal*, helped develop a lively public sphere: he championed the celebration of the centenary of the siege in 1788–89 and was almost certainly the printer of an early edition of *The Rights of Man, Part I*; he was also involved in the annual Bastille Day celebrations and in the temporary revival of Volunteering. He helped cultivate a distinctly emollient attitude towards Catholic political relief among many city freemen. By 1796 there were some in Douglas's circle of friends who had moved from being patriot Volunteers to republican democrats, their plans being to seize control of the city. Derry became the dynamo encouraging the spread of United organization across the more prosperous parts of the north-west, and the depth of support across both Presbyterian and Catholic districts was sufficiently great to alarm government allies. However Douglas sold his paper to a government supporter, and when news of the French armada reached the city at the end of 1796, the Corporation set about repairing and re-hanging the gates (although the professional military view was that the city could not be defended against French cannon). Once again the gates were closed during the hours of darkness. A small group of radicals within the city still had plans for a northern insurrection during 1797, but the national leadership kept the brakes on. The local leadership was subsequently penetrated by informers, then stripped of their civic freedom, imprisoned, and bounced out of the city. Most went to the United States. But the retribution meted out by Crown forces on their many foot soldiers in the countryside was far more brutal.[25]

As a consequence no rebel army from any quarter arrived to test Derry's gates in '98. Yet the cascade of events that led up to the events of that year had 'closed the gates', there and elsewhere – not, as in 1688, an act of heroic defiance against an engulfing Catholic army, but in a virtual and more profound sense, the closure of an idea. For the creation of a civil society that would transcend religious division and of an Irish polity that could draw its legitimacy from 'the whole people of Ireland' had seemed a real possibility to many of those men and women who reached adulthood in the 1770s and 1780s, not least to the thousands who had paraded in Volunteer uniform and to the tens of thousands who watched their colourful plumage. It had been, in Padhraig Higgins's phrase, a period of 'denser political space', a moment of unprecedented political engagement. But the religious tensions unleashed by the democratic politics of the 1790s collapsed such hopes of a common cause, and old ghosts returned to divide civil society and to re-fortify the virtual barriers. The polity itself was dissolved by parliamentary union in 1801.[26]

11
PARTINGS

On the evening of 10 September 1825 the principal streets on Dublin's east side were bathed in gaslight for the first time. Within a few weeks all the city's arteries were lit up and the 6,000 old street-lamps discarded. The manufacture and distribution of oil or coal-gas for public and domestic illumination was a new technology, developed in wartime England and pioneered in London. Despite signs of an early transfer of the new technology to Dublin, there had been more than seven years of talk and litigation while citizens lamented 'the deplorable state of darkness' before the Irish capital entered the age of gas lighting (although Dublin in 1825 was ahead of most big cities outside Britain). Gas installation was also underway in Drogheda, Cork, Waterford and Limerick's Newtown Pery, all anticipating safer streets at a lower cost. Where once walls and toll-gates had declared the boundaries of cities, now the nocturnal divide was between the darkness of the *banlieu* and the amply lit city sidewalks. And it was largely English capital as well as English science that drove this revolution.

Gaslight came a century and a quarter after the first communal lighting schemes in Dublin: from the 1690s there had been a variety of arrangements both there and in the Munster cities, none of which proved satisfactory, whether through poor oversight of the contractors, inadequate finance or petty vandalism. In Dublin there had been incremental improvements in luminosity and in the level of coverage during the eighteenth century, but servicing the shark-oil, rapeseed or tallow lamps remained labour intensive, costly and troublesome. Efficiency improved with the reform of Dublin Corporation's Paving Board in 1784, but the Liberties were only brought within the Board's control in 1808, after which time the lamp standards, 'formerly crowded together . . . [were] now judiciously distributed over every part of the city'. And in Cork, where there had been

400 lights in 1743, reforms in the 1780s expanded the coverage and by 1820 there were some 3,000. 'Within the lights' became a new marker for city limits, all the more pronounced when the 'brilliance' of gas-lit streets arrived.[1]

Belfast turned to gas even more swiftly. Lighting and other utilities (including the watch system) had been actively managed in the town since 1800 by statutory commissioners and, under them, an elected and far more active Police Committee. By the 1810s the latter had strengthened its role and assumed modest planning functions as well as exercising moral oversight of the streets, and the town's first quasi-sectarian riot in 1813 no doubt increased their vigilance. They agreed a contract with London ironmongers in 1822 for the new technology and in the following autumn, two years before Dublin, 14 miles of gas pipes 'to our lamps, shops, factories, inns and private houses' went 'live' and the streets lit up.[2]

But as high streets became brighter, many houses in older neighbourhoods, particularly in the southern cities, were darkened. An over-crowded underworld in the murky lanes, courts and alleys was nothing new, but the deliberate blocking out of daylight was. The specific cause was the window tax, an old and unpopular levy in England, which had been introduced into Ireland in 1799 as a wartime measure. Houses with fewer than six windows were exempt, but all larger houses, even when crowded with multiple 'roomkeepers', were included. The tax principally affected urban dwellers: Dublin and the nine provincial centres generated between them approximately three-quarters of net tax receipts, and in some towns window tax probably exceeded all locally imposed utility taxes. In 1799/1800, the only year for which such data exist, just under half of Belfast houses had sufficient windows to be taxed, and Limerick, Waterford and Derry were not far behind; the ratios for Dublin and Cork are not extant, but it appears that of our ten centres the laggards were Galway (less than a third with six or more windows), Kilkenny, and Drogheda, where only 15 per cent of its houses reached the threshold (see Appendix 7).

Doubtless there were anomalies in the administration of the new tax, but such a ranking is suggestive: despite recent rapid growth, much of Belfast's housing stock was clearly multi-storied; it also points to the substantial number of larger houses in the Munster ports, set against the far more modest housing stock in Kilkenny and Drogheda. Reinforcing this impression are the hearth-tax returns, available for seven of our ten centres in the three years 1797/98 and 1799/1800. All single-hearth houses in the country had been exempted from

Figure 26 The 'S[outh]-W[est] view of the town of Galway' from the Claddagh district, drawn by P. Duggan for James Hardiman's *History of Galway* (1820).

the hearth tax since 1791, and in the seven cities and towns more than half of *all* householders were now exempt from the tax: Limerick had the lowest exemption level, Drogheda once again the highest, suggesting a proliferation there of single-storey cabins on the margins. The hearth tax was another impost chiefly felt in the towns; Dublin city contributed around a third of national revenue accruing from the two taxes during the wars. But window tax was much the heavier burden, all the more so as it was regularly increased, notably in 1811, stirring up protests in the capital.

RECESSION

With the coming of peace there was a concerted campaign in Westminster, led by Dublin and Cork MPs, to have the great war-tax abolished. Older inner-city parishes carrying historically high valuations at a time of falling property values were seen as particularly disadvantaged. A large proportion of the windows in poorer streets in Dublin, Limerick and possibly elsewhere were now partly bricked up (this only gave tax relief from 1816), and the consequent 'putrid air' and lack of ventilation was believed to have greatly exacerbated the deadly typhus epidemic that afflicted Dublin and most Irish cities in 1816–17. The reduction and then cancellation of the window tax in 1822 reflected the impact of such concerns.[3]

The torrent of post-war complaint about taxation, local and national, was symptomatic of deeper changes underway. Indeed the high level of tax exemption already evident in every city in 1800 was indicative of the brittleness of most urban economies even then, coming after the sharp economic downturn of 1797, the collateral effects of '98, and the food crisis of 1799. During the Napoleonic Wars urban poverty almost certainly intensified everywhere south of Belfast. This was principally the result of the differential effects of inflation on urban incomes, rentiers gaining, most wage-earners losing out, although construction workers and service sector workers benefited from the wartime agricultural boom. But most urban artisans across the textile sector (apart from cotton weavers) lost status and income. This was first evident in Dublin, Cork and Limerick, but after 1815 in Kilkenny and Drogheda as well. A wave of commercial bankruptcies in 1810, principally affecting cotton and woollen manufacturers in Dublin and Cork, was a warning of things to come.

The comprehensive post-war fall in agricultural prices hit both farmer and landlord, and this contributed to a sharp rise in migration to town and city, now less a search for new opportunities, more a refuge migration from an under-employed and agitated countryside. The decade after Waterloo was a time of troubles for most rural sectors, and for those who had a stake in the land the worst came in 1820: a tidal wave of bankruptcies that summer was precipitated by the collapse of the Roches' Bank in Cork. That brought down no less than seven other private banks – two in Limerick, one other in Cork, and one each in Waterford, Kilkenny, Clonmel and Dublin, leaving only two banks of any size still trading in the Munster cities. But for those without a stake in the land, the abnormal seasons, multiple harvest failures and encompassing fevers of 1816–17 were the time of greatest extremity, the worst since the 1740s (and they were repeated on a smaller scale in the south and west in 1821–22). The consequential inflow of 'rejected country cottiers' to the cities was blamed, perhaps too quickly, as the source of the 'fever plague'. But the breakdown in urban public health in 1817 was also the result of general food shortages, coming at a time of soaring artisan unemployment. Nevertheless the severity of the fall in urban business activity reflected a general collapse in rural demand and consumer spending.[4]

The most tangible legacy of the post-war crisis in Dublin was the Mendicity Institution, established in January 1818 to document, clothe, feed and employ able-bodied beggars on the capital's streets (but not to house them). 'The Mendicity' was an eighteenth-century response to a nineteenth-century crisis. It was technically a non-denominational voluntary association of wealthy merchants and professionals that included a handful of Catholic churchmen, but it was in fact a typically Protestant-led initiative that depended on the voluntary efforts of a few and the munificence of the settled citizenry at large. Charity concerts and newspaper appeals were used for early fund-raising, but public subventions – via the city Grand Jury – were soon necessary to sustain operations. But the Mendicity had a flair for publicity (as when in the first year it paraded some 2,000 registered beggars through the east-side streets to whip up support). The precedent was immediately followed in Limerick.

CHARITABLE PURPOSES

Exactly a century previously a group of surgeons had established the first 'charitable infirmary' in Dublin, and since 1718 at least a dozen other 'voluntary' hospitals were opened in the capital, plus at least treble that number of dispensaries and asylums (for unmarried mothers, widows, the blind, servants, and the elderly). All of these initiatives were the work of voluntary groups, some with denominational affiliation, most without, but very few had more than token Catholic representation. Parliamentary largesse was crucial for some, notably the largest, the Lying-in Hospital, which became a city landmark. Its luscious celebration of philanthropy in the magnificent stuccowork of the hospital chapel embodied the underlying ideology of many of these initiatives – the Christian duty of giving to the poor, who would always be there to receive. By any measure the quantum of charities in Dublin was impressive, and indeed this became something of a city boast, but provincial emulation followed: the first voluntary infirmaries were established in Waterford (in 1740), Cork (1744), Limerick (1773), and Belfast (1774), and by 1818 there were at least eleven hospitals in the nine provincial centres.

The great expansion of voluntary hospitals mirrored similar initiatives in eighteenth-century England and Scotland, but the standards of management of Irish city hospitals at the end of the period stood favourable comparison with Britain. Almost all Irish physicians who entered the profession before 1800 had been educated in the world outside – in Edinburgh, Leiden, Paris or

Rheims; thus the 'Medical Enlightenment' embodied in these initiatives can be seen as a reflection of the distinctive openness of the medical profession to new thinking in the world outside.[5]

The Mendicity was the third attempt to provide a workhouse for able-bodied beggars in Dublin; the first establishment (1702) became the city's Foundling Hospital, the second, the House of Industry (1773), a multi-purpose agency that increasingly specialized in aiding those who could not work. All such eighteenth-century foundations had started as voluntary bodies and depended on 'an economy of concerts, assemblies and subscriptions', helped by bequests, lotteries and, particularly, charity sermons (one estimate of the 1790s reckoned that no less than £50,000 a year was raised in Dublin by such sermons). But most welfare bodies ended up, after 1800 if not before, dependent on subventions from the city (in the form of Grand Jury grants levied on all householders) or from the state (in the form of parliamentary grants), or both. The first hospital to become entirely dependent on parliamentary support was the large Lock hospital in Dublin's south docklands, which from 1792 catered principally for female patients suffering from sexually transmitted diseases. Government support for other charitable trusts was always slow in coming, but Dublin institutions, even in post-Union times, always found it easier to extract such support than did the provincial ones.

The sophistication and complexity of voluntary action can be read in several ways: the great bequests of Doctors Steevens, Dun and Swift, each of which was sufficient (sooner or later) to fund the construction of a city hospital in Dublin, reflected the particular religious and professional beliefs of the donors. But most of the new ventures, in Dublin and elsewhere, were strongly reactive, the response at times of food crisis to the presence of denizens and strangers begging on the streets, and to the fear of the famine diseases that invariably followed in their wake: 'motives of self-preservation and public policy operated to enforce the suggestions of benevolence'. The enormity of the Frost Famine of 1740–41 influenced the establishment of the first Cork infirmary (the North) and may have been the trigger for Mosse and his maternity hospital project in Dublin, an idea born in bad times which blossomed to greater things in the expansive 1750s. Dublin's two fever hospitals, the Hardwicke and the much larger Cork St, were established shortly after the food crisis of 1799–1801: the latter, laid out on a 3-acre site, aimed 'to relieve the destitute poor afflicted with fever, and to check the progress of contagion'; it attracted an initial public subscription of more than £9,000, with several of the wealthiest business names among the trustees.[6]

20. Elaborate mausolea and obelisks memorializing several of Belfast's principal merchant dynasties (notably the Greggs, Cunninghams and Batesons) populate Knockbreda churchyard, and they are silhouetted in Andrew Nicholl's *Belfast from Knockbreda church*.

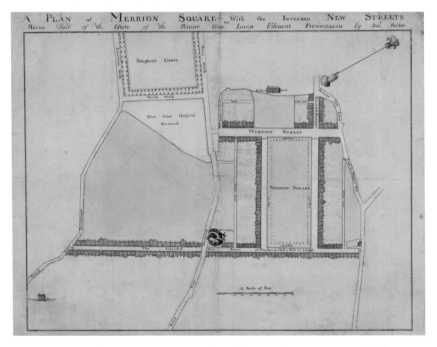

21. An early draft of plans in 1764 to transform the FitzWilliam estate on Dublin's southside and create a new rectilinear square and the future 'Georgian mile', Fitzwilliam St.

22. Unfinished prospect: Samuel Brocas sr, *The bishop's palace and Mall*, Waterford, *c.* 1812.

23. Michael Shanahan's controversial new bridge across Cork's North Channel, which included a drawbridge (R) to allow continuing access for shipping to the higher quays.

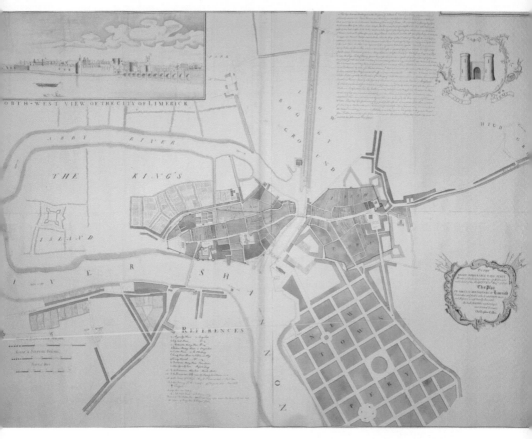

24. David Ducart's original plan for Newtown Pery does not survive, and whether it was faithfully reproduced or significantly adapted by his assistant Christopher Colles in this, the latter's map of the city in 1769, remains unknown.

25. The iconic image of the just-completed showpiece: Thomas Malton, *Custom House, Dublin*, 1791.

Houses designed by G.R Pain Architect
for site between Academy St. and French Church St. –

26. In an echo of the designs favoured by Dublin's Wide Streets Commissioners, one of Cork's principal post-war architects, G.R. Pain, proposed a striking integrated facade for a set of three shops on the Academy St/Patrick St intersection, *c.* 1825. It seems a simpler facade was chosen.

27. Joseph Tudor's *A prospect of the Library of Trinity College, Dublin* (1753) gives a birds-eye view from the west and includes an ensemble of older College buildings and, in the distance, Ringsend, Irishtown, Dublin Bay and Howth.

28. A new street trade – newsprint: Hugh Douglas Hamilton, *Rare news in the Evening Post*, c. 1760.

29. Both Waterford's Custom House (L) and the Exchange beside it were quite old by the time J.T. Serres painted the scene in 1787, but the adjacent quay remained the epicentre of the port and was the stage for confrontations over food exports.

30. The carnivalesque riot in John Nixon's characterization of life on Dublin's Patrick St (*c.* 1790) may exaggerate but does not deceive.

31. The ambitious scale of Belfast's new Arthur Square theatre, opened in 1793, is striking, but its subsequent repeated closures reflected a polarized community.

32. The political dominance of the Beresfords in Co. Waterford was less evident in the city of Waterford, but the choice of James Gandon to design the new county and city court house-and-gaol on Ballybricken Green certainly indicated direct Beresford influence. This led to the construction of a very fine composite building (1784–87), but some sixty years later it was completely demolished.

33. The opening of the great Foyle bridge in 1791 hastened the development of Derry city south-east of the walls and new quays were built, but the most valuable property still lay within the old city.

34. The Belfast Charitable Society, founded in 1752, opened a workhouse for the town's able-bodied poor in 1774, at a time when other cities were establishing similar 'houses of industry' after the passage of enabling legislation in 1772. But the striking location for the charity, prominently overlooking the town, was unusual.

35. Sackville St, Dublin, the great boulevard envisaged by Luke Gardiner sr in the 1740s, only became a completed reality in Napoleonic times, and the decision to erect the great commemorative pillar for Horatio Nelson on the street (1806–9) and to locate the General Post Office nearby (1814–17) reinforced the sense that this was now the centre of the post-Union city.

36. Despite the very constricted site in Dublin's Marlborough St, the Catholic metropolitan church or 'Pro-Cathedral' (1814–25) became an unambiguous statement of changing times. Its chaste Doric order reflected the instincts of Archbishop John Troy (1739–1823), the champion of the building project for nearly forty years. However the influence of John Sweetman, brewer, art connoisseur and exiled United Irishman, in the choice of design remains tantalizingly unclear.

37. 'An extraordinary woman and loves to be thought so': Martha McTier's two-edged verdict on the Countess of Moira in 1797. She was second only to Emily, Duchess of Leinster as an exceptionally well-connected and widely read society hostess, but unlike the duchess she continued to frequent her Usher's Island mansion in Dublin for more than half a century. She was a patron of literature and young writers (including Maria Edgeworth), and of culture and the arts, and was close to but never compromised by her radical friends, although she allowed Moira House to become a discreet political sanctuary in the 1790s and 1803.

38. Like many canal projects, there was a huge time-lag between the inception of the Limerick navigation project in the 1760s and the first realization of its commercial value in the 1820s, when services linking the city to middle and lower Shannon began to operate. At the time of this unattributed painting (c. 1826) the canal stores were quite overshadowed by the nearby Lock Flour Mill and the Canal Brewery, but no other development was visible on the swampy north-east side of the city.

PARTINGS

BELFAST APART?

The Belfast Charitable Society, a consortium of leading merchants, opened a small fever hospital in 1794; twenty years earlier it had overseen the building of a poor-house, orphanage and infirmary. But unlike the relatively obscure locations of Cork's infirmary or Dublin's House of Industry, the trustees chose an elevated site for their building with an elegant sub-Palladian facade and spire (see Plate 34). Robert Joy, co-owner of the *News Letter*, was responsible for the design and, together with the other families who had promoted the project, he remained intimately involved with the institution. Following the precedent of the Rotunda, the Society let out its elegant rooms for hire and it was also financially innovative, becoming contractors for the supply of piped water to the town in 1792 and later in the decade opening a civic cemetery on its property. As in other workhouses, the Society employed its able-bodied inmates, but in 1777, a little unusually, Joy and a partner set up cotton-spinning and carding machines within the building. The children employed to work these novel devices became the pioneers of the cotton industry in Ireland.[7]

Half a century later the Belfast skyline was very different, dominated by a small number of multi-storey buildings, most of them steam-powered cotton-spinning mills, and they formed part of an integrated cotton economy built on private capital that developed in the inner Belfast region; it was completely dependent on the overseas supply of both coal and cotton. By the 1820s a few were experimenting with machine weaving, but the handloom was still dominant: since the 1780s young migrants in their thousands had been drawn to settle around the mills and the cotton printing yards. The Springfield mill was the first in town to install a steam engine (*c.* 1791), from which time milling enterprises had grown in scale and number, almost all of them dependent on female and juvenile labour, with the male workforce staying at the domestic handloom. Dubourdieu estimated in 1812 that there were some 16,500 cotton weavers in and around Belfast, taking work from several dozen manufacturers. However, the post-war recession hit hard and there were unprecedented labour disputes in 1815–17. But weavers' earnings recovered strongly until the sharp recession of 1825–26. According to one contemporary audit, close on a third of all the capital employed in Belfast trade and manufacturing was by then invested in the cotton and linen firms.

The largest of the Belfast cotton spinning mills, the six-storey giant in York St erected in 1824 by Thomas and Andrew Mulholland, marked the high point for an industry that had powered the growth of Belfast since the 1780s, creating new suburbs across the river and to the west, and re-casting the business community. The Mulhollands' father had come from poor beginnings, and many of the other cotton manufacturers had an artisan or shop-keeping background. In a highly volatile market, business failure was very common and partnerships short-lived. Then, in June 1828, their great mill was destroyed by fire. The accident was the catalyst for the ever-enterprising Mulhollands to abandon cotton and use the insurance money to construct a huge flax mill instead, incorporating the new technology of wet-spinning. It was a success and they were quickly copied, from which time Belfast emerged to become the 'linenopolis' of Europe.[8]

The Mulhollands' great investments had involved English and Scottish partners; several of the pioneering Belfast cotton manufacturers in the 1780s and '90s had come from across the water, and there was a continuing inflow of skilled operatives from the north of England and Scotland to the town and environs. Belfast's inherited strengths, its broad-based expertise in the finishing and wholesaling of fine linen, its relatively strong but informal capital market, its close ties with Lancashire and the Clyde, and its direct trading links with the United States and the Caribbean had created an attractive habitat for investment in fine cottons. The industry was, on balance, a valuable apprenticeship for Belfast, and the profits accumulated in cotton powered the take-off of the factory linen industry.

In the South cotton was something of a false dawn. In the 1780s the Irish Parliament, the Linen Board and the Dublin Society had all actively encouraged the creation of out-of-town 'Manchester manufactories' (vertically integrated cotton enterprises) in villages near Dublin, partly as a measure of import substitution, partly as a way of drawing 'turbulent' weavers out of the Liberties. This was replaced in the early 1790s by a policy favouring higher import tariffs on printed calico and muslin, immediately stimulating heavy investment in spinning and cotton printing. There were twenty-three cotton print-yards operating in Ireland by 1800, more than half of which were near Cork city or Dublin; thousands of weaving jobs were created by these enterprises, but when Sadliers, the largest Cork firm, failed in 1801 the wider manufacture thereabouts abruptly withered. Employment in all branches of the Dublin manufacture peaked at around 9,000 by 1809, and only in Belfast did the demand for cotton wool and yarn remain resilient up until the late 1820s.

There were however several common factors in the Irish manufacture of cotton. The first was labour costs: this was the one area where Irish firms had comparative advantage over English and Scottish competitors (at least in the unskilled categories), and the huge numbers employed in spinning shops and print-yards, north and south, were predominantly women and children with little or no bargaining power. The second was the palpable uncertainty as to the effects of free trade, whenever it might come, on their market dominance, for it was the Irish consumer on whom they all primarily depended, and that in itself was a great weakness. The Union compromise of 1800 had allowed for a staggered reduction of import tariffs on most commodities, beginning in 1808, with the final removal scheduled for 1820; this was delayed but was finally implemented in 1824, a time when the wholesale prices of cotton cloth were falling internationally. A recession in 1825 became the depression of 1826. Belfast's army of cotton weavers were badly affected, but the large-scale dumping of cheap English cottons on the Dublin market was the proverbial last straw. Free trade (and the currency amalgamation of 1826) arrived at the worst possible moment for the vulnerable textile sectors, and in the autumn of that year all Dublin's hospitals and fever sheds were under siege with thousands awaiting admission, arising from a public health crisis that flowed directly from industrial collapse. Only a bespoke silk and poplin industry survived.[9]

THE NEW DISPENSATION

In the southern and western cities the economic future now lay with food processing and alcohol production, and the proliferation of tall grain stores and drying kilns in every port (including Sligo and Galway) reflected the massively increased volumes of wheat, flour and oats being collected and despatched to Scotland and the north of England in the post-war years. Parallel to this the scale of maltings, flour mills and distilleries was transformed within a generation. But the leviathans in the sector were the porter breweries: in Dublin and Cork a handful of firms capitalized on tax and regulatory changes in the 1790s and helped cultivate a new taste among townspeople for local ale and porter.

In Dublin the Guinness brewery, half a century old in 1809, was by then responsible for a quarter of all malt liquor sales made by the city's top nine breweries, and it was far ahead of its competitors; production fell back after the war, but the firm's flour-mills in nearby Kilmainham helped maintain profits. Beginning in the mid twenties Guinness began to export 'Dublin porter' to Liverpool, Bristol and London, and by 1840 around 60 per cent of its sales of porter were being made in England. The dominant Cork brewery, Beamish & Crawford, was located within the old city; it expanded spectacularly during the French wars and controlled an even larger share of civil and military consumption in Cork than did Guinness in Dublin, and remained the largest brewery in the country until the 1830s. But after the wars, output fell and the firm diversified into tied houses, property and flour-milling; their vast Lee Flour Mills, erected in the late 1820s, were among the largest in the country and dominated the western approaches to the city. Both firms were heavily capitalized enterprises, prudently managed and built up through the reinvestment of profits; in these respects they differed from the typically short-lived 'capital manufactories' of the eighteenth century. And they differed also in that the labour force was relatively modest; both breweries were located near some of the poorest neighbourhoods of their cities, yet they had very limited impact in alleviating local unemployment.[10]

The economies of scale that both firms exploited were greatly facilitated by transport improvements: in the case of the Guinness brewery, the Grand Canal became the principal corridor for sourcing malt and barley from their prime suppliers in the south Midlands, and both Cork and Dublin brewers were beneficiaries of the transport revolution on the Irish Sea in the 1820s that resulted from the introduction of steam-powered paddle steamers. The first scheduled cross-channel passenger services linked Belfast with Greenock (1818) and with Liverpool (1819), and Cork with Bristol (1821), while small shipbuilders and iron-founders in the two ports were quick to compete with English suppliers in the manufacture of marine steam engines. But the greatest opportunity lay in the provision of the fast and regular links between Dublin, Liverpool and Holyhead. Both Liverpool and Dublin capital was involved, but it was principally a Dublin story: passenger and mail cross-channel services ran intermittently from 1820, but the major breakthrough came with the opening of an all-weather service to Liverpool by the City of Dublin Steam Packet Company, designed primarily for cargo; this became a daily service in 1826, and the fourteen vessels involved by 1830 represented a capital investment of a quarter million pounds. Charles Wye Williams (1779–1886), a Dublin-born gentleman engineer, 'reckless and brash', was the key figure in building up the company and his involvements stretched far beyond the Irish Sea.

With the shipping revolution of the 1820s (and the completion of major road and bridge construction in Wales), travelling time between Dublin and London was almost halved, and the impact of this on Anglo-Irish trade was profound and immediate. For the new English consumer industries, the Irish market was opened up anew; for Irish provincial merchants, distance from their suppliers was shrunk, and transaction costs – with customs duties now gone – dramatically lowered. But it was the trade in live cattle and pigs, in eggs and flour, that brought most profit to the shipping companies, benefiting Drogheda and Waterford as well as Dublin's North Wall, but offering little consolation to the butchers, the coopers and the tallow chandlers in the heart of Cork and Dublin when faced with the eclipse of the old processing industries. In the longer run Belfast was the greatest gainer by the transport revolution, its share of ship tonnage invoiced rising at a time when all southern ports except Waterford were losing ground.

In the bitter political debates of the 1830s over the consequences of parliamentary union, advocates of Repeal blamed the dismantling of tariffs between 1816 and 1824 as the cause of the collapse of the old textile industries of the southern towns, but the causes of de-industrialization were complex and ran much deeper. The shift in the international terms of trade between farm products and factory products in favour of the former, now being driven by British industrialization, hollowed out artisan economies. Much of what had created wealth in the eighteenth-century city was ebbing away.[11]

CAPITAL MATTERS

Gaslights and steamships, free trade and cheap cotton were facilitated by a financial system that was itself undergoing rapid change. During the French wars and the era of cash suspension by the Bank of Ireland, there had been a mushrooming of small private banks, most of which had issued their own bank notes. The majority were short-lived, but the crash of summer 1820 was distinctive because it brought down some of the largest banks in a short number of weeks, businesses unable to adapt to deflationary times or to the Bank of Ireland's tighter controls over money supply. Among the many wartime banks, three were established in Belfast in 1808–09 that were nothing exceptional in themselves, building on smaller eighteenth-century predecessors, except that for the first time their bank paper managed to dislodge the persistent preference for gold specie that had been a distinguishing feature of the Ulster economy. The turbulence of 1820 reached the Belfast banks, but all three survived. Then, in the wake of legislation liberalizing Irish banking in 1821 and 1824, one of them, Montgomery's, was re-launched as a joint-stock venture, the Northern Bank.

This was modelled on well-tried Scottish precedent and the share call was over-subscribed: of the 221 who became its first shareholders, 87 per cent were from east Ulster, 54 per cent specifically Belfast-based. In 1827 the two other private banks joined forces in a defensive alliance to become the Belfast Banking Company; this entity was more strongly embedded in the linen trade and drew on a wider geographical field of investors, but shareholders were drawn almost entirely from the province of Ulster. Slow to push operations outside Belfast, both banks projected their influence through nominated agents in larger Ulster towns. Their successful capitalization signalled both the strength and confidence of the town's business and professional classes, and for several years their shares traded at a hefty premium – even though, as Philip Ollerenshaw has revealed, control over both firms remained in the hands of the old partners.

In Dublin the Bank of Ireland's monopoly, although trimmed, still determined the banking landscape. The circulation of its bank paper through most of the country had increased dramatically after 1820 but because of its conservative reputation, both financially and politically, there was growing resentment of its power. Thus, parallel to the launch of the Northern, a consortium of Catholic and Quaker merchants established the Hibernian Bank in Dublin with a capital set at a million pounds (identical to the combined capital of the two Belfast banks); in the initial call in 1824, £563,550 was raised for this 'opposition' bank; remarkably, 23 per cent of the sum came from 229 merchants and professionals based in Kilkenny and the Munster cities, and 7.5 per cent from 112 subscribers in Drogheda, Galway and Sligo; a mere £300 were subscribed in Belfast and nothing in Derry.

The promoters had to turn to London for additional financial support, but once in operation the Hibernian was restricted by the Bank of Ireland's privileges and remained little more than a deposit and discount office, much to the frustration of provincial investors who had expected it to fill the vacuum left by the bank failures of 1820. However, it was an English-managed and English-funded initiative, the Provincial Bank of Ireland (1826), that brought new-style branch banking and a professional cadre of managers (mainly Scots) to the provinces, with branches set up in all but one of the principal urban centres within a year (Drogheda at first lost out, being within the 50-mile zone where the Bank of Ireland enjoyed monopoly privileges over banknote issue, and the Bank only opened a branch there in 1834). Shares in the Provincial were far more volatile than those of the Belfast banks, and neither it nor the Bank of Ireland, which moved hesitantly into branch banking, had much impact in

Belfast. That reflected a deeper shift in the North away from its old dependence on Dublin for the discounting of bills and other banking services. Cotton millers and linen manufacturers in the Belfast region were now integrated financially as well as commercially with cross-channel markets, and the progressive weakening of links with Dublin was just one element in fracturing the formerly unchallenged national role of Dublin's money market.[12]

MOVING OUTWARDS

Dublin became a destination for travellers after the French wars, with a succession of guidebooks presenting the city in strongly positive terms with a lively season (now in spring) and some forty hotels, several of them refurbished taverns, in the central city area. The legacy of public building and street improvements from the previous century was now supplemented by a spate of new churches (of all denominations), public monuments of war heroes (Nelson, Wellington), hospitals, prisons and barracks, with several of the principal Wide Streets projects – notably Sackville St – only now being completed (see Plate 35). An enormous Greek revival Catholic 'pro-cathedral' was emerging a stone's throw from the Beresfords' townhouse in Marlborough St – changing times indeed (see Plate 36).

Yet there was a compelling trope that the few writers of fiction of the period who wove Dublin into their plots (Maria Edgeworth and Lady Morgan, Charles Maturin and John Banim) could resist: Dublin had changed, had lost its old aristocratic heart, its *raison d'être*, since the Union. Edgeworth was optimistic that a reformed urban society could now emerge, whereas Morgan characterized the capital in 1818 as 'still, silent, and void'. And Sir Jonah Barrington's widely read *Personal Recollections*, which first appeared in 1827, helped establish the conventional belief that pre-Union Dublin was a raffish world, now lost.[13]

Those who visited the new home of the Mendicity Institution, Moira House on Usher's Quay, saw it as a compelling symbol of Dublin's fall. In the 1780s and 1790s it had been the site of the liveliest literary and political salon in the city and, before that, the location for Neapolitan excess, all courtesy of the redoubtable Countess of Moira (1731–1808). But in the early 1820s it became a forbidding-looking workhouse, and its remarkable transformation played to the powerful romantic narrative of civic nemesis (see Plate 37).[14]

Social change in the capital city was however far more complex: Dublin like several of the older English cities was painfully adjusting to the new industrial order, some districts and some types of property decaying, others adapting to the expansion of government and the professions. Demand for very large private houses, especially those in old parts of the city like Usher's Quay, fell in the wake of the Union, but property in the east of the city and the suburbs appreciated, and speculative residential development – particularly in the south-east – continued up until 1815, then recovered in the 1820s.

But there was a continuing haemorrhage out of the old neighbourhoods by all those who could afford it, not just from decaying secondary streets but from the commercial arteries of old Dublin, from the once-fashionable quays, from Thomas St, Capel St and Pill Lane; the reputation of parts of the Gardiner estate, including even Henrietta St, was declining. Population density throughout these neighbourhoods as reported in the 1821 census was still exceptionally high by Irish urban standards (mean household size exceeded 14 in 8 old city parishes), and in the first street directories of the 1830s the trade of increasing numbers of houses in the old city was listed simply as 'tenements'. The movement of the better off was at first a short-distance one, with new developments on the east side of the Gardiner estate attracting such migrants. In Cork, *haute bourgeois* families and those of independent means who had once populated the heart of the city were disappearing by 1830 – to the high ground to the north-east of the city or to the south-east and along the Blackrock road – while in Limerick, the expansive gridiron of Newtown Pery was able to accommodate those decamping from the old twin-walled town, although English Town with its markets and civic institutions remained a socially mixed neighbourhood (see Plate 38).[15]

Several elements, by no means unique to Irish cities, were combining to drive this process: the bourgeois anxiety engendered by the growing squalor of the back streets and the prevalence of fever in formerly mixed neighbourhoods, made worse by the decay of so many artisan industries; the well-grounded belief in the health benefits of fresh air, clean water and sea-bathing; the social cachet of living beside social peers, worshipping in a respectable church, and proximity to respectable private schools; and, for those who moved out of the city altogether, the prospect of lower local taxes beyond the city and the lure of open ground, private gardens and a prospect of sea or mountain. The first Dublin suburban retreats were built on higher ground on the north side, and in Cork the popularity of the neighbourhood of Sunday's Well overlooking the Lee had begun early in the eighteenth century. In both cities the process accelerated in the last decades of the century; by the mid 1830s there were at least 670 stand-alone villas or 'seats' outside the metropolis located in Co. Dublin parishes within 20 kilometres of the Circular Road, some of which may have originally been summer retreats, but by then nearly all were the main residence of professional and business families who worked in the city. In the case of Cork the scattering had started later and was confined to half a dozen parishes to the east and south-east of the city: there were around 180 such residences in the mid thirties overlooking the Harbour and its inlets or nestled along the wooded Glanmire valley.[16]

The centrifugal movement of wealthier households came at a cost: development outside the canals and Circular Road weakened Dublin Corporation's tax base (this became a much more acute issue later), and altered land values, sometimes to the detriment of the poor occupying sites on the edge of common land or along suburban routes. The responsibilities of the Dublin police as reconstituted in 1808 were extended far beyond the city limits (from a radius of 2 to 8 miles from Dublin Castle and enlarging the 'police district' from 12 to 201 square miles), and out-of-town sites of popular recreation – Donnybrook and Palmerstown fairs, Crumlin Commons, Kilmainham, the Phoenix Park and Finglas – were subject to an increasing degree of suspicion and surveillance, reflecting strident clerical hostility, both Catholic and Protestant, and lay disapproval of the once-tolerated excesses associated with carnival and sporting events.[17]

These two outward movements from Dublin – that of the predominantly upper-class families discarding their oversized homes in the years after parliamentary union, and (more gradually) that of the *haute bourgeoisie* transposed to green acres in Co. Dublin – profoundly affected civic society in the capital. In one sense, lawyers and doctors, bankers and brewers stepped into the shoes of the aristocratic families in terms of providing leadership in philanthropic and cultural bodies, and Dublin in that respect was becoming more like the provincial cities where associational culture had been intrinsically bourgeois all along. But these were families who now were increasingly resident outside town; their investment of time and money in the public life of the city was therefore more selective, particularly when central government was taking an ever-greater role in the governance and financing of public institutions within the city.

RIVAL STORIES

What overlay all such considerations was the changed political climate. Religious acrimony across the public sphere had become deeply pervasive by the 1820s. What seemed like the old equilibrium in civil society – the uncontested dominance of Protestants – had been broken by the unresolved legacies of 1798 and the Union, by the expectation of Catholic Emancipation and then its denial, and by the growth of Catholic wealth during the wars (particularly in Dublin and Cork). Then, in the early 1820s came the sudden revitalization of Catholic politics, thanks principally to Daniel O'Connell: in a few tumultuous years he adapted the methods of 1792 and harnessed mass Catholic support to push for the unfinished business of Catholic Emancipation. Coming at a time of extreme sectarian tension in the countryside, of mounting hostility between the Established Church and a far more assertive Catholic hierarchy, the institutions of civil society were more profoundly split than ever before: in the southern cities, party divisions and religious divisions did not quite coincide but the degree of polarization evident within Dublin and Cork was uniquely intense.

However, in Belfast and Derry, despite very considerable Catholic immigration since 1800, middle-class Catholics were still very few; the political divide there was rather between Tory and reformer, and the cause of reform carried much of its language from the past. But, as Wright has argued, the cultural influence of the reformist liberal elite in Belfast began to weaken in the 1820s as the town's religious demography changed and evangelical sermons became ever louder. And, culturally as well as commercially, it was becoming more a British- than an Irish-seeming place, its intimate links with Dublin weakening.[18]

Belfast was an outlier demographically as well: immigration from its east Ulster hinterland was accelerating in the 1820s, whereas elsewhere, apart from greater Dublin, the long expansionary movement into the cities was losing momentum, a generation before absolute decline became a defining feature of Irish towns in the decades after the Great Famine. Given the voracious demand for industrial labour, the doubling of Belfast's official population between 1821 and 1841 is easily explained, but accounting for the pattern of deceleration or decline elsewhere is less straightforward, and the story may be slightly different in each case. But two inter-related factors are common to all: the narrowing of employment prospects across many urban sectors which impacted wages and immigration, and the growing appeal of emigration (and its falling cost) for embattled urban artisans. Out-migration to England was of course nothing new, but it became a matter of regular comment in the 1820s.[19]

Figure 27 The view (*c.* 1841) from Derry's walls down Fahan St and into the (by then) burgeoning Bogside.

KNOWLEDGE TRANSFERRED

The emigration from Irish cities in this era raises another set of questions: whether urban emigrants took with them distinctive skills, social attitudes or cultural attributes that may have influenced host societies, whether in Britain or North America. Did indeed Ireland's unusual urban history over the previous century and a half register at all in the world outside? Unfortunately, the many scholars who have studied the social and cultural impact of the Irish diaspora have rarely focused on the geographical origins of migrants within Ireland or sought to distinguish between the already urbanized and wholly rural migrants, so answers must wait. But a few provisional observations are possible.

The migration *into* Irish cities of skilled outsiders, English, Scottish, French and Dutch, so much a feature of the seventeenth century, had been critical in the development of the luxury crafts and of several staple manufactures (from the salting of beef to the bleaching of fine linen). Incentivizing this migration had been one element of the state's drive to anglicise, protestantize and economically develop Irish society. Some of the incomers' new ways of making and doing were widely shared from the beginning, while some were tightly protected, whether by guild monopoly, apprenticeship regulation or tight family networks. In the long run, however, there was a vast extension of technical know-how as Irish cities grew in scale, complexity and bourgeois wealth, and this infusion of technical expertise from advanced sectors in the neighbouring island remained critical in launching the capitalized industries of the late eighteenth century.

Yet in this long process the new ways of making and doing were altered, adapted and shaped within a singular urban world where the traumatic events of the seventeenth century had left a profound impress. One business elite, the Old English, had been entirely displaced, and another, of mixed ancestry, evolved within an environment of religious repression and economic opportunity. Yet nothing was quite what it seemed, and nothing was quite the same from city to city: the relative anonymity of the capital city stood in contrast to the intimacy of most provincial centres. And none of them were the same, from, at one extreme, the sleepy Catholic-dominated world of Galway, its trading families conscious of old pedigrees and suspicious of its untamed hinterland, to the other, the dynamic but unsettled state of Belfast, where Episcopalians controlled the formal institutions of the town, Presbyterians its trade and manufacture, and the small Catholic element provisioned the citizenry with food and drink, but were invisible in the public sphere.

Thus those who departed from these urban communities may have had a diversity of stories to tell, but there are some common features. To take the first group that departed, the Catholic mercantile diaspora to the Continent in the seventeenth century: they created a multilateral network of traders and a tradition of international mobility that persisted until the end of the eighteenth century; the lineaments of this trading system in Atlantic Europe and the Caribbean are now known, but not how it measures up against other pre-industrial diasporas, and it is not clear whether the success of Irish merchant houses in trans-imperial brokerage (like the remarkable Fitzgerald clan in mid-century London or Saule and Hennessy in Cognac) reflects on family lessons learnt at home, or on risk-taking and rule-breaking in the world outside. There are however a few clear-cut instances where Irish technical expertise was transplanted: Waterford tanners who settled in the Basque country and transformed the industry there in the early eighteenth century; Dublin mezzotint engravers who in the 1740s brought their new techniques to London and to greater fame; woollen weavers from Dublin and Cork who were recruited in the 1750s to settle in Guadalajara where they formed the basis of a royal manufactory; Dublin wallpaper manufacturers who were pioneers in Bordeaux and Philadelphia; silk weavers and dyers who brought skills back to industrializing England.[20]

But that is a limited audit. Outside the technical sphere there were subtle and more significant instances of the expatriation of skills and ideas, possibly in urban construction, probably in labour relations, and certainly in publishing, political protest, associational culture and education.

The great public buildings of eighteenth-century Dublin are associated with a small number of outstanding English and Continental architects, stuccodores and carpenters, most of whom remained in the country. But through a well-regulated apprenticeship system, the exemplary training provided by the Dublin Society schools of design, and the architectural literacy of some of their patrons, the technical standards and the aesthetic sensibility of Irish practitioners in the business of building came to be of a high order in the second half of the eighteenth century. And a few of those trained in Dublin made a mark far afield: James Hoban left in the 1780s to greater things in Washington, and James O'Donnell shortly after 1800 reproduced Dublin-style brick terraces in State St, New York, and later Dublin Gothic in Montreal's huge Catholic cathedral. Dublin's Wide Streets Commissioners, influenced by London, Paris and possibly Lisbon, garnered praise from visitors, but whether their bespoke solutions for Dublin were copied elsewhere has not been revealed; however one Commissioner, Andrew Caldwell, sought to influence plans for re-ordering the centre of Liverpool in 1802. And the draughtsman of the plan for Limerick's Newtown Pery in 1769, Christopher Colles, may have carried his plans abroad: he emigrated to New York shortly before the Revolution and advised on the city's water supply, then and later. Whether his experience in plotting the grid-iron streets for Limerick was shared with the New York Commissioners for laying out the new street system for Manhattan in 1811 remains a distant possibility.[21]

Building craftsmen were among the most peripatetic of skilled workers and were often invisible in the historical record. By contrast journeymen in the textile and clothing trades were among the earliest to organize and fought the most visible battles to protect wages and apprenticeship. They did this without harnessing exclusive religious or sectarian symbols to the cause. That long tradition of organization and, from the 1790s, of politicization was carried across the Irish Sea, although the precise contribution of organized Irish labour to English labour history remains unclear. But from 1795 to 1848 the impact of urban Irish radicalism in its many guises on revolutionary stirrings in London and the north-west was recurring, and Chartism would have been very different without its Irish ingredients.[22]

The repertoire of more general civic protest – whether over food prices or against obnoxious public figures – was similar to the patterns of British protest in the eighteenth century, although there was no parallel in Ireland to the extreme violence of the Porteous Riots in Edinburgh or the Gordon Riots in London. But what was distinctive in Ireland were the protests, rhetorical and physical, against imported goods that rivalled home production, which had welled up intermittently from the 1710s: the focus was almost entirely on the issue of imported luxury clothing, and protests were always strongest in Dublin, drawing on the support of the 'virtuous' female consumer. As O'Dowd has argued, the consumer boycotts of British goods in America prior to the Revolution were certainly prefigured in Ireland, whether or not these tactics were consciously copied in New England. There was continuity in America between the patriotic consumerism of the pre-Revolutionary era and the championing of muscular protectionism in the early United States, a cause in which émigré Irish radicals took the lead, notably Mathew Carey: his extravagant championing of tariffs in Dublin in 1784 and his scabrous attacks on those who opposed them led to his forced departure to Philadelphia; a generation later he became one of the most fearsome advocates of high tariffs to protect the fledgling American economy. And Carey's career epitomized the successful transfer of book-making and publishing: he was only one of more than a hundred Irish printers and booksellers who had a second life in late eighteenth- and early nineteenth-century America, although his success and reputation outshone all others.[23]

Import substitution had also been the mission of the Dublin Society since its inception in the 1730s, although its tactics were the polar opposite to the confrontational politics of political reformers. But the Dublin Society was seen outside Ireland as a model of enlightened voluntary action, combining philanthropy and public subvention, and it attracted interest in Britain and the

American colonies in the pre-revolutionary era. However, its greatest urban project – the schools of design – got far less attention externally than their sponsorship of spinning schools and of silk warehouses, which in the long run mattered far less.

A more covert Irish initiative in voluntary association was in the development of freemasonry, not that the movement was a specifically Irish phenomenon, although Irish membership was proportionately higher than anywhere else in the British dominions. But at a crucial moment in its development, freemasonry took an Irish turn, specifically with a breakaway network that drew its authority from the 'Antient' Grand Lodge established in London in 1751; over the next sixty years these lodges outgrew all those affiliated to the older English Grand Lodge. The importance here, as Ric Berman has shown, was that the 'Antient' lodges in England were socially far more diverse than the established and largely upper-class 'modern' ones, and in London at least, large numbers of lodges operated as friendly societies for native and immigrant tradesmen (including many Irish). From the beginning, freemasonry had been rather more inclusive in Ireland, with prominent Catholic and *converso* membership. The key man in the London 'Antient' Lodge was for several decades its secretary, Laurence Dermott (1720–91), a younger brother of Anthony Dermott, co-founder of the Catholic Committee and one of the wealthiest merchants in Dublin. The benign but absorbing ceremonies of masonry, which Dermott elaborated in his manual *Ahiman Rezon* (London, 1756) and which went into at least fifteen editions with printings in Dublin, Drogheda and Belfast, helped popularize a fraternal organization that side-stepped the divisions of party and religion. But of course freemasonry also provided the template for a rather different fraternal organization that began to spread at the turn of the century, one which side-stepped social divisions by unifying the initiated around a powerful religious message – in other words, the Orange Order, itself soon to become another great Irish export.[24]

But the voluntary association of greatest transnational impact was the Catholic teaching order, starting with Nano Nagle's efforts in Cork city. Her order, the Presentation Sisters, was still in a very precarious state at the time of her death until it received a papal brief of approval in 1791. But by 1800 there were six foundations in the country, the start of a remarkable proliferation of girls' schools with a strong religious ethos, where teaching was provided entirely by religious sisters. Its arrival in Waterford city prompted the foundation of a similar society for the education of poor Catholic boys, the initiative of a mid-ranking merchant and widower, Edmund Rice (1766–1844). His system of schooling, delivered by a well-disciplined lay order of teachers, developed more slowly, but by 1821 his Institute, the Christian Brothers, was operating schools in Waterford, Dublin, Cork and Limerick cities, and was poised for greater things. It proved to be the ideal vehicle for widening educational access at a time when demand was growing but the ability of poor parents to pay was declining. The template of these organizations was adapted and refined over the following thirty years within Ireland (with the establishment in Dublin of a province of the Loreto order in 1822, and the founding of the Sisters of Mercy there in 1827). By mid century the Irish teaching orders were already becoming an international phenomenon, strongest where Irish émigrés were settling but with, as it seemed, an infinite capacity for growth, destined to become one element in Catholic Ireland's 'spiritual empire'. All had their genesis in an urban setting.[25]

SACRED AND SECULAR

New churches, in neoclassical, Greek revival or Gothic idiom, were a feature of every Irish urban centre in the early nineteenth century. At least sixteen Catholic, ten Anglican, and seven dissenting churches were built or rebuilt within the capital city and its inner suburbs between 1810 and 1850, marking out the changing religious demography in what was perhaps the greatest wave of church building in the city's history before the mid twentieth century. And denominational rivalries were played out from the skyline to the schoolroom in other cities too.

Yet for all that, the secular Enlightenment had left its mark. One symbol was Leinster House, from 1815 the capacious new home of the Dublin Society and venue for celebrity lectures and exhibitions on the arts and sciences: in 1828 some 3,000 people attended the Society's scientific lectures and almost 30,000 visited its museums of geology, art or natural history. But socially the Society was 'old regime'. By contrast, the *haute bourgeoisie* in provincial cities, notably Cork and Belfast, were determined from the time of the Union to challenge Dublin's cultural monopoly and to elevate science and high culture in their own domain. Despite the raucous political divisions, in large measure they succeeded in both places. Leadership came from wealthier merchants, medics and manufacturers rather than gentry or the law (as in Dublin). The goal in each case was the creation of an institution of higher education and learning: the Belfast Academical

Institution, established in 1808, had a promising start under William Drennan, but it was forced to trim its ambitions, and the Royal Cork Institution, for all its strengths as a centre of the arts and popular science, was not the basis for a university. But a generation later, Sir Robert Peel's government accepted the case for a new secular Irish university, the Queen's University, with campuses established in Belfast, Cork and Galway (in 1844). The fact that the Catholic hierarchy subsequently decided to condemn them as 'godless colleges' stunted the early development of those in Cork and Galway, but each of the three institutions survived to become enduring centrepieces in their city's development and a counterweight to Dublin's cultural dominance. Their appearance was a vindication of those rarest of commodities in Union Ireland, cross-party civic patriotism and open minds. The case for Limerick was canvassed strongly, but despite the central role of Waterford's Thomas Wyse MP (1791–1862) in securing the new university, no one argued for a university college for Waterford, birthplace of the Christian Brothers and the one Irish city where confessional rivalries had always been weak and where civic culture had transcended denomination.[26]

CONCLUSION

At least 150 histories of English towns were published in the course of the eighteenth century, an impressive literature that prompted almost no imitation in Ireland. Apart from Walter Harris's posthumous and woefully incomplete history of *Dublin* (1766), and John Ferrar's *Limerick* (1767, expanded in 1787), Irish cities found no chroniclers to celebrate their growth. It has been suggested that this striking Anglo-Irish contrast may reflect deep differences in the urban culture of the two countries, with English civic society successfully distancing itself from the convulsions of civil war and party conflict, whereas in Ireland the legacy of confiscation and religious discrimination may have destroyed any sense of common identity or shared history among the urban elites. This is plausible, and indeed the contrast between the profusion of topographical paintings and engravings of pre-industrial English towns and the very small crop of images of urban life in Ireland outside Dublin is also suggestive. Only in the superb mid-century Irish town maps produced by John Rocque, Bernard Scalé and their team of mainly Huguenot surveyors and engravers – of Dublin and Cork, Kilkenny and Waterford (as well as of Armagh and Newry, though of more modest proportions) – do we find a sense that Irish urbanism was worthy of celebration and that Irish towns were distinctive sites of improvement. Their work influenced a few imitators, with fine maps of Limerick (1769 and 1786), Belfast (1791) and Derry (1799).[1]

But surprisingly the study of the urban past did flourish in post-Union Ireland, when there was a sudden flush of publications on Irish towns. One of the most reflective was that on Galway, published in Dublin in 1820. Its author James Hardiman, lawyer, archivist, antiquarian and pioneering folklorist, presented it to his readers as a work of revelation, demonstrating the rich and heretofore hidden antiquity of 'the capital of Connaught', an urban world that in his judgment had been crushed over the previous two centuries by penal laws and English mercantilist legislation but that now, in a more enlightened age, was entering a renaissance. Within a few years, his *Galway* history shared the shelf with at least eight other Irish urban histories, including Warburton, Whitelaw and Walsh's vast tomes on *Dublin* (1818) that had been more than a decade in the making. Most were substantial antiquarian and topographical works, but they were unschematic in their treatment, and their appearance was in no way coordinated. Their authors were all local men drawn from across the religious spectrum and from a variety of professional and bourgeois occupations; none was unduly partisan, a pride of place reacting perhaps against the divisive passions of the age. However, the fashion soon passed, and even with the revival of topographical antiquarianism later in the nineteenth century few of the concerns of urban history (other than in Kilkenny and Dublin) received scholarly notice.[2]

The irony is that the moment of optimistic self-reflection exemplified by Hardiman marked not so much a renaissance, but the closing stages of the long cycle of urban demographic growth that has been the focus of this study. The tide would soon recede for Galway; indeed, all provincial centres outside Ulster were close to their maxima in terms of population in the 1820s, reaching a human scale not to be surpassed in some cases until far into the next century. This was not because they had once again become more deadly than the countryside, although the great cholera epidemic of 1832, a particularly urban scourge, caused nationwide apocalyptic fears: nine-tenths of Sligo's residents fled the town within a few days, and it killed an estimated 4,478 in Dublin city, over five times the death rate in London. But in the long run, urban growth outside Ulster was reversed because provincial cities were no longer the industrial hubs and vibrant processing centres drawing in new labour from their hinterlands. Instead they served as the stepping-stones for the mass movement out of the countryside seeking betterment far afield.[3]

The short-lived bloom in Irish urban history coincided with less visible but profound changes in the cultural habits of city-dwellers. Many of the eighteenth-century developments set out in this study had contributed to the formation of a broadly anglophone middle-class culture, influenced by but differentiated from aristocratic values and habits, alive to international fashions and practices, and affected by, but not wholly defined by, religious confession. Participation in that culture had been restricted not by birth or creed, but by wealth, education, deportment and material display, as was evident in the theatre, the masonic lodge, the assembly rooms and the race meeting. Catholic participation in this urban world, limited in the first half of the century, accelerated from the 1770s but, as we have seen, it was fracturing, perhaps before 1800, certainly by the 1820s. Convivial friendships across the religious divide of course continued among the *haute bourgeoisie* (and strikingly so in Galway and Limerick), but they were eroded by the foregrounding of religious beliefs and practices in all denominations, by the raw divisiveness of new-style electoral politics (notably in Dublin and Cork) and by the increasingly aggrieved tone of the demand for full Catholic Emancipation and the right to sit in Parliament. The all-consuming 'Catholic question' rumbled on for three decades until 1829, during which time municipal government in all but Galway, Limerick and Waterford was dominated, if not monopolized, by the opponents of Emancipation, and even in Waterford fewer than a quarter of freemen were Catholic.

The presence of liberal Protestants undoubtedly weakened the forces of polarization, not least in Limerick and Waterford where the marathon career of Sir John Newport (MP for the city from 1803 to 1832) set the tone, but the political logjam over Emancipation was intensified by the novel religious tensions of the 1820s: on the one hand, the increasingly powerful evangelical wings of both major Protestant denominations, with talk of a 'second reformation' and a new commitment to proselytism; on the other, an increasingly assertive Catholic hierarchy, which for the most part was supportive of O'Connell's mobilization of the Catholic masses. The visibly greater wealth of Catholic merchants in the southern cities in the post-war era was used to amplify the moral case for Catholic parliamentary membership – and to some Protestant eyes such evidence was deeply unsettling.[4]

The Cork annalist Francis Tuckey, writing in 1838, looked back wistfully on the 'unaffected sociability and a taste for public amusements' in the eighteenth-century city, when assemblies were held twice a week in the Assembly House and weekly concerts in a music hall, and contrasted all this with his own era:

A great change has taken place in these matters; the general reserve and exclusiveness of modern manners now confine frivolous amusements chiefly to private houses, and with the aid of an increasing religious spirit, have extinguished these establishments ... In private society,

CONCLUSION

Protestants and Roman Catholics have little intercourse with one another; political differences now separate them rather more than formerly . . .[5]

Perhaps truer of *petite* than *haute bourgeoisie*, these 'differences' were in part a consequence of exclusive schooling, both elementary and advanced. They were certainly reinforced by the deeper religiosity of the age as confessional boundaries became far less permeable. By the 1820s, perhaps earlier, the churches, chapels and meeting houses of rival creeds were taboo spaces for non-members, even for funerals. And with intensified Protestant concern over Sabbath observance, another point of difference was exposed, as John Bicheno noted of Sundays in Cork city in 1830: 'the public walks . . . are not frequented by Protestants, but are filled with crowds of Catholics'.[6]

'The ancient and national exercise called hurling'[7] had always been a Sunday pastime, and in the eighteenth century, like wrestling matches, cockfighting and football, it had been tolerated on the grassy edges of the cities, whatever the day of the week. Such occasions often attracted large crowds, and up until the 1770s hurling matches had been patronized by upper-class gambling

Figure 28 'Cork from the Mardyke walk' (1806), with a distant view of the newly completed Barracks overlooking the city.

enthusiasts as well. But with sabbatarianism on the increase, with more effective policing, and with growing Catholic clerical disapproval of all rough-house conviviality, there was a noticeable decline in large sporting activities adjacent to the cities in the early nineteenth century, and this reduced the social occasions for communal interaction.[8]

Those most affected were the artisan and labouring classes. Subtle and slow-burning changes in what was deemed respectable behaviour were undermining these, and much older, recreational practices. The movement was spearheaded by the Churches, but it was a slow process: Archbishop Carpenter had attempted to prohibit attendance at St John's Eve festivities in Kilmainham in 1786, but not until the 1830s did its popularity fade. Writing in 1839 of the slaughter-yard district above Blarney Lane in Cork, John Windele could still celebrate the raucous calendar customs associated with the place, May-Day mumming, Skellig night and whipping the herring on Easter Saturday, but he noted their decline in recent years: 'The day may not be far distant when the very memory of these things shall pass away.' And the great temperance movement of the early 1840s and the Great Famine that followed helped to achieve just that.[9]

This cultural shift in social manners, curbing practices that conflicted with the emerging norms of respectability, new work disciplines and the polarizing of gender roles, was of course not just a local urban phenomenon but is familiar to all students of nineteenth-century western Europe. The impulse was common across all religious denominations, and although Irish cities may have been the first to be influenced by such trends, the drive for bourgeois respectability became universal in Ireland across creed and region in the course of the nineteenth century. It preceded – but was related to – the waning of aristocratic values and upper-class power within Irish society, and was a time when, in Ciaran O'Neill's characterization, the 'polished middle classes . . . [had] finally wrested control of the poor from the rich through control of philanthropy, charity and education . . .' This was seen earliest in the case of Presbyterian Belfast, perhaps last in the case of vice-regal Dublin.

The shift illustrates a perennial theme of this study, one perhaps so obvious that it requires little emphasis: the enduring influence of the metropole. For as we have seen, it was English and Scottish fashions, ideas, consumer preferences and technical know-how that profoundly affected all departments of Irish urban society during the long eighteenth century. The sheer proximity of Irish port cities to the urban hubs of England and Scotland was crucial in sustaining that influence, given the almost total freedom of movement of gentry and merchants, artisans and labourers to criss-cross the Irish Sea, and the closeness of this relationship was reinforced by the coming of free trade and the transport and banking revolutions of the 1820s. Indeed, Irish urban development and the wider commercialization of Irish farming had been driven first and foremost by demand from Britain and its colonies, and without the continuing strength of that imperial economy or the technological innovations that drove it to new heights, or indeed the military power that underpinned it, the Irish urban cycle would have been a far more modest phenomenon.[10]

But it was never a one-way traffic: Irish urban communities were never the passive recipients or reactive transmitters of knowledge and ideas flowing across the Irish Sea. The argument here has been that Irish cities in general, and Dublin and Belfast in particular, were the sites where indigenous, English, Scottish and Continental influences interacted, sometimes with unique results, and herein lies their distinctive story, whether it is their role in engineering the revolution in literacy and language change, or the contribution of urban laity in shaping and resourcing the roll-back of the Reformation and laying the foundations for the remarkable recovery of institutional Catholicism in the nineteenth century.

The colonial backdrop and peculiar and unstable religious make-up of Irish cities make that history and those interactions unique in western Europe, but the challenges and solutions that emerged were not unique and sometimes, as we have suggested, the ideas and practices incubated in Irish cities had a bearing on urban histories far afield.

APPENDICES

The Scale of Irish City Walls, *c.* 1700

	Length of walls/ditches (m.)	Space enclosed (hect.)
Derry	1,325	13
Sligo		[15-20]
Galway	1,325	13
Limerick	3,025	27.5
Cork	1,625	14
Waterford	2,150	23
Kilkenny	4,150	43.5
Dublin	*c.*1,750	20
Drogheda (north and south of river)	3,545	43
Belfast	[1,500-2,000]	[30-35]

Source: Based on data in Avril Thomas, *The Walled Towns of Ireland* (Dublin, 1992), II, 'Gazetteer'.
Note: Perimeter lengths here include quayside walls where they existed. The fortification surrounding Belfast was 'a bastion rampart and ditch' erected in 1641/2, but that around Sligo was only a 'retrenchment', erected in 1689.

APPENDICES

Urban Population Data 1660/61

	Urban poll-tax payers	Estimated civilian population
Derry	810	2,349
Sligo	488	1,415
Galway	n.a.	
Limerick	1,367	3,964
Cork	2,430	7,627
Waterford	865	2,508
Kilkenny	1,311	3,802
Dublin	[?12,000]	[34,800]
Drogheda	1,231	3,570
Belfast	589	1,708

Source: Séamus Pender, ed. *A Census of Ireland circa 1659*, with introduction by W.J. Smyth, 2nd ed. (Dublin, 2002), pp. xiv, xxxi, xxxiii, 8, 123–4, 191–2, 263, 349, 373, 432–2, 474–5, 597.

Notes: I follow W.J. Smyth's meticulous reassessment of what was formally described as the 1659 census, and have applied the median of his suggested multipliers (2.9) to convert those enumerated for poll tax (in Column 1) into population totals.

This choice of multiplier must remain somewhat speculative, both for the reasons Smyth has set out, and for wider demographic considerations. The latter include the presumably atypical age profile of urban populations at the end of a period of war, plague and ethnic displacement when immigrants, whether local or English, who had repopulated the cities in the 1650s, were presumably young adults in the main. Their marital status and gender balance can only be guessed at, and there is little information on household structure and dependency ratios. However, see Dickson, 'No Scythians Here: Women and marriage in seventeenth-century Ireland', in *Women in Early Modern Ireland*, eds. Margaret MacCurtain and Mary O'Dowd (Edinburgh, 1991), pp. 227–32; Brian Gurrin, *Pre-census Sources for Irish Demography* (Dublin, 2002), pp. 73–5. The case for a multiplier of at least this order is strengthened by the evidence of the Dublin bills of mortality, which survive for eight years in the Restoration period (R.A. Butlin, 'The Population of Dublin in the Late Seventeenth Century', *Irish Geography*, v (1965), 56–7).

Taking the provincial poll-money figures individually: Derry's figures relate to all streets and lanes but not to the city Liberties; Sligo's figures relate to the 'town' only; Limerick's relate to returns for the south ward, middle ward, north wards; Cork's figures relate to the walled city and the suburbs but I have excluded the garrison as it was not consistently included elsewhere; Waterford's returns are for the west ward, south ward, and north ward; Kilkenny's returns are for the city wards and extramural city parishes and streets outside; Drogheda's returns are for the city and Liberties minus the garrison; Belfast's returns are for 'town' and quarters. The poll-tax returns for two Dublin parishes are missing, so I have followed Smyth's suggested figure for the total population of the city (Pender and Smyth, *1659 Census*, p. xxxiii]. For slightly different estimates for Cork city, see Mark McCarthy, in John Crowley et al. *Atlas of Cork City* (Cork, 2005), pp. 122–6.

Table 2.1: Notes on the 1821 Census Totals:

Galway: the total for the urban population is somewhat suspect in that 32.4 per cent of persons in occupations are returned in agriculture (although presumably this includes the large Claddagh fishing suburb).

Limerick: the total is also suspect in that 30.2 per cent of persons in occupations are returned in agriculture. I have only included the urban parishes 1–4, 16–17, 21–22 (8 in all) out of the total for the city and Liberties (note that I am adopting the parish numbering used in the *Census* report).

Cork: the very large city Liberties have bedevilled pre-1841 estimates of city population; I have used the returns for parishes 1, 3, 12–13, 20–22 (7 in all) out of the total of 22 parishes in the city and Liberties.

Waterford: I have only included the urban parishes 1–10 and 13 (11 in all) out of the total for the Liberties of the city.

Dublin: the Dublin total is that proposed by the 1821 enumerators in the 'The Metropolis of Ireland section' (*1821 Census*, pp. xx–xxiii), and includes the emerging suburbs of Chapelizod village, Clontarf town, Drumcondra, Glasnevin village, Kilmainham, Islandbridge, Ranelagh, Rathmines, Milltown and Harolds Cross.

Belfast: includes Cromac but not Ballymacarett, for which there is no separate data.

APPENDIX 4

Dublin Bills of Mortality

Years	Total burials	Baptisms as % burials	Under 16 as % total	Fevers as % total	Smallpox as % total	Measles as % total
1682/83	2,154	48.5	57.0	24.5	6.6	5.7
1695 [3rd/4th qtrs.]	715	79.6		40.1		
1696 [2nd, 3rd, 4th qtrs.]	2,047	44.2		26.8	34.1	
1697 [2nd, 3rd, 4th qtrs.]	1,375	61.5		35.9	1.1	0.5
? 1697/98	1,947	51.3		35.1	1.0	
? 1698	2,412	48.1		28.7	29.3	
1712	2,184	32.8	52.9	22.1	10.7	
1713	2,809	43.2	54.8	17.1	15.3	4.4
1714	2,960	45.2	58.7	19.4	20.5	5.4
1715	2,689	41.6	55.6	19.1	22.0	4.5
1716	2,679	41.7	58.0	18.2	19.6	9.9
1717	3,021	38.0	56.3	21.1	22.3	4.0
1718	2,462	49.5	49.8	6.1	15.2	4.2
1752	1,844	94.0	45.8	19.1	13.6	6.8
1753	1,825	100.7	38.0	25.3	13.2	1.7
1754	1,897	93.4	41.4	21.8	15.4	1.7
1755 [1st qtr.]	702	78.8	40.7	25.8	14.5	1.3

Sources: 1666–1680: Sir William Petty, *Several Essays in Political Arithmetick*, 4th edn (London, 1755), p. 42; 1682/3: Sir William Petty, *Further Observations on the Dublin Bills of Mortality* (London, 1683); *Census of Ireland, 1851*, V, Report on Deaths, p. 504; 1695–1698: 'Documents Relating to the Dublin Bills of Mortality...' (Bodleian Lib., Oxford, MS Rawl. C 406 [NLI Mic p. 2819]), pp. 93–6; 1712–18: B.L. Add. MS 21,138, f.64, reprinted in *CARD*, VII, p. 578; 1752–1755: *Dublin Weekly Bills of Mortality*, 1752–5 [Gilbert Collection, Dublin City Libraries]; William Wilde, 'Miscellanea', in *Assurance Magazine*, III,1 (1853), 251. See also, John Rutty, *A Chronological History of the Weather and Seasons, and of the Prevailing Diseases in Dublin...* (London, 1770), pp. 127–8, 338.

APPENDICES

Table 2.5: Irish cities: Sources for religious composition

In column [1] the 1660 figures relate to civilian adults levied for poll tax, and the convention of equating the figures given for 'Irish' inhabitants as the Catholic population has been followed here: Séamus Pender, ed. *A Census of Ireland circa 1659*, 2nd edn with introduction by W.J. Smyth (Dublin, 2002). See also Appendix 2, above.

In column [2], data for Galway [houses] are from 1724: Bernadette Cunningham, 'A Galway Hearth Money Roll for 1724', in *JGAHS*, lvi (2004), 60–74; data for Kilkenny are from 1731: William Tighe, *Statistical Observations Relative to the County of Kilkenny . . .* (Dublin, 1802), p. 458; and data for Sligo are from 1749: Marie-Louise Legg, *The Elphin Census, 1749* (Dublin, 2004), pp. 524–39.

In column [3], apart from Belfast, all data are taken from Brian Gurrin, Kerby A. Miller and Liam Kennedy, eds. *The Irish Religious Censuses of the 1760s: Catholics and Protestants in Eighteenth-century Ireland* (Dublin: forthcoming, 2021); all apart from Drogheda (1764/5) and Derry (1771) relate to 1766. I am very grateful to the editors for permission to use data from this project in advance of publication. The data for Belfast are from Hyndman's survey of 1757: John Dubourdieu, *Statistical Survey of the County of Antrim* (Dublin, 1812), p. 507.

In column [4], all data come from the 1834 educational returns: *First Report of the Commissioners of Public Instruction, Ireland* (Parl. papers, 1835, XXXIII).

Table 8.1: Provincial imprints, newspapers, circulating libraries and booksellers: 1701–1824

Column 1: *Total recorded titles* – Toby Barnard, *Brought to Book . . .* (Dublin, 2017), p. 271, based on *Eighteenth-Century Short Title Catalogue* (ESTC) listings as in 2015.

Column 2: *Newspaper titles and dates* – E.R.McC. Dix, 'Printing in Cork in the First Quarter of the Eighteenth Century', in *Proc. RIA*, xxxvi, C (1921), 10–15; R.L. Munter, *A Hand-list of Irish Newspapers 1685–1750* (London, 1960); J.R.R. Adams, *The Printed Word and the Common Man . . .* (Belfast, 1987), pp. 34–6; Gerard Long, ed. *Books beyond the Pale . . .* (Dublin, 1996); James O'Toole, *Newsplan*, 2nd edn (London and Dublin, 1998). *Note*: The very poor survival of short-lived pre-1750 newspapers makes totals for Cork and Waterford tentative.

Column 3: *Circulating Libraries* – based on K.A. Manley, *Irish Reading Societies and Circulating Libraries Founded before 1825: Useful knowledge and agreeable entertainment* (Dublin, 2018).

Column 4: *Booksellers/stationers* – Pigot & Co.'s *City of Dublin and Hibernian Directory* (London and Manchester, 1824). *Note*: The criteria used in *Pigot's Directory* to distinguish between book-sellers, stationers and related trades were not consistently applied, making these figures no more than indicative.

APPENDICES

Percentage of Houses Exempt from State Taxes in Provincial Cities: 1798–1800

	Hearth tax exemption 1797/8–1799/1800	Window tax exemption 1799/1800
Derry	57.0	60.2
Sligo	n.a.	
Galway	70.4	69.7
Limerick	53.1	53.7
Cork	n.a.	
Waterford	56.6	56.6
Kilkenny	65.9	74.2
Drogheda	84.9	85.0
Belfast	58.4	51.4

Source: JHCI, XIX, append., dccclvii, dccclxi.

NOTES

INTRODUCTION

1. I.D. Whyte, 'Scottish and Irish Urbanisation in the Seventeenth and Eighteenth Century: A comparative perspective', in S.J. Connolly, et al., eds. *Conflict, Identity and Economic Development: Ireland and Scotland 1600–1939* (Preston, 1995), pp. 14–28; Peter Clark, *European Cities and Towns 400–2000* (Oxford, 2009), pp. 128–31. The estimate for Ireland in 1821 is 9.95 per cent, adapted from A.J. Fitzpatrick & W.E. Vaughan, *Irish Historical Statistics: Population 1821–1971* (Dublin, 1978), pp. 28–41. There was a modest increase in the proportion living in cities and towns of over 5,000 between the 1821 and 1841 census: in the latter census 10.57 per cent were resident there: Fitzpatrick & Vaughan, op. cit.

2. Gearóid MacNiocaill, 'Socio-economic Problems in the Late Medieval Irish Town', in David Harkness & Mary O'Dowd, eds. *The Town in Ireland* (Belfast, 1981), pp. 7–22; Peter Borsay & Lindsay Proudfoot, 'The English and Irish Urban Experience, 1500–1800 . . .', in Borsay & Proudfoot, eds. *Provincial Towns in Early Modern England and Ireland: Change, convergence and divergence* (Oxford, 2002), pp. 7, 21–7; Clark, *European Cities*, pp. 110–37; David Dickson, 'Towns and Cities', in Eugenio F. Biagini & Mary E. Daly, eds. *The Cambridge Social History of Modern Ireland* (Cambridge, 2017), pp. 112–28.

3. Disputes since the nineteenth century as to the city's correct name have mirrored acute local political divisions, but the currently neutral appellation of Derry/Londonderry has not been used here. In the eighteenth century the county was invariably referred to as Londonderry, the diocese as Derry, and in the written record the city sometimes as Derry but more usually Londonderry, or London-Derry. However, the shorter version, reflecting vernacular usage then and now, is used throughout this work. Cf. [George Douglas], *Derriana: A Collection of Papers Relative to the Siege of Derry* (London-Derry, 1794).

4. W.J. Smyth, *Map-making, Landscapes and Memory: A geography of colonial and early modern Ireland c.1530–1750* (Cork, 2006), pp. 254–60.

5. T.C. Barnard, 'An Irish Urban Renaissance?', in John Hinks & Catherine Armstrong, eds. *The English Urban Renaissance Revisited* (Newcastle upon Tyne, 2018), pp. 172–87.

6. Philip Knowles, 'Continuity and Change in Urban Culture: A case study of two provincial towns, Chester and Coventry c.1600–c.1750' (D.Phil., Leicester University, 2001), p. 124; T.C. Barnard, *Making the Grand Figure: Lives and possessions in Ireland, 1641–1770* (New Haven & London, 2004), pp. 113, 118.

7. A.C. Hepburn, *Contested Cities in the Modern West* (Basingstoke, 2004), p. 2.

8. Cf. R.J. Morris, 'Urban Ulster since 1600', in Liam Kennedy & Andrew R. Holmes, eds. *Ulster since 1600: Politics, economy and society* (Oxford, 2013), pp. 121–39.

CHAPTER 1 THE WALLS COME DOWN

1. John Ferrar, *An History of the City of Limerick . . .* (Limerick, 1767), p. 56.

2. Avril Thomas, *The Walled Towns of Ireland* (Dublin, 1992), I, pp. 130–3.
3. Anthony Sheehan, 'Irish Towns in a Period of Change, 1558–1625', in Ciaran Brady & Raymond Gillespie, eds. *Natives and Newcomers: The making of Irish colonial society 1534–1691* (Dublin, 1986), pp. 110–11; Raymond Gillespie, 'Urban Destruction by War in Early Modern Ireland', in Martin Körner, ed. *Destruction and Reconstruction of Towns . . .*, II (Berne, 2000), p. 280; Kenneth Nicholls, 'Sixteenth- and Early Seventeenth-Century Cork', in J.S. Crowley et al., eds. *Atlas of Cork City* (Cork, 2005), p. 117; Yair Mintzker, *The Defortification of the German City 1689–1866* (New York, 2012), pp. 43–82.
4. Christine Casey, 'Art and Architecture in the Long Eighteenth Century', in Kelly, *Cambridge History of Ireland*, III, pp. 407–10. The Londonderry tapestry is reproduced in F.G. Hall, *The Bank of Ireland 1783–1946* (Dublin, 1949), plate 57.
5. The Knight of Glin & James Peill, *Irish Furniture: Woodwork and carving in Ireland from the earliest times to the Act of Union* (New Haven & London, 2007), pp. 66–7; Patrick Walsh, *The Making of the Irish Protestant Ascendancy: The life of William Conolly, 1662–1729* (Woodbridge, 2010), passim. Baillie also supplied furnishings for Castletown. Van Beaver was so described on the frame of the tapestry of George II acquired by the Weavers Guild in 1738 (Glin & Peill, op cit., p. 76).
6. *CSP Dom., 1672*, pp. 513–15; Toby Barnard, 'Identities, Ethnicity and Tradition among Irish Dissenters, c.1650–1750', in Kevin Herlihy, ed., *The Irish Dissenting Tradtion, 1650–1750* (Dublin, 1995), pp. 42–3; W.P. Kelly, 'The Forgotten Siege of Derry, March–August 1649', in William Kelly, ed. *The Sieges of Derry* (Dublin, 2001), pp. 34–49; *A Census of Ireland circa 1659*, ed. Séamus Pender (2nd edn, Dublin, 2002), pp. 123–4; Avril Thomas, ed. *IHTA, XV: Derry-Londonderry*, (Dublin, 2005), p. 4; Ian McBride, *The Siege of Derry in Ulster Protestant Mythology* (Dublin, 1997), p. 25.
7. T.G. Fraser, 'The Siege: Its history and legacy, 1688–1888', in Gerard O'Brien, ed. *Derry and Londonderry: History and society* (Dublin, 1999), p. 379; John Childs, *The Williamite Wars in Ireland 1688–1691* (London, 2007), pp. 75–9, 90–1.
8. John Mackenzie, *A Narrative of the Siege of London-Derry: Or, the late memorable transactions of that city, faithfully represented . . .* (London, 1690), pp. 4–6, 48; William Hamill, *A View of the Danger and Folly of Being Publick-spirited, and Sincerely Loving One's Country. In the deplorable case of the Londonderry and Innishkilling regiments* (London, 1721), p. 45; McBride, *Siege of Derry*, pp. 16, 18; Colin Thomas, 'Demographic Trends and Socio-economic Characteristics, 1650–1900', in O'Brien, *Derry and Londonderry*, pp. 362–7; Childs, *Williamite Wars*, pp. 85–6, 116, 135; Thomas, *Derry-Londonderry*, pp. 2–4; A.J. Smyth, 'The Social and Economic Impact of the Williamite War on Ireland, 1688–91' (Ph.D. thesis, University of Dublin, 2012), p.18; Peter Barry, 'The Journeys of Samuel Molyneux in Ireland 1708–1709', in *Anal. Hib.*, xlvi (2015), 30–1.
9. Fraser, 'The Siege', pp. 380–7; Childs, *Williamite Wars*, pp. 109, 138, 224.
10. Mackenzie, *Narrative*, pp. 28–30; Hamill, *View of the Danger*, pp. 11–12; J.R.R. Adams, *The Printed Word and the Common Man: Popular culture in Ulster 1700–1900* (Belfast, 1987), p. 70; Brian Lacey, *Siege City: The story of Derry and Londonderry* (Belfast, 1990), pp. 113–37; McBride, *Siege of Derry*, pp. 28–31; *ODNB*, 'John Mitchelburne'; *DIB*, 'John Mitchelburne'; *ESTC*, 'Ireland Preserv'd'.
11. [Jacques Louis] De Latocnaye, *Promenade d'un français dans l'Irlande* (Dublin, 1797), pp. 23–4; John Gamble, *Society and Manners in Early Nineteenth-Century Ireland*, ed. Breandán Mac Suibhne (Dublin, 2011), pp. 362–3. Cf. McBride, *Siege of Derry*, p. 39.
12. [John Mitchelburne], *Ireland Preserv'd: Or the siege of London-Derry . . .* (London, n.d. [1705]), preface, pp. [x], [xii], [23]; McBride, *Siege of Derry*, pp. 19–20, 36–7; Fraser, 'The Siege', pp. 386–7; Walsh, *Protestant Ascendancy*, p. 36. Conolly, when acting as a Lord Justice in 1717, refused to accept that the financial claims of the veterans should be a charge on the Irish establishment: Hamill, *View of the Danger*, p. 67.
13. Diary of Col. Samuel Moore 1844–5, 8 June 1844 [in private possession]; Londonderry City council book, 2 Nov. 1797 (Derry City Council Archives); MacKenzie, *Narrative of the Siege*, p. 6.

14. Travel journal of Daniel Beaufort, 1787, ff 53–5 (TCD MS 4027); *Quarters of the Army in Ireland for Anno 1733* (n.p., n.d.); T[erence] O'Rorke, *History of Sligo: Town and county* (Dublin, n.d. [1889]), pp. 209–21; J.G. Simms, *Jacobite Ireland 1685–91* (London, 1969), pp. 131–2, 238–9; Mary O'Dowd, *Early Modern Sligo 1568–1688* (Belfast, 1991), pp. 146, 149–64; Thomas, *Walled Towns*, II, pp. 238–9; Childs, *Williamite Wars*, pp. 347–64; D.A. Fleming, *Politics and Provincial People: Sligo and Limerick, 1691–1761* (Manchester, 2010), pp. 203–5; Fiona Gallagher & Marie Louise Legg, eds. *IHTA, XXIV: Sligo* (Dublin, 2012), pp. 1–3, 14; J.J. Cronin & Pádraig Lenihan, 'Wars of Religion, 1641–1691', in Jane Ohlmeyer, ed. *Cambridge History of Ireland*, II (Cambridge, 2018), p. 253.

15. J.T. Gilbert, *A Contemporary History of Affairs in Ireland, from 1641 to 1652 . . .* (Dublin, 1879–80), p. xv; Rev. J. Rabbitte, 'Galway Corporation MS.C', in *JGAHS*, xv, 3/4 (1932/3), 85–6; R.A. Butlin, 'Land and People c. 1600', in T.W. Moody, F.X. Martin & F.J. Byrne, eds. *A New History of Ireland*, III: *Early Modern Ireland 1534–1691* (Oxford, 1976), p. 159; Thomas, *Walled Towns*, II, pp. 106–7; Gearóid Mac Niocaill, 'Medieval Galway: Dependence and liberty', in Howard B. Clarke, ed. *Irish Cities* (Cork, 1995), pp. 126–34; Paul M. Kerrigan, *Castles and Fortifications in Ireland 1485–1945* (Cork, 1995), p. 94; Mary Ann Lyons, 'The Emergence of an Irish Community in Saint-Malo, 1550–1700', in Thomas O'Connor, ed. *The Irish in Europe 1580–1815* (Dublin, 2001), pp. 108, 111–12, 116; Cronin & Lenihan, 'Wars of Religion', pp. 251–2.

16. T.C. Barnard, *Cromwellian Ireland: English government and reform in Ireland 1649–1660* (Oxford, 1975), pp. 55–7; Thomas, *Walled Towns*, II, pp. 110–13; Paul Walsh, 'The Topography of the Town of Galway in the Medieval and Early Modern Periods', in Gerard Moran & Raymond Gillespie, eds. *Galway: History and society* (Dublin, 1996), pp. 58–63, 94; Cunningham, 'From Warlords to Landlords: Political and social change in Galway 1540–1640', in ibid., pp. 115–17; Patrick Melvin, 'The Galway Tribes as Landowners and Gentry', in ibid., pp. 320–4; Sheila Molloy, 'The Transfer of Power 1642–1702', in ibid., pp. 219–21; James Kelly, 'The Politics of Protestant Ascendancy: County Galway 1650–1832', in ibid., pp. 231–2; Jacinta Prunty, ed. *IHTA, XXVIII: Galway* (2016), p. 4; John Cunningham, *Conquest and Land in Ireland: The transplantation to Connacht, 1649–80* (Woodbridge, 2011), pp. 57–63, 92–5; David Brown & Micheál Ó Siochrú, 'The Cromwellian Urban Surveys, 1653–1659', in *AH*, lxix (2016), 40–1.

The Irish Act of Explanation (1665), which had offered redress to a minority of the thousands of Catholic landowners dispossessed by the Commonwealth, ruled out any restoration of property lying within the walled towns: 'whereas the corporations of Ireland are now planted with English, who have considerably improved at their own charges, and brought trade and manufacture into that our kingdom and by their settlement there do not a little contribute to the peace and settlement of that country, the disturbing or removal of which English would in many respects be very prejudicial, that all such of the popish religion, of any corporations in Ireland, who have been for public security dispossessed of their estates within any corporation, shall be forthwith reprised in forfeited lands, tenements and hereditaments, near the said corporations . . .' [sect. 18].

17. Simms, *Jacobite Ireland*, pp. 230–6; Harman Murtagh, 'Galway and the Jacobite War', in *Irish Sword*, xii (1975), 2–4, 9–10; Sheila Mulloy, 'Galway in the Jacobite War', in *JGAHS*, xl (1985), 1–19; Kerrigan, *Castles and Fortifications*, p. 124; Walsh, 'Topography of Galway Town', pp. 30–1, 61–4, 72, 94; Mulloy, 'Transfer of Power', pp. 221–5; Kelly, 'County Galway', pp. 232–7; Eoin Kinsella, 'In Pursuit of a Positive Construction: Irish Catholics and the Williamite articles of surrender, 1690–1701', in *ECI*, xxiv (2009), 22–35.

18. *Statutes of Ireland*: 4 George I, chap. xv, preamble; James Hardiman, *The History of the Town and County of the Town of Galway*, 2nd edn (Galway, 1926), pp. 175, 177–9; 'Report on the State of Popery, Ireland, 1731; Diocese of Tuam', in *AH*, iii (1914), 145–6; W.P. Burke, *Irish Priests in Penal Times*, 2nd edn (Shannon, 1969), pp. 419–22; Walsh, 'Topography of Galway Town', pp. 64–6; James Mitchell, 'The Catholics of Galway 1708–13: A commentary on a report by Don Giovanni Donato Mezzafalce', in *JGAHS*, lxi (2009), 84–5, 99; Prunty, *IHTA, Galway*, pp. 4–5; Barry, 'Journeys of Samuel Molyneux', pp. 44–5.

Sect. 23 of 2 Anne (1703–4), chap. 6, set out the terms, and sect. 28 (perhaps as an afterthought) excused seamen, fishermen and day labourers holding property worth less than

£2 p.a. from the act. Burke, however, claimed that the act restricted its terms to twenty 'trading merchants'; that may have been the number who actually registered (Burke, *Irish Priests*, p. 412).

19. Thomas, *Walled Towns*, II, pp. 144–5, 150–3; James Burke, 'The New Model Army and the Problems of Siege Warfare. 1648–51', in *IHS*, xxvii (1990–1), 19–29; Kerrigan, *Castles and Fortifications*, pp. 43–4; Rolf Loeber & Geoffrey Parker, 'The Military Revolution in Seventeenth-Century Ireland', in Jane Ohlmeyer, ed. *Ireland from Independence to Occupation 1641–1660* (Cambridge 1995), pp. 68–9, 81; Cunningham, *Transplantation and Land*, pp. 22–3, 62; Cronin & Lenihan, 'Wars of Religion', p. 266.

20. Diary of Col. Michael Stephens, 9 Sept. 1691, in John T. Gilbert, ed. *A Jacobite Narrative of the War in Ireland* (Shannon, 1971); Simms, *Jacobite Ireland*, pp. 163–72, 243–58; Childs, *Williamite Wars*, pp. 105, 241–60, 365–84; Kerrigan, *Castles and Fortifications*, pp. 118, 124–5, 126–8; Cronin & Lenihan, 'Wars of Religion', pp. 260, 262–3.

21. *Quarters of the Army, 1733*; Ferrar, *History of Limerick*, pp. 67, 72; Burke, *Irish Priests*, p. 394; Eamon O'Flaherty, 'Three Towns: Limerick since 1691', in Clarke, *Irish Cities*, pp. 177–81; id., 'An Urban Community and the Penal Laws: Limerick 1690–1830', in John Bergin et al., *New Perspectives on the Penal Laws* (Dublin, 2011), pp. 200–4, 205; Nini Rodgers, *Ireland, Slavery and Anti-slavery 1612–1865* (Basingstoke, 2007), p. 136; Fleming, *Politics and Provincial People*, pp. 58–60, 203, 222; Eamon O'Flaherty, ed. *IHTA, XXI: Limerick* (2010), pp. 7–8, 24, 27.

22. John A. Murphy, 'The Expulsion of the Irish from Cork in 1644', in *JCHAS*, lxix, (1964), 123–131; Barnard, *Cromwellian Ireland*, pp. 52–3; Michael MacCarthy-Morrogh, *The Munster Plantation: English migration to southern Ireland 1583–1641* (Oxford, 1986), pp. 240–3; Thomas, *Walled Towns*, II, p. 61; Mark McCarthy, 'Turning a World Upside Down . . . The city of Cork during the 1640s and 1650s', in *Irish Geography*, xxxiii, 1 (2000), 37–55; id., 'The Evolution of Cork's Built Environment, 1600–1700', in Crowley et al., *Atlas of Cork City*, pp. 121–6; Kenneth Nicholls, 'The Anglo-Normans and Beyond', and 'Sixteenth- and Early Seventeenth-Century Cork', in ibid., pp. 110, 113–18; David Dickson, *Old World Colony: Cork and south Munster 1630–1830* (Cork & Madison, 2005), pp. 8–9, 19.

23. Thomas, *Walled Towns*, II, pp. 60–7; Colin Rynne, *The Archaeology of Cork City and Harbour* . . . (Cork, 1993), pp. 63–8; Kerrigan, *Castles and Fortifications,* pp. 33, 35–6, 55–6, 60, 117.

24. Simms, *Jacobite Ireland*, pp. 177–82; Kenneth Ferguson, 'The Army in Ireland from the Restoration to the Act of Union' (Ph.D., University of Dublin, 1981), pp. 119–21; Diarmuid Ó Murchadha, 'The Siege of Cork in 1690', in *JCHAS*, xcv (1990), 4–5; Kerrigan, *Castles and Fortifications*, p. 125; Maurice F. Hurley, 'Below Sea Level in the City of Cork', in Clarke, *Irish Cities*, pp. 44–54; Dickson, *Old World Colony*, pp. 117–18; McCarthy, 'Cork's Built Environment, 1600–1700', p. 120; *ODNB*, 'John Churchill, Duke of Marlborough'.

25. Survey of Cork City Walls, 1733 (Cork Archives Insitute, www.corkarchives.ie/media /SM646digitalcopy.pdf); Thomas, *Walled Towns*, II, p. 63; Cal McCarthy, *Cork Harbour* (Dublin, 2019), pp. 43–57.

26. Patrick O'Flanagan, 'Beef, Butter, Provisions and Prosperity . . .', in Crowley, *Atlas of Cork City*, pp. 141–67.

27. J.P. Prendergast, *The Cromwellian Settlement of Ireland* (Dublin, 1875), p. 298; Barnard, *Cromwellian Ireland*, pp. 53–5, 68; id., *Making the Grand Figure*, pp. 88–9; Butlin, 'Land and People c. 1600', p. 161; J.H. Andrews, 'Land and People, c.1685', in Moody et al., *New History of Ireland*, III, p. 476; Kerrigan, *Castles and Fortifications*, pp. 41–3, 60, 82, 116; Loeber & Parker, 'Military Revolution', pp. 68–9; Cunningham, *Conquest and Land*, pp. 15–17; Susan Flavin, *Consumption and Culture in Sixteenth-Century Ireland: Saffron, stockings and silk* (Woodbridge, 2014), pp. 43–7.

28. Charles Smith, *The Antient and Present State of the County and City of Waterford . . .* (Dublin, 1746), p.170n.; Mark Girouard, *Town and Country* (New Haven & London, 1992), p. 154; Childs, *Williamite Wars*, p. 239; *DIB*, 'John Barrett'; Kinsella, 'In Pursuit of a Positive Construction', pp. 12–19, 21–22; Brian Murphy, 'The Waterford Catholic Community in the Eighteenth Century' (NUI, UCD, MA, 1997), p. 17. Barrett went on to join in the disastrous defence of Cork city.

29. Thomas Covey, *A Scheme for Building a Bridge over the River Suire at the City of Waterford* (Waterford 1770), p. 77.

30. J.G.A. Prim, 'An Attempt to Identify the Persons Who Issued Tradesmen's Tokens in Kilkenny', in *TKAS*, ii, 1 (1852), 159–176; J.P. Prendergast, 'The Clearing of Kilkenny, anno 1654', in *JKSEIS*, iii, 2 (1861), 326–44; Neely, *Kilkenny: An urban history, 1391–1843* (Belfast, 1989), pp. 124–5, 132–3; Fearghus Ó Fearghail, 'The Catholic Church in County Kilkenny, 1600–1800', in William Nolan & Kevin Whelan, eds. *Kilkenny: History and society* (Dublin, 1990), pp. 213–21; Thomas, *Walled Towns*, I, p. 136; John Bradley, 'From Frontier Town to Renaissance City: Kilkenny, 1500–1700', in Peter Borsay & Lindsay Proudfoot, eds. *Provincial Towns in Early Modern England and Ireland . . .* (Oxford, 2002), pp. 36–8, 41–51; Flavin, *Consumption and Culture*, pp. 23, 47–8.

31. Neely, *Kilkenny: An urban history, 1391–1843* (Belfast, 1989), pp. 134–46; Ó Fearghail, 'Catholic Church in Kilkenny', pp. 221–33.

    For the drastic decline of Ormond finances and of the duke's local political influence after the 1690s: D.W. Hayton, 'Dependence, Clientage and Affinity: The political following of the second Duke of Ormonde', in Toby Barnard & Jane Fenelon, eds. *The Dukes of Ormonde, 1610–1745* (Woodbridge, 2000), pp. 222–37.

32. Kerrigan, *Castles and Fortifications*, p. 104; Thomas, *Walled Towns*, II, p. 84; Loeber & Parker, 'Military Revolution', pp. 68–71, 78–9; Gillespie, 'Urban Destruction', p. 281; David Dickson, *Dublin: The making of a capital city* (London, 2014), pp. 60–71.

33. Barnard, *Cromwellian Ireland*, p. 68; Dickson, *Dublin*, p. 76.

34. Thomas, *Walled Towns*, II, p. 84; John Montague, 'A Shopping Arcade in Eighteenth-Century Dublin . . .', in *IADS*, x (2007), 234–5; Colm Lennon, ed. *IHTA, XIX: Dublin, part II, 1610–1756* (Dublin, 2008), pp. 2–4; Dickson, *Dublin*, pp. 50–1, 55–8; Robin Usher, *Protestant Dublin 1660–1760: Architecture and iconography* (Basingstoke, 2012), pp. 31–2, 46.

    In 1672 the claim was made that 'the revenue was much increased and the city much enriched, as appears by the newly erected buildings, whereby the city, since the Restoration, is enlarged almost one-half' (Mayor, sheriffs commons and citizens of Dublin to King Charles, 4 June 1672: TNA, SP 30/F, f.631).

35. Ferguson, 'Army in Ireland', pp. 116–17; Keegan, *Walled Towns*, II, pp. 108, 115–6, 122; Lennon, *IHTA, Dublin* II, pp. 2–4; Dickson, *Dublin*, pp. 97–104; James Kelly & Mary Ann Lyons, *The Proclamations of Ireland 1660–1820* (Dublin, 2014), II, pp. 219–20.

36. Thomas, *Walled Towns*, II, pp. 82, 84, 86–7; Lennon, *IHTA, Dublin*, II, pp. 2–3, 24–5; Dickson, *Dublin*, pp. 122–3, 215, 226–9.

37. *A Discription of Tredagh in Ireland with the Antiquity, Scituation, Natural Strength and Fortifications of the Said Place . . .* (n.p., 1689), p.1; Rev. T[homas] Grogan, ed. *The Council Book of the Corporation of Drogheda . . . 1649–1734* (Drogheda, 1915), p. 43; Barnard, *Cromwellian Ireland*, p. 68; Gerard Rice, 'Four Wills of the Old English Merchants of Drogheda,1654–1717', in *JCLAHS*, xx, 2, (1982), 96–105; Thomas, *Walled Towns*, II, pp. 72–9; Christine Casey & Alistair Rowan, *The Buildings of Ireland: North Leinster* (London,1993), p. 233; Michael Perceval-Maxwell, *The Outbreak of the Irish Rebellion of 1641* (Dublin 1994), pp. 36, 40.

38. *At a General Session of the Peace Held in and for the County of the Town of Drogheda . . . on . . . the 7th Day of October, 1708 . . .* (n.p., n.d., [1708]), pp. 1–2; Simms, *Jacobite Ireland*, pp. 125–6, 145, 152; Childs, *Williamite Wars*, pp. 158–9, 211, 229; Kinsella, 'In Pursuit of a Positive Construction', pp. 12–13, 16–19, 21–2, 34–5.

39. C.J. Woods, ed. *Charles Abbot's Tour through Ireland and North Wales . . . 1792* (Dublin, 2019), p. 21; 'O'Connor's Journal', *c.*1794 (TCD, MS 2568), f.12; John D'Alton, *The History of Drogheda: With its environs . . .* (Dublin, 1844), p. 85; Casey & Rowan, *North Leinster*, pp. 233, 236–7; Kieran Campbell, 'Drogheda from St. John's Hill by Francis Place, 1698', in *JLAHS*, xxvi, 4 (2008), 475.

40. George Benn, *A History of the Town of Belfast: From the earliest times to the close of the eighteenth century* (London, 1877), pp. 98–9, 102–44, 122–3; Raymond Gillespie & Stephen Royle, eds. *IHTA, XII: Belfast, Part I* (Dublin, 2003), pp. 1–3.

41. Benn, *Belfast*, pp. 128–33, 161–8.

42. Ibid., pp. 162–68, 263; Gillespie & Royle, *IHTA, Belfast I*, pp. 2–6; Raymond Gillespie, *Early Belfast: The origins and growth of an Ulster town to 1750* (Belfast, 2007), pp. 129–31, 143, 159–60, 167–73.

43. Burke, 'The New Model Army', pp. 4–8; K. Cullen et al., 'Battered but Unbowed: Dundee during the seventeenth century', in C. McKean, B. Harris & C. Whatley, eds. *Dundee: Renaissance to Enlightenment* (Dundee, 2009), pp. 61–3.

44. Andrews, 'Land and People, *c.*1685', pp. 475–6.

45. Sligo, Cork, Waterford, Dublin and Belfast: Thomas, *Walled Towns*, II, passim. Future urban archaeology may help to date the timing of this process more precisely.

46. J.G.A. Prim, 'The Market Cross of Kilkenny', in *TKAS*, ii, 2 (1853), 219–230; C.D. Milligan, *The Walls of Derry: Their building, defending, preserving*, II (Londonderry, 1950), pp. 88–91; Daniel Dowling, *Waterford Streets Past and Present* (Waterford, 1998), pp. 38, 63–4; John R. Bowen & Conor O'Brien, eds. *A Celebration of Limerick Silver* (Cork, 2007), p. 23; Gallagher & Legg, *IHTA, Sligo*, p. 2; Mary Clarke, *The Dublin City Portrait Collection: Patronage, politics and patriotism 1693–2013* (Dublin, 2016), pp. 22–9; Alison FitzGerald, *Silver in Georgian Dublin: Making, selling, consuming* (Abingdon, 2017), pp. 6, 24, 165–7.

    The market cross in Drogheda was demolished in the 1660s, but the Jacobite corporation attempted to have a replacement erected: D'Alton, *Drogheda*, I, pp. 108–7; II, p. 291.

CHAPTER 2 PEOPLING THE CITIES

1. *Dublin Chronicle*, 15 Jan. 1788; G.K., 'Description of Belfast', in *WHM*, 1789, 697–9; *Anthologia Hibernica*, I (Jan.–June 1793), 329; J.H. Andrews, 'The Oldest Map of Dublin' in *Proc. RIA*, lxxxiii, C (1983), 226–9; Dickson, *Old World Colony*, p.122; id., *Dublin*, pp. 171–2.

2. For Derry evidence of high residential turnover: Colin Thomas, 'The City of Londonderry: Demographic trends and socio-economic characteristics, 1650–1900', in O'Brien, *Derry and Londonderry*, p. 372.

3. Rev. James Whitelaw, *An Essay on the Population of Dublin* ... (Dublin, 1805); Patrick Fagan, 'The Population of Dublin in the Eighteenth Century ..', in *ECI*, vi (1991), 144–7; Richard S. Harrison, *Dr John Rutty (1698–1775) of Dublin: A Quaker polymath of the Enlightenment* (Dublin, 2011), pp. 193–207.

4. *A Census of Ireland circa 1659*, ed. Séamus Pender, with introduction by W.J. Smyth, 2nd edn (Dublin, 2002), pp. xv–xl; *DIB*, 'Sir William Petty'.

5. Dickson, 'Town and City', in Eugenio F. Biagini & Mary E. Daly, eds. *Cambridge Social History of Modern Ireland* (Cambridge, 2017), pp. 122–4. The British figure is extrapolated from Table 14.4 in John Langton, 'Urban Growth and Economic Change, c.1688–1841', in Clark, *Cambridge Urban History*, II, p. 473. If London is excluded, the rate falls to 0.6 per cent p.a.

6. Holy Trinity Cork, and St Mary's Limerick (Church of Ireland), registers (NAI, Mics 23 and 15); Michael Drake, 'The Irish Demographic Crisis of 1740–41', in *Historical Studies VI*, ed. T.W. Moody (London, 1968), pp. 119–22; James Kelly, 'Harvests and Hardship: Famine and scarcity in Ireland in the late 1720s', in *Studia Hibernica*, xxvi (1992), 70, 82–95; Chris Galley, 'A Model of Early Modern Urban Demography', in *EHR*, xlviii, 3 (1995), 448–51, 465–68; id., *The Demography of Early Modern Towns: York in the sixteenth and seventeenth centuries* (Liverpool, 1998), p. 173; Pádraig Lenihan, 'War and Population, 1649–52', in *IESH*, xxiv (1997), 9–13; Pamela Sharpe, 'Population and Society 1700–1840', in *Cambridge Urban History of Britain*, II: *1500–1800*, ed. Peter Clark (Cambridge, 2007), pp. 504–5; Clark, *European Cities and Towns, 400–2000* (London, 2009), pp. 159–61. See also review by Leonard Schwarz of Richard Lawton & Robert Lee, eds. *Population and Society in Western European Port-Cities c. 1650–1939* (Liverpool, 2002), in *Urban History*, xxxi, 1 (2004), 157–8.

    On inward disease transmission: James Sims, *Observations on Epidemic Disorders* ... (London, 1773), pp. 36–8, quoted in K.H. Connell, *The Population of Ireland, 1750–1845* (Oxford, 1950), pp. 209–10.

7. Connell, *Population of Ireland*, pp. 208–20; Dickson, *Cork*, p. 309; Romola Davenport, Leonard Schwarz & Jeremy Boulton, 'The Decline of Adult Smallpox in Eighteenth-Century London', in *EHR*, lxiv, 4 (2011), 1301, 1307–10.

8. 'Documents relating the Dublin bills of mortality . . .' (Bodleian Lib., Oxford, MS Rawl. C 406 [N.L.I. Mic p2819]), p. 92; *Dublin Gazette*, 23–26 June, 10–14 July, 4–7 Aug. 1733; Fagan, 'Population of Dublin', p. 154; Kelly, 'Harvests and Hardship', 95; Richard T. Vann & David Eversley, *Friends in Life and Death: The British and Irish Quakers in the demographic transition* (Cambridge, 1992), p. 212; Sharpe, 'Population and Society', pp. 512–13; Thomas, 'Derry', 108; Davenport et al., 'Adult Smallpox', 1291; Davenport et al., 'Urban Inoculation and the Decline of Smallpox Mortality in Eighteenth-Century Cities', in *EHR*, lxix, 1 (2016), 196–8. Cf. Valerie Morgan & William Macafee, 'Mortality at Magherafelt, Co. Derry in the Early Eighteenth Century Reappraised', in *IHS*, xxiii, 89 (1982), 52–3, reporting child deaths constituting 75 per cent of deaths among both Church of Ireland and Dissenter parishioners; Clodagh Tait, 'Causes of Death and Cultures of Care in Co. Cork: The evidence of Youghal parish registers 1660–1720', in John Cunningham, ed. *Early Modern Ireland and Medicine* (Manchester, 2019), pp. 135–7, where in the sickly years of 1713 and 1718 child deaths reached 72 and 63 per cent respectively.
9. St Patrick's Waterford (Church of Ireland) registers (NAI, Mic. 11); St Catherine's Dublin (Church of Ireland) registers (RCB Library); *Dublin Gazette*, 29 July–2 Aug. 1740; *Census of Ireland, 1851, V, Report on Deaths*, p. 504; Connell, *Population of Ireland*, p. 209; Vann & Eversley, *Friends*, pp. 210–13; Dickson, *Arctic Ireland: The extraordinary story of the great frost and forgotten famine of 1740–41* (Belfast, 1997), p. 45. See Appendix 4 for bills of mortality sources and data.
10. J. Warburton, J. Whitelaw & R. Walsh, *History of Dublin* (London, 1818), I, pp. 589, 591, 596; W.D. Wodsworth, *A Brief History of the Ancient Foundling Hospital of Dublin . . .* (Dublin, 1876), pp. 34, 36–9, 41, 48, 52; Joseph Robins, *The Lost Children: A study of charity children in Ireland, 1700–1900* (Dublin, 1980), pp. 17, 22; Raymond Refaussé, *The Register of the Parish Church of St Thomas, Dublin 1750 to 1791* (Dublin, 1994); Dickson, *Dublin*, p. 120; Alysa Levene, *Childcare, Health and Mortality at the London Foundling Hospital 1741–1800* (Manchester, 2007), pp. 102–6; Karen Sonnelitter, *Charity Movements in Eighteenth-Century Ireland: Philanthropy and improvement* (Woodbridge, 2016), pp. 155–63. Less extreme ratios of child/'daughter of'/'son of' deaths were registered for St Patrick's Waterford (Church of Ireland), where between 1733 and 1744 the child proportion of total burials was 34.9 per cent (NAI, Mic. 11); and in St Mary's Limerick, (Church of Ireland), where between 1727 and 1753 the proportion was 41.2 per cent (NAI, Mic. 15).
11. D.E.C. Eversley, 'The Demography of the Irish Quakers 1630–1830', in J.M. Goldstrom & L.A. Clarkson, eds. *Irish Population, Economy and Society: Essays in honour of the late K.H. Connell* (Oxford, 1982), pp. 61, 80; Vann & Eversley, *Friends*, p.195; P. Griffiths et al., 'Population and Disease, Estrangement and Belonging, 1540–1700', in Clark, *Cambridge Urban History*, II, pp. 208–9. The estimate of a 40 per cent *urban* share in the Quaker Irish sample is my own, based on the distribution of families between Quaker meetings, and if anything understates the urban component in the eighteenth century.
12. Cormac Ó Gráda, 'Dublin's Demography in the Early Nineteenth Century: Evidence from the Rotunda', in *Population Studies*, xlv, 1 (1991), 46–9.
13. The ratio of excess burials over births between 1666 and 1680 was 164 to 100; in 1697 and 1698, 201; between 1712 and 1718, 240; and between 1752 and 1754, 104 (for sources see Appendix II). Wilde cites totals in bills (apparently not extant) for 1760, 1766 and 1768 where the ratios were 116 to 100, 106 and 104 respectively: William Wilde, 'Miscellanea', in *Assurance Magazine*, 3, 1 (1853), 251. On nursing: *The Tryal of Neale Molloy, esq; and Vere Molloy, His Wife . . .* (Dublin, 1763), p. 12; S.J. Connolly, 'Family, Love and Marriage . . .', in Margaret MacCurtain & Mary O'Dowd, eds. *Women in Early Modern Ireland* (Edinburgh, 1991), pp. 286–7; Erin Bishop, *The World of Mary O'Connell 1778–1836* (Dublin, 1999), pp. 64–7; Angela Bourke et al., eds. *The Field Day Anthology of Irish Writing*, IV (Cork, 2002), p. 902; Griffiths et al., 'Population and Disease', and Sharpe, 'Population and Society', in Clarke, *Cambridge Urban History*, II, pp. 201–3, 506.
14. Thomas, 'Demographic Trends', pp. 362–64; id., 'Family Formation in a Colonial City: Londonderry, 1650–1750', in *Proc. RIA*, c, C, (2000), 92. In St Patrick's Waterford (Church of Ireland) register, baptisms averaged 16.3 p.a. in 1731–40 compared with 101.0 burials p.a., almost certainly reflecting the large-scale burial of non-communicants there: NAI, Mic. 11.

15. Fagan, 'Population of Dublin', 125–6, 151; Whitelaw, *Essay on Population*, p. 14; Sharpe, 'Population and Society', pp. 496, 499.

    One problem with Whitelaw's template in 1798 was that the return of servants was linked to the return of 'upper or middle class' households, and no allowance was made for servants (i.e. apprentices) living in 'lower class' households. Servants, male, female and juvenile, made up 9.4 per cent of Dublin city population in 1841: *Census of Ireland, 1841*.

16. 'State of Lisburn, 1779', in Robinson Papers (Dublin City Libraries, Pearse St., Gilbert MS 36), p. 334; L.A. Clarkson, 'Household and Family Structure in Armagh City', in *Local Population Studies*, xx (1978), 27–9; id., 'Armagh Town in the Eighteenth Century', in Brenda Collins, Philip Ollerenshaw & Trevor Parkhill, eds. *Industry, Trade and People in Ireland 1650–1950: Essays in Honour of W.H. Crawford* (Belfast, 2005), pp. 56, 66; Marie-Louise Legg, *The Census of Elphin, 1749* (Dublin, 2004), pp. 524–39.

17. St Patrick's Waterford (Church of Ireland) registers (NAI, Mic. 11); Thomas, 'Family Formation', 94–7, 98–100.

18. Moira Corcoran, 'A Drogheda Census List of 1798', in *JCLAHS*, xvii, 2 (1970), 94; L.A. Clarkson, 'The Demography of Carrick-on-Suir, 1799', in *Proc. RIA*, lxxxvii, C (1987), 14–36; id., 'Love, Labour and Life: Women in Carrick-on-Suir in the late eighteenth century', in *IESH*, xx (1993), 23–4.

19. *Census of Ireland, 1821*. For the figures for Dublin: Fagan, 'Population of Dublin', 151; for Sligo: Legg, *Elphin*, pp. 524–39; for Lisburn: 'State of Lisburn, 1779'; for Kilkenny: William Tighe, *Statistical Observations Relative to the County of Kilkenny . . .* (Dublin, 1802), p. 458.

20. L.A. Clarkson, 'The Carrick-on-Suir Woollen Industry in the Eighteenth Century', in *IESH*, xvi (1989), 27–9, 37, 40; Thomas, 'Family Formation', 96; Sharpe, 'Population and Society', pp. 493–4.

21. John Cunningham, *Conquest and Land in Ireland: The transplantation to Connacht, 1649–1680* (Woodbridge, 2011), pp. 92–3.

22. *Statutes of Ireland*, 14 & 15 Charles II, c. 13; 4 William & Mary, c.2; Dickson, 'Huguenots in the Urban Economy of Eighteenth-Century Dublin and Cork', in C.E.J. Caldicott, Hugh Gough & J-P. Pittion, eds. *The Huguenots and Ireland: Anatomy of an emigration* (Dublin, 1987), pp. 321–32; Jacqueline Hill, *From Patriots to Unionists: Dublin civic politics and Irish Protestant patriotism, 1660–1940* (Oxford, 1997), pp. 32–3, 36; Raymond Gillespie, ed. *The Vestry Records of the Parishes of St Catherine and St James, Dublin, 1657–92* (Dublin, 2004), p. 17; Raymond Hylton, *Ireland's Huguenots and their Refuge, 1662–1745: An unlikely haven* (Brighton and Portland, 2005); Dickson, *Dublin*, pp. 112–13. Both the 1662/3 and 1703/4 statutes were limited to seven years from the dissolution of the sitting parliament.

23. Vincent Kinane, 'Printers' Apprentices in Eighteenth- and Nineteenth-Century Dublin', in *Irish Booklore*, x (1993), 111–14; Kevin Whelan, *The Tree of Liberty . . .* (Cork, 1997), p. 77; Patrick Wallis, Cliff Webb & Chris Minns, 'Leaving Home and Entering Service: The age of apprenticeship in early modern London', in *Continuity and Change*, xxv, 3 (2010), 377–404; Edward Whelan, 'Native versus Newcomer . . . in Dublin, 1600–1800', in *DHR*, lxiii, 1 (2010), 75; Raymond Gillespie, 'Making Belfast 1600–1750', in S.J. Connolly, ed. *Belfast 400: People, place and history* (Liverpool, 2014), p. 158; Brian Gurrin, 'Population and Emigration, 1730–1845', in Kelly, *CHI*, III: *1730–1880*, p. 222. The mean age of matriculants to Trinity College Dublin between 1685 and 1750 was 17.1: David Hannigan, 'The University of Dublin 1685–1750: A study of matriculation records' (M.A. dissertation, Maynooth University, 1995), p. 56.

24. Toby Barnard, *A New Anatomy of Ireland: The Irish Protestants 1649–1770* (New Haven and London, 2003), pp. 263–4, 306–9, 314–16; FitzGerald, *Silver*, pp. 42–47, 52–3.

25. By contrast, the migration field for eighteenth-century Edinburgh was growing at this time, especially for female migrants: Sharpe, 'Population and Society', p. 497.

26. J. Wareing, 'Changes in the Geographical Distribution of the Recruitment of Apprentices to the London Companies, 1486–1750', in *Journal of Historical Geography*, vi (1980), 242, 245–7; Griffiths et al., 'Population and Disease', pp. 198–9.

27. NLI MS 12,131; Mary Pollard, *A Dictionary of Members of the Dublin Book Trade 1550–1800* (London, 2001); FitzGerald, *Silver*, pp. 47, [221–2].

28. On the changing ratio of full to quarter brothers in Dublin's St Luke's Guild: Pollard, *Dictionary*, pp. xi-xii.

29. Maureen Wall, *Catholic Ireland in the Eighteenth Century . . .*, ed. Gerard O'Brien (Dublin, 1989), pp. 63–5, 175; Fagan, 'Population of Dublin', p. 133; Rowena V. Dudley, 'Dublin's Parishes 1660-1729: The Church of Ireland parishes and their role in the civic administration of the city' (Ph.D., University of Dublin, 1995), pp. 270–1, 276; Hill, *Patriots to Unionists*, pp. 33–8; Pollard, *Dictionary*, pp. xxvi-xxviii; FitzGerald, *Silver*, pp. 12–3, 55.

   For a protest from the Liberties c.1712 against 'the arbitrary power of the master and wardens of the corporations [i.e. guilds]' over apprenticeship rules, see Dudley, op. cit., pp. 270–1. For complaints that Catholic merchants were accepting Protestant apprentices in Limerick in the 1750s: David Fleming, 'Limerick's Eighteenth-Century Economy', in Irwin & Ó Tuathaigh, *Limerick*, p. 171.

30. Colm Lennon, 'Religious and Social Change in Early Modern Limerick: The testimony of the Sexton family papers', in Liam Irwin, Gearóid Ó Tuathaigh & Matthew Potter, eds., *Limerick: History and Society* (Dublin, 2009), pp. 122–3; O'Flaherty, 'An Urban Community and the Penal Laws', pp. 203–4.

31. John Patten, 'Patterns of Migration and Movement of Labour to Three Pre-industrial East Anglian Towns', in *Journal of Historical Geography*, ii (1976), 111–29.

   For an indication as to how limited migration fields may have been, see John Mannion's map of the geographical origins of emigrants embarking at Waterford for Newfoundland in the eighteenth and early nineteenth centuries: Map 16 in F.H.A. Aalen, Kevin Whelan & Matthew Stout, eds. *Atlas of the Irish Rural Landscape*, 2nd edn (Cork, 2011), p. 377.

32. Norman Gamble, 'The Business Community and Trade of Belfast 1767-1800' (Ph.D. dissertation, University of Dublin, 1978), p. 104; Sharpe, 'Population and Society', pp. 494–5; Michael E. Smith, 'Peasant Mobility, Local Migration and Pre-modern Urbanization', in *World Archaeology*, xlvi, 4 (2014), 528.

33. Papers regarding the Dublin workhouse, 1725–6 (Marsh's Library, Dublin, MS Z.3.1.1), p. clv; *Anthologia Hibernica*, i (Jan.–June 1793), 26.

34. Copy, William Colles to Thomas Pryor [sic], 29 Feb. 1744/5, in Prim papers (NAI, MS 1A.55.83); *Dublin Gazette*, 3 June 1729; Griffiths et al., 'Population and Disease', p. 199; David Fleming & John Logan, eds. *Pauper Limerick: The register of the Limerick House of Industry 1774–93* (Dublin, 2011).

   Cork city's House of Industry, opened in 1777, had slightly larger capacity than that of Limerick: Colman O Mahony, *In the Shadows: Life in Cork 1750–1930* (Cork, 1997), pp. 23–5.

35. Richard Lucas, *The Cork Directory for the Year 1787, Including the Adjacent Out-ports . . .*, 2 vols (Cork, [1787–8]); Pender, *Census*, pp. 195, 265, 350.

36. 'Report on the State of Popery, Ireland, 1731; Diocese of Tuam', in *AH*, iii (1914), 146–7; Brian Ó Dalaigh, *Ennis in the Eighteenth Century: Portrait of an urban community* (Blackrock, 1995), pp. 30–1.

37. *First report of the Commissioners of Public Instruction, Ireland* (Parl. papers, 1835, XXXIII).

38. Baptismal registers, St Andrew's parish, Dublin [Catholic] (NLI, Mic p6605); S.J. Connolly, *Religion, Law and Power: The making of Protestant Ireland 1660–1760* (Oxford, 1992), pp. 145, 147; Fagan, 'Population of Dublin', 131, 149. Note that interpretation of the St Andrew's figures is complicated by the existence of separate registers kept by two of the clergy.

39. St Peter's, Drogheda [Catholic], baptism and marriage register (NLI); Tighe, *Kilkenny*, p. 458; Dickson, 'Inland City: Reflections on eighteenth-century Kilkenny', in Nolan & Whelan, *Kilkenny*, pp. 274–81, 335–6. Cf. Fagan, 'Population of Dublin', 131, 146–7. By comparison, the number of baptisms in St Patrick's Church of Ireland parish register in Waterford grew much more modestly in each decade between 1731 and 1758: NAI, Mic. 11.

40. Ian d'Alton, *Protestant Society and Politics in Cork, 1812–1844* (Cork, 1980), pp. 32–4. Fagan has suggested a sharp difference between Catholic and Protestant household size in Dublin in the 1710s, with Catholic homes around 40 per cent larger, on the supposition of contrasting fertility levels or of greater numbers of lodgers in Catholic houses. He also posited a peak Protestant population of 75,000 that was reached in the early 1730s, falling

back to 58,000 by 1766. The fertility differential is plausible but unproven, but the mid-century decline in Protestant numbers, if indeed true, would be puzzling and could only be explained by marked changes in Protestant migration patterns: Fagan, 'Population of Dublin', 131, 149. The Church of Ireland register for St Mary's Limerick, indicates declining numbers of baptisms in the 1740s and early 1750s: St Mary's Limerick (Church of Ireland) parish registers (NAI, Mic. 15).

41. Aubry de la Mottraye, *Voyages en anglois et en françois* . . . (Dublin, 1732), p. 468; Joseph Rogers, *An Essay on Epidemic Diseases, More Particularly on the Endemial Epidemics of the City of Cork* . . . (Dublin, 1734), p. 42; J. Landers, *Death and the Metropolis: Studies in the demographic history of London 1670–1830* (Cambridge, 1993), pp. 160, 468; G.J. Lyne & M.E. Mitchell, 'A Scientific Tour through Munster: The travels of Joseph Woods, architect and botanist, in 1809', in *NMAJ*, xxvii (1985), 23.

42. William Strong, Dublin, to Nathaniel Hawes, 5 Aug.1684, listed in Fonsie Mealy, Book Auction Catalogue, 29 May 2017, lot 489; *Dublin Gazette*, 2–5 Aug. 1760; *Cork Chronicle*, 23 March 1767; Ferrar, *History of Limerick*, p. 65; F.H. Tuckey, *The County and City of Cork Remembrancer* (Cork, 1837), pp. 135, 145, 166, 171, 215; Daniel Dowling, *Waterford Streets Past and Present* (Waterford, 1991), p. 23. For ribbon development around Limerick: O'Flaherty, *IHTA, Limerick*, map 15 [William Eyres, 1752]; for Belfast suburbs, Gamble. 'Belfast Merchant Community', pp. 16, 139; Royle & Gillespie, *IHTA, Belfast*, pp. 4, 6, map 8 [1757], map 10 [1815]; Gillespie, *Early Belfast*, pp. 146–8.

43. Fagan, 'Population of Dublin', 123, 128, 134, 138; Dickson, *Dublin*, pp. 597–8fn.; Colm Lennon & John Montague, *John Rocque's Dublin: A guide to the Georgian city* (Dublin, 2010), pp. 1, 30–3.
    In 1834 Dublin's old mural parishes were over 79.2 per cent Catholic compared to 71.7 per cent in all the parishes outside the mural line: *First Report, Public Instruction*.

44. 'Population of Ireland, 1788' (University of London, Senate House Library MS 1127, A1); Whitelaw, *Essay on Population*, p. 14; R.A. Butlin, 'The Population of Dublin in the Late Seventeenth Century', in *Irish Geography*, v (1965), 59–62; Nuala Burke, 'An Early Modern Suburb: The estate of Francis Aungier, Earl of Longford', in *Irish Geography*, vi, 4 (1972), 365–85; Fagan, 'Population of Dublin', 143; Edel Sheridan-Quantz, 'The Multi-centred Metropolis: The social topography of eighteenth-century Dublin', in Peter Clark & Raymond Gillespie, eds. *Two Capitals: London and Dublin 1500–1840* (Oxford, 2001), pp. 277–80.

45. For contrasts in house valuations within Limerick *c*.1850: O'Flaherty, *IHTA, Limerick*, map 24. For Cork valuations: Crowley, *Atlas of Cork*, p. 163. The parish with highest valuation was Christ Church/Holy Trinity, the population of which was 33.7 per cent Protestant in 1834.

46. Warburton, *Dublin*, II, p. 1073n.; *CARD*, VII, p. 95; Edward McParland, 'The Papers of Bryan Bolger, Measurer', in *DHR*, xxv (1972), 122; Lennon & Montague, *John Rocque's Dublin*, pp. 70–1; Dickson, *Dublin*, pp. 84, 94–5, 228–9; Leslie Tomory, *The History of the London Water Industry, 1580–1820* (Baltimore, 2017), pp. 102–4, 123, 188.

47. De Latocnaye, *Promenade d'un français dans l'Irlande*, pp. 86–7; John Ferrar, *An History of Limerick* . . ., 2nd edn (Dublin, 1787), p. 129; R.W.M. Strain, *Belfast and its Charitable Society* . . . (Oxford, 1961), pp. 182–99, 237–9; O Mahony, *In the Shadows*, pp. 58–62; Colin Rynne, *Industrial Ireland 1750–1930: An archaeology* (2006), pp. 411–50.

CHAPTER 3   THE KEYS OF THE KINGDOM

1. Joseph Johnston, *Bishop Berkeley's Querist in Historical Perspective* (Dundalk, 1970), p. 148.
2. L.M. Cullen, *Anglo-Irish Trade 1660–1800* (Manchester, 1968), pp. 97–102; id., 'The Evolution of Mercantile Cultures and Values in Western Europe in the Seventeenth and Eighteenth Centuries . . .', in Simonetta Cavaciocchi, ed. *Fiere e mercati nella integrazione delle economie Europee secc. XIII-XVIII* (Prato, 2001), pp. 1001–38; Jon Stobart, 'Personal and Commercial Networks in an English Port: Chester in the early eighteenth century', in *Journal of Historical Geography*, xxx (2004), 288–90.

3. Cullen, *Anglo-Irish Trade*, passim; id., 'Problems in and Sources for the Study of Irish Economic Fluctuations, 1660–1900', in *IESH*, xli (2014), 1–13; Patrick Walsh, *The South Sea Bubble and Ireland: Money, banking and investment 1690–1721* (Woodbridge, 2014), passim.

4. Dickson, 'Society and Economy in the Long Eighteenth Century', in Kelly, *CHI*, III, pp. 155–67.

5. TNA/CUST/15; Conrad Gill, *The Rise of the Irish Linen Industry* (Oxford, 1925), pp. 339–42.

6. Cullen, 'Economic Fluctuations', 1–19; Dickson, 'Society and Economy', pp. 159–70.

7. Cullen, 'The Irish Merchant Communities of La Rochelle, Bordeaux and Cognac in the Eighteenth Century', in Cullen & Paul Butel, *Négoce et industrie en France et en Irlande aux XVIIIe et XIXe siècles* (Paris, 1980), pp. 54–60; id., *Economy, Trade and Irish Merchants at Home and Abroad 1600–1988* (Dublin, 2012), pp. 165–92; James Kelly, ed. *The Letters of Lord Chief Baron Edward Willes . . . 1757–1762* (Aberystwyth, 1990), pp. 83–4, 86–7; Truxes, *Irish-American Trade*, p. 87; John Bergin, 'Irish Catholics and their Networks in Eighteenth-Century London', in *Eighteenth-Century Life*, xxxix, 1 (2015), 78–9.

   On young merchants travelling as supercargoes from Restoration Belfast: Jean Agnew, *Belfast Merchant Families in the Seventeenth Century* (Dublin, 1996), pp. 140–1.

8. Dickson, *Old World Colony*, pp. 114–16, 118. Goold had invested heavily in the Restoration land market and was Jacobite mayor of the city in 1687/8; he lost all his real property after the war in disputed circumstances, but three decades of legal wrangling and shortly before his death in 1728 he received a royal bounty: id., pp. 80, 118.

9. James Waller, Cork, to Edward Southwell, 16 March 1693/4: Southwell papers (BL, Add. MS 38,147); J. S. Bromley, 'The Jacobite Privateers in the Nine Years War', in A. Whiteman, J. S. Bromley & P.G.M. Dickson, eds. *Statesmen, Scholars and Merchants: Essays in eighteenth-century history presented to Dame Lucy Sutherland* (Oxford, 1973), pp. 23–5; Dickson, *Old World Colony*, p. 160; Liam Murphy, *Waterford Merchants and their Families on Distant Shores: Waterford traders in Spain and France 1600–1800* (Dublin, 2018), p. 215.

10. Thomas M. Truxes, *Irish-American Trade 1660–1783* (Cambridge, 1988), p. 78; Gerard O'Brien, ed. *Irish Catholics in the Eighteenth Century: Collected essays of Maureen Wall* (Dublin, 1989), p. 87; Dickson, *Old World Colony*, pp. 122–3, 138–43, 160, 166–9, 646, 655, 658, 660.

11. Paul G.E. Clemens, 'The Rise of Liverpool, 1665–1750', in *EHR*, xxix, 2 (1976), 213; Kenneth Morgan, *Bristol and the Atlantic Trade in the Eighteenth Century* (Cambridge, 1993), p. 123; Joseph Leydon, 'The Irish Provisions Trade to the Caribbean, c.1650–1780: An historical geography' (Ph.D. dissertation, University of Toronto, 1995), pp. 118–19, 207, 235–7, 241; Dickson, *Old World Colony*, pp. 118, 149–50, 545, fn. 6; Rodgers, *Ireland, Slavery and Anti-slavery*, pp. 131–3; James O'Shea, ed. *Letterbook of Richard Hare, Cork Merchant 1771–1772* (Dublin, 2013), pp. xiv-xvi, 253. Waterford, Limerick and Galway together recorded just under 40 per cent of Cork's total tonnage in the first quarter of the eighteenth century, and just over 56 per cent in the final quarter: TNA, CUST/1.

12. TNA, CUST/1; *The New Cork Directory, for the Year 1795* (Cork, 1795); Truxes, *Irish-American Trade*, pp. 77–8; Morgan, *Bristol and the Atlantic Trade*, p. 45; Dickson, *Old World Colony*, pp. 149–53, 158–9.

    The figure of 140 merchants includes timber and wine merchants: *Cork Directory, 1795*; 142 was the total number listed in Richard Lucas, *The Cork Directory: For the year 1787 . . .* (Cork, [1787]). Leading Cork merchants whose rise to great wealth seems to have occurred in wartime include Edward Hoare (in the Nine Years War), John Anderson (in the American War of Independence), Daniel Callaghan (in the Napoleonic Wars), and possibly Richard Hare (in the Seven Years War).

13. Dickson, *Old World Colony*, pp. 116, 123, 150–1, 155–6.

14. Memorandum book of David Rochford, 1798: Caulfield Papers, MS 43 (UCC Archives); Dickson, *Old World Colony*, pp. 152, 160–3, 168–9; Richard S. Harrison, 'Quaker Enterprise', in Crowley et al., *Atlas of Cork City*, pp. 171–4; Jan Parmentier, 'The Sweets of Commerce: The Hennessys of Ostend . . .', in Dickson, Parmentier & Jane Ohlmeyer, eds. *Irish and Scottish Mercantile Networks in Europe and Overseas in the Seventeenth and Eighteenth Centuries* (Gent, 2007), pp. 72–82.

15. Maurice Lenihan, *Limerick, its History and Antiquities . . .* (Dublin, 1866), pp. 229, 473, 552, 596, 708; Richard Hayes, 'Some Old Limerick Wills', in *NMAJ*, ii (1940–1), 73; Eoin O'Kelly, *The Old Private Banks of Munster* (Cork, 1959), pp. 98–109; David Fleming, 'Limerick's Eighteenth-Century Economy', in Irwin & Ó Tuathaigh, *Limerick*, p. 169.

16. Samuel Monsell, Limerick, to Thomas Lynch Fitzjames, 26 Oct. 1722, Monsell Letterbook (UL, Special Collections P.29), f. 5; Richard Lucas, *A General Directory of the Kingdom of Ireland*, II (Cork, 1788), pp. 161–79; Dwight E. Robinson, 'Secrets of British Power in the Age of Sail: Admiralty records of the coasting fleet', in *American Neptune*, xlviii, 1 (1988), 8. For Limerick's dependence on Dublin for the supply of sugar, wine and imported spirits: Cullen, *Anglo-Irish Trade*, pp. 14–15.

17. Monsell, Limerick, to Widow Sampson & Samuel Browne, 16 Oct. 1722: Monsell Letterbook, f. 2; Rodgers, *Ireland, Slavery and Anti-slavery*, pp. 104, 142–3.

18. Truxes, *Irish-American Trade*, p. 87; Hill, *Building of Limerick*, pp. 80–2; Rodgers, *Ireland, Slavery and Anti-slavery*, pp. 96, 112–13, 132–3; Fleming, 'Limerick's Economy', pp. 163–5, 167–71; O'Flaherty, 'An Urban Community and the Penal Laws', pp. 206–8; id., *IHTA, Limerick*, p. 8; *DIB*, 'Francis Arthur'; Cullen, *Economy, Trade and Irish Merchants*, pp. 160–1, 201; Woods, *Abbot's Tour*, p. 81. For the unusually prolific references linking Limerick merchants with smuggling, both along the Shannon Estuary and on the Isle of Man (before 1764): Rodgers, *Ireland, Slavery and Anti-slavery*, p. 104; Fleming, *Politics and Provincial People*, pp. 175–81.

19. John Mannion, 'The Waterford Merchants and the Irish-Newfoundland Provisions Trade, 1770–1820', in Cullen & Butel, *Négoce et industrie*, pp. 38–9; id., 'The Maritime Trade of Waterford in the Eighteenth Century', in William J. Smyth & Kevin Whelan, eds. *Common Ground: Essays on the historical geography of Ireland* (Cork, 1988), pp. 209–15, 219, 223; Patrick O'Flanagan & Julian Walton, 'The Irish Community at Cádiz during the Late Eighteenth Century', in Howard B. Clarke, Jacinta Prunty & Mark Hennessy, eds. *Surveying Ireland's Past: Multidisciplinary essays in honour of Anngret Simms* (Dublin, 2004), pp. 361–5; Parmentier, 'The Sweets of Commerce', p. 71; Guy Saupin, 'Les réseaux commerciaux des irlandais de Nantes sous le règne de Louis XIV', and Maria del Carmen Lario, 'The Irish Traders of Eighteenth-Century Cádiz', in Dickson et al., *Irish and Scottish Mercantile Networks*, pp. 118–27, 129–30, 214–27; Scott Talbott, '"Such unjustifiable practices"?: Irish trade, settlement and society in France 1688–1715', in *EHR*, lxvii, 2 (2014), 573–4; Bergin, 'Irish Catholics and London', 79, 81; Murphy, *Waterford Merchants and Their Families*, pp. 62–3, 65–6, 76–81, 118–19, 171–2. In the 1773 census of Cádiz, of the 226 Irish people whose origin was noted, 72 came from Waterford and 47 per cent came from the south-east (Waterford, Kilkenny or Wexford): O'Flanagan & Walton, op. cit., pp. 373–4.

20. Brian Murphy, 'The Waterford Catholic Community in the Eighteenth Century' (MA, NUI, UCD, 1997), pp. 11–13, 62; [Eamonn McEneany & Rosemary Ryan], *Waterford Treasures: A guide . . .* (Waterford, 2004), pp. 152–3; Murphy, *Waterford Merchants*, pp. 238–9.

21. Mannion, 'Irish-Newfoundland Provisions Trade', pp. 29–34, 42; id., 'Maritime Trade', pp. 215–17; id., 'Vessels, Mariners and Seafaring: Patterns of voyages in Waterford commerce 1766–1771', in William Nolan & Thomas P. Power, eds. *Waterford: History and society* (Dublin, 1992), pp. 381–4, 387–8; id., 'Irish Migration and Settlement in Newfoundland: The formative phase, 1697–1732', in *Newfoundland and Labrador Studies*, xvii, 2 (2001), 261–2.

22. Covey, *Scheme for Building a Bridge*, p. 13.

23. Woods, *Abbot's Tour*, pp. 63–4; Truxes, *Irish-American Trade*, pp. 84–5; Mannion, 'Maritime Trade', pp. 212–15, 218–19.

24. L.M. Cullen, 'The Overseas Trade of Waterford as seen from a Ledger of Courtenay and Ridgway', in *JRSAI*, lxxxix, 2 (1958), 168–78; id., *Anglo-Irish Trade*, pp. 69–70; Mannion, 'Irish-Newfoundland Provisions Trade', pp. 30–4, 36–7; id., 'Maritime Trade', p. 221.

25. Mannion, 'Irish-Newfoundland Provisions Trade', pp. 38, 41; id., 'Maritime Trade', pp. 211, 218–19; id., 'Vessels, Mariners and Seafarers', pp. 394–6; Hubert Gallwey, 'Bartholomew Rivers of Waterford, Banker, and his Kindred', in *Decies*, xii (Sept. 1979), 56–8; Truxes,

Irish-American Trade, pp. 84–5; Patrick Grogan, 'Some Aspects of Lemuel Cox's Bridge . . .', in *Decies*, lv (1999), 30–1.

26. See David Heeb in 'Reviews', in *Journal of Urban History*, xxv, 6 (1999), 868–70.

27. Tighe gave parish population data for Co. Kilkenny for 1731 and 1800, but noted disarmingly of the city total returned for 1800 that they 'were numbered some years ago, and are below the real amount': Tighe, *Kilkenny*, p. 461n.

28. L.M. Cullen, 'The Social and Economic Evolution of Kilkenny in the Seventeenth and Eighteenth Centuries', and Dickson, 'Inland City: Reflections on eighteenth-century Kilkenny', in Nolan & Whelan, *Kilkenny*, pp. 274–81, 333–45; Neely, *Kilkenny*, pp. 190–1, 194–5; David Broderick, *The First Toll-roads: Irelands turnpike roads 1729–1858* (Dublin, 2002), pp. 66–7.

   On the mode of carriage for coal to Dublin in the 1740s: W.R. Chetwood, *A Tour through Ireland . . .* (Dublin, 1748), pp. 203–4.

29. Lucas, *General Directory, 1788*, pp. 134–44; Neely, *Kilkenny*, p.153.

30. Neely, *Kilkenny*, pp. 184, 192–4, 208–9; *DIB*, 'William Colles'; Tony Hand, 'Supplying Stone for the Dublin house', in Christine Casey, ed. *The Eighteenth-Century Dublin Town House: Form, function and finance* (Dublin, 2010), pp. 84–5, 89–91, 96, plate 9.

CHAPTER 4   NORTHERN TURN

1. J.R.R. Adams, *Merchants in Plenty: Joseph Smyth's Belfast Directories of 1807 and 1808* (Belfast, 1991); Agnew, *Belfast Merchant Families*, pp. 15–16, 33; Thomas M. Truxes, ed. *Letterbook of Gregg & Cunningham: Merchants of New York and Belfast 1756–1757* (Oxford, 2001), p. 20; Gillespie, *Early Belfast*, pp. 128–9.

2. Isaac Macartney, Belfast, to John Bucke, 12 March 1704/5, Isaac Macartney Letterbook, 1704–6 (PRONI, D501/1); Agnew, *Belfast Merchant Families*, pp. 120, 123–4, 128–31, 139, 162–4, 180–92, 236, 209–52. Black George became a Presbyterian a few years before his death in 1702: id., pp. 94–104. On the Black family and the evolution of their transnational family network: James Livesey, *Civil Society and Empire: Ireland and Scotland in the eighteenth-century Atlantic world* (New Haven & London, 2010), pp. 130–53.

3. Gamble, 'Business Community of Belfast', pp. 10, 259, 269, 277–80, 292–3; Leydon, 'The Irish Provisions Trade', p. 280; Truxes, *Gregg & Cunningham*, p. 20. According to Abbot in 1792, there were then 80 ships belonging to the port: Woods, *Abbot's Tour*, pp. 30–1.

4. Agnew, *Belfast Merchant Families*, pp. 65–7; Gamble, 'Belfast Business Community', pp. 18, 20.

5. Agnew, *Belfast Merchant Families*, pp. 127–34; Gamble, 'Belfast Business Community', pp. 34, 41–8, 412, 414. Around 18 per cent of the entries in Smyth's *Directory* of 1807 were partnerships, compared to approximately 7 per cent in the Dublin directories of the 1790s: Adams, *Joseph Smyth's Belfast Directories*. For partnerships in Waterford: Mannion, 'Irish-Newfoundland Trade', p. 39.

6. Agnew, *Belfast Merchant Families*, pp. 44–7; Gamble, 'Belfast Merchant Community', pp. 143–5, 197, 297, 309, 404–5; Truxes, *Irish-American Trade*, pp. 81, 107, 114, 136, 140, 142; id., *Gregg & Cunningham*, pp. 38–56; Barnard, *Making the Grand Figure*, p. 114; Gillespie & Royle, *IHTA, Belfast*, p. 4; Gillespie, 'Making Belfast 1600–1750', pp. 129–30.

7. There is a striking precedent in early eighteenth-century Liverpool where a cluster of major public initiatives was pushed through by the town's small merchant community: Clemens, 'Rise of Liverpool, 1665–1750', p. 217.

8. Gamble, 'Belfast Business Community', pp. 69–72, 81, 85–91, 124, 157, 161, 172, 201. Mrs McTier, no fan of old Waddell Cunningham (or of slave-traders), referred to him in the last months of his life as a 'cunning dark-souled uncle': Gamble, op. cit., p. 30.

9. *JHCI*, VIII, append. p. clxiii; Arthur Young, *A Tour of Ireland . . .* (Dublin, 1780), II, pp. 206, 216–17; R.J. Dickson, *Ulster Emigration to Colonial America 1718–1775* (London, 1966), pp. 10, 23n., 32–3, 60–2, 115, 144, 238–81; Gamble. 'Belfast Business Community', p. 305; Truxes, *Irish-American Trade*, pp. 81–2, 136, 140–1; Brian Lacey, *Siege City: The story of Derry and Londonderry* (Belfast, 1990), pp. 148–9, 163–4; Patrick Griffin, *The People with*

No Name: Ireland's Ulster Scots, America's Scots Irish, and the creation of a British Atlantic world 1689–1764 (Princeton, 2001), pp. 91–3; Kerby Miller, Arnold Schrier, Bruce D. Bolling & David N. Doyle, *Irish Immigrants in the Land of Canaan . . . 1675–1815* (Oxford, 2003), p. 537; Benjamin Bankhurst, *Ulster Presbyterians and the Scots Irish Diaspora, 1750–1764* (Basingstoke, 2013), pp. 129–30.

10. *JHCI*, VIII, append. p. clxiii; Cullen, *Anglo-Irish Trade*, p. 66; Kelly, *Willes's Letters*, p. 107; Dickson, *Old World Colony*, pp. 131–5; Robert Gavin, William Kelly & Dolores O' Reilly, *Atlantic Gateway: The port and city of Londonderry since 1700* (Dublin, 2009), pp. 5, 12, 18, 23–4. On the north-west's dominant position in flax cultivation *c.*1796: W.J. Smyth, 'Flax Cultivation in Ireland . . .', in Smyth & Whelan, *Common Ground*, pp. 237–40.

11. Londonderry Corporation minutes, 8B (1765–80), pp. 111, 116–7, 123, 129 (https://www.nidirect.gov.uk/publications/corporation-minute-book-volume-8b-1765-1780); Andrew Ferguson to William Aitkin, 28 Feb. 1775, Ferguson Letterbook 1775–80 (PRONI, D1130/1); *JHCI*, VIII, append. p. clxiii; Col. [Thomas] Colby, *Ordnance Survey of the County of Londonderry*, I: *Memoir of the city . . . of Londonderry* (Dublin, 1837), pp. 130–1; Edith Mary Johnston-Liik, *History of Irish Parliament . . .* (Belfast, 2002), IV, pp. 424–5; Truxes, *Irish-American Trade*, p. 136; John Dooher & Michael Kennedy, eds. *The Fair River Valley: Strabane through the ages* (Belfast, 2000), pp. 106–7; Barnard, *New Anatomy of Ireland*, p. 164; Donal Ó Drisceoil & Diarmuid Ó Drisceoil, *Beamish & Crawford: The history of an Irish brewery* (Cork, 2015), pp. 20–2, 217; IAA, Dictionary of Irish Architects, 'Lemuel Cox'. On the importance of choosing efficient collectors: Patrick Walsh, 'The Fiscal State in Ireland 1691–1780', in *HJ*, lvi, 3 (2013), 641.

12. Steph[en] Bennett, Londonderry, to James Alexander, 30 Apr. 1782, Caledon Papers (PRONI, D2433/B/1/2/4); Charles W. Janson, *The Stranger in America* (London, 1807), pp. 452–3; Maldwyn Jones, 'Ulster Emigration, 1783–1815', in E.R.R. Green, ed., *Essays in Scotch-Irish History* (London, 1969), pp. 49–61; Johnston-Liik, *History of the Irish Parliament*, III, pp. 77–9; Gavin et al., *Atlantic Gateway*, pp. 20–1; Woods, *Abbot's Tour*, pp. 41–4. Another family from the north-west, the Stewarts, later marquesses of Londonderry, began their social climb to greatness after Alexander Stewart (1697–1781) married Mary Cowan, heiress both of her father John Cowan, a Derry merchant, and of her step-brothers, William and Robert, for a while a Lisbon-based merchant but who made his fortune in India, culminating in his governorship of Bombay (1729–34): Johnston-Liik, op. cit., pp. 332–3; *ODNB*, 'Sir Robert Cowan'.

13. Address of the principal inhabitants of Market St, Sligo, 5 Oct. 1785, O'Hara Papers (PRONI, T2812/20/34); Daniel Beaufort, Notes on a Tour of Ireland, 1787/8 (TCD, MS 4027), f.53; Andrew Maiben, Sligo, to [John Foster], 30 Sept. 1790, Foster Papers (PRONI, D562/5299); [Robert Stephenson], *The Reports and Observations of Robert Stephenson, Made to the . . . Trustees of the Linen Manufacture, for . . . 1760, and 1761* (Dublin, 1762), p. 69; Hugh Fenning, 'The Journey of James Lyons from Rome to Sligo, 1763–65', in *Coll. Hib.*, xi (1968), 106; Truxes, *Irish-American Trade*, pp. 87–8, 121, 210; Barnard, *New Anatomy of Ireland*, pp. 256–7; Fleming, *Politics and Provincial People*, pp. 21, 42–3, 205; Dickson & Fleming, eds. 'Charles O'Hara's Observations on County Sligo, 1752–73', in *Anal. Hib.*, xlvi (2015), 95, 97, 107–8, 113, 119.

14. *JHCI*, XIV, append. pp. ccxciii–ccxcvii; J.T. Dolan & Daniel Lynch, 'Drogheda Trade and Customs, 1683', in *JCLAHS*, iii, 1 (1912), 83–103; id., 'Exports from Drogheda in 1683', in *JCLAHS*, iii, 3 (1914), 250–8; Gill, *Linen Industry*, p. 39; Ada K. Longfield, *Anglo-Irish Trade in the Sixteenth Century* (London, 1929), pp. 90, 92; John FitzGerald, 'The Drogheda Textile Industry, 1780–1820', in *JCLAHS*, xx (1981), 36–48; id., 'Drogheda Merchants of the Eighteenth Century', in *Journal of the Old Drogheda Society*, v (1986), 21–6; Gamble, 'Belfast Merchant Community', p. 52; Truxes, *Irish-American Trade*, pp. 85, 199, 207; Ned McHugh, 'The Port of Drogheda, 1790–1850: An era of regeneration and resurgence', in *JCLAHS*, xxvi, 2 (2006), 175–6, 179–80.

In the desperate winter of 1788/9 French orders were received and flour from the great Slane Mill was despatched from Drogheda on three vessels to Bordeaux: A.P.W. Malcomson, *John Foster (1740–1828): The Politics of Improvement and Prosperity* (Dublin, 2011), p. 384;

James Kelly, *Food Rioting in Ireland in the Eighteenth and Nineteenth Centuries: The 'moral economy' and the Irish crowd* (Dublin, 2017), pp. 34–7, 47–8, 51, 95–8, 104–5, 108, 122, 150, 163.

15. Edward Wakefied, *An Account of Ireland, Statistical and Political* (London, 1812), II, p. 616; Fitzgerald, 'Drogheda Merchants', p. 24; Malcomson, *Foster* (1978), pp. 168–71, 181; id., *Politics of Improvement*, pp. 82–3; McHugh, 'Port of Drogheda', pp. 179–80; *DIB*, 'Henry Singleton'; Barnard, *Brought to Book: Print in Ireland 1680–1784* (Dublin, 2017), pp. 326–7.

   Robert Hardman, a merchant in 1683, was presumably three generations senior to Edward Hardman (+1814), the last of the family to play a major commercial role in the town; FitzGerald has estimated that during the years 1779–1809 Edward Hardman's gross income totalled £36,000: Malcomson, *Foster* (1978), p. 169.

16. William Drennan, [Dublin], to Martha McTier, 22 Aug. 1800, in Jean Agnew, ed. *The Drennan-McTier Letters, II: 1794–1801* (Dublin, 1999), p. 623; [Andrew O'Reilly], *Reminiscences of an Emigrant Milesian* (London, 1853), III, pp. 222–5; Warburton et al., *Dublin*, II, p. 987; W.A. Thomas, *The Stock Exchanges of Ireland* (Liverpool, 1986), p. 89; Malcomson, *Politics of Improvement*, p. 83; Cullen, *Economy, Trade and Irish Merchants*, p.194.

17. On Charles Campbell: Nuala Burke, 'Dublin 1600–1800: A study in urban morphogenesis' (Ph.D. dissertation, University of Dublin, 1972), pp. 212–13.

18. *Some Reasons Humbly Offered for Establishing a Yarn-Market in the City of Dublin . . .* (Dublin, 1736), p. 16; Ada K. Longfield, 'History of the Irish Linen and Cotton Printing Industry in the 18th Century', in *JRSAI*, 7th ser., VII, 1 (1937), 33–4; Cullen, *Anglo-Irish Trade*, pp. 58–66; Dickson. 'The Place of Dublin in the Eighteenth-Century Irish Economy', in T.M. Devine & David Dickson, eds. *Ireland and Scotland 1600–1850 . . .* (Edinburgh, 1983), pp. 182–4; Agnew, *Belfast Merchant Families*, pp. 52, 184–5; Truxes, 'London's Irish Merchant Community . . .', in Dickson et al., *Irish and Scottish Merchant Networks*, pp. 278–9, 286. One estimate was that by 1760, £400,000 'in specie' was taken north annually from Dublin, 'mostly from the banks' to finance the linen trade: *Letter on Public Credit*, p. 10.

19. *An Alarm to the Citizens of Dublin* (Dublin, 1787), pp. 26–8; *WHM*, 1792, II, 385–6; Warburton et al., *Dublin*, II, pp. 1124–5; Thomas P. O'Neill, 'Discoverers and Discoveries: The penal laws and Dublin property', in *DHR*, xxxvii, 1(1983), 5–6; Eileen Byrne, ed. *The Convert Rolls*, 2nd edn (Dublin, 2005), pp. 436–7.

   Another young shop assistant working on the street at the time was John Keogh, employed by Widow Lincoln's haberdashery; Keogh, like Byrne, rose to national political prominence as a Catholic leader: O'Brien, *Collected Essays of Maureen Wall*, p. 81.

20. *Wilson's Dublin Directory*, 1763, 1766, 1767, 1771; *WHM*, 1792, II, 385–6; *Irish Magazine*, 1811, 19–20, 72–3; Gilbert, *Dublin*, I, pp. 354–5; William Drennan, Marlborough St [Dublin], to Martha McTier, – Jan, [1795], 17 April 1801, in *The Drennan-McTier Letters*, II, pp. 120, 698; T.W. Moody, R.B. McDowell & C.J. Woods, eds. *The Writings of Theobald Wolfe Tone, I: 1763–98* (Oxford, 1998), pp. 167n., 233, 287, 314, 324n.; L.M. Cullen, *The Irish Brandy Houses of Eighteenth-Century France* (Dublin, 2000), pp. 48–9; L.A. Clarkson & E. Margaret Crawford, *Feast and Famine: A history of food and nutrition in Ireland 1500–1920* (Oxford, 2001), pp. 51–2; Thomas Bartlett, ed., *Revolutionary Dublin, 1795–1801: The Letters of Francis Higgins to Dublin Castle* (Dublin, 2004), pp. 97–8, 193; Lisa-Marie Griffith, 'Social Mobility and the Middling Sort: Dublin Merchants, 1760–1800' (Ph.D. dissertation, University of Dublin, 2008), pp. 69–84; Cullen, *Economy, Trade and Irish Merchants*, p. 206.

   Byrne's second marriage to a Protestant (and potential heiress) Maryanne Roe in 1797 was a matter of ribald comment in the city: Henrietta Battier, *An Irregular Ode to Edward Byrne, Esq. of Mullinahack . . .* (Dublin, 1797); W.J. Fitzpatrick, *Curious Family History: Or, Ireland before the Union* (Dublin, 1880), pp. 195–9. One of Byrne's sons went bankrupt in Liverpool: Gilbert, *Dublin*, II, p. 245. Byrne's new house, now 37 North Great George's St, survives substantially intact.

21. Nathaniel Clements, Dublin, to Robert Wilmot, 12 March 1754 (PRONI, T3019/2286); Cullen, *Anglo-Irish Trade*, pp. 163–4, 200n.; id., *Princes and Pirates: The Dublin Chamber of Commerce, 1783–1983* (Dublin 1983), pp. 34–40; id., 'The Evolution of Mercantile Cultures', p. 1024; Bergin, 'Irish Catholics in London', 82–3.

22. Jacqueline Hill, 'Dublin Corporation, Protestant Dissent and Politics 1660–1800', in Kevin Herlihy, ed. *The Politics of Irish Dissent 1650–1800* (Dublin, 1997), pp. 30–2; *DIB*, 'Benjamin Burton'.

23. Benjamin Geale account-book, 1779–1803 (NLI, MS 2286); Cullen, *Princes and Pirates*, pp. 25–8; id., 'The Evolution of Mercantile Culture', pp. 1006–8; id., *Economy, Trade and Society*, pp. 194–6; Truxes, *Irish-American Trade*, pp. 85–6; *A Directory of Dublin for the Year 1738* (Dublin, 2000); Griffith, 'Social Mobility', pp. 27–8; Dickson, *Dublin*, pp. 124–6.

    250 Dublin merchants were listed as declaring confidence in the local banks after news that Edinburgh had been captured by the advancing Jacobite army: *FDJ*, 5 Oct. 1745.

24. *CSPI 1669/70*, p. 683; Dickson. 'Place of Dublin', p. 190n.

25. *A Letter from a Shop-keeper in Dublin to His Grace the Duke of Bedford . . . on Public Credit* (Dublin, 1760), pp. 7–10; Malcomson, *Clements: Government and the Governing Elite*, pp. 158–9; *DIB*, 'Benjamin Burton'; Rowena Dudley, 'The Failure of Burton's Bank and its Aftermath, in *IESH*, xl (2013), 1–30; Cullen, *Economy, Trade and Irish Merchants*, pp. 211–16.

    For Damer's supposedly fabulous wealth at the time of death in 1720: Patrick Fagan, *Second City: Portrait of Dublin 1700–1760* (Dublin, 1986), pp. 251–2.

26. Dickson, *Dublin*, pp. 126–7. On the northerners and Dublin, see Agnew, *Belfast Merchant Families*, pp. 174–5, 184–5.

27. *Wilson's Dublin Directory, 1768, 1794*; *Lucas's Directory, 1787*; *Cork Directory, 1795*; Wakefield, *Account of Ireland*, II, p. 785; Philip Ollerenshaw, *Banking in Nineteenth-Century Ireland: The Belfast Banks 1825–1914* (Manchester, 1987), pp. 5–6; W.N. Osborough, 'The Regulation of the Admission of Attorneys and Solicitors in Ireland, 1600–1866', in Daire Hogan & W.N. Osborough, eds. *Brehons, Serjeants and Attornies: Studies in the history of the Irish legal profession* (Dublin, 1990), pp. 123–5; Fagan, *Catholics in a Protestant Country*, pp. 102–18; Barnard, *New Anatomy of Ireland*, 122–7; Dickson, *Old World Colony*, pp. 81–2, 276, 421.

28. Edward McParland, 'James Gandon and the Royal Exchange Competition, 1768–69', in *JRSAI*, cii, 1 (1972), 58–72; id., *Gandon*, p. 38; Cullen, *Princes and Pirates*, pp. 34–44; Christine Casey, *The Buildings of Ireland: Dublin – The City Within the Grand and Royal Canals . . .* (New Haven & Dublin, 2005), pp. 361–4.

29. Cullen, *Anglo-Irish Trade*, pp. 45–53, 174.

30. *Wilson's Dublin Directory for the Year 1776* (Dublin, 1776); Warburton et al., *Dublin*, II, pp. 989–91; Cullen, *Anglo-Irish Trade*, pp. 117–18; Robinson, 'Secrets of British Power in the Age of Sail', 8; Dickson, *Dublin*, pp. 220–1; Arthur Gibney, *The Building Site in Eighteenth-Century Ireland*, eds. Livia Hurley & Edward McParland (Dublin, 2017), pp. 122–3. Slightly over half of the regular trading vessels using Dublin port in 1726 were Dublin-based: *CARD*, VII, pp. 338–9.

31. 'Brief for the Inhabitants of the City of Dublin . . . against a Petition for the Building of a New Bridge', 17 February 1752, Foster Papers (PRONI D562/7694).

32. Edward McParland, 'Strategy in the Planning of Dublin, 1750–1800', in Paul Butel & L.M. Cullen, *Cities and Merchants: French and Irish perspectives on urban development 1500–1900* (Dublin, 1986), pp. 97–107; Michael Brown, 'The Location of Learning in Mid-Eighteenth-Century Dublin', in Muriel McCarthy & Anne Simmons, eds. *Marsh's Library: A mirror to the world* (Dublin, 2009), pp. 113–16; Dickson, *Dublin*, pp. 218–19.

33. F.G. Hall, *The Bank of Ireland 1783–1946* (Dublin, 1949), pp. 41–3, 508–10; Jacqueline Hill, 'The Politics of Privilege: Dublin Corporation and the Catholic question 1792–1823', in *Maynooth Review*, vii (1982), 23–6; id., *Patriots to Unionists*, pp. 231–3; Cullen, *Princes and Pirates*, pp. 45–55; id., 'The Evolution of Mercantile Culture', pp. 1031, 1035; Griffith, 'Social Mobility', pp. 80–1; Dickson, *Dublin*, pp. 211–12, 245.

34. 'Vessels arrived from the West Indies at Dublin, 1799', and 'A list of vessels belonging to Dublin' [c.1800]: Foster Papers (PRONI D207/31/16/19); [Denys Scully], *A Statement of the Penal Laws, Which Aggrieve the Catholics of Ireland . . .*, 2nd edn (Dublin, 1812), p. 327; O'Brien, *Collected Essays of Maureen Wall*, pp. 81–2; Leydon, 'The Irish Provisions Trade', p. 314; Dickson, *Dublin*, p. 296; Cullen, *Economy, Trade and Irish Merchants*, pp. 121–4, 161, 174; Griffith, 'Social Mobility', pp. 29n., 158, 160, 265.

35. *Some Considerations on the Laws Which Incapacitate Papists from Purchasing Lands ...* (Dublin, 1739), pp. 23–4; William Stevens, *Hints to the People, Especially to the Inhabitants of Dublin ...* (Dublin, 1799), pp. 25–6; *Linen Board Minutes, 1803*, pp. 52–3; Wakefield, *Account of Ireland*, II, pp. 546, 624; P.B. Eustace & O. C. Goodbody, eds. *Quaker Records, Dublin: Abstracts of wills* (Dublin, 1957), pp. 15–16, 30–2, 83; O'Brien, *Collected Essays of Maureen Wall*, pp. 89–90; Dickson, 'Large-scale Developers and the Growth of Eighteenth-Century Irish Cities', in Butel & Cullen, *Cities and Merchants*, pp. 114–16, 119–20; Kelly, *Catholic Merchant Community*, p. 38; Bernard Neary, *The Candle Factory: Five hundred years of Rathbornes, master chandlers* (Dublin, 1998), pp. 28–31, 145–8; A.P.W. Malcomson, *Nathaniel Clements: Government and the governing elite in Ireland 1725-1775* (Dublin, 2009), pp. 24–5; *DIB*, 'Joseph Leeson'; Murphy, *Waterford Merchants*, pp. 67, 85–6, 101–2, 243–5; Dickson, *Dublin*, pp. 235, 280–1; Karina Holton, *Valentine Lawless, Lord Cloncurry, 1773-1853 ...* (Dublin, 2018), pp. 17–21.

On Leonard McNally's merchant grandfather, who invested in urban property in Dublin but lost it all because of hostile discoveries: Henry MacDougall, *Sketches of Irish Political Characters* (Dublin, 1799), p. 256.

CHAPTER 5   WORKSHOP, WAREHOUSE AND THE PRMACY OF DUBLIN

1. Dickson, 'Aspects of the Rise and Decline of the Irish Cotton Industry', in L.M. Cullen & T.C. Smout, eds. *Comparative Aspects of Scottish and Irish Economic and Social History 1600-1900* (Edinburgh, [1978]), pp. 104–6, 113; id., *Dublin*, pp. 280–1.
2. Barnard, *Making the Grand Figure*, pp. 310–44; Dickson, *Dublin*, pp. 52–4, 125–6; Flavin, *Consumption and Culture*, pp. 262–7; Aidan Clarke, ed. *The 1641 Depositions, IV: Dublin* (Dublin, 2017), pp. 256–8, 289–92. The limited evidence on excise returns points to a similar picture, with Dublin contributing 34 per cent of the national total in 1692, 51 per cent in 1730: Patrick Walsh, 'Enforcing the Fiscal State ....', in Aaron Graham & Walsh, eds. *The British Fiscal-military States, 1660-c.1783* (Abingdon, 2016), pp. 141–2.
3. *Limerick Directory, 1769*, pp. 41–2; Robert Herbert, 'The Trade Guilds of Limerick', in *NMAJ*, ii (1940–1), 122, 131; Hill, *Patriots to Unionists*, pp. 26, 31; C.D.A. Leighton, *Catholicism in a Protestant Kingdom ...* (Dublin, 1994), pp. 70–1; Fleming, *Politics and Provincial People*, pp. 130–3, 139, 150. In Drogheda there were seven trade 'fraternities' with customary rights of nomination to the common council of the Corporation; in Kilkenny, there were seven until the 1660s, and four thereafter; in Limerick fifteen; and in Cork fifteen: Grogan, *Council Book of Drogheda*; Neely, *Kilkenny*, pp. 101–2, 114, 122, 137–8, 143–4; Herbert, 'Trade Guilds', 122, 125; William O'Sullivan, *The Economic History of Cork City ...* (Cork, 1937), pp. 306–7.
4. O'Brien, *Collected Essays of Maureen Wall*, pp. 63–72; Sean Murphy, 'The Lucas Affair: A study of municipal and electoral politics in Dublin, 1742–9' (M.A. dissertation, NUI [UCD], 1981), p. 37; Leighton, *Catholicism in a Protestant Kingdom*, pp. 70, 72–4; Hill, *Patriots to Unionists*, pp. 25–6, 31–7, 40; Fleming, *Politics and Provincial People*, pp. 131–2; Alison FitzGerald, *Silver in Georgian Dublin: Making, selling, consuming* (Abingdon, 2017), pp. 12–13n.
5. Hill, *Patriots to Unionists*, p. 26; S.R. Epstein, 'Craft Guilds, Apprenticeship, and Technological Change in Pre-industrial Europe', in *JEH*, lviii (1998), 684–713; Gibney, *The Building Site*, pp. 20–5.
6. John O'Keeffe, *Recollections of the Life of John O'Keeffe* (London, 1826), I, pp. 38–44; Mary Clark & Raymond Refaussé, eds. *Directory of Historic Dublin Guilds* (Dublin, 1993); Leighton, *Catholics in a Protestant Kingdom*, pp. 71–3, 84; Hill, *Patriots to Unionists*, pp. 27–9, 41, 44, 194–5, 389–90; Alison FitzGerald & Conor O'Brien, 'The Production of Silver in Late Eighteenth-Century Dublin', in *IADS*, iv (2001), 16; Dickson, *Dublin*, pp. 73, 232; Timothy Murtagh, 'Dublin's Artisans and Radical Politics, 1779–1803' (Ph.D. dissertation, University of Dublin, 2015), pp. 152–3. For an unofficial riding of the franchises in Limerick in 1762: Fleming, *Politics and Provincial People*, pp. 138–9.

7. Hill, *Patriots to Unionists*, pp. 29, 205, 207; Fagan, *Catholics in a Protestant Country*, pp. 85–100; Barnard, *New Anatomy*, pp. 130–42; Susan Mullaney, 'The 1791 Irish Apothecary's Act: The first nationwide regulation of apothecaries . . .', in *ECI*, xxv (2010), 177–190; id., 'The Evolution of the Medical Professions in Eighteenth-Century Dublin', in Cunningham, *Early Modern Ireland and Medicine*, pp. 233–48.

8. Jacob M. Price, 'Summation: The American Panorama of Atlantic Port Cities', in Franklin W. Knight & Peggy K. Liss, eds. *Atlantic Port Cities: Economy, culture and society in the Atlantic world, 1650–1950* (Knoxville, 1991), pp. 265–6; Toby Barnard, 'Lawyers and the Law in Late Seventeenth-century Ireland', in *IHS*, xxviii, 111 (May 1993), 260, 274; Raymond Gillespie, 'Dublin 1600–1700', in Peter Clark & Bernard Lepetit, eds. *Capital Cities and their Hinterlands in Early Modern Europe* (Aldershot, 1996), pp. 86–7; Edward McParland, *Public Architecture in Ireland 1680–1760* (New Haven & London, 2001), pp. 91–4; Barnard, *Making the Grand Figure*, p. 87; Stapleton, 'The Merchant Community in Dublin', p. 77; The Knight of Glin & James Peill, *Irish Furniture . . .* (New Haven & London, 2007), pp. 33–7; Dickson, *Dublin*, pp. 97–8.

9. Jessica Cunningham, 'Dublin's Huguenot Goldsmiths, 1690–1750', in *IADS*, xii (2009), 179, fn. 22.

10. Dickson & Richard English, 'The La Touche Dynasty', in Dickson, *The Gorgeous Mask: Dublin 1700–1850* (Dublin, 1987), pp. 17–18; Dickson, 'Death of a Capital? Dublin and the consequences of Union', in Clark & Gillespie, *Two Capitals*, pp. 123–4; Hylton, *Ireland's Huguenots and their Refuge*, pp. 118–22; Cunningham, 'Dublin's Huguenot Goldsmiths, 1690–1750', 162–77; Dickson, *Dublin*, p. 113, 579 fn.15.

11. J.H. C[ottingham], *Observations on the Projected Union . . .* (Dublin, 1798), p. 31; Richard Jebb, *A Reply to a Pamphlet, Entitled, Arguments for and against an Union*, 3rd ed. (Dublin, 1799), pp. 33–5; Dickson, 'Place of Dublin', p. 186; id., *Dublin*, p. 260; D.W. Hayton, 'Introduction', in Hayton, ed. *The Irish Parliament in the Eighteenth Century: The long apprenticeship* (Edinburgh, 2001), pp. 23–5.

12. A.K. Longfield, 'History of the Irish Linen and Cotton Printing Industry in the 18th century', in *JRSAI*, lxvii (1937), 26–56; Eoin Magennis, 'Corn, Coal and Canals: Parliaments and the disposal of public monies 1695–1772', in Hayton, ed., *Irish Parliament in the Eighteenth Century*, pp. 73–8.

13. *General and Citizen's Almanack . . .* (Dublin, 1763), p. 75; *The Accounts of the Dublin Society . . . Commencing . . . June, 1750* (Dublin, [1764]); *An Appendix to the Proceedings of the Dublin Society, Containing, the Appointment of a Standing Select Committee of Commerce, and a Report* (Dublin, 1773), p. 15; Warburton et al., *Dublin*, II, pp. 976–84; Martyn J. Powell, *The Politics of Consumption in Eighteenth-century Ireland* (Basingstoke, 2005), pp. 46, 54, 76–80; Barnard, 'The Dublin Society and other Improving Societies, 1731–85', in James Kelly & Martyn J. Powell, eds. *Clubs and Societies in Eighteenth-Century Ireland* (Dublin, 2010), pp. 57–65; ibid., *Brought to Book*, pp. 172–6; Claudia Kinmouth, 'Rags, Riches and Recycling: Material and visual culture of the Dublin Society, 1731–81', in *IADS*, xxi (2018), 75–95.

The allocations made by the Dublin Society in 1764 reveal their priorities: £2,030 to silk premia and £300 to the warehouse; £1800 to fine woollens; £1,650 to linen printing; £600 to the glass manufacture; £500 to iron-related trades; £500 to earthenware; £200 to paper manufacture; £200 to brewing; £200 to the leather trades; £200 to brass and copper trades; £100 to optical goods; and £20 to flint-cutters: *The Application of Eight Thousand Pounds Granted by Parliament to the Dublin Society for the Encouragement of Certain Manufactures, 1764* (Dublin, [1764]).

14. Edward Synge, *Universal Beneficence: A sermon preached in the parish-church of St Luke, Dublin . . .* (Dublin, 1721), pp. 2–3, 26–7; Walsh, *South Sea Bubble and Ireland*, pp. 120–1; L.M. Cullen, 'Swift's *Modest Proposal* (1729): Historical context and political purpose', in D.W. Hayton & Andrew R. Holmes, eds. *Ourselves Alone: Religion, society and politics in eighteenth- and nineteenth-century Ireland . . .* (Dublin, 2016), pp. 42–60.

15. TNA, CUST/15; *Wilson's Dublin Directory, 1793*.

16. Book of Brothers, 1722–44: Dublin Weavers Guild; minute-book (1734–60), 1 July 1751: Dublin Weavers Guild (RSAI); *Dublin Mercury*, 14–17 Jan. 1769; Catherine Cox, 'Women

and Business in Eighteenth-Century Dublin: A case study', in Bernadette Whelan, ed., *Women and Paid Work in Ireland 1500–1930* (Dublin, 2000), pp. 35–7; Barnard, *New Anatomy of Ireland*, p. 245; Ó Gráda, *Georgian Dublin*, pp. 234–5; Murtagh, 'Dublin's Artisans', p. 56.

17. TNA, CUST/15; Arthur Young, *A Tour in Ireland . . . made in the years 1776, 1777 and 1778, and brought down to the end of 1779* (Dublin, 1780), II, append. pp. 95–100; *Considerations on the Silk Trade of Ireland . . . Addressed to the Dublin Society* (Dublin, 1778); Cullen, *Anglo-Irish Trade*, pp. 51–2; Dickson, 'Place of Dublin', p. 182; id., *Dublin*, pp. 185–6.

18. [Joseph Fenn], *First Volume of the Instructions Given in the Drawing School Established by the Dublin Society* (Dublin, 1769); O'Keeffe, *Recollections*, I, pp. 3, 11–20; Powell, *Politics of Consumption*, pp. 76–8; Johnston, *Bishop Berkeley's Querist*, p. 131; Gitta Willemson, *The Dublin Society Drawing Schools: Students and awards winners 1746–1876* (Dublin, 2000); Dickson, *Dublin*, pp. 187–8; Gibney, *The Building Site*, pp. 58, 85.

19. FitzGerald & O'Brien, 'Production of Silver', 10–26, 34–40; FitzGerald, *Silver in Georgian Dublin*, pp. 88–90, 98, 111–14, 142–3, 164–5, 173, 184, fn.32, [226–7]. A very high figure of 42,557 oz. assayed in 1697/8 seems an outlier and was presumably a consequence of the currency turbulence in England and the undervaluation of sterling coin: Cunningham, 'Huguenot Goldsmiths', 166.

20. O'Sullivan, *Economic History of Cork City*, pp. 120–2; John R. Bowen & Conor O'Brien, *Cork Silver and Gold: Four centuries of craftsmanship* (Cork, 2005), pp. 180–6, 200; id., *Celebration of Limerick's Silver*, pp. 15, 190–7; id., 'The Goldsmiths of Waterford', in *Decies*, lxiii (2007), 155–62; FitzGerald, *Silver in Georgian Dublin*, pp. [223–5]. Note that absence of provincial newspapers before 1750 and of directories before 1787 must partly explain the jump in Cork and Limerick silversmiths after mid century.

21. W.G. Stuart, *Watch and Clockmakers in Ireland*, ed. D.A. Boles (Celbridge, 2000); Morgan Kelly & Cormac Ó Gráda, 'Adam Smith, Watch Prices, and the Industrial Revolution', in *Quarterly Journal of Economics*, cxxxi, 4 (Nov., 2016), 1727–52.

22. *FDJ*, 8–12 Sept. 1752, and *Limerick Chronicle*, 28 Sept. 1780, quoted in Glin & Peill, *Irish Furniture*, pp. 290, 281; Read, 'Penroses of Woodhill', 88; Peter Francis, *Irish Delftware: An illustrated history* (London, 2000), pp. 41–64; David Skinner, *Wallpaper in Ireland 1700–1900* (Tralee, 2014), pp. 59–60, 74, 81–5, 87–90.

23. Thomas Denton, 'A Perambulation . . . 1687–8 . . .', in Lennon, *IHTA, Dublin*, II, p. 37; William Baer, 'Early Retailing: London's shopping exchanges 1550–1700', in *Business History*, xlix, 1 (2007), 30–1.

24. *Wilson's Dublin Directory, 1768*; Clé Lesger, 'Patterns of Retail Location and Urban Form in Amsterdam in the Mid-eighteenth Century', in *Urban History*, xxxviii, 1 (2011), 31–4. The 28 bakers named in the first Cork directory were less widely scattered, with almost half (13) in two streets (South Main St and Mallow Lane): *Lucas's Cork Directory, 1787*.

25. *Considerations on the Silk Trade*, pp. 17–18; *Dublin Mercury*, 7–10 Jan. 1769; *DEP*, 16 March 1797, 23 Aug. 1798; *James Malton's Dublin Views in Colour*, intro. Maurice Craig (Dublin, 1981); Edward McParland, 'Malton's Views of Dublin: Too good to be true?', in Brian P. Kennedy & Raymond Gillespie, eds. *Ireland: Art into History* (Dublin, 1994), pp. 20–3; Sarah Foster, '"Ornament and Splendour": Shops and shopping in Georgian Dublin', in *IADS*, xv (2012), 14–18; Lennon & Montague, *John Rocque's Dublin*, pp. 22–3; Gibney, *The Building Site*, pp. 219–20, 229, 232–3. Among the specialist shops 'free of the 5 and 10 per cent' in the Dublin Custom House in 1794, i.e. enjoying a duty concession designed for wholesale merchants, 14 were grocers/tobacconists, 6 woollen drapers and/or haberdashers, 5 dealt in hardware/earthenware, and 4 ironmongers: *Wilson's Dublin Directory, 1794*.

26. Charles Stewart, ed. *Travels of Mirza Abu Taleb Khan in Asia, Africa and Europe during the Years 1799, 1800, 1801 . . .* (London, 1814), I, pp. 139–41; Eoin Bourke, ed. *"Poor Green Erin": German travel writers' narratives on Ireland . . .*, 2nd edn (Frankfurt am Main, 2013), pp. 33–4.

    The occupations chosen for Table 5:1 are drawn from those used in Jon Stobart & Leonard Schwarz, 'Leisure, Luxury and Urban Specialization in the Eighteenth Century', in *Urban History*, xxxv, 2 (2008), 216–36.

27. Andrew Ferguson [Derry] to Henry Jackson, 5 Sept., 5 Dec. 1775, 15 Oct. 1776: Ferguson Letterbook 1775–80 (PRONI, D1130/1); John D'Alton, *The History of the County of Dublin*

(Dublin, 1838), p. 808; Michael Durey, *Transatlantic Radicals and the Early American Republic* (Lawrence, Kansas, 1997), pp. 104–5, 167; *DIB*, 'Henry Jackson'; Dickson, *Dublin*, pp. 243–4, 284.

28. Cissie Fairchilds, 'The Production and Marketing of Populuxe Goods in Eighteenth-Century Paris', in John Brewer & Roy Porter, eds., *Consumption and the World of Goods* (London, 1993), pp. 228–46; William Laffan, ed., *The Cries of Dublin Drawn from Life by Hugh Douglas Hamilton, 1760* (Dublin, 2003); Dickson, *Dublin*, p. 185.

29. 'Alexander the Coppersmith', *Remarks upon the Religion, Trade, Government, Police, Customs, Manners and Maladys of the City of Corke* (Cork, 1737, rep., 1974), pp. 78–9; Patrick O'Flanagan, 'Beef, Butter, Provisions and Prosperity . . .', in Crowley et al., *Atlas of Cork City*, pp. 156–8. 37 per cent of the city's gateage tolls in 1725/6 were collected in Mallow Lane: Thomas Pembrock's mayoralty book (Cork City Library: www.corkpastandpresent.ie /history/mayoral%20booke), p.320.

30. Warburton et al., *Dublin*, II, pp. 1123–8; William Martin, *A Commercial Guide through Dublin for 1825 . . .* (Dublin, 1825), pp. 196–8, 212–19; Colin Smith, 'The Wholesale and Retail Markets of London, 1660–1840', in *EHR*, lv, 1 (2002), 33–5, 42, 46; *Cries of Dublin (1760)*, passim.

31. *IHTA, Belfast*, I, pp. 28–9; *IHTA, Derry/Londonderry*, pp. 29–30; *IHTA, Limerick*, p. 37; *IHTA, Galway*, p. 26; *IHTA, Drogheda*, pp. 48–9. Excavations at St Peter's Market in Cork have revealed evidence of brick wall-ovens where several eighteenth-century houses stood: Hurley, 'Post-medieval Archaeology of Cork', p. 124.

32. Caulfield, *Cork Council Book*, pp. 288, 694, 711, 714, 736, 873, 875, 883, 917, 1063, 1073.

33. Dickson, *Old World Colony*, pp. 386–7; James Kelly, 'The Consumption and Sociable Use of Alcohol in Eighteenth-Century Ireland', in *Proc. RIA*, cxv (2015), C, 219–30.

34. Memoranda on Irish Revenue, 1693–4: Evelyn Papers (BL, Add. MS 78,452, f.14r); Sir William Petty, *Political Survey of Ireland . . .* (London, 1719), pp. 13, 115; John Rutty, *A Natural History of Dublin* (Dublin, 1771), p. 13; *Parliamentary Register of Ireland . . .*, XIII (Dublin, 1795), p. 469; *Pigot and Co.'s City of Dublin and Hibernian Provincial Directory for 1824* (Manchester, 1824); E.B. McGuire, *Irish Whiskey: A history of distilling in Ireland* (Dublin, 1973), pp. 97, 158–63; Elizabeth Malcolm, 'The Rise of the Pub', in J.S. Donnelly & Kerby A. Miller, eds. *Irish Popular Culture 1650–1850* (Dublin, 1998), pp. 60–6; DIB, 'Joseph Leeson (1660–1741)'; Kelly, 'Consumption and Use of Alcohol', 240, 242–4; Seán Magee, 'Sweetman Breweries in Eighteenth-Century Dublin', in *DHR*, lxviii, 1 (2015), 113–126. The total in 1824 of 505 vintners etc. includes Kilmainham, Clontarf and Ringsend, but excludes those listed for Chapelizod, Palmerstown, Milltown, Blackrock and Kingstown. Limerick and Waterford had the lowest per capita number of vintners, followed by Dublin, Cork and Belfast, which had proportionately almost twice the number returned for Limerick. Note that Gilbert, who limited his *History* to the inner city, listed some 110 taverns: Gilbert, *History of Dublin*, III, append. pp. 76–8.

35. Cullen, 'The Huguenots from the Perspective of the Merchant Networks of W. Europe (1680–1790) . . .', and Dickson, 'Huguenots in the Urban Economy', in Caldicott et al., *Huguenots and Ireland*, pp. 138–43, 324; Cullen, *Economy, Trade and Irish Merchants*, pp. 194, 197–200; Dickson, 'Place of Dublin', pp. 180–1; id., *Old World Colony*, p. 156; Hylton, *Ireland's Huguenots*, p. 124; Kelly, 'Consumption and Use of Alcohol', 236.
    There was a late surge of wine merchants in Cork, 11 being listed in 1795, but only 3 of these were recognized at the Custom House as importers: *Cork Directory, 1795*.

36. A.P.W. Malcomson, *The Pursuit of the Heiress: Aristocratic marriage in Ireland 1740–1840*, 2nd edn (Belfast, 2006), p. 46; Kelly, 'Consumption and Use of Alcohol', 231–5; L.M. Cullen, 'The Boyds in Bordeaux and Dublin', in Truxes, *Ireland, France and the Atlantic*, pp. 56–62.

37. *BNL*, 12 March 1754, p. 2; Gilbert, *History of Dublin*, I, pp. 94–6; Nodlaig P. Hardiman & Máire Kennedy, eds. *A Directory of Dublin for the Year 1738* (Dublin, 2000), p. 83; Cullen, *The Irish Brandy Houses*, pp. 42–56; Kelly, 'Consumption and Use of Alcohol', 232; L.M. Cullen, John Shovlin & Thomas Truxes, eds., *The Bordeaux-Dublin Letters, 1757* (Oxford, 2013), pp. 34–9.

1. [Theobald M'Kenna], *A Letter Containing Some Loose Hints on . . . an Establishment for the Roman Catholic Religion in Ireland* (Dublin, 1801), p. 32; Gilbert, *History of Dublin*, pp. 314–15.

2. 'Report on the State of Popery, Ireland, 1731: Diocese of Tuam', in *AH*, iii (1914), 125–6, 153, 155; 'Report on the State of Popery, 1731: Diocese of Dublin', in *AH*, iv (1915), 132–3, 138; Hugh Fenning, 'The Journey of James Lyons from Rome to Sligo, 1763–65', in *Coll. Hib.*, xi (1968), 109; P.J. Corish, *The Catholic Community in the Seventeenth and Eighteenth Centuries* (Dublin, 1981), pp. 78–80, 83, 89, 100; James Kelly, 'The Impact of the Penal Laws', in Kelly & Dáire Keogh, eds., *History of the Catholic Diocese of Dublin* (Dublin, 2000), pp. 144–66; O'Flaherty, 'An Urban Community and the Penal Laws', pp. 211–13; Prunty, *IHTA, Galway*, p. 20.

3. Smith, *State of Waterford*, p. 181; 'The Humble Petition and Remonstrance of the Roman Catholic Inhabitants of This City [Waterford, *c.*1701]', in *JRSAI*, vi (1860), 128; 'Report on the State of Popery, Ireland, 1731', in *AH*, ii (1913), 131; Brady, *Catholics in the Eighteenth-Century Press*, p. 99; Nuala Burke, 'A Hidden Church? The structure of Catholic Dublin in the mid-eighteenth century', in *AH*, xxxii (1974), 81–92; Evelyn Bolster, *A History of the Diocese of Cork from the Penal Era to the Famine* (Cork, 1989), pp. 52–3; Hugh Fenning O.P., *The Irish Dominican Province, 1698–1797* (Dublin, 1990), pp. 411–12; Ó Fearghail, 'Catholic Church in Kilkenny', p. 227; Patrick Fagan, *An Irish Bishop in Penal Times: The chequered career of Sylvester Lloyd OFM, 1680–1747* (Dublin, 1993), pp. 178–9; Dickson, *Old World Colony*, pp. 256–8; id., *Dublin*, pp. 110–11, 146; Emmet Larkin, *The Pastoral Role of the Roman Catholic Church in Pre-Famine Ireland, 1750–1850* (Dublin, 2006), p. 138; O'Flaherty, 'An Urban Community and the Penal Laws', pp. 216–17; Prunty, *IHTA, Galway*, p. 20; Usher, *Protestant Dublin*, pp. 90–2; Lennon & Montague, *John Rocque's Dublin*, pp. 66–7.

4. Casey, 'Art and Architecture in the Long Eighteenth Century', pp. 434–5.

5. Brady, *Catholics in the Eighteenth-Century Press*, p. 225; Fenning, 'The Journey of James Lyons from Rome to Sligo', 106; id., 'Letters from a Jesuit in Dublin . . . 1747–48', in *AH*, xxix (1970), 137, 154; id., *The Undoing of the Friars of Ireland . . .* (Louvain, 1972), pp. 147–8, 161–7, 185; Burke, 'Hidden Church?', 81–2, 87–9; Corish, *Catholic Community*, pp. 85, 90, 103; Kelly, 'Impact of the Penal Laws', p. 168; Larkin, *Pastoral Role*, pp. 141–3; Cormac Begadon, 'The Renewal of Catholic Religious Culture in Eighteenth-Century Dublin', in John Bergin et al., *New Perspectives on the Penal Laws* (Dublin, 2011), pp. 240–1, 243–6; Toby Barnard, 'A Saint for Eighteenth-Century Dublin? Father John Murphy', in Salvador Ryan & Clodagh Tait, eds., *Religion and Politics in Urban Ireland c.1500–c.1750: Essays in Honour of Colm Lennon* (Dublin, 2016), pp. 228–36.

6. Charles O'Conor to Daniel O'Conor, 3 March 1756; O'Conor to John Curry, 21 May 1756, 25 Dec. 1759, in C.C. Ward, *The Letters of Charles O'Conor of Belanagare*, I (n.p., 1980), pp. 11, 13–14, 87; *Dublin Gazette*, 15–17 Nov., 27 Nov.-1 Dec., 11–15 Dec. 1759; Brady, *Catholics in the Eighteenth-Century Press*, pp. 100–1; Des Cowman, 'Thomas ("Bullocks") Wyse: A Catholic industrialist during the Penal Laws', in *Decies*, xxiv (1983), 9–13; O'Brien, *Collected Essays of Maureen Wall*, pp. 65–6; Robert E. Burns, *Irish Parliamentary Politics in the Eighteenth Century*, II: *1730–1760* (Washington, 1990), p. 45; Patrick Fagan, *Divided Loyalties: The question of an oath for Irish Catholics in the eighteenth century* (Dublin, 1997), pp. 63–4, 70–1, 125–6; Kelly, 'Impact of the Penal Laws', pp. 152–9. The 1760 address was published in the *London Gazette* (3–7 Feb. 1761) without signatories.

7. *Dublin Gazette*, 28 June–1 July, 1–5 July 1740; *Wilson's Dublin Directory, 1790*; Usher, *Protestant Dublin*, pp. 61–9; Barnard, *New Anatomy*, p. 270.

8. H.A. Wheeler & M.J. Craig, *The Dublin City Churches of the Church of Ireland* (Dublin, 1948); McParland, *Public Architecture*, pp. 38, 42–9; Usher, *Protestant Dublin*, pp. 76–90. In addition to the stock of parish churches in Dublin, there were at least eight Church of Ireland chapels attached to institutions and one chapel of ease all active before 1800: Craig & Wheeler, *Dublin Churches*, pp. 43–5.

9. Christine Casey & Alistair Rowan, *The Buildings of Ireland: North Leinster* (London, 1993), pp. 237–8; McParland, *Public Architecture*, pp. 42, 44; Connolly, *Belfast 400*, p. 165; *IHTA, Sligo*, pp. 4, 13; Ned McHugh, ed. *IHTA, XXIX: Drogheda* (2019), pp. 5, 25.

10. Smith, *Cork*, I, pp. 378–7; Tuckey, *Cork Remembrancer*, pp. 126–9, 185; McParland, *Public Architecture*, pp. 38, 42; Colin Rynne, 'Shandon', in Crowley et al., *Atlas of Cork City*, pp. 142–4; Roger Stalley, 'Reconstructions of the Gothic Past: The lost cathedral of Waterford', in *IADS*, xvi (2013), 94–131; *DIB*, 'Peter Browne'.

11. McParland, *Public Architecture*, pp. 42; Girouard, *Town and Country*, pp. 156–62; [McEneany & Ryan], *Waterford Treasures*, pp. 151–3; *DIB*, 'John Roberts'.

12. C.H. Crookshank, *History of Methodism in Ireland*, I: *Wesley and His Times* (Belfast, 1885), pp. 107, 201, 272, 288, 310, 396, 403, 426; 'Report on the State of Popery, Ireland, 1731', in *AH*, ii (1913), 131, and iv (1915), 142; S.J. Connolly, *Priests and People in Pre-Famine Ireland, 1780–1845* (Dublin, 1982), pp. 196–8; David Hempton, 'Methodism in Irish Society, 1770–1830', in *TRHS*, xxxvi (1986), 122–5, 135–6; Kelly, 'Impact of the Penal Laws', pp. 162–3; MacGrath, *Ireland and Empire*, p. 113; *DIB*, 'John Wesley', 'Thomas Kelly'; Thomas O'Connor, 'Catholic and Protestant Dublin Weavers before the Spanish Inquisition, 1745–54', in Ryan & Tait, *Religion and Politics in Urban Ireland*, pp. 221–3; Barnard, 'Father John Murphy', pp. 230, 233; id., *Brought to Book*, p. 213.

13. McBride, *Eighteenth-Century Ireland*, pp. 76–84.

14. S.J. Connolly, *Religion, Law and Power: The making of Protestant Ireland 1660–1760* (Oxford, 1992), pp. 159–71; Barnard, 'Identities, Ethnicity and Tradition', pp. 29–48; R. Finlay Holmes, 'The Reverend John Abernethy . . .', in Herlihy, ed., *The Religion of Irish Dissent, 1650–1800* (Dublin, 1996), pp. 100–11; Jacqueline Hill, 'Dublin Corporation, Protestant Dissent and Politics, 1660–1800', in Herlihy, ed. *The Politics of Irish Dissent, 1659–1800* (Dublin, 1997), p. 113; Michael Brown, *Francis Hutcheson in Dublin, 1719–1730* (Dublin, 2002), pp. 26–9, 52–3, 79–80; Fergus Whelan, *Dissent into Treason: Unitarians, king-killers and the Society of United Irishmen* (Dingle, 2010), pp. 91–2; Robert Whan, *The Presbyterians of Ulster 1680–1730* (Woodbridge, 2013), pp. 122, 158, 186–7; Michael Brown, *The Irish Enlightenment* (Cambridge, MA & London, 2016), pp. 28–53.

15. Charles O'Hara to Lady Mary O'Hara, 26 March 1758: O'Hara papers (PRONI, T2812/10/25); O'Keeffe, *Recollections*, I, p. 32; C. H. Irwin, *A History of Presbyterianism in Dublin and the South and West of Ireland* (London, 1890), pp. 172, 192, 212–13, 236–7, 290–1, 302–3; Steven ffeary-Smyrl, '"Theatres of Worship": Dissenting meeting house in Dublin, 1650–1750', in Kevin Herlihy, ed. *The Irish Dissenting Tradition, 1650–1750* (Dublin, 1995), pp. 49–64; R. Finlay Holmes, 'The Reverend John Abernethy . . .', in Herlihy, ed., *The Religion of Irish Dissent, 1650–1800* (Dublin, 1996), pp. 100–11; Jacqueline Hill, 'Dublin Corporation, Protestant Dissent and Politics, 1660–1800', in Herlihy, *Politics of Irish Dissent*, pp. 34–8; Kenneth Ferguson, 'Rocque's Map and the History of Nonconformity in Dublin: A search for meeting houses', in *DHR*, lviii, 2 (2005), 129–65; Brown, *Irish Enlightenment*, pp. 28–53.

   Abernethy was, however, an Irish speaker, an admirer of Bishop Bedel, and supportive of conversion: *Persecution Contrary to Christianity* . . . (Dublin, 1735), p. 165.

16. G. Andrew Forrest, 'Religious Controversy within the French Protestant Community in Dublin 1692–1716', in Herlihy, *Irish Dissenting Tradition*, pp. 100–9; Richard S. Harrison, 'Some Eighteenth-Century Quaker Families', in *JCHAS*, civ (1999), 117–20; id., *Merchants, Mystics and Philanthropists: 350 years of Cork Quakers* (Cork, 2006), pp. 169–70, 178–9; Hylton, *Ireland's Huguenots*, pp. 189–92; Dickson, *Old World Colony*, p. 168; id., *Dublin*, pp. 90–1.

17. Neal Garnham, *The Courts, Crime and the Criminal Law in Ireland, 1692–1760* (Dublin, 1996), pp. 27–32; Raymond Gillespie, 'Urban Parishes in Early Seventeenth-Century Ireland: The case of Dublin'; Rowena Dudley, 'The Dublin Parish, 1660–1730', and Toby Barnard, 'The Eighteenth-Century Parish', in Elizabeth Fitzpatrick & Raymond Gillespie, eds. *The Parish in Medieval and Early Modern Ireland* (Dublin, 2006), pp. 228–41, 277–96, 306–7, 310–11, 315–16, 323.

For Cork Corporation allowing the parishes to determine whether or not to come together in an agreement with a private contractor for lighting the city in 1780: Caulfield, *Council Book of Cork*, pp. 959–60.

18. Catholics were formally excluded from voting in vestries from 1726, as were all dissenters from 1774; however, the latter prohibition was reversed in 1776 and Catholic attendance appears to have begun in the 1780s: Barnard, 'The Eighteenth-Century Parish', p. 305; Bartlett, *Revolutionary Dublin*, pp. 109–10.

19. Imelda Brophy, 'Women in the Workforce', in Dickson, *Gorgeous Mask*, pp. 51–63; Catherine Cox, 'Women and Business in Eighteenth-Century Dublin: A case study', in Bernadette Whelan, ed., *Women and Paid Work in Ireland 1500–1930* (Dublin, 2000), pp. 32–43; Mary O'Dowd, *A History of Women in Ireland, 1500–1800* (Harlow, 2005), pp. 114–30; Barnard, *New Anatomy of Ireland*, p. 275.

20. *Census of Ireland, 1841*; Niall Ó Ciosáin, *Print and Popular Culture in Ireland 1750–1850* (Basingstoke, 1997), pp. 35, 211–12; Rab Houston, 'The Literacy Myth?: Illiteracy in Scotland 1630–1760', in *Past & Present*, xcvi (1982), 99–100; id., *Literacy in Early Modern Europe* (Harlow, 2002), pp. 145, 170; Cormac Ó Gráda, 'School Attendance and Literacy in Ireland before the Great Famine', in Garret FitzGerald, *Irish Primary Education in the Early Nineteenth Century* (Dublin, 2013), pp. 113–23. Drogheda also reported a high proportion of semi-literate older women, but the size of the relevant cohort is very small.

21. T.C. Barnard, 'Learning, the Learned and Literacy in Ireland, 1660–1760', in Barnard, Dáibhí Ó Croinín & Katharine Simms, eds., *'A Miracle of Learning': Studies in manuscripts and Irish learning – Essays in honour of William O'Sullivan* (Aldershot, 1998), pp. 220–1; Houston, *Literacy in Europe*, p. 171; Raymond Gillespie, *Reading Ireland: Print, reading and social change in early modern Ireland* (Manchester, 2005), pp. 41–5; John Rees, *The Leveller Revolution: Radical Political Organization in England 1640–1650* (London, 2017). Note, however, that only about two-thirds of the poor tradesmen who partook of Dean Swift's petty credit scheme in the 1720s and 1730s signed their name: Brendan Twomey, 'Personal Financial Management in Early Eighteenth-Century Ireland: Practices, participants and outcomes' (Ph.D. dissertation, University of Dublin, 2018), pp. 209–11, and personal information from Dr Twomey.

For the high illiteracy of most of the women and some of the men who supplied the Channel Row convent with foodstuffs in the 1720s and 1730s: Bernadette Cunningham, *Gentlemen's Daughters in Dublin Cloisters: The social world of nuns in early eighteenth-century Dublin* (Dublin, 2018), pp. 21–2.

22. Warburton et al., *Dublin*, pp. 564–78, 602–18; 'Report of the Commissioners of Irish Education Enquiry, 1791', in *Royal Commission to Inquire into Endowments, Funds and Condition of Schools Endowed for Purpose of Education in Ireland* (Parl. papers, 1857–58, XXII, 2336), part 3, pp. 355–6, 376; Barnard, 'Learning, the Learned and Literacy', p. 219; id., *New Anatomy of Ireland*, p. 310; id., *Brought to Book*, pp. 78–9.

'The Incorporated Society for Promoting English Working Schools in Ireland' which governed the 60-odd charter schools was given financial assistance by Dublin Corporation and two of their schools were built near the capital (at Santry and Clontarf) but they were both isolated from the city; Kilkenny and Waterford Corporations each founded charter schools near their cities: Kenneth Milne, *The Irish Charter Schools 1730–1830* (Dublin, 1997), pp. 31, 36, 347–8.

23. Warburton et al., *Dublin*, pp. 776–7, 802–3, 806–13, 852–66; 'Report on Popery, 1731: Dublin', 131–48; John Brady, 'Catholic Schools in Dublin in 1787–8', in *Reportorium Novum*, i, 1 (1955), 193–6; Rowena Dudley, 'Dublin's Parishes 1660–1729: The Church of Ireland parishes and their role in the civic administration of the city' (Ph.D. dissertation, University of Dublin, 1995), p. 203; David Hayton, 'Did Protestantism Fail in Early Eighteenth-Century Ireland?', in Alan Ford, James McGuire & Kenneth Milne, eds. *As by Law Established: The Church of Ireland since the Reformation* (Dublin, 1995), pp. 184–6; FitzGerald, *Irish Primary Education*, pp. 63, 71; Rosemary Raughter, 'A Discreet Benevolence: Female philanthropy and the Catholic resurgence in eighteenth-century Ireland', in *Women's History Review*, vi, 4 (1997), 472.

Investigations in the 1820s revealed some cross-denominational enrolment in confessional schools (both in town and countryside): FitzGerald, op. cit., p. 77. The 1788/1815 comparison is based on parish returns provided for the 1791 inquiry and on those complied by Robert Walsh *c.*1816, both of which have some gaps and rounding of figures: Brady, 'Catholic Schools', 193-6; Warburton et al., *Dublin*, p. 866. For the 1731 returns I am relying on the parish returns, not the less complete ones supplied by the Lord Mayor: 'Report on Popery, 1731: Dublin', 131-48.

24. T.J. Walsh, *Nano Nagle and the Presentation Sisters* (Dublin, 1959), pp. 44-54, 130-59; Peadar McCann, 'Charity Schooling in Cork City in the Late 18th and Early 19th Centuries', in *JCHAS*, lxxxvi (1981), 30-7, 109-15, and lxxxvii (1982), 51-7; M.P. Magray, *The Transforming Power of the Nuns: Women, religion and cultural change in Ireland 1750-1900* (New York & Oxford, 1998), pp. 8-9, 16-17, 40, 117; O'Dowd, *History of Women*, p. 219; Jessie Castle & Gillian O'Brien, ' "I Am Building a House": Nano Nagle's Georgian convents', in *IADS*, xix (2016), 57-75. On the growth of schooling in Cork's hinterland: Dickson, *Old World Colony*, pp. 440-1.

25. Henry Maule, Cork, to [Jane] Bonnell, 31 Dec. 1722: Smyth of Barbavilla papers (NLI, MS 41,580/30); 'Report on the State of Popery in Ireland, 1731', in *AH*, iv (1915), 171-2; Seán Peitíd, 'The Rev. Henry Maule of Shandon and the Charity School Movement', in *JCHAS*, lxxii (1972), 107-16; Peadar McCann, 'Cork's Eighteenth-Century Charity Schools . . .', in *JCHAS*, lxxxiv (1979), 102-11; Hannigan, 'University of Dublin 1685-1750', p. 34; Barnard, *New Anatomy of Ireland*, pp. 310-11; Dickson, *Old World Colony*, pp. 211-12; *DIB*, 'Henry Maule'.

26. Samuel Whyte, *The Shamrock, or Hibernian Cresses* (Dublin, 1772); Oliver Moore, *The Staff Officer: Or, the soldier of fortune . . .* (London, 1831), pp. 2-4; *Pigot's Directory, 1824*; Tuckey, *Cork Remembrancer*, pp. civ-cv; S.F. Petit, 'The Royal Cork Institution . . .', in *JCHAS*, lxxxi (1976), 77; O'Dowd, *Women in Ireland*, pp. 210-17; *ODNB*, 'Thomas Dix Hincks'; *DIB*, 'John Austin'; 'Sisson Darling'; 'Thomas Sheridan (1687-1738)'; 'Theobald Wolfe Tone'; Barnard, *Brought to Book*, p. 86. For fine detail on the curriculum, discipline and charges in a private academy that seems to have had a short life: *An Abstract of the Course of Education, Taught at the Royal Military and Marine Academy, at Belmont on Summer-Hill, Dublin . . . under the direction of David Bates* (Dublin, 1794).

27. Charles Smith, *The Antient and Present State of the County and City of Cork* (Dublin, 1750), I, p. 364; Lucas, *Cork Directory, 1787*; Lucas, *General Directory, 1788*; *Pigot's Directory, 1824*; D. Ó Donnabháin, 'The Munster Academy, 1772-1792', in *JCHAS*, lxix (1964), 101-12; Kennedy, 'At the Exchange', pp. 154-5; Barnard, *Brought to Book*, pp. 86, 280-3, 292.

By 1788 Cork was credited with 30 academies, Limerick 24, Waterford 19, Belfast 15, and the other centres with less than 10 each. On Timothy Delany offering Geography to the girls in Mrs Lloyd's Boarding School in Cork: *Hibernian Chronicle*, 30 Dec. 1771.

28. 'Irish Education Enquiry, 1791', p. 343; Michael Quane, 'Drogheda Grammar School', in *JCLAHS*, xv, 3 (1963), 231.

29. [S.S. Millin?], *Eighteenth-Century Belfast* (n.d., n.p. (*c.*1925)], pp. 3-5, 94-8; A.T.Q. Stewart, *Belfast Royal Academy: The first century 1785-1885* (Belfast, 1985), pp. 10-16; Adams, *Printed Word*, pp. 15-18; T.C. Barnard, 'Educating Eighteenth-Century Ulster', in Hayton & Holmes, *Ourselves Alone*, pp. 114-23; *IHTA, Belfast*, pp. 32-3; *DIB*, 'James Crombie'; 'William Bruce'; 'David Manson'; Barnard, *Brought to Book*, pp. 89-90.

30. Ó Fearghail, 'Catholic Church in Kilkenny', pp. 247-8; Raughter, 'A Discreet Benevolence', 465-87; Cunningham, *Gentlemen's Daughters*, passim; McHugh, *IHTA, Drogheda*, p. 59. The Poor Clares seem to have maintained a small presence in Galway throughout the century – despite intermittent harassment in the early years.

31. O'Keeffe, *Recollections*, I, p. 30; Brady, *Catholics in the Eighteenth-Century Press*, pp. 222, 225, 231-2; Barnard, *Brought to Book*, p. 214; *DIB*, 'Cornelius Nary'.

32. Brady, *Catholics and Catholicism*, pp. 266-7; Brian Boydell, 'Music', in Ian Campbell Ross, ed. *Public Virtue, Public Love: The early years of the Dublin Lying-in Hospital* (Dublin, 1986), pp. 96-124; id., 'Music, 1700-1850', in Moody & Vaughan, *NHI*, IV, pp. 568-71, 574-98, 608-9, 614-21; id., *Rotunda Music in Eighteenth-Century Dublin* (Blackrock, 1992),

pp. 148–60; *DIB*, 'Tommaso Giordani'; Dickson, *Dublin*, pp. 157–9; Sonnelitter, *Charity Movements*, pp. 90–2; Michael Griffin, *Live from the Conniving House: Poetry and music in eighteenth-century Dublin* (Dublin, 2019), pp. 1–28.

33. Brief on Minister's Money, St Werburgh's Dublin, 1714: Foster Papers (PRONI, D562/483–5); Rutty, *Natural History of Dublin*, pp. 15–16; Wakefield, *Account of Ireland*, II, pp. 791–2; Gamble, *Society and Manners*, pp. 46–7; Lydia Wilson, ed., *Knockbreda: Its monuments and people* (Belfast, n.d.); Linzi Simpson, 'Post-medieval Archaeology in Dublin', in Horning et al., *Post-medieval Archaeology*, p. 87; Ó Gráda, *Georgian Dublin*, pp. 163–4.

34. Bolster, *Diocese of Cork*, pp. 278–9; Eamon Phoenix, *Two Acres of Irish History . . . Friar's Bush and Belfast, 1570–1918* (Belfast, 1988), pp. 25–7; Thomas, *IHTA, Derry/Londonderry*, p. 19.

35. Warburton et al., *Dublin*, p. 1175; O'Keeffe, *Recollections*, I, pp. 21–2; Julian C. Walton, 'Pictorial Decoration on East Waterford Tombstones', in *Decies*, xiv (May, 1980), 75–81; Sean Murphy, *St James's Graveyard Project* (Dublin, 1988), 32–3, 38–44; id., *Bully's Acre and Royal Hospital Kilmainham Graveyards: History and inscriptions* (Dublin, 1989), p. 15; id., 'Burying Poor and Gentry: St James's church and graveyard', in Lisa Marie Griffith & Ciaran Wallace, eds., *Grave Matters: Death and dying in Dublin, 1500 to the present* (Dublin, 2016), pp. 139–45; Maurice Hurley, 'Christianity, Churches and Burial Places', in Crowley et al., *Atlas of Cork City*, pp. 89–90. Probably three eighteenth-century Catholic archbishops of Dublin (Byrne, Murphy and Lincoln) and several of the first Dominican sisters in Channel Row were buried in St James's graveyard, as was the leading Catholic merchant Anthony (Mc)Dermott and the celebrated madame, Mrs Leeson. Archbishop Carpenter was buried in St Michan's: *DIB*.

CHAPTER 7 PROJECTS AND PROJECTIONS

1. Copy, [William Smyth], Dublin, to [James Smyth], [-] June [1711]: Smyth of Barbavilla Papers (NLI, MS 41,582/1); *CARD*, VI, p. 583; Burke, 'Dublin', pp. 132, 138, 146, 157, 163; *IHTA, Dublin*, II, pp. 3–4; Dickson, *Dublin*, pp. 83–9, 97–8. An agreement that the Crown should lease Chichester House (for 99 years) was only concluded in 1673: Charles II to [the Earl of Essex], 22 March 1673: *CSP Dom.*, XV: Mar–Oct 1673, p. 391.

2. Lennon & Montague, *Rocque's Dublin*, pp. 42–3, 46–7; Burke, 'Dublin', pp. 150–1; Desmond McCabe, *St Stephen's Green, Dublin, 1660–1875* (Dublin, 2011), pp. 53, 55, 78–81, 92, 95–6.

3. *CARD*, V, frontispiece; Johnston-Liik, *History of Irish Parliament*, III, pp. 261–2; Robin Usher, 'Domestic Architecture, the Old City and the Suburban Challenge, c.1660–1700', in Casey, *The Dublin Town House*, pp. 64–6; Dickson, *Dublin*, pp. 86–7.

4. Andrew Bigelow, *Leaves from a Journal . . .* (Boston, 1821), p. 66; H.A. Gilligan, *History of the Port of Dublin* (Dublin, 1988), pp. 21–8; Stewart, *Travels of Mirza Abu taleb Khan*, pp. 148–9; Dickson, *Dublin*, pp. 170–1.

5. Petition, Order and Report from the Committee of the Ballast Office, July–Aug. 1713; Notes on suit, H.M. *v.* Sir John Rogerson [I], n.d. [c.1715]; copy, will of Sir John Rogerson [II], July 1741; brief for Richard Benson and others, 23 Dec. 1757: Erne Papers (PRONI, D1939/24/5/7; 24/5/20; 24/13; 24/2/4); *DIB*, 'Sir John Rogerson I'.
   The still incomplete reclamation of the site c.1757 is pictured in Gabrielli Ricciardelli's 'View of Dublin' from the harbour entrance: Anne Crookshank & the Knight of Glin, *Ireland's Painters 1600–1940* (New Haven & London, 2002), p. 78.

6. *CARD*, VII, pp. 30–4, 51, 259–60; IX, pp. 120–2; B.P. Bowen, 'The North Strand', in *DHR*, xi (1950), 53–7, 83–4; Burke, 'Dublin 1600–1800', pp. 283–4, 398; Lennon & Montague, *Rocque's Dublin*, pp. 30–3. Even in 1773 there was almost no building evident: Bernard Scalé, *Survey of the City, Harbour, Bay and Environs of Dublin* (Dublin, 1773).

7. William Smyth, Dublin, to Ralph Smyth, 29 Oct., 2 Nov. 1751: Smyth of Barbavilla Papers (NLI, 41,591/1); Thomas Waite, Dublin Castle, to Sir Robert Wilmot, 22 Feb. 1752: Wilmot Papers (PRONI, T3019/1851); *A Letter to T --- P ---, esq. Concerning a New Bridge* (n.p., 1751); John Bush, *Hibernia Curiosa: A letter from a gentlemen in Dublin . . .* (Dublin, 1769), pp. 13–14; Maurice Craig, *Dublin 1660–1860* (London, 1952), p. 179; Edward McParland,

'Strategy in the Planning of Dublin, 1750–1800', in Cullen & Butel, *Cities and Merchants*, pp. 97–9; Malcomson, *Clements: Government and the Governing Elite*, pp. 23–30, 125–7, 132–7, 203–4; id., *Nathaniel Clements 1705–77: Politics, Fashion and Architecture in Mid-eighteenth century Ireland* (Dublin, 2015), pp. 11–38, 40, 60, 64–9; *DIB*, 'Luke Gardiner'; Dickson, *Dublin*, pp. 140–3, 162–3; Lennon & Montague, *John Rocque's Dublin*, pp. 26–7.

8. Gardiner Papers (NLI, Collection List No. 67); Burke, 'Dublin', pp. 220–2, 283–4, 302–5; Dickson, 'Large-scale Developers and the Growth of Eighteenth-Century Irish Cities', in Butel & Cullen, *Cities and Merchants*, pp. 115–16; Casey, *Buildings of Dublin*, pp. 200–4; Usher, *Protestant Dublin*, pp. 188–96; Malcomson, *Nathaniel Clements: 1705–77* pp. 35–80.

9. The great house was sold by the family to the Dublin Society in 1815, and a century later it became the Houses of the Oireachtas, the Irish Free State parliament, in 1922.

10. Casey, *Buildings of Dublin*, pp. 391–2, 577–9; Eve McAulay, 'Some Problems in Building on the FitzWilliam Estate . . .', in *IADS*, ii (1999), 99–117; Frederick O'Dwyer, 'Architecture, Politics and the Board of Works, 1760–1860', in *IADS*, v (2002), 122–9; Finola O'Kane, ' "Bargains in View": The Fitzwilliam family's development of Merrion Square', in Casey, *The Dublin Town House*, pp. 98–109; Dickson, *Dublin*, pp. 166–7; Malcomson, *Nathaniel Clements 1705–77*, pp. 109–10, 112.

11. Jane Meredith, 'Letters between Friends: Lord Charlemont's library and other matters', in *IADS*, iv (2001), 56–67; Casey, *Buildings of Dublin*, pp. 149–50, 206, 220–30; Anthony Duggan, 'Parnell Square', in Mary Clark & Alaistair Smeaton, eds. *The Georgian Squares of Dublin: An architectural history* (Dublin, 2006), pp. 7–31; Dickson, *Dublin*, pp. 227–8.

12. Casey, *Buildings of Dublin*, pp. 149–50, 205–6; Dickson, *Dublin*, pp. 226–7; Ó Gráda, *Georgian Dublin*, pp. 120–1.

13. McParland, 'The Wide Streets Commissioners . . .', in *Bulletin of the Irish Georgian Society*, xv (1972), 1–9; id., 'Strategy in the Planning of Dublin', pp. 97–101; Pollard, *Dictionary*, pp. 125–6; Casey, *Buildings of Dublin*, pp. 443–4; *DIB*, 'George Semple'; Dickson, *Dublin*, pp. 181–2; Malcomson, *Nathaniel Clements (1705–77)*, pp. 67–9; Gibney, *The Building Site*, pp. 162–6; John Montague, 'From Rome to Paris and London: Searching for the European roots of the Wide Streets Commissioners', in *IADS*, xxi (2018), 53–73; IAA, Dictionary of Irish Architects, 'George Semple'.

14. Pollard, *Dictionary*, pp. 125–6; Casey, *Buildings of Dublin*, pp. 443–4; Sarah Rhiannon Drumm, ' "Fine Rooms Increase Wants": Town houses of Irish MPs', in Casey, *The Dublin Town House*, p. 138; Dickson, *Dublin*, pp. 182–3.

15. Christine Casey, 'The Dublin Domestic Formula', and Conor Lucey, 'Classicism or Commerce? The town house interior as commodity', in Casey, *The Dublin Town House*, pp. 46–58, 236–48.

16. Brendan Twomey, 'Speculative Property Development in Eighteenth-Century Dublin', and Usher, 'Domestic Architecture', in Casey, *The Dublin Town House*, pp. 32–3, 35–6, 65–72; Malcomson, *Nathaniel Clements (1705–77)*, pp. 34, 36; Gibney, *The Building Site*, pp. 24–6, 34, 55, 84–5, 270–2. On the divergence of Irish, specifically Dublin, building practices from English conventions, fully evident by the 1740s: Gibney, op. cit., pp. 269–70.

17. Samuel Lewis, *A Topographical Dictionary of Ireland* (London, 1837), II, p. 110; Burke, 'Dublin', pp. 183, 219; Hugo Read, 'The Penroses of Woodhill, Cork: An account of their property in the city', in *JCHAS*, lxxxv (1980), 80–5.

18. Smith, *Waterford*, pp. 155–6, 187–8, 194–7; 23 & 24 Geo. III, c. 52, sects. 25–9; *WHM*, 1794, II, 357; *A Langable, or Rental . . . of the lands, tithes, and revenues, belonging to the mayor, sheriffs, and citizens of the city of Waterford* (Waterford, 1794); Read, 'Penroses of Woodhill', 79–80; J.S. Carroll, 'Old Waterford Newspapers', in *Decies*, xxii (Jan. 1983), 59; Ian W.J. Lumley, 'The Georgian Townhouses of Waterford . . .', in *Decies*, xxxiv (1987), 49–60; Dowling, *Waterford Streets*, pp. 1–3, 6, 30, 32, 55, 76, 78, 113–16, 121–2, 150–1, 157–9; Thomas P. Power, 'Electoral Politics in Waterford City, 1692–1832', and Kenneth Milne, 'The Corporation of Waterford in the Eighteenth Century', in Nolan & Power, *Waterford*, pp. 231–2, 337; Girouard, *Town and Country*, pp. 154–66; Jack Burtchaell, 'Waterford', in Loeber et al., *Art and Architecture*, IV, pp. 473–4; Woods, *Abbot's Tour*, pp. 63–4. The Waterford Wide Streets legislation was 23 & 24 Geo. III, c. 52, sects. 25–9.

19. Edward McParland, *James Gandon, Vitruvius Hibernicus* (London, 1985), pp. 146–9; Kelly, *Willes Letters*, p. 44; [Hugh Maguire, ed.], *An Introduction to the Architectural Heritage of County Waterford* (Dublin, 2004), pp. 21–33; IAA, Dictionary of Irish Architects, 'John Roberts'.

Roberts was fortunate that the Corporation seems to have had a distinctly relaxed attitude to the funding of capital projects: Milne, 'Corporation of Waterford', pp. 336–7.

20. Read, 'Penroses of Woodhill', 80–5; Máire Kennedy, 'At the Exchange: The eighteenth-century book trade in Cork', in Charles Benson & Siobhán Fitzpatrick, eds. *That Woman! Studies in Irish Bibliography: A festschrift for Mary 'Paul' Pollard* (Dublin, 2005), pp. 140–5; Kieran Hickey, 'Flooding in the City', and Richard Harrison, 'Quaker Enterprise', in Crowley et al. *Atlas of Cork City*, pp. 25, 173; http://corkorigins.ie/maps/.

21. 'Mayoralty Book of Thomas Pemberton', pp. 131, 189–92, 306, 312–14; Smith, *Cork*, I, pp. 375–6, 405–6, 408–9; John Rocque, *A Survey of the City and Suburbs of Cork* (Dublin, 1759); *CEP*, 15 Aug. 1763; Joseph Connor, *A Map of the City and Suburbs* (n.p., 1774); John Windele, *Historical and Descriptive Notices of the City of Cork and its Vicinity . . .*, 2nd edn (Cork, 1849), pp. 25–7; Caulfield, *Cork*, p. 970; Eugene Carberry, 'The Development of Cork City', in *JCHAS*, xlviii (1943), 73–9; Mark Bence-Jones, 'Old Town Revisited: A city of vanished waterways', in *Country Life*, cxlii (1967), 250; James Kelly, 'A Tour in the South of Ireland in 1782', in *NMAJ*, xxix (1987), 60; Patrick O'Flanagan, 'Transformation . . .', and 'Beef, Butter, Provisions and Prosperity . . .', in Crowley et al., *Atlas of Cork City*, pp. 100–3, 149–67; John Logan, ' "Dropped into This Kingdom from the Clouds": The Irish career of Davis Dukart, architect and engineer, 1761–81', in *IADS*, x (2007), 36–9.

Precise dating of George St is unknown, but the bridge leading directly from the old city (Tuckey's Lane) to the beginning of what became George's St was constructed by William Dunscombe in 1698, which suggests that the line of the street may have been decided then: Tuckey, *Cork Remembrancer*, p. 122.

22. 'Mayoralty Book of Thomas Pembrock', p. 131; *Hibernian Chronicle*, 26 Dec. 1771; Tuckey, *Cork Remembrancer*, pp. 190, 202–3, 217; Caulfield, *Cork*, pp. 728, 772–3; *DIB*, 'Michael Shanahan'.

23. Smith, *Cork*, I, p. 413; *JHCI*, VII, pp. 35–6, 214; VIII, pp. 24, 304; IX, p. 425; X, p. 25; XI, pp. 86–7, xciv; Daniel Beaufort, *Memoir of a Map of Ireland . . .* (Dublin, 1792), p. 96; Caulfield, *Cork*, pp. 867, 882, 1058–60; Lewis, *Topographical Dictionary*, I, p. 416; Tuckey, *Cork Remembrancer*, p. 128; Samuel Andrews, 'A Map of the Slob Belonging to the Corporation of Cork &c., dated August 1780', *JCHAS*, xxxiv (1929), 116; Louise Harrington, 'The Work of Cork's Wide Streets Commissioners in Washington St', in *IADS*, xv (2012), 113–4.

24. Smith, *Cork*, I, pp. 409–10; 5 Geo. III c.24, sect. 12; Dan[iel] Murphy, *A Survey of the City and Suburbs of Cork* ([Cork], 1788); *HC*, 17 Feb. 1791; de Latocnaye, *Promenade*, p.100; Tuckey, *Cork Remembrancer*, pp. 146–7, 205; Caulfield, *Cork*, p. 1070; Read, 'Penroses of Woodhill', 89–93; J.H. Andrews, *Plantation Acres: An historical study of the Irish land surveyors* (Belfast, 1985), p. 355; Gerard J. Lyne, 'Lewis Dillwyn's Visit to Waterford, Cork and Tipperary in 1809', in *JCHAS*, xci (1986), 91; Peter Murray, *Illustrated Summary Catalogue of the Crawford Municipal Art Gallery* (Cork, 1992), p. 197; Kelly, 'A Tour in 1782', 59; Harrison, *Merchants, Mystics and Philanthropists*, pp. 58–9; Harrington, 'Cork's Wide Streets Commissioners', 99–117; Frank Keohane, 'Cork', in Loeber et al., *Art and Architecture*, IV, p. 451; IAA, Dictionary of Irish Architects, 'Daniel Murphy'. The Cork improvement act of 1765 was 5 Geo. III, c. 24, sect. 12.

25. O'Flaherty, *IHTA, Limerick*, p. 8.

26. *JHCI*, VII, append. pp. lxiv, lxvii; VIII, pp. 219, 513, 515; A.P.W. Malcolmson, 'Speaker Pery and the Pery Papers', in *NMAJ*, xvi (1973/4), 33–6; Hill, *Building of Limerick*, pp. 71–6, 78–9, 81–5, 94; Johnston-Liik, *History of Irish Parliament*, VI, pp. 55–9; *ODNB*, 'Edmond Sexton Pery'; Fleming, *Politics and Provincial People*, pp. 82–3, 96–7.

Parliamentary funding for the Shannon navigation began in 1755, and in 1759 for improvement of the city quays; these grants were before Pery's election as a city MP in 1761, but after he had first entered the Commons as MP for the pocket borough of Wicklow.

27. John Ferrar, *An History of Limerick* . . . 2nd ed. (Limerick, 1787), p. xviii; Leonardo Benevolo, *The Architecture of the Renaissance* (London, 1978), II, pp. 849–55, 1053; Hill, *Building of Limerick*, pp. 87–8; id., 'David Ducart and Christopher Colles . . .', in *IADS*, ii (1999), 119–45; Logan, 'Davis Dukart', 40–8, 83n.

28. *Limerick Chronicle*, 26 Oct. 1769; Lenihan, *History of Limerick*, pp. 50–1, 370, 380; Hill, *Building of Limerick*, pp. 87–27, 135–41; *IHTA, Limerick*, pp. 8–10.

29. McHugh, *IHTA, Drogheda*, pp. 6–8; Livia Hurley, 'Drogheda', in Loeber et al., *Art and Architecture*, IV, p. 453; Casey & Rowan, *North Leinster*, p. 242.

30. *JHCI*, VIII, p. clxiii; Colby, *Memoir of Londonderry*, pp. 128–31, 134–5; Thomas, *IHTA, Derry/Londonderry*, pp. 6–7, 34.

31. Hardiman, *Galway* (2nd edn), pp. 292–3; M. Hayes-McCoy, 'The Eyre Documents . . .', in *JGAHS*, xx (1942), 68; xxiii (1949), 147–53; J.F. Cunningham, 'Patterns of Social Change in a Provincial Capital: Galway, *c.*1800–1914 (Ph.D. dissertation, NUI (Galway), 2001), pp. 17–18; Paul Walsh, 'The Post-medieval Archaeology of Galway, 1550–1850', in Horning et al., *Post-medieval Archaeology*, p. 162; Prunty, *IHTA, Galway*, Map 21; Prunty, 'Galway', in Loeber et al., *Art and Architecture*, IV, p. 462.

32. James MacParlan, *Statistical Survey of the County of Sligo* (Dublin, 1802), p. 70; Lewis, *Topographical Dictionary*, II, p. 568; Derry O'Connell, 'The Arrival at Sligo . . .', in Martin A. Timoney, ed., *A Celebration of Sligo* (Sligo, 2007), pp. 257–62; Gallagher & Legg, *IHTA, Sligo*, pp. 4–5.

33. *WHM*, 1792, II, 195; C.E.B. Brett, *Buildings of Belfast* (London, 1967), pp. 5–7, 11–12; Gamble, 'Belfast Business Community', pp. 138, 142–5, 153, 161, 165–9; Gillespie, *Early Belfast*, pp. 132, 147–51, 160, 168–73; Gillespie & Royle, *IHTA, Belfast*, I, pp. 4–8; *DIB*, 'Arthur Chichester (1739–1799)'; Connolly, *Belfast 400*, pp. 161–78.

34. Minute-book of First Belfast Congregation (PRONI, MIC 1B/2/2), 23 April, 12 May 1781; Brett, *Buildings of Belfast*, p. 6; Gamble, 'Belfast Business Community', pp. 139–40, 146, 148–9; Peter Roebuck, 'The Donegall Family and the Development of Belfast 1600–1850', in Cullen & Butel, *Cities and Merchants*, pp. 130–5; R.T. Campbell & Stephen A. Royle, 'East Belfast and the Suburbanization of North-west County Down . . .', in Lindsay Proudfoot, ed. *Down: History and Society* (Dublin, 1997), pp. 636–40; *IHTA, Belfast*, I, p. 8.

35. Dickson, *Dublin*, p. 262. Some 137 acts of parliament relating to Dublin were passed between 1770 and the Union: Rob Goodbody, ed. *IHTA, Dublin, III*: XXIX (Dublin, 2014), p. 1.

36. *An Alarm to the Citizens of Dublin* (Dublin, 1787), pp. 23–4; McParland, 'Strategy in the Planning of Dublin', pp. 103–4; id., *Gandon*, pp. 41–9, 72–4; Gilligan, *Port of Dublin*, pp. 51–6; Dickson, *Dublin*, pp. 218–222; James Kelly, 'Representations of the Revenue Commissioners with Respect to a "New Custom House" in Dublin, 1771–81', in *IADS*, xxi (2018), 137–60.
    Note that, after the burning of the Custom House in 1921 during the War of Independence, it was completely rebuilt with the only noticeable external change being the dome, grey Irish limestone being used in place of the original Portland: Casey, *Buildings of Dublin*, pp. 145–6.

37. 22 George II (Ir.), *c.*15; *Letters addressed to Parliament, and to the public in general, on various improvements of the metropolis* . . . (Dublin, 1787), p. 90; William Guthrie, *An Improved System of Modern Geography* . . . [Chambers' edition] (Dublin, 1789), p. 437; McParland, 'Wide Streets Commissioners', 10–24; id., 'Strategy in the Planning of Dublin', pp. 104–6; Dickson, *Dublin*, pp. 222–5; Casey, 'Art and Architecture in the Long Eighteenth Century', p. 444.

38. McParland, *Gandon*, pp. 95–6, 149–64; id., 'Strategy in the Planning of Dublin', p. 103; Dickson, *Dublin*, p. 225.

39. John Coleman, 'Luke Gardiner (1745–98): An Irish dilettante', in *Irish Arts Review Yearbook*, xv (1999), 161–8; Casey, *Buildings of Dublin*, pp. 200–4; *DIB*, 'Luke Gardiner [1st Viscount Mountjoy]'; Dickson, *Dublin*, pp. 227–8; *IHTA, Dublin III*, p. 2, map 10.

40. V.T.H. & D.R. Delany, *The Canals of the South of Ireland* (Newton Abbot, 1966), pp. 32–47; Dickson, *Dublin*, pp. 228–31. Wakefield estimated the total sum granted by the Irish Parliament to canal and waterway construction up to 1800 at £379,388: Wakefield, *Account of Ireland*, I, p. 638.

41. Murray Fraser, 'Public Building and Colonial Policy in Dublin, 1760–1800', in *Architectural History*, xxviii (1985), 108–13; McParland, 'Strategy in the Planning of Dublin', pp. 105–6; Jane Meredith, 'Andrew Caldwell (1733–1808)' (M.Litt. dissertation, University of Dublin, 2005), pp. 151–6; Dickson, *Dublin*, pp. 218–20, 597n.
42. *Parliamentary Register . . . of the House of Commons of Ireland* [XV] (Dublin, 1796), p. 23.
43. [Thomas Malton?], *Letters Addressed to Parliament and to the Public in General; On various improvements in the metropolis* (Dublin, 1787); McParland, *Gandon*, pp. 31–2, 94–6; Casey, *Buildings of Dublin*, pp. 141–6; Dickson, *Dublin*, pp. 221–2.

CHAPTER 8 FOOD FOR THOUGHT

1. McParland, *Public Architecture*, pp. 145–58; Pollard, *Dictionary*, pp. 358–60; Máire Kennedy, 'Reading the Enlightenment in Eighteenth-Century Ireland', in *ESC*, xlv, 3 (2012), 364–5; Peter Fox, *Trinity College Library Dublin: A history* (Cambridge, 2014), pp. 51–7, 64–7; K.A. Manley, *Irish Reading Societies and Circulating Libraries Founded before 1825: Useful knowledge and agreeable entertainment* (Dublin, 2018), p. 20.
2. R.B. McDowell & D.A. Webb, *Trinity College Dublin 1592–1952 . . .* (Cambridge, 1982), pp. 37–49; Hannigan, 'University of Dublin', pp. 7–10, 20, 25, 90, 98, 102; Brown, *Irish Enlightenment*, pp. 212–20; Mullaney, 'Evolution of the Medical Professions', pp. 240–1.
3. *Wilson's Dublin Directory, 1768*; Diarmaid Ó Catháin, 'John Fergus M.D.: Eighteenth-Century doctor, book collector and Irish scholar', in *JRSAI*, cxviii (1988), 139–62; Mary Pollard, *Dublin's Trade in Books 1550–1800* (Oxford, 1989), pp. 214–6; id., *Dictionary*, pp. 532–4; *Dublin Directory, 1738*; Barnard, 'Libraries and Collectors, 1700–1800', in Raymond Gillespie & Andrew Hadfield, eds. *The Oxford History of the Irish Book*, III: *The Irish Book in English 1550–1800* (Oxford, 2006), pp. 111–34; Barnard, *Brought to Book*, pp. 342, 345–6; Kennedy, 'Reading the Enlightenment', 355–78.
4. Hugh Gough, 'Book Imports from Continental Europe in Late Eighteenth-Century Ireland: Luke White and the *Société Typographique de Neuchâtel*', in *Long Room*, xxxviii (1993), 35–48; Kennedy, 'Reading the Enlightenment', 357, 367; id., 'Huguenot Readers in Eighteenth-Century Ireland', and Allison Neill-Rabaux, 'A Literary Journal: Imitator of the *Bibliothèque raisonnée?*', in Jane McKee & Randolph Vigne, eds. *The Huguenots: France, Exile and Diaspora* (Eastbourne, 2013), pp. 173–80, 185–92.
5. R.L. Munter, *A Hand-list of Irish Newspapers 1685–1750* (London, 1960), pp. x, 29; Pollard, *Dublin's Book Trade*, pp. 119, 197–203; id., *Dictionary*, pp. 532–4; Graham Gargett, 'List of Books Connected with the French Enlightenment, 1700–1800', in Gargett & Sheridan, eds. *Ireland and the French Enlightenment 1700–1800* (New York & Basingstoke, 1999), pp. 243–84; McParland, *Public Architecture*, pp. 156, 161; Brown, *Hutcheson in Dublin*, pp. 101–5, 110, 121–2; Kennedy, 'Reading the Enlightenment', 366; Dickson, *Dublin*, pp. 150, 176; Barnard, *Brought to Book*, pp. 18, 57–8, 64–5, 306.
6. Munter, *Hand-list of Irish Newspapers*, p. viii; id., *The History of the Irish Newspaper 1685–1760* (Cambridge, 1967), pp. 67–90; Robert E. Ward, *Prince of Dublin Printers: The letters of George Faulkner* (Lexington, KY, 1972); Pollard, *Dictionary*, pp. 198–206; Richard Sher, *The Enlightenment and the Book: Scottish authors and their publishers in eighteenth-century Britain, Ireland and America* (Chicago & London, 2006), pp. 459–67, 500–2; Kennedy, 'Reading the Enlightenment', 356–7; Dickson, *Dublin*, p. 150; Barnard, *Brought to Book*, pp. 350–5.
7. Gilbert, *History of Dublin*, p. 315; James Kelly, 'The State and the Control of Print in Eighteenth-Century Ireland', in *ECI*, xxiii (2008), 150, 162–5; S.J. Connolly, *Divided Kingdom: Ireland 1630–1800* (Oxford, 2008), p. 449.
8. Joshua Dawson, Dublin Castle, to [George] Dodington, 13 Nov. 1708: Blenheim Papers (BL, Add. MS 61,633, f.132); R[ichard] Challoner, *The Morality of the Bible . . .* (Dublin, 1765), pp. [vi–xvi]; Corish, *Catholic Community*, pp. 86–7, 89; Fagan, *Catholics in a Protestant Country*, pp. 165–6, 184–6; Livesey, *Civil Society and Empire*, p. 103; Begadon, 'Catholic Religious Culture', pp. 229–39; Nicholas M. Wolf, 'Advocacy, the Enlightenment and the Catholic Print Trade in Mathew Carey's Dublin', in *Éire-Ireland*, xlix, 3/4 (2014), 256–69;

Barnard, 'Father John Murphy', pp. 226–8, 244–7; id., *Brought to Book*, pp. 206–15, 223, 360–1.

The earliest extant edition of a Catholic devotional work published by Bowes appears to be J.J. Hornyold, *The Decalogue Explain'd*... (Dublin, 1746), which attracted 233 subscribers of whom 17 per cent were clergy and only two were merchants.

9. Pollard, *Dictionary*, pp. 315–16; Sher, *Enlightenment and the Book*, p. 498; Kennedy, 'Reading the Enlightenment', 371; Barnard, *Brought to Book*, p. 67; Manley, *Reading Societies*, pp. 57–6, 61–5, 71.

10. *JHCI*, XII, p. lxiv; Munter, *History of the Irish Newspaper*, pp. 85–8; Adams, *Printed Word*, pp. 29–34; Pollard, *Book Trade*, pp. 159–61, 190–1; Barnard, 'Print Culture 1700–1800', in Gillespie & Hadfield, *The Irish Book in English 1550–1800*, pp. 51–3; Kennedy, 'At the Exchange', pp. 145–51; Manley, *Reading Societies*, pp. 65–8.

11. Adams, *Printed Word*, pp. 26, 43–8; Barnard, *Brought to Book*, pp. 301, 311; James Kelly, 'Sport and Recreation', in Kelly, *CIH: III*, pp. 496–8; Manley, *Reading Societies*, pp. 33, 37–9, 150.

12. Máire Kennedy, 'Eighteenth-Century Newspaper Publishing in Munster and South Leinster', in *JCHAS*, ciii (1998), 67–88; id., 'At the Exchange', pp. 145–61; Hugh Fenning, 'The Catholic Press in Munster in the Eighteenth century', in Long, *Books beyond the Pale*, pp. 26–7; Jennifer Moore, 'John Ferrar, 1742–1804', and Máire Kennedy, 'William Flyn (1740–1811) ...', in John Hinks et al., eds. *Periodicals and Publishers: The newspaper and journal trade 1750–1914* (Newcastle, DE & London, 2009), pp. 47–62, 75–91; *DIB*, 'Henry Sheares'; Dickson, *Dublin*, pp. 148–9; Michael Griffin, ed. *The Collected Poems of Laurence Whyte* (Lewisburg, 2016), pp. 21–3; Barnard, *Brought to Book*, pp. 274–96.

13. Martha McTier, [Belfast], to William Drennan, [22 May 1797]: Agnew, *Drennan-McTier Letters*, II, p. 314; Brian Inglis, *The Freedom of the Press in Ireland 1784–1841* (London, 1954), pp. 19–49, 98–104; Munter, *History of the Irish Newspaper*, pp. 169–91; Adams, *Printed Word*, p. 36; Kevin Whelan, 'The United Irishmen, the Enlightenment and Popular Culture', in Dickson, Dáire Keogh & Kevin Whelan, eds. *The United Irishmen: Republicanism, radicalism and rebellion* (Dublin, 1993), p. 278; Pollard, *Dictionary*, pp. 552–3; Kennedy, 'At the Exchange', p.148; Dickson, *Old World Colony*, pp. 466–7; id., *Dublin*, p. 250; Barnard, *Brought to Book*, pp. 301–2; Manley, *Reading Societies*, pp. 50–6.

14. Warburton et al., *History of Dublin*, II, pp. 874–5; Adams, *Printed Word*, pp. 33–4, 48–9, 86, 90, 98–107; Dickson, 'Paine and Ireland', in Dickson et al., *The United Irishmen*, pp. 137–50; Nancy Curtin, *The United Irishmen: Popular politics in Ulster and Dublin 1791–1798* (Oxford, 1994), pp. 179–81, 191–7; Ó Ciosáin, *Print and Popular Culture*, pp. 87–99, 158–66; id., 'Printing in Irish and Ó Súilleabháin's *Pious Miscellany*', in Long, *Books beyond the Pale*, pp. 87–99; Andrew Carpenter, ed. *Verse in English from Eighteenth-Century Ireland* (Cork, 1998), pp. 7–10, 19–20; Antonia McManus, *The Irish Hedge School and its Books, 1695–1831* (Dublin, 2004), pp. 147–69, 218–24; Barnard, 'Print Culture', and Andrew Carpenter, 'Literature in Print, 1550–1800', in Gillespie & Hadfield, *The Irish Book in English 1550–1800*, pp. 49–51, 315–16; Barnard, *Brought to Book*, p. 212.

15. James W. Phillips, *Printing and Bookselling in Dublin 1670–1800* (Dublin, 1998), pp. 30–1; Pollard, *Dictionary*, pp. 415–16; Fenning, 'Catholic Press in Munster', pp. 19–27; Joanna Archbold, '"The Most Extensive Literary Publication Ever Printed in Ireland": James Moore and the publication of the *Encyclopaedia Britannica* in Ireland, 1790–1800', in Gillian O'Brien & Finola O'Kane, eds. *Georgian Dublin* (Dublin, 2008), pp. 175–87; Frank A. Kafker & Jeff Loveland, 'The Publisher James Moore and his Dublin Edition of the "Encyclopaedia Britannica"', in *ECI*, xxvi (2011), 115–39; Dickson, *Dublin*, pp. 202–4; Barnard, *Brought to Book*, pp. 290–2, 350.

The estimate of Moore's remarkable output is drawn from Kafker and Loveland's calculations of 617 imprints by 'J. Moore' or 'James Moore' over this period, allowing each volume of a series and of serials to be counted as separate items: op. cit., 118–19.

16. Pollard, *Dictionary*, p. 416; Máire Kennedy, 'Women and Reading in Eighteenth-Century Ireland', in Bernadette Cunningham & Máire Kennedy, eds. *The Experience of Reading: Irish historical perspectives* (Dublin, 1999), pp. 79–93; id., 'At the Exchange', pp. 155–6; O'Dowd,

Women in Ireland, pp. 213, 215–17, 220, 223–5; Joanna Archbold, 'Irish Periodicals in their Atlantic Context, 1770–1830' (Ph.D. dissertation, University of Dublin, 2008), pp. 180–6; Padhraig Higgins, *A Nation of Politicians: Gender, patriotism, and political culture in late eighteenth-century Ireland* (Madison, 2010), pp. 178–201; Barnard, *Brought to Book*, pp. 76, 233–4, 311, 315, 327, 337–8, 373.

    At least two Dublin periodicals, *Le magazin à la mode* in 1777/8 and the *New Magazine* in 1799, and one in Cork, William Flyn's *Modern Monitor* (1771), made a pitch for female readers: Archbold, 'Irish Periodicals', pp. 180–3; Barnard, *Brought to Book*, p. 284.

17. R.C. Cole, *Irish Booksellers and English Writers 1740–1800* (London, 1986), pp. 148–72; Pollard, *Dublin Book Trade*, pp. 153–7, 203–9, 211; Sher, *Enlightenment and the Book*, pp. 467–86, 497–8; Dickson, *Dublin*, p. 285; Manley, *Reading Societies*, pp. 75–7.
18. Pollard, *Book Trade*, pp. 159, 161; Kennedy, 'At the Exchange', p. 156.

CHAPTER 9 ORDER AND DISORDER

1. Ferguson, 'Army in Ireland', p. 98; Mairead Dunlevy, *Dublin Barracks: A brief history . . .* (Dublin, 2002), pp. 12–33; Casey, *Buildings of Dublin*, pp. 247–9; McParland, *Public Architecture*, pp. 123–34, 140–1; Fleming, *Politics and Provincial People*, pp. 192–3, 198–9; Charles Ivar McGrath, *Ireland and Empire 1692–1770* (Abingdon, 2012), pp. 77–88, 113–21, 166; McBride, *Eighteenth-Century Ireland*, p. 46.
2. The Lords Justices, Dublin Castle, to the Earl of Sunderland, 30 July 1715: Blenheim Papers (BL, Add. MS 61,633, f.125); *Four Letters Originally Written in French, Relating to the Kingdom of Ireland . . .* (Dublin, 1739), p. 26; Smith, *Cork*, p. 408; Duke of Bedford, Woburn Abbey, to William Pitt, 29 Aug. 1758, in Lord John Russell, ed. *Correspondence of John, Fourth Duke of Bedford . . .* (London, 1843), II, p. 363; Kelly, *Willes Letters*, p. 47; Jacinta Prunty, *Dublin Slums, 1800–1925: A study in urban geography* (Dublin, 1999), p. 32; Gillespie, *Early Belfast*, pp. 144–5; Neal Garnham, *The Militia in Eighteenth-Century Ireland: In defence of the Protestant interest* (Woodbridge, 2012), pp. 35–72; James Kelly, *Sport in Ireland, 1600–1840* (Dublin, 2014), p. 245; Loeber, *Art and Architecture*, IV, pp. 240–1; Dickson, *Dublin*, pp. 122–3; Timothy D. Watt, *Popular Protest and Policing in Ascendancy Ireland, 1691–1761* (Woodbridge, 2018), pp. 34–40.
3. *Animadversions on the Street Robberies in Dublin . . .* (Dublin, 1765), pp. 5–7; Connolly, *Religion, Law and Power*, pp. 221–4; Brian Henry, *Dublin Hanged: Crime, law enforcement and punishment in late eighteenth-century Dublin* (Dublin, 1994), pp. 19, 100; Garnham, *Courts, Crime and Criminal Law*, pp. 155–6, 161–3; Nicholas Rogers, *Mayhem: Post-war crime and violence in Britain, 1748–53* (New Haven & London, 2012), pp. 41–50.

    By comparison, in Cork city and county in the years 1780 to 1787, thirty people were executed (two-thirds for theft, burglary or false possession), and thirty were sentenced to transportation: Thomas Newenham, *A View of the Natural, Political and Commercial Circumstances of Ireland* (London, 1809), append. pp. 43–4.

4. *FJ*, 28–30 Aug. 1790, 25–27 Aug. 1791, 2 Sept. 1800; *FLJ*, 27–31 Aug. 1791; Gamble, *Society and Manners*, pp. 44–6; Henry, *Dublin Hanged*, pp. 100–2, 123–7, 135–6, 173–84; Séamus Ó Maitiú, *The Humours of Donnybrook: Dublin's famous fair and its suppression* (Blackrock, 1995), pp. 14–16, 20–3, 31–2, 35–8; 'Introduction', in Peter Jupp & Eoin Magennis, eds. *Crowds in Ireland c.1720–1920* (Basingstoke, 2000), pp. 3–12; Neal Garnham, 'Police and Public Order in Eighteenth-century Dublin', in Clark & Gillespie, *Two Capitals*, pp. 81–91; id., 'Riot Acts, Popular Protest, and Protestant Mentalities in Eighteenth-Century Ireland', in *HJ*, xl, 2 (2006), 415–17; Kelly, *Sport in Ireland*, pp. 278–80; Milne, 'Corporation of Waterford', p. 343. Quite against the tide, Waterford city received statutory powers to establish a parish watch system in 1784: 23 & 24 Geo. III, c. 52, sects. 31–8.
5. *Corke Journal*, 21 April 1755, 30 April 1764; *FJ*, 30 April 1785, 5 June 1790; Tuckey, *Cork Remembrancer*, pp. 128, 143 153, 162; Caulfield, *Cork*, pp. 693, 701; O Mahony, *In the Shadows*, pp. 20–1; Vincent Morley, *Irish Opinion and the American Revolution 1760–1783* (Cambridge, 2002), pp. 92, 128, 182, 255–6; James Kelly, *The Liberty and Ormond Boys:*

Factional riot in eighteenth-century Ireland (Dublin, 2005); id., '"Ravaging Houses of Ill Fame": Popular riot and public sanction in eighteenth-century Ireland', in Hayton & Holmes, *Ourselves Alone*, pp. 84–103; Watt, *Popular Protest*, pp. 180–203.

6. *The Supplement* [London], 9–11 Jan., 1709–10; Dickson, *Old World Colony*, p. 379; Kelly, *Proclamations of Ireland*, II, pp. 616–17, 623–4; id., *Food Rioting*, pp. 29–32, 113, 143–4, 212–14; John Walter, 'The Politics of Protest in Seventeenth-Century England', in M.T. Davis, ed., *Crowd Actions in Britain and France from the Middle Ages to the Modern World* (Basingstoke, 2015), p. 60; Tait, 'Causes of Death in . . . Youghal', pp. 135–7.

7. Archbishop Hugh Boulter, Dublin, to the Duke of Newcastle, 13 March 1728/9, in Kenneth Milne & Paddy McNally, eds. *The Boulter Letters* (Dublin, 2016), pp. 267–8; Kelly, *Food Rioting*, pp. 34–7; Watt, *Popular Protest*, p. 87.

8. Eoin Magennis, 'In Search of the "Moral Economy": Food scarcity in 1756–57 and the crowd', in Jupp & Magennis, *Crowds in Ireland*, pp. 198–207; Kelly, *Food Rioting*, pp. 98–9, 101–2, 117, 137, 150–1, 163–4, 167–8, 169n.; Watt, *Popular Protest*, pp. 124–5.

9. Dominic Farrell, Waterford, to Daniel Mussenden, 23 April 1757: Mussenden Papers (PRONI, D354/851); Boulter, Dublin, to Baron Carteret, 8 March 1728/9, in Milne & McNally, *Boulter Letters*, pp. 266–7; Caulfield, *Cork*, pp. 584, 595, 598, 601–5, 608–9, 803–4; Gilbert, *CARD*, VIII, pp. 289–91, 323, 385; Drake, 'Demographic Crisis', pp. 105–6, 114–5; Magennis, 'Food Scarcity in 1756–57', pp. 203–4; Dickson, *Dublin*, pp. 179–80; Kelly, *Food Rioting*, pp. 34–47, 93–9, 131, 138, 149, 192–200; Murtagh, 'Dublin's Artisans', pp. 191–2; Watt, *Popular Protest*, pp. 53, 109–12.

10. C.R. Dobson, *Masters and Journeymen: A prehistory of industrial relations 1717–1800* (London, 1980), pp. 21–2, 140–1; Watt, *Popular Protest*, pp. 163–4.
    Dobson lists 28 labour disputes in Dublin between 1728 and 1800 (two-thirds in textiles or clothing), and 2 in Cork: op. cit, pp. 154–70.

11. *Weekly Journal or British Gazetteer*, 17 Aug. 1728; *London Journal*, 17 Aug. 1728; 'Irish Combination Act', 3 Geo. II, c.14; Kelly, *Liberty and Ormond Boys*, p. 20; Dickson, *Dublin*, p. 242; Watt, *Popular Protest*, pp. 165–9; Murtagh, 'Dublin's Artisans', pp. 53–4.

12. *Limerick Chronicle*, 23 Feb. 1769; *FDJ*, 13–15, 15–17 June 1780; *JCHI*, X, pp. 101–2; John Latimer, *The Annals of Bristol in the Eighteenth Century* (Bristol 1893), pp. 70–1; O'Sullivan, *Economic History of Cork*, pp. 216–7; Maurice O'Connell, 'Class Conflict in a Pre-industrial Society: Dublin in 1780', in *Irish Ecclesiastical Record*, ciii (1965), 97–105; Dickson, 'Aspects of the Irish Cotton Industry', pp. 101–3; id., *Dublin*, pp. 210–11; Smyth, *Men of No Property*, p. 145; Henry, *Dublin Hanged*, pp. 60–76; Patrick Walsh, 'Club Life in Late Seventeenth- and Early Eighteenth-Century Ireland', in Kelly & Powell, *Clubs and Societies*, pp. 43–6; Murtagh, 'Dublin's Artisans', pp. 33–5, 63, 84, 120, 131, 142–3, 183–4, 204.

13. *FJ*, 2–6 March 1771, 16 April 1784; *Middlesex Journal*, 5–7 March 1771; Tuckey, *Cork Remembrancer*, pp. 182, 187; O'Connell, 'Class Conflict', 104; James O'Donovan, 'The Anatomy of the Volunteers in Cork, 1775–1782: I', in *JCHAS*, lxxxvii (1982), 31–2, 36–8; Stanley Palmer, *Police and Protest in England and Ireland 1780–1850* (Cambridge, 1988), pp. 117–36; Neely, *Kilkenny*, pp. 161–4; James Kelly, 'A Secret Return of the Volunteers of Ireland in 1784', in *IHS*, xxvi (1988–9), 281, 284, 286, 289, 291; Hill, *Patriots to Unionists*, pp. 198–200; Henry, *Dublin Hanged*, pp. 60–76, 137–53; Dickson, *Old World Colony*, pp. 437–8, 443–7; id., *Dublin*, pp. 197–200, 204–5, 214–17; Ruan O'Donnell, 'The United Irishmen in Limerick, 1791–8', in Irwin et al., eds., *Limerick*, p. 185; Murtagh, 'Dublin's Artisans', pp. 42, 72, 81, 90–3, 116–17, 150–1.

CHAPTER 10 THE SHUTTING OF THE GATES

1. Inglis, *Freedom of the Press*, pp. 52–74; Morley, *Irish Opinion*, pp. 138, 236–7, 256–7; Bartlett, *Revolutionary Dublin*, pp. 18, 44; Bankhurst, *Ulster Presbyterians*, pp. 31–41; Padhraig Higgins, 'Mathew Carey, Catholic Identity, and the Penal Laws', and James Kelly, 'Mathew Carey's Irish Apprenticeship: Editing the *Volunteers Journal*, 1783–84', in *Éire-Ireland*, xlix, 3/4 (2014), 176–200, 206–43; Barnard, *Brought to Book*, pp. 71–2.

2. *Private Correspondence of David Garrick* (London, 1835), II, p. 309; Mrs Mathews, *Memoirs of Charles Mathews, Comedian* (London, 1839), I, p. 107; Gilbert, *Dublin*, II, pp. 201–4; William S. Clark, *The Irish Stage in the County Towns, 1720–1800* (Oxford, 1966), pp. 114–15, 306, 342; Christopher Morash, *A History of Irish Theatre 1601–2000* (Cambridge, 2002), pp. 58–66, 71–2; Helen M. Burke, *Riotous Performances: The struggle for hegemony in Irish theater, 1712–1784* (Notre Dame, IN, 2003), pp. 183–208, 242–52, 260–80; Higgins, *Nation of Politicians*, pp. 75, 262n.

3. Clark, *Irish Stage*, pp. 51–2, 54–6, 59, 63–8, 113–17, 121–3, 132–8, 155–6, 160, 195–6, 271, 285; Burke, *Riotous Performances*, pp. 263–5, 281–90.
   At different times in his career the intriguing but ill-fated Owenson managed theatres in Derry, Galway, Kilkenny and Sligo: W.J. Fitzpatrick, *Lady Morgan, Her Career, Literary and Personal...* (London, 1860), pp. 54–5, 62–3, 66; *DIB*, 'Robert Owenson'.

4. Woods, *Abbot's Tour*, p. 32; J. H. Stewart, 'The Fall of the Bastille on the Dublin Stage', in *JRSAI*, lxxxiv (1954), 78–91; Gamble, 'Belfast Business Community', p. 116; Marianne Elliott, *Wolfe Tone: Prophet of Irish independence* (New Haven & London, 1989), pp. 134–47, 172–78; Nancy J. Curtin, 'Symbols and Rituals of United Irish Mobilisation', in Hugh Gough & David Dickson, eds., *Ireland and the French Revolution* (Blackrock, 1990), pp. 69–70; id., *United Irishmen*, p. 229; A.T.Q. Stewart, *A Deeper Silence: The hidden origins of the United Irish movement* (London, 1993), pp. 146–8, 154–60; *DIB*, 'Richard Daly'; Kevin L. Dawson, *The Belfast Jacobin: Samuel Neilson and the United Irishmen* (Dublin, 2017), pp. 9–11, 19–29, 35–8, 35–9; Ian McBride, 'Protestant Dissenters, c.1690–1800', in Kelly, *Cambridge History of Ireland*, III, pp. 326–7.

5. Thomas Bartlett, *The Rise and Fall of the Irish Nation: The Catholic question 1690–1830* (Dublin, 1992), pp. 127–72; Hill, *Patriots to Unionists*, pp. 218–36; Dickson, *Dublin*, pp. 234–8.

6. Clark, *Irish Stage*, pp. 67, 142, 160–1, 214, 216–17, 275–6, 281–3; J.C. Greene, *Theatre in Belfast 1736–1800* (Bethlehem, MD, 2000), pp. 268–71; id., *Theatre in Dublin 1745–1820: A calendar of performances* (Bethlehem, MD, 2011), V, pp. 2780–1, 2793, 2809, 3027; Helen Burke, 'Jacobin Revolutionary Theatre and the Early Circus: Astley's Dublin amphitheatre', in *International Federation for Theatre Research*, xxxi, 1 (2006), 1–16; Bartlett, *Revolutionary Dublin*, p. 203. On the rising popularity in Dublin during the 1790s of 'panorama' shows involving vast canvases featuring wartime victories and imperial success: Kevin & Emer Rockett, *Magic Lantern, Panorama and Moving Picture Shows in Ireland 1786–1909* (Dublin, 2011), pp. 92–117.

7. C. J. Woods, 'The Personnel of the Catholic Convention, 1792–3', in *AH*, lvii (2003), 26–76; Moody et al., *Works of Tone*, I, pp. 355, 361–70, 398; Thomas Bartlett, '"So Many Wheels within Wheels": The 1793 Catholic Relief act revisited', in Hayton & Holmes, *Ourselves Alone*, pp. 126–36. The Roman Catholic Relief Act was 33 Geo. III, *c*.21 in the Statutes of Ireland.

8. De Latocnaye, *Promenade d'un français dans l'Irlande*, p. 74; Ryland, *History of Waterford*, pp. 160–1; R.G. Thorne, ed., *The History of Parliament: The House of Commons, 1790–1820*, IV (London, 1986), pp. 663–4; Thomas P. Power, 'Electoral Politics in Waterford City, 1692–1832', in Nolan & Power, *Waterford*, pp. 245, 247–50.

9. *Report of the Trial of Richard Maher, of the City of Waterford, esq. M.D. for High Treason and Disaffection...* (Dublin, 1798); Ryland, *History of Waterford*, p. 100; Sir Richard Musgrave, *Memoirs of the Different Rebellions in Ireland...*, 4th edn, Steven W. Myers & Dolores E. McKnight, eds. (Fort Wayne IN, 1995), pp. 649–53; *DIB*, 'Thomas Hussey'.

10. O'Kelly, *Old Private Banks of Munster*, pp. 84–7; Ruan O'Donnell, 'The United Irishmen in Limerick, 1791–98', in Irwin et al., *Limerick*, pp. 185–6, 191, 196, 207; Michael Durey, 'William Maume: United Irishman and informer in two hemispheres', in *ECI*, xviii (2003), 130–6; O'Flaherty, 'An Urban Community and the Penal Laws', pp. 221–3; *DIB*, 'Francis Arthur'; 'Richard McCormick'.

11. *HC*, 9 April 1772, 30 Nov. 1789; Tuckey, *Cork Remembrancer*, pp. lxxxiv–lxxxvi, xciii–xcix, 160; Máire Kennedy, 'William Flyn', pp. 75–91; Dickson, *Old World Colony*, pp. 164–5, 368, 443–7; Petri Mirala, 'Masonic Sociability and its Limitations: The case of Ireland', and David

Fleming, 'Clubs and Societies in Eighteenth-Century Munster', in Kelly & Powell, *Clubs and Societies*, pp. 329–30, 439.

12. Kennedy, 'The Cork Library Society . . .', in *JCHAS*, xciv (1989), 56–73; O'Mahony, *In the Shadows*, pp. 11–12, 15–6; Dickson, *Old World Colony*, pp. 375–7, 442; Fleming, 'Clubs and Societies', p. 445; Manley, *Reading Societies*, pp. 105–6, 210–11.

13. *NS*, 29 Sept.–3 Oct. 1792; *HC*, 17, 24 Sept., 11, 15, 18, 22, 25, 29 Oct. 1792; Hugh Fenning O.P., 'Some Broadsides, Chiefly from Cork 1709–1821', in *Coll. Hib.*, xxxviii (1996), 120–2.

14. *CEP*, 17, 21 Jan. 1793; *HC*, 15 April 1793; *DEP*, 16 June 1795; Dickson, *Old World Colony*, pp. 455–70; Durey, 'William Maume', 123–8; *DIB*, 'Arthur O'Connor', 'Henry Sheares'.

15. D'Alton, *History of Drogheda*, I, p. 51; II, p. 370; Malcomson, *Politics of Anglo-Irish Ascendancy*, pp. 182–7; Kevin Whelan, 'Catholics, Politicisation and the 1798 Rebellion', in R. Ó Muirí, ed. *Irish Church History Today* (Armagh, 1990), p. 75; id., *The Tree of Liberty: Radicalism, Catholicism and the construction of Irish identity 1760–1830* (Cork, 1996), pp. 77, 114; Jim Smyth, *The Men of No Property: Irish radicals and popular politics in the late eighteenth century* (Basingstoke, 1992), pp. 60, 76, 105–7; Dáire Keogh, *'The French Disease': The Catholic Church and radicalism in Ireland, 1790–1800* (Dublin, 1993), pp. 191–2, 194–6; Bartlett, *Rise and Fall of the Irish Nation*, pp. 184–5; Fenning, 'Some Broadsides', 123–5; Moira Corcoran, 'Three Eighteenth-Century Drogheda Letters', 29–35; Fergus O'Dowd, 'An Account of the Insurrection of 1792 in Drogheda', and 'The Trial of John Bird . . . 1794', in Anon., *Drogheda and 1798* (Drogheda, 1998), pp. 11, 17–29, 33–63; Patrick Fagan, *The Diocese of Meath in the Eighteenth Century* (Dublin, 2001), pp. 178–85; Bartlett, *Revolutionary Dublin*, p.18.

Father Martin was captured in south Wicklow during the Rising when on an errand for the Leinster leadership; he made a somewhat empty confession, was imprisoned for more than three years in Kilmainham, escaped, then disappeared without trace: Keogh, op. cit., pp. 194–6.

16. Smyth, *Men of No Property*, pp. 61, 108, 161; Cullen, 'Social and Economic Evolution of Kilkenny', pp. 284–7.

17. Gamble, 'Belfast Business Community', pp. 91, 415; Stewart, *Deeper Silence*, pp. 185–6; Curtin, *United Irishmen*, pp. 118, 134, 142, 146–7; David Miller, 'Radicalism and Ritual in East Ulster', in Thomas Bartlett et al., eds., *1798: A bicentennial perspective* (Dublin 2003), pp. 202–4; Dawson, *Neilson*, pp. 56–8.

18. Smyth, *Men of No Property*, pp. 145–50; Whelan, *Tree of Liberty*, pp. 77–80; Murtagh, 'Dublin's Artisans', pp. 175–6, 197, 213–14, 219, 221–4, 254–5, 267.

19. *WHM* 1797, 191; Curtin, *United Irishmen*, pp. 126–43, 289–91; Allan Blackstock, *An Ascendancy Army: The Irish Yeomanry 1796–1834* (Dublin, 1998), pp. 88–91, 98–9, 118, 131–4, 137–9; Bartlett, *Revolutionary Dublin*, pp. 14–68; *DIB*, 'Oliver Bond', 'Thomas Braughall', 'Richard McCormick', 'Henry Jackson'; Dickson, *Dublin*, pp. 243–6, 248–9; Murtagh, 'Dublin's Artisans', pp. 138–9, 262.

20. *BNL*, 25–9 Aug. 1794; *FDJ*, 8 Sept. 1795; *WHM*, 1795, 286; D.A. Chart, 'The Irish Levies during the Great French War', in *Eng. HR*, xxxii (1917), 499; Ferguson, 'Army in Ireland', pp. 73–5, 96, 171–3; Morley, *Irish Opinion*, pp. 143–4, 183, 262, 304–5; Fleming, *Politics and Provincial People*, pp. 196–7, 214; McGrath, *Ireland and Empire*, pp. 147–9; Roger Morriss, *The Foundations of British Maritime Ascendancy: Resources, logistics and the state, 1755–1815* (Cambridge, 2012), Table 6.2; J. Ross Drancy, *The Myth of the Press Gang: Volunteers, impressment and the naval manpower problem in the late eighteenth century* (Woodbridge, 2015), pp. 50–1, 80, 84, 151; Thomas Bartlett, 'Ireland During the Revolutionary and Napoleonic Wars', in Kelly, *Cambridge History of Ireland: III*, pp. 75–6; Murtagh, 'Dublin's Artisans', pp. 194, 258–9, 277–8; Watt, *Popular Protest*, p. 90.

21. Gamble, 'Belfast Business Community', pp. 79n., 91, 415, 417; Bartlett, *Revolutionary Dublin*, pp. 30–8, 55–7, 67; *DIB*, 'Henry Joy McCracken'; Connolly, *Belfast 400*, pp. 184–5; Dickson, *Dublin*, p. 243.

22. Blackstock, *Ascendancy Army*, pp. 148–50; Bartlett, *Revolutionary Dublin*, pp. 57–8, 347–75; Dickson, *Dublin*, pp. 247–57.

1,069 men surrendered in Dublin city, but over 70 of these had addresses outside the city and suburbs: Bartlett, op. cit., pp. 347–75.

23. *Sligo Journal*, 28 May 1793, reprinted in *FJ*, 30 May–1 June 1793; Nuala Costello, ed. 'James Little's Diary of the French Landing in 1798', in *Anal. Hib.*, xi (1941), 111; Musgrave, *Memoirs of the Different Rebellions*, pp. 566–7; Liam Kelly, *A Flame Now Quenched: Rebels and Frenchmen in Leitrim 1793–1798* (Dublin, 1998), pp. 88–93.

24. Hardiman, *History of Galway*, p. 196.

25. Londonderry Corporation minutes, 1793–1817, p. 56 (https://www.nidirect.gov.uk /publications/corporation-minute-book-volume-10b-1793-1817); *WHM*, 1797, 381–2; Clark, *Irish Stage*, pp. 214–15; Lacey, *Siege City*, pp. 154–8, 162–3; Breandán Mac Suibhne, 'Up and Not Out: Why did north-west Ulster not rise in 1798?', in Cathal Póirtéir, ed. *The Great Irish Rebellion of 1798* (Cork 1998), pp. 83–98; id., 'Politicization and Paramilitarism: North-west and south-western Ulster, c.1772–98', in Bartlett et al., *1798*, pp. 243–78; Gerald R. Hall, *Ulster Liberalism, 1778–1876: The middle path* (Dublin, 2011), pp. 43–9; Bankhurst, *Ulster Presbyterians*, p. 130; Woods, *Abbot's Tour*, pp. 41–4.

26. James Livesey, *Civil Society and Empire: Ireland and Scotland in the eighteenth-century Atlantic world* (New Haven & London, 2009), pp. 185, 205; McBride, *Eighteenth-Century Ireland*, pp. 377–81; Higgins, *Nation of Politicians*, p. 8.

CHAPTER 11 PARTINGS

1. 6 Geo. I, c.18; *FJ*, 2 Jan., 22 Oct. 1822; 21 March, 31 Oct. 1823; 23 July, 29 Oct., 16 Nov. 1824; 13 April, 10 Sept. 1825; Warburton et al., *Dublin*, II, p. 1076n; Lewis, *Topographical Dictionary*, II, p. 269; Johnson, *Birth of the Modern*, pp. 159–60; Rynne, *Industrial Ireland*, pp. 422–6; *IHTA, Limerick*, p. 46; Tom Spalding, 'Sun-fish and Coal-gas: Public lighting in Cork city, 1718–1826', in *IADS*, xiii (2010), 61–77; Leslie Tomory, *Progressive Enlightenment: The origins of the gaslight industry, 1780–1820* (Cambridge, MA, 2012), pp. 117–20, 236–7; Finnian Ó Cionnaith, *Exercise of Authority . . .* (Dublin, 2015), pp. 90–9.

2. Minutes of the [Belfast] Police Committee, 1818–19 (PRONI LA/7/2BA/1/4); [W.H. Crawford], *Problems of a Growing City: Belfast 1780–1870* (Belfast, 1973), pp. 29–39, 61–79.

3. *JHCI*, XIX, append., pp. dccclvii, dccclxi; *House of Commons Debates*, 5 May 1819 (Hansard, XL, cols 126–48); *Return of the Net Amount of Window and Hearth Tax in the City of Dublin, 1815–18* (Parl. papers 1819, XVI [357]); *Return of Number of Officers Employed for Collection of Revenue in the City and County of Dublin, 1806–8 and 1816–18* (Parl. papers 1819, XVI [359]); *Account of the Number of Houses in Ireland Subject to Tax on Windows 1805–10* (Parl. papers, 1821 XIX [213]; *Account of the Amount of Duties on Houses and Windows in the United Kingdom, 1792–1821* (Parl. papers, 1822, XX [227]), p. 2; Marquess of Londonderry, ed. *Memoirs and Correspondence of Viscount Castlereagh* (London, 1849), III, pp. 433–4; M.E. Gleeson, 'Dr John Geary . . .', in *Old Limerick Journal*, xxiv (1988), 25–6; Hill, *Patriots to Unionists*, p. 267; Laurence M. Geary, *Medicine and Charity in Ireland 1718–1851* (Dublin, 2004), pp. 73–7, 83–7; Rob Goodbody, ' "Tax upon Daylight": Window tax in Ireland', in *IADS*, ix (2006), 87–97; J.J. Wright, *The 'Natural Leaders' and Their World: Politics, culture and society in Belfast c.1801–1832* (Liverpool, 2012), p. 90; Malcomson, *Politics of Improvement*, pp. 245–6.

   Robert Walsh, writing c. 1812, estimated that in the city of Dublin hearth and window taxes together raised £180,000, at a time when *local* taxes only raised around £160,000: Warburton et al., *Dublin*, II, p. 1171.

4. Thomas Brodigan, Drogheda, to Henry Goulburn, 25 May 1824 (NAI, CSO/RP/1824/1363); [Horatio Townsend], *A View of the Agricultural State of Ireland in 1815 . . .* (Cork, 1816), pp. 10–11; *Commission of Inquiry into the Poorer Classes in Ireland*, Appendix C, part ii (Parl. papers, 1836 [30]), pp. 24, 32, 45, 88–9; Gamble, *Society and Manners*, pp. 54–5; K.H. Connell, *The Population of Ireland 1750–1845* (Oxford, 1950), pp. 227–34; O'Kelly, *Private Banks of Munster*, pp. 26–8; Cullen, *Economic History of Ireland*, pp. 101–4; G.L. Barrow, *The Emergence of the Irish Banking System 1820–1845* (Dublin, 1975), pp. 17–23; John Post, *The Last Great Subsistence Crisis in the Western World* (Baltimore & London, 1977), pp. 129–31; Audrey Woods, *Dublin Outsiders: A history of the Mendicity Institution 1818–1998* (Dublin, 1998), pp. 12–73; Prunty, *Dublin Slums*, p. 33; Ó Gráda, *New Economic History*, pp. 56–7, 63,

156–8, 161, 293; Geary, *Medicine and Charity*, pp. 79–80, 83–7; Dickson, *Old World Colony*, pp. 486–8; id., *Dublin*, p. 315.

5. Warbuton et al., *Dublin*, II, pp. 669–798; Connell, *Population of Ireland*, p. 196; Geary, *Medicine and Charity*, pp. 16, 18, 20, 31–2; Dickson, *Dublin*, pp. 299, 315; Sonnelitter, *Charity Movements*, pp. 78–98.

6. William Guthrie, *A New System of Modern Geography . . .*, 1st American edn (Philadelphia, 1794), p. 380; Elizabeth Malcolm, *Swift's Hospital: A history of St. Patrick's Hospital, Dublin, 1746–1989* (Dublin, 1989), pp. 9–55; Prunty, *Dublin Slums*, pp. 25–31; Toby Barnard, 'Public and Private Uses of Wealth in Ireland, *c.*1660–1760', in Jacqueline Hill & Colm Lennon, eds. *Luxury and Austerity* (Dublin, 1999), pp. 66–7; Geary, *Medicine and Charity*, pp. 26–8, 33, 36–8, 77, 80–5; *DIB*, 'Richard Steevens', 'Sir Patrick Dun'; Dickson, *Dublin*, p. 314.

7. R.W.M. Strain, *Belfast and its Charitable Society: A story of urban social development* (Oxford, 1961); Connolly, *Belfast 400*, pp. 167–9.

8. Estimates of capital employed in various Irish towns, *c.*1822/4, Liverpool Papers (BL, Add. MS 38,368); John Dubourdieu, *Statistical Survey of the County of Antrim* (Dublin, 1812), pp. 400–12; Wakefield, *Ireland*, pp. 699, 704–5; *Poor Inquiry*, Appendix C, part i (Parl. papers, 1836, XXX), pp. 5–6; E.R.R. Green, *The Lagan Valley 1800–50: A Local History of the Industrial Revolution* (London, 1949), pp. 96–105, 110, 179; H.D. Gribbon, *The History of Water Power in Ulster* (Newton Abbot, 1969), pp. 110–19; Gamble, 'Belfast Business Community', pp. 22, 55, 146, 288, 317, 322, 341, 373–87, 411; Andy Bielenberg, *Ireland and the Industrial Revolution . . . . 1801–1922* (Abingdon, 2009), pp. 24–5, 206n.–7n.; *DIB*, 'Andrew Mulholland'; Wright, '*Natural Leaders*', pp. 42–3; Stephen A. Royle, 'Workshop of the Empire, 1820–1914', in Connolly, *Belfast 400*, pp. 208–9.

9. Francis White, *Report and Observations on the State of the Poor of Dublin* (Dublin, 1833), p. 13; Timothy O'Neill, 'The State, Poverty and Distress in Ireland, 1815–45' (Ph.D. dissertation, NUI [UCD], 1971), pp. 64, 169–73; Dickson, 'Irish Cotton Industry', pp. 100–15; id., 'Death of a Capital?', pp. 128–30; David O'Toole, 'The Employment Crisis of 1826', in Dickson, *Gorgeous Mask*, pp. 157–71; Cormac Ó Gráda, 'Industry and Communications, 1801–45', in W.E. Vaughan, ed., *NHI*, V: *1801–70* (Oxford, 1989), pp. 139, 142; id., *New Economic History*, p. 277; Andy Bielenberg, *Cork's Industrial Revolution 1780–1880: Development or Decline?* (Cork, 1991), pp. 22–5, 34–6; do., *Ireland and Industrial Revolution*, pp. 24–6.

10. *Report from the Committee on the Petition of Brewers of Dublin . . .* (Parl. papers, 1810–11, V), p. 7; Patrick Lynch & John Vaizey, *Guinness's Brewery in the Irish Economy 1759–1876* (Cambridge, 1960), pp. 89–90, 92, 119–24, 140; Cullen, *Economic History of Ireland*, p. 123; Ó Gráda, 'Industry and Communications', pp. 135, 156; Dickson, *Old World Colony*, pp. 388–9, 393; Rynne, *Industrial Ireland*, pp. 262–3; Bielenberg, *Ireland and the Industrial Revolution*, pp. 77–80, 83; Ó Drisceoil & Ó Drisceoil, *Beamish & Crawford*, pp. 34–79, 374–5.

11. Dickson, 'Death of a Capital?', pp. 115–16; Rynne, *Industrial Ireland*, pp. 280–4; P.M. Solar, 'Shipping and Economic Development in Nineteenth-Century Ireland', in *EHR*, lix (2006), 725–40; Dickson, *Dublin*, p. 289.

12. *FJ*, 22 Nov. 1824; Cullen, *Economic History of Ireland*, pp. 102–3, 125–9; Barrow, *Irish Banking System*, pp. 61–82, 215; Ollerenshaw, *Banking in Nineteenth-Century Ireland*, pp. 9–30; Ó Gráda, 'Industry and Communications', p. 152; id., *New Economic History*, p. 58.

13. Wakefield, *Account of Ireland*, II, pp. 784–9; Dickson, 'Death of a Capital?', pp. 116–17; Gillian O'Brien, ' "What Can Possess You To Go To Ireland": Visitors' perceptions of Dublin, 1800–30', and Sharon Murphy, ' "Beauties and Defects": Maria Edgeworth's representations of Georgian Dublin', in O'Brien & O'Kane, *Georgian Dublin*, pp. 17–29, 146–51; Claire Connolly, *A Cultural History of the Irish Novel 1790–1829* (Cambridge, 2012), pp. 38–45, 60–2, 80–1; Dickson, *Dublin*, pp. 273–4. But for a sense of transgressive public behaviour in post-union Dublin: *The Grand Masquerade: Or, the Devil in Dublin: Containing several curious anecdotes of those public characters who graced the private masqued ball of the Lady Mayoress on the 9th and 10th of Feb. 1810* ([Dublin], [1810]).

14. O'Dowd, *History of Women*, pp. 46, 222–3; Aidan O'Boyle, 'The Earls of Moira: Their property and architectural interests', in *Artefact*, i (2007), 70–9.

15. Samuel Rosborough, *Observations on the State of the Poor of the Metropolis* (Dublin, 1801), p. 42; *Poor Inquiry*, Appendix C, part i, pp. 23–4; Angela Fahy, 'Residence, Workplace and Patterns of Change: Cork 1787–1863', in Cullen & Butel, *Cities and Merchants*, pp. 47–50; Cullen, 'The Growth of Dublin 1600–1900', in F.H.A. Aalen & Kevin Whelan, eds. *Dublin City and County: From prehistory to present* (Dublin, 1992), pp. 265–7, 272; O'Flaherty, *IHTA, Limerick*, pp. 8–9; Finola O'Kane, '"The Appearance of a Continued City": Dublin's Georgian suburbs', in O'Brien & O'Kane, *Georgian Dublin*, pp. 114–26; Dickson, *Dublin*, pp. 276–8, 373; Laura Johnstone. '"On One Level to the Eye": Visions for suburbia on the Longford de Vesci estate', in *IADS*, xviii (2015), 84–92; Gurrin, 'Population and Emigration', in Kelly, *CHI*, III, pp. 221–2.

16. Windele, *Historical Notices of Cork*, pp. 43–4; Kelly, *Willes's Letters*, p. 21; Ó Gráda, *Georgian Dublin*, pp. 90–6. These estimates are drawn from the parish entries in Lewis, *Topographical Dictionary*.

17. Stanley H. Palmer, *Police and Protest in England and Ireland 1780–1850* (Cambridge, 1988), pp. 152–9; Seamas Ó Maitiú, *The Humours of Donnybrook . . .* (Blackrock, 1995), pp. 12–33; Kelly, *Sport in Ireland*, pp. 264–6, 278–9.

18. Wakefield, *Account of Ireland*, II, pp. 734–5; Tuckey, *Cork Remembrancer*, pp. c–ci; D'Alton, *Protestant Society in Cork*, pp. 28–36; Hill, *Patriots to Unionists*, pp. 277–80, 330–45; Dickson, *Old World Colony*, pp. 476–80; Gerald Hall, *Ulster Liberalism, 1778–1876* (Dublin, 2011), pp. 66–77; Jonathan Wright, '*Natural Leaders*', pp. 49–105; Murtagh, 'Dublin's Artisans', p. 337.

19. *Poor Inquiry*, Appendix G (Parl. papers, 1836, XXXIV), pp. vii, 21, 25, 71; Fitzpatrick & Vaughan, *Irish Historical Statistics*, pp. 27–41; Dickson, 'Town and City', in Eugenio F. Biagini & Mary E. Daly, eds. *Cambridge Social History of Modern Ireland* (Cambridge, 2017), pp. 122–41.

20. David Alexander, 'The Dublin Group: The mezzotint engravers in London, 1750–1775', in *QBIGS*, xvi, 3 (1973), 73–89; F.E. Williams, 'The Irish in the East Cheshire Silk Industry, 1851–61', in *Transactions of the Historical Society of Lancashire and Cheshire*, cxxxvi (1986), 101–6, 123; Amaia Bilboa Acedos, *The Irish Community in the Basque Country c.1700–1800* (Dublin, 2003); Cullen, *The Irish Brandy Houses*; id., 'The Two George Fitzgeralds of London, 1718–1759', in Dickson et al., *Irish and Scottish Mercantile Networks*, pp. 251–70; Skinner, *Wallpaper in Ireland*, pp. 84–91; Thomas O'Connor, 'Spanish Subornment of English and Irish Textile Workers, 1749–56', in Truxes, *Ireland, France and the Atlantic*, pp. 194–209.

21. Matthew Baigell, 'James Hoban and the First Bank of the United States', in *JSAH*, xxviii, 2 (1969), 135–6; Franklin Toker, 'James O'Donnell: An Irish Georgian in America', in *JSAH*, xxix, 2 (1970), 132–43; Hill, 'Ducart and Colles', 129–31; Kenneth T. Jackson & David S. Dunbar, eds. *Empire City: New York through the centuries* (New York, 2002), pp. 116–23; Meredith, 'Andrew Caldwell', p. 69; Deborah Popper, 'A Notable Precursor: Christopher Colles and the mapping of America' in *Old Kilkenny Review*, lx (2008), 78–88.

22. Dorothy Thompson, 'Ireland and the Irish in English Radicalism before 1850', in James Epstein & Thompson, eds. *The Chartist Experience . . .* (London, 1982), pp. 120–51; Ian McCalman, *Radical Underworld: Prophets, revolutionaries and pornographers in London, 1795–1840* (Cambridge, 1988), pp. 10–17, 61; John Belchem, 'Nationalism, Republicanism and Exile: Irish emigrants and the revolutions of 1848', in *Past & Present*, cxlvi (1995), 125–34; Dickson, 'Death of a Capital?', pp. 126–8; Donald M. MacRaild, *The Irish in Britain 1800–1914* (Dundalk, 2006), pp. 67–9; Murtagh, 'Dublin's Artisans', pp. 185, 385–6.

23. Cole, *Irish Booksellers and English Writers*, pp. 148–90; David Wilson, *United Irishmen, United States: Immigrant radicals in the early Republic* (Dublin, 1998), pp. 90–2; Powell, *Politics of Consumption*, pp. 173–6, 181–7; Higgins, *Nation of Politicians*, pp. 111–15, 223–9; Mary O'Dowd, 'Politics, Patriotism and Women in Eighteenth-Century Ireland, Britain and Colonial America, c.1700–1780', in *Journal of Women's History*, xxii, 4 (2010), 21–5; Sarah Foster, '"An Honourable Station . . .": Retailing, consumption and economic nationalism in Dublin, 1720–85', in O'Brien & O'Kane, *Georgian Dublin*, pp. 32–44; Eoin Magennis,

'Mathew Carey, "Protecting Duties", and the Dublin Crowd in the Early 1780s', in *Eire-Ireland*, l, 3/4 (2015), 173–98.

24. Fagan, *Catholics in a Protestant Country*, pp. 126–58; Petri Mirala, 'Masonic Sociability and Its Limitations: The case of Ireland', in Kelly & Powell, *Clubs and Societies*, pp. 315–31; Ric Berman, 'The London Irish and the Antients Grand Lodge', in *Eighteenth-Century Life*, xxxix, 1 (2015), 103–30.

25. J.E. Bicheno, *Ireland and its Economy . . .* (London, 1830), pp. 280–5; Walsh, *Nano Nagle*, pp. 47–8; Barry Coldrey, *Faith and Fatherland: The Christian Brothers and the development of Irish nationalism 1838-1921* (Dublin, 1988), pp. 14–19; Magray, *Transforming Power*, pp. 8–10; *DIB*, 'Ignatius Rice'.

26. John A. Murphy, *The College: A history of Queen's/University College Cork 1845-1995* (Cork, 1995), pp. 3–48; Terry Eagleton, *Crazy Jane and the Bishop and Other Essays on Irish Culture* (Cork, 1998), pp. 158–211; Dickson, "Second City Syndrome . .', in S.J. Connolly, ed., *Kingdoms United? Great Britain and Ireland since 1500* (Dublin, 1999), pp. 99, 102–8; id., *Dublin*, pp. 288–9.

CONCLUSION

1. Walter Harris, *The History and Antiquities of the City of Dublin . . .* (London and Dublin, 1766); John Ferrar, *An History of the City of Limerick . . .* (Limerick, 1767, 1787); J.H. Andrews, *Plantation Acres: An historical study of Irish land surveyors* (Belfast, 1985), pp. 342–6; Thomas, *IHTA, Derry/Londonderry*, Map 17; Gillespie & Royle, *IHTA, Belfast, part I*, Map 9; O'Flaherty, *IHTA, Limerick*, Maps 18, 19; Rosemary Sweet, 'Provincial Culture and Urban Histories in England and Ireland During the Long Eighteenth Century', in Borsay & Proudfoot, *Provincial Towns*, pp. 223–39; Dickson, 'Town and City', 112–13.

   The urban sections of Charles Smith's major histories of Co. Waterford (1746) and Cork (1750) were however quite substantial.

2. James Hardiman, *The History of the Town and County of the Town of Galway . . .* (Dublin, 1820), v-viii; James Warburton, James Whitelaw & Robert Walsh, *History of the City of Dublin . . .* 2 vols. (London, 1818); Samuel McSkimin, *The History and Antiquities of the County and Town of Carrickfergus . . .* (Belfast, 1811); James Stuart, *Historical Memoirs of the City of Armagh . . .* (Newry, 1819); [George Benn], *The History of the Town of Belfast . . .* (Belfast, 1823); R.H. Ryland, *The History, Topography and Antiquities of the County and City of Waterford* (London, 1824); L.C. Johnston, *History of Drogheda . . .* (Drogheda, 1826); Patrick Fitzgerald & J.J. McGregor, *The History, Topography, and Antiquities, of the County and City of Limerick*, 2 vols (Dublin, 1826–7); F.H. Tuckey, *The County and City of Cork Remembrancer . . .* (Cork, 1837).

   Benn's history of Belfast was the only one to be re-issued later in the century. The most weighty additions to Irish urban history after this period came with the publication of the records of a number of the unreformed municipal councils – including Dublin, Cork and Belfast – but John Gilbert's *History of Dublin*, 3 vols. (Dublin, 1854–9) and the many articles on Kilkenny that appeared from 1849 in the *Transactions of the Kilkenny Archaeological Society* were the most important contributions.

3. O'Neill, 'State, Poverty and Distress', pp. 66–74; id., 'A Bad Year in the Liberties', in Elgy Gillespie, ed. *The Liberties of Dublin* (Dublin, 1973), pp. 82–3; S.J. Connolly, 'The "Blessed Turf": Cholera and popular panic in Ireland', in *IHS*, xxiii (1983), 214–232.

4. Estimates of capital employed in various Irish towns, *c.*1822/4: Liverpool Papers (BL, Add. MS 38,368); S.J. Connolly, *Priests and People in Pre-famine Ireland 1780-1845* (Dublin, 1982), p. 27; d'Alton, *Protestant Society in Cork*, pp. 128–37; Thorne, *House of Commons, 1790-1820*, IV, pp. 663–7; Barnard, 'Public and Private Uses of Wealth', pp. 69–76; id., *Making the Grand Figure*, p. 120; Kelly, *Sport in Ireland*, pp. 502, 515.

5. Tuckey, *Cork Remembrancer*, pp. c-ci. Tuckey was a young Cork attorney at the time of writing.

6. Bicheno, *Ireland and its Economy*, p. 209; Connolly, *Priests and People*, p. 123; id., 'Mass Politics and Sectarian Conflict, 1823-30', in Vaughan, *NHI*, V, pp. 74–5.

7. NAI, CSO/RP/1829/358.
8. Kelly, *Sport in Ireland*, pp. 204, 262–8, 277–82, 309–10, 353–4.
9. Windele, *Historical Notices of Cork*, pp. 38–9; Connolly, *Priests and People*, pp. 144; id., 'Mass Politics', pp. 89–90; Dickson, 'City, Seasons and Society', in Crowley et al., *Atlas of Cork*, pp. 127–34.
10. Connolly, *Priests and People*, pp. 171–2; Ciaran O'Neill, 'Bourgeois Ireland, or, on the Benefits of Keeping One's Hands Clean', in Kelly, *CHI*, III, p. 518.

SELECT BIBLIOGRAPHY

PRINTED PRIMARY SOURCES AND SOURCE COLLECTIONS

Brown, David, and Ó Siochrú, Micheál. 'The Cromwellian Urban Surveys, 1653–1659', in *AH*, lxix (2016)

Carpenter, Andrew, ed. *Verse in English from Eighteenth-Century Ireland* (Cork: University Press, 1998)

Cullen, L.M., Shovlin, John, and Truxes, Thomas, eds. *The Bordeaux-Dublin Letters, 1757* (Oxford: University Press, 2013)

Fitzpatrick, A.J., and Vaughan, W.E. *Irish Historical Statistics: Population 1821–1971* (Dublin: RIA, 1978)

Gamble, John. *Society and Manners in Early Nineteenth-Century Ireland*, ed. Breandán Mac Suibhne (Dublin: Field Day, 2011)

Gilbert, Sir John, and Gilbert, R.M. *Calendar of the Ancient Records of Dublin*, 19 vols. (Dublin: Dublin Corporation, 1889–1944)

Griffin, Michael. *The Collected Poems of Laurence Whyte* (Lewisburg, PA: Bucknell University Press, 2016)

Irish Historic Towns Atlas fascicles (Dublin: RIA) –
No. X, *Kilkenny*, ed. John Bradley (2000); no. XII, *Belfast, part 1: To 1840*, eds. Raymond Gillespie & Stephen Royle (2003); no. XV, *Derry/Londonderry*, ed. Avril Thomas (2005); no. XIX, *Dublin, part 2: 1619–1756*, ed. Colm Lennon (2008); no. XXI, *Limerick*, ed. Eamon O'Flaherty (2010); no. XXIV, *Sligo*, eds. Fiona Gallagher & Marie Louise Legg (2012); no. XXVI, *Dublin, part 3: 1756–1847*, ed. Rob Goodbody (2014); no. XXVIII, *Galway*, ed. Jacinta Prunty (2016); no. XXIX, *Drogheda*, ed. Ned McHugh (2019)

Journals of the House of Commons of Ireland, 1613–1800, 19 vols (Dublin, 1796–1800)

Kelly, James. *Proceedings of the Irish House of Lords, 1771–1800*, 3 vols (Dublin: IMC, 2008)

Kelly, James, and Lyons, Mary Ann. *The Proclamations of Ireland, 1660–1820*, 5 vols. (Dublin: IMC, 2014)

Kennedy, Liam, and Solar, Peter M. *Irish Agriculture: A price history from the mid-eighteenth century to the eve of the First World War* (Dublin: RIA, 2007)

Laffan, William, ed. *The Cries of Dublin Drawn from Life by Hugh Douglas Hamilton, 1760* (Dublin: Irish Georgian Society, 2003)

Lewis, Samuel. *A Topographical Dictionary of Ireland*, 2 vols (London: S. Lewis & Co., 1837)

Lucas, Richard. *A General Directory of the Kingdom of Ireland* (Cork: J. Cronin, 1788)

Parliamentary papers (United Kingdom):
Census of Ireland, 1821 [1824, XII]
Royal Commission to Inquire into Municipal Corporations (Ireland) [1835, XXVII-XXVIII]
Census of Ireland, 1841 [1843, XXIV]

SELECT BIBLIOGRAPHY

Reports of the Commissioners for Inquiring into the Condition of the Poorer Classes in Ireland [1836, XXX–XXXIV]

Pender, Séamus, ed. *A Census of Ireland circa 1659*, with intro. by W.J. Smyth (2nd edn Dublin: IMC, 2002)

Pigot and co.'s City of Dublin and Hibernian Provincial Directory for 1824 (Manchester: Pigot & Co., 1824)

Young, Arthur. *A Tour in Ireland, with General Observations on the State of that Kingdom . . .* (Dublin: Messrs Whitestone et al., 1780)

SECONDARY SOURCES: GENERAL IRISH URBAN HISTORY

Andrews, J.H. *Plantation Acres: An historical study of the Irish land surveyor* (Belfast: Ulster Historical Foundation, 1985)

Archbold, Johanna. 'Irish Periodicals in their Atlantic Context, 1770–1830' (Ph.D., University of Dublin, 2008)

Barnard, T.C. *Cromwellian Ireland: English government and reform in Ireland 1649–1660* (Oxford: University Press, 1975)

—— 'Lawyers and the Law in Late Seventeenth-Century Ireland', in *IHS*, xxviii, 111 (May 1993)

—— *A New Anatomy of Ireland: The Irish Protestants 1649–1770* (New Haven & London: Yale University Press, 2003)

—— *Making the Grand Figure: Lives and possessions in Ireland, 1641–1770* (New Haven & London: Yale University Press, 2004)

—— *Brought to Book: Print in Ireland, 1680–1784* (Dublin: Four Courts Press, 2017)

Barrow, G.L. *The Emergence of the Irish Banking System 1820–1845* (Dublin: Gill & Macmillan, 1975)

Bartlett, Thomas. *The Rise and Fall of the Irish Nation: The Catholic question 1690–1830* (Dublin: Gill & Macmillan, 1992)

Bartlett, Thomas, et al., eds. *1798: A bicentennial perspective* (Dublin: Four Courts Press, 2003)

Bielenberg, Andy. *Ireland and the Industrial Revolution: The impact of the Industrial Revolution on Irish industry, 1801–1922* (Abingdon: Routledge, 2009)

Brown, Michael. *The Irish Enlightenment* (Cambridge, MA and London: Harvard University Press, 2016)

Butel, Paul, and Cullen, L.M., eds. *Cities and Merchants: French and Irish perspectives on urban development 1500–1900* (Dublin: Dept. of History, TCD, 1986)

Casey, Christine. 'Art and Architecture in the Long Eighteenth Century', in Kelly, *Cambridge History of Ireland*, III

Clark, William S. *The Irish Stage in the County Towns, 1720–1800* (Oxford: University Press, 1966)

Clarke, Howard B., ed. *Irish Cities* (Cork: Mercier Press, 1995)

Clarkson, L.A., and Crawford, E. Margaret. *Feast and Famine: A history of food and nutrition in Ireland 1500–1920* (Oxford: University Press, 2001)

Connolly, S.J. *Religion, Law and Power: The making of Protestant Ireland 1660–1760* (Oxford: University Press, 1992)

—— *Divided Kingdom: Ireland 1630–1800* (Oxford: University Press, 2008)

Corish, P.J. *The Catholic Community in the Seventeenth and Eighteenth Centuries* (Dublin: Educational Co., 1981)

Crookshank, Anne, and Glin, The Knight of. *Ireland's Painters 1600–1940* (New Haven & London: Yale University Press, 2002)

Cullen, L.M. *Anglo-Irish Trade 1660–1800* (Manchester: University Press, 1968)

—— *An Economic History of Ireland since 1660* (London: Batsford, 1972)

—— *The Emergence of Modern Ireland, 1600–1900* (London: Batsford, 1981)

—— *Economy, Trade and Irish Merchants at Home and Abroad 1600–1988* (Dublin: Four Courts Press, 2012)

—— 'Problems in and Sources for the Study of Economic Fluctuations, 1660–1900', in *IESH*, xli (2014)

310

—— and Butel, Paul, eds. *Négoce et industrie en France et en Irlande aux XVIIIe et XIXe siècles* (Paris: Éditions du Centre national de la recherche scientifique, 1980)

Cunningham, Bernadette, and Kennedy, Máire, eds. *The Experience of Reading: Irish historical perspectives* (Dublin: Library Association of Ireland, 1999)

Curtin, Nancy. *The United Irishmen: Popular politics in Ulster and Dublin 1791–1798* (Oxford: University Press, 1994)

Dickson, David. 'Town and City', in Eugenio F. Biagini and Mary E. Daly, eds. *Cambridge Social History of Modern Ireland* (Cambridge: University Press, 2017)

—— 'Society and Economy in the Long Eighteenth Century', in Kelly, ed., *Cambridge History of Ireland*, III

—— Keogh, Dáire and Whelan, Kevin, eds. *The United Irishmen: Republicanism, radicalism and rebellion* (Dublin: Lilliput Press, 1993)

—— Parmentier, Jan, and Ohlmeyer, Jane, eds. *Irish and Scottish Mercantile Networks in Europe and Overseas in the Seventeenth and Eighteenth Centuries* (Gent: Academia Press, 2007)

Drake, Michael. 'The Irish Demographic Crisis of 1740–41', in *Historical Studies VI*, ed. T.W. Moody (London: Routledge & Kegan Paul, 1968)

Gargett, Graham and Sheridan, Geraldine, eds. *Ireland and the French Enlightenment 1700–1800* (New York & Basingstoke: Macmillan, 1999)

Garnham, Neal. *The Courts, Crime and the Criminal Law in Ireland, 1692–1760* (Dublin: Irish Academic Press, 1996)

Geary, Laurence M. *Medicine and Charity in Ireland 1718–1851* (Dublin: UCD Press, 2004)

Gibney, Arthur. *The Building Site in Eighteenth-Century Ireland*, eds. Livia Hurley and Edward McParland (Dublin: Four Courts Press, 2017)

Gillespie, Raymond. 'Urban Destruction by War in Early Modern Ireland', in Martin Körner, ed. *Destruction and Reconstruction of Towns . . .* II (Berne: Haupt, 2000)

—— and Hadfield, Andrew, eds. *The Oxford History of the Irish Book*, III: *The Irish book in English 1550–1800* (Oxford: University Press, 2006)

Glin, The Knight of, and Peill, James. *Irish Furniture: Woodwork and carving in Ireland from the earliest times to the Act of Union* (New Haven & London: Yale University Press, 2007)

Graham, B.J., and Proudfoot, L.G., eds. *An Historical Geography of Ireland* (London: Sage, 1993)

Gurrin, Brian. 'Population and Emigration, 1730–1845', in Kelly, *Cambridge History of Ireland*, III

Hayton, David, ed. *The Irish Parliament in the Eighteenth Century: The long apprenticeship* (Edinburgh: University Press, 2001)

—— and Holmes, Andrew, eds. *Ourselves Alone? Religion, society and politics in eighteenth- and nineteenth-century Ireland: Essays presented to S.J. Connolly* (Dublin: Four Courts Press, 2016)

Herlihy, Kevin, ed. *The Irish Dissenting Tradition, 1650–1750* (Dublin: Four Courts Press, 1995)

—— ed. *The Religion of Irish Dissent, 1650–1800* (Dublin: Four Courts Press, 1996)

—— ed. *The Politics of Irish Dissent, 1659–1800* (Dublin: Four Courts Press, 1997)

Higgins, Padhraig. *A Nation of Politicians: Gender, patriotism, and political culture in late eighteenth-century Ireland* (Madison, WI: University of Wisconsin Press, 2010)

Hill, Jacqueline, and Lennon, Colm, eds. *Luxury and Austerity* (Dublin: UCD Press, 1999)

Hylton, Raymond. *Ireland's Huguenots and their Refuge, 1662–1745: An unlikely haven* (Brighton and Portland: Sussex Academic Press, 2005)

Inglis, Brian. *The Freedom of the Press in Ireland 1784–1841* (London: Faber & Faber, 1954)

Johnston-Liik, Edith Mary. *History of the Irish Parliament 1692–1800: Commons, constituencies and statutes*, 6 vols (Belfast: Ulster Historical Foundation, 2002)

Kelly, James. 'Harvests and Hardship: Famine and scarcity in Ireland in the late 1720s', in *Studia Hibernica*, xxvi (1992)

—— 'The State and the Control of Print in Eighteenth-Century Ireland', in *ECI*, xxiii (2008)

—— *Sport in Ireland, 1600–1840* (Dublin: Four Courts Press, 2014)

—— 'The Consumption and Sociable Use of Alcohol in Eighteenth-Century Ireland', in *Proc. RIA*, Vol. 115, C (2015)

—— *Food Rioting in Ireland in the Eighteenth and Nineteenth Centuries: The 'moral economy' and the Irish crowd* (Dublin: Four Courts Press, 2017)

—— *Cambridge History of Ireland*, III: *1730–1880* (Cambridge: University Press, 2018)

—— and Powell, Martyn J., eds. *Clubs and Societies in Eighteenth-Century Ireland* (Dublin: Four Courts Press, 2010)

Kennedy, Máire. 'Reading the Enlightenment in Eighteenth-Century Ireland', in *ESC*, xlv, 3 (2012)

Leighton, C.D.A. *Catholicism in a Protestant Kingdom: A study of the Irish* ancien régime (Dublin: Gill & Macmillan, 1994)

Loeber, Rolf, Campbell, Hugh, Hurley, Livia, Montague, John, and Rowley, Ellen, eds. *Art and Architecture of Ireland*, IV: *Architecture 1600-2000* (Dublin, New Haven & London: RIA & Yale University Press, 2016)

Long, Gerard, ed. *Books beyond the Pale: Aspects of the provincial book trade in Ireland before 1850* (Dublin: Library Association of Ireland, 1996)

Magray, M.P. *The Transforming Power of the Nuns: Women, religion and cultural change in Ireland 1750-1900* (New York: Oxford University Press, 1998)

Malcomson, A.P.W. *The Pursuit of the Heiress: Aristocratic marriage in Ireland 1740-1840*, 2nd edn (Belfast: Ulster Historical Foundation, 2006)

McBride, Ian. *Eighteenth-Century Ireland: The isle of slaves* (Dublin: Gill, 2009)

McGrath, Charles Ivar. *Ireland and Empire, 1692-1770* (Abingdon: Routledge, 2012)

McGuire, James, ed. *Dictionary of Irish Biography*, 9 vols (Cambridge: University Press, 2010)

Moody, T.W., Martin, F.X., and Byrne, F.J., eds. *A New History of Ireland*, III: *Early modern Ireland 1534-1691* (Oxford: University Press, 1976)

—— and Vaughan, W.E., eds. *A New History of Ireland*: IV: *Eighteenth-Century Ireland, 1691-1800* (Oxford: University Press, 1986)

Morash, Christopher. *A History of Irish Theatre 1601-2000* (Cambridge: University Press, 2002)

Morley, Vincent. *Irish Opinion and the American Revolution, 1760-1783* (Cambridge: University Press, 2002)

Munter, R.L. *The History of the Irish Newspaper 1685-1760* (Cambridge: University Press, 1967)

O'Brien, Gerard, ed., *Irish Catholics in the Eighteenth Century: Collected essays of Maureen Wall* (Dublin: Geography Publications, 1989)

Ó Ciosáin, Niall. *Print and Popular Culture in Ireland 1750-1850* (Basingstoke: Macmillan, 1997)

O'Dowd, Mary. *A History of Women in Ireland, 1500-1800* (Harlow: Longman, 2005)

Ó Gráda, Cormac. 'Industry and Communications, 1801-45', in Vaughan, *NHI*, V

—— *Ireland: A New Economic History 1780-1939* (Oxford: University Press, 1995)

Powell, Martyn J. *The Politics of Consumption in Eighteenth-Century Ireland* (Basingstoke: Palgrave Macmillan, 2005)

—— 'Civil Society, *c.*1700–*c.*1850', in Kelly, *Cambridge History of Ireland*, III

Rodgers, Nini. *Ireland, Slavery and Anti-slavery 1612-1865* (Basingstoke: Palgrave Macmillan, 2007)

Ryan, Salvador, and Tait, Clodagh, eds., *Religion and Politics in Urban Ireland c.1500-c.1750: Essays in honour of Colm Lennon* (Dublin: Four Courts Press, 2016)

Rynne, Colin. *Industrial Ireland 1750-1930: An archaeology* (Cork: Collins Press, 2006)

Skinner, David. *Wallpaper in Ireland 1700-1900* (Tralee: Churchill House Press, 2014)

Smyth, A.J. 'The Social and Economic Impact of the Williamite War on Ireland, 1688-91' (Ph.D. thesis, University of Dublin, 2012)

Smyth, Jim. *The Men of No Property: Irish radicals and popular politics in the late eighteenth century* (Basingstoke: Macmillan, 1992)

Solar, P.M. 'Shipping and Economic Development in Nineteenth-Century Ireland', in *EHR*, lix (2006)

Thomas, Avril. *The Walled Towns of Ireland*, 2 vols (Dublin: Irish Academic Press, 1992)

Truxes, Thomas M. *Irish-American Trade 1660-1783* (Cambridge: University Press, 1988)

Vann, Richard T., and Eversley, David. *Friends in Life and Death: The British and Irish Quakers in the demographic transition* (Cambridge: University Press, 1992)

Vaughan, W.E. *A New History of Ireland*, V: *1801-70* (Oxford: University Press, 1989)

Walsh, Patrick. 'The Fiscal State in Ireland 1691-1780', in *HJ*, lvi, 3 (2013)

SELECT BIBLIOGRAPHY

Watt, Timothy D. *Popular Protest and Policing in Ascendancy Ireland, 1691–1761* (Woodbridge: Boydell & Brewer, 2018)

Whelan, Kevin. *The Tree of Liberty: Radicalism, Catholicism and the construction of Irish identity 1760–1830* (Cork: University Press, 1996)

SECONDARY SOURCES: COMPARATIVE AND TRANSNATIONAL

Alexander, David. 'The Dublin Group: The mezzotint engravers in London, 1750–1775', in *QBIGS*, xvi, 3 (1973)

Baer, William. 'Early Retailing: London's shopping exchanges 1550–1700', in *Business History*, xlix, 1 (2007)

Belchem, John. 'Nationalism, Republicanism and Exile: Irish emigrants and the revolutions of 1848', in *Past & Present*, cxlvi (1995)

Benevolo, Leonardo. *The Architecture of the Renaissance* (London: Routledge & Kegan Paul, 1978)

Bergin, John. 'Irish Catholics and their Networks in Eighteenth-Century London', in *Eighteenth-Century Life*, xxxix, 1 (2015)

Borsay, Peter, ed. *The Eighteenth-Century Town: A reader in English urban history 1688–1820* (Harlow: Longman, 1990)

—— and Proudfoot, Lindsay, eds. *Provincial Towns in Early Modern England and Ireland: Change, convergence and divergence* (Oxford: University Press, 2002)

Brewer, John, and Porter, Roy, eds. *Consumption and the World of Goods* (London: Routledge, 1994)

Chalklin, C.W. *The Provincial Towns of Georgian England: A study of the building process 1740–1820* (London: Edward Arnold, 1974)

Clark, Peter. *European Cities and Towns 400–2000* (Oxford: University Press, 2009)

—— ed., *The Cambridge Urban History of Britain*, II: *1500–1800* (Cambridge: University Press, 2007)

—— and Lepetit, Bernard, eds. *Capital Cities and their Hinterlands in Early Modern Europe* (Aldershot: Scolar Press, 1996)

—— and Gillespie, Raymond, eds. *Two Capitals: London and Dublin, 1500–1840* (Oxford: University Press, 2001)

Clemens, Paul G.E. 'The Rise of Liverpool, 1665–1750', in *EHR*, xxix, 2 (1976)

Cole, R.C. *Irish Booksellers and English Writers 1740–1800* (London: Continuum, 1986)

Connolly, S.J., ed. *Kingdoms United? Great Britain and Ireland since 1500: Integration and diversity* (Dublin: Four Courts Press, 1999)

—— Houston, Rab, and Morris, R.J., eds. *Conflict, Identity and Economic Development: Ireland and Scotland 1600–1939* (Preston: Carnegie, 1995)

Cullen, L.M., and Smout, T.C., eds. *Comparative Aspects of Scottish and Irish Economic and Social History 1600–1900* (Edinburgh: John Donald, [1978])

Davenport, Romola, Schwarz, Leonard, and Boulton, Jeremy. 'The Decline of Adult Smallpox in Eighteenth-Century London', in *EHR*, lxiv, 4 (2011)

Davis, M.T., ed. *Crowd Actions in Britain and France from the Middle Ages to the Modern World* (Basingstoke: Palgrave Macmillan, 2015)

Devine, Thomas M., and Dickson, David, eds. *Ireland and Scotland, 1600–1850: Parallels and contrasts in economic and social development* (Edinburgh: John Donald, 1983)

—— and Jackson, Gordon, eds. *Glasgow*, I: *Beginnings to 1830* (Manchester: University Press, 1995)

De Vries, Jan. *European Urbanization 1500–1800* (London: Methuen, 1984)

Durey, Michael. *Transatlantic Radicals and the Early American Republic* (Lawrence, KS: University Press, 1997)

Epstein, James, and Thompson, Dorothy, eds. *The Chartist Experience: Studies in working-class radicalism and culture, 1830–60* (London: Macmillan, 1982)

Epstein, S.R. 'Craft Guilds, Apprenticeship, and Technological Change in Pre-industrial Europe', in *JEH*, lviii (1998)

SELECT BIBLIOGRAPHY

Galley, Chris. 'A Model of Early Modern Urban Demography', in *EHR*, xlviii, 3 (1995)

—— *The Demography of Early Modern Towns: York in the sixteenth and seventeenth centuries* (Liverpool: University Press, 1998)

Garrioch, David. *The Making of Revolutionary Paris* (Berkeley & London: University of California Press, 2002)

Graham, Aaron, and Walsh, Patrick, eds. *The British Fiscal-military States, 1660–c.1783* (Abingdon: Routledge, 2016)

Griffin, Patrick. *The People with No Name: Ireland's Ulster Scots, America's Scots Irish, and the creation of a British Atlantic world 1689–1764* (Princeton: University Press, 2001)

Hepburn, A.C. *Contested Cities in the Modern West* (Basingstoke: Palgrave Macmillan, 2004)

Hinks, John, and Armstrong, Catherine, eds. *The English Urban Renaissance Revisited* (Newcastle upon Tyne: Cambridge Scholars Publishing, 2018)

Houston, Rab. *Literacy in Early Modern Europe* (Harlow: Longman, 2002)

Knight, Franklin W., and Liss, Peggy K., eds. *Atlantic Port Cities: Economy, culture and society in the Atlantic world, 1650–1950* (Knoxville, TN: University of Tennessee Press, 1991)

Konvitz, Josef W. *Cities and the Sea: Port city planning in early modern Europe* (Baltimore, MD: Johns Hopkins University Press, 1978)

Landers, John. *Death and the Metropolis: Studies in the demographic history of London 1670–1830* (Cambridge: University Press, 1993)

Lawton, Richard, and Lee, Robert, eds. *Population and Society in Western European Port-cities c.1650–1939* (Liverpool: University Press, 2002)

Lee, Robert. 'The Socio-Economic and Demographic Characteristics of Port Cities: A typology for comparative analysis?', in *Urban History*, xxv, 2 (1998)

Lesger, Clé. 'Patterns of Retail Location and Urban Form in Amsterdam in the Mid-Eighteenth Century', in *Urban History*, xxxviii, 1 (2011)

Levene, Alysa. *Childcare, Health and Mortality at the London Foundling Hospital 1741–1800* (Manchester: University Press, 2007)

Leydon, Joseph. 'The Irish Provisions Trade to the Caribbean, c.1650–1780: An historical geography' (Ph.D. dissertation, University of Toronto, 1995)

Lis, Catharina. *Social Change and the Labouring Poor: Antwerp 1770–1860* (New Haven & London: Yale University Press, 1986)

Livesey, James. *Civil Society and Empire: Ireland and Scotland in the eighteenth-century Atlantic world* (New Haven & London: Yale University Press, 2010)

McCalman, Ian. *Radical Underworld: Prophets, revolutionaries and pornographers in London, 1795–1840* (Cambridge: University Press, 1988)

McKean, C., Harris, B., and Whatley, C., eds. *Dundee: Renaissance to Enlightenment* (Dundee: University Press, 2009)

McKee, Jane, and Vigne, Randolph, eds. *The Huguenots: France, exile and diaspora* (Eastbourne: Sussex University Press, 2013)

Miller, Kerby, Schrier, Arnold, Bolling, Bruce D., and Doyle, David N. *Irish Immigrants in the Land of Canaan: Letters and memoirs from colonial and revolutionary America 1675–1815* (New York: Oxford University Press, 2003)

Mintzker, Yair. *The Defortification of the German City, 1689–1866* (New York: Cambridge University Press, 2012)

Mokyr, Joel. *The Enlightened Economy: An economic history of Britain 1700–1850* (New Haven & London: Yale University Press, 2009)

Morgan, Kenneth. *Bristol and the Atlantic Trade in the Eighteenth Century* (Cambridge: University Press, 1993)

Morriss, Roger. *The Foundations of British Maritime Ascendancy: Resources, logistics and the state, 1755–1815* (Cambridge: University Press, 2010)

Nash, Gary B. *The Urban Crucible: The northern sea-ports and the origins of the American Revolution* (Cambridge, MA: Harvard University Press, 1978)

Nash, R.C. 'Irish Atlantic Trade in the Seventeenth and Eighteenth Centuries', in *William and Mary Quarterly*, xlii, 3 (1985)

O'Connor, Thomas, ed. *The Irish in Europe 1580–1815* (Dublin: Four Courts Press, 2001)

314

SELECT BIBLIOGRAPHY

O'Dowd, Mary. 'Politics, Patriotism and Women in Eighteenth-Century Ireland, Britain and Colonial America, c.1700–1780', in *Journal of Women's History*, xxii, 4 (2010)

Patten, John. 'Patterns of Migration and Movement of Labour to three Pre-industrial East Anglian towns', in *Journal of Historical Geography*, ii (1976)

Prendergast, Amy. *Literary Salons across Britain and Ireland in the Long Eighteenth Century* (Basingstoke: Palgrave Macmillan, 2015)

Roche, Daniel. *The People of Paris: An essay in popular culture in the eighteenth century* (Leamington Spa: Berg, 1987)

Sher, Richard. *The Enlightenment and the Book: Scottish authors and their publishers in eighteenth-century Britain, Ireland and America* (Chicago & London: Chicago University Press, 2006)

Smith, Colin. 'The Wholesale and Retail Markets of London, 1660–1840', in *EHR*, lv, 1 (2002)

Stobart, Jon. 'Personal and Commercial Networks in an English Port: Chester in the early eighteenth century', in *Journal of Historical Geography*, xxx (2004)

Thorne, R.G., ed. *The History of Parliament: The House of Commons, 1790–1820* (London: Secker & Warburg, 1986)

Tomory, Leslie. *Progressive Enlightenment: The origins of the gaslight industry, 1780–1820* (Cambridge, MA: MIT Press, 2012)

—— *The History of the London Water Industry, 1580–1820* (Baltimore, MD: Johns Hopkins University Press, 2017)

Truxes, Thomas M., ed. *Ireland, France and the Atlantic in a Time of War: Reflections of the Bordeaux-Dublin Letters, 1757* (Abingdon: Routledge, 2017)

Wareing, J. 'Changes in the Geographical Distribution of the Recruitment of Apprentices to the London Companies, 1486–1750', in *Journal of Historical Geography*, vi (1980)

Wilson, David A. *United Irishmen, United States: Immigrant radicals in the early Republic* (Dublin: Four Courts Press, 1998)

Youngson, A.J. *The Making of Classical Edinburgh 1750–1840* (Edinburgh: University Press, 1966)

PRIMARY AND SECONDARY SOURCES FOR SPECIFIC CITIES AND TOWNS

Belfast

Adams, J.R.R. *The Printed Word and the Common Man: Popular culture in Ulster 1700–1900* (Belfast: Institute of Irish Studies, QUB, 1987)

—— *Merchants in Plenty: Joseph Smyth's Belfast Directories of 1807 and 1808* (Belfast: Ulster Historical Foundation, 1991)

Agnew, Jean. *Belfast Merchant Families in the Seventeenth Century* (Dublin: Four Courts Press, 1996)

—— ed. *The Drennan-McTier Letters*, 3 vols (Dublin: IMC, 1999)

Benn, George. *A History of the Town of Belfast: From the earliest times to the close of the eighteenth century* (London: Marcus Ward, 1877)

Brett, C.E.B. *Buildings of Belfast* (London: Weidenfeld & Nicolson, 1967)

Connolly, S.J., ed. *Belfast 400: People, place and history* (Liverpool: University Press, 2014)

Dawson, Kevin L. *The Belfast Jacobin: Samuel Neilson and the United Irishmen* (Dublin: Irish Academic Press, 2017)

Gamble, Norman. 'The Business Community and Trade of Belfast 1767–1800' (Ph.D. dissertation, University of Dublin, 1978)

Gillespie, Raymond. *Early Belfast: The origins and growth of an Ulster town to 1750* (Belfast: Ulster Historical Foundation, 2007)

Green, E.R.R. *The Lagan Valley 1800–50: A local history of the Industrial Revolution* (London: Faber & Faber, 1949)

Strain, R.W.M. *Belfast and its Charitable Society: A story of urban social development* (Oxford: University Press, 1961)

Truxes, Thomas M., ed. *Letterbook of Gregg & Cunningham: Merchants of New York and Belfast 1756–1757* (Oxford: British Academy, 2001)

Whan, Robert. *The Presbyterians of Ulster 1680–1730* (Woodbridge: Boydell & Brewer, 2013)

Wright, J.J. *The 'Natural Leaders' and their World: Politics, culture and society in Belfast c.1801–1832* (Liverpool: University Press, 2012)

Cork

Bielenberg, Andy. *Cork's Industrial Revolution, 1780–1880: Development or decline?* (Cork: University Press, 1991)

Bolster, Evelyn. *A History of the Diocese of Cork from the Penal Era to the Famine* (Cork: Tower Books, 1989)

Caulfield, Richard. *Council Book of the Corporation of the City of Cork from 1609 . . .* (Guildford: J. Billing & Sons, 1876)

Crowley, John, Devoy, Robert, Linehan, Denis, and O'Flanagan, Patrick, eds. *Atlas of Cork City* (Cork: University Press, 2005)

D'Alton, Ian. *Protestant Society and Politics in Cork, 1812–1844* (Cork: University Press, 1980)

Dickson, David. *Old World Colony: Cork and south Munster 1630–1830* (Cork: University Press, 2005)

Harrison, Richard. *Merchants, Mystics and Philanthropists: 350 years of Cork Quakers* (Cork: Sitka Press, 2006)

Kennedy, Máire. 'At the Exchange: The eighteenth-century book trade in Cork', in Charles Benson and Siobhán Fitzpatrick, eds. *That Woman! Studies in Irish bibliography: A festschrift for Mary 'Paul' Pollard* (Dublin: Lilliput Press, 2005)

Keohane, Frank. *The Buildings of Ireland: Cork – City and County* (New Haven & London: Yale University Press, 2020)

Lucas, Richard. *The Cork Directory for the Year 1787, including the Adjacent Out-ports . . .* (Cork: J.Cronin, [1787])

McCarthy, Mark. 'Turning a World Upside Down . . .: The city of Cork during the 1640s and 1650s', in *Irish Geography*, xxxiii (2000)

Ó Drisceoil, Donal, and Ó Drisceoil, Diarmuid, *Beamish & Crawford: The history of an Irish brewery* (Cork: Collins Press, 2015)

O Mahony, Colman. *In the Shadows: Life in Cork 1750–1930* (Cork: Tower Books, 1997)

O'Shea, James, ed. *Letterbook of Richard Hare, Cork Merchant 1771–1772* (Dublin: IMC, 2013)

O'Sullivan, William. *The Economic History of Cork City from the Earliest Times to the Act of Union* (Cork: University Press, 1937)

Smith, Charles. *The Antient and Present State of the County and City of Cork* (Dublin: J. Exshaw, 1750)

Tuckey, F.H. *The County and City of Cork Remembrancer* (Cork: Osborne Savage & Son, 1837)

Windele, John. *Historical and Descriptive Notices of the City of Cork and its Vicinity . . .* (2nd edn, Cork: Bradford & Son, 1849)

Derry

Colby, Col. [Thomas]. *Ordnance Survey of the County of Londonderry*, I: *Memoir of the City . . . of Londonderry* (Dublin: Hodges & Smith, 1837)

Gavin, Robert, Kelly, William, and O'Reilly, Dolores. *Atlantic Gateway: The port and city of Londonderry since 1700* (Dublin: Four Courts Press, 2009)

Lacey, Brian. *Siege City: The story of Derry and Londonderry* (Belfast: Blackstaff Press, 1990)

McBride, Ian. *The Siege of Derry in Ulster Protestant Mythology* (Dublin: Four Courts Press, 1997)

Mac Suibhne, Breandán. 'Up and Not Out: Why did north-west Ulster not rise in 1798?', in Cathal Póirtéir, *The Great Irish Rebellion of 1798* (Cork: Mercier, 1998)

O'Brien, Gerard, ed. *Derry and Londonderry: History and society* (Dublin: Geography Publications, 1999)

Thomas, Colin. 'Family Formation in a Colonial City: Londonderry, 1650–1750', in *Proc.RIA*, c, C (2000)

SELECT BIBLIOGRAPHY

Drogheda

Casey, Christine, and Rowan, Alistair. *The Buildings of Ireland: North Leinster* (London: Penguin, 1993)

D'Alton, John. *The History of Drogheda: With its environs . . .* (Dublin: John D'Alton, 1844)

FitzGerald, John. 'The Drogheda Textile Industry, 1780–1820', in *JCLAHS*, xx (1981)

Grogan, Rev. T[homas]. *The Council Book of the Corporation of Drogheda . . . 1649–1734* (Drogheda: Independent, 1915)

Malcomson, A.P.W. *John Foster: The politics of the Anglo-Irish ascendancy* (Oxford: University Press, 1978)

Dublin

Aalen, F.H.A., and Whelan, Kevin. *Dublin City and County: From prehistory to present* (Dublin: Geography Publications, 1992)

Bartlett, Thomas, ed. *Revolutionary Dublin, 1795–1801: The letters of Francis Higgins to Dublin Castle* (Dublin: Four Courts Press, 2004)

Begadon, Cormac. 'The Renewal of Catholic Religious Culture in Eighteenth-Century Dublin', in John Bergin et al., *New Perspectives on the Penal Laws* (Dublin: Eighteenth-Century Ireland Society, 2011)

Boydell, Brian. *Rotunda Music in Eighteenth-Century Dublin* (Blackrock: Irish Academic Press, 1992)

Branagan, Michael. *Dublin Moving East, 1708–1844: How the City Took Over the Sea* (Dublin: Wordwell, 2020)

Brown, Michael. *Francis Hutcheson in Dublin, 1719–1730* (Dublin: Four Courts Press, 2002)

Burke, Nuala. 'Dublin 1600–1800: A Study in Urban Morphogenesis' (Ph.D., University of Dublin, 1972)

—— 'A Hidden Church? The structure of Catholic Dublin in the mid-eighteenth century', in *AH*, xxxii (1974)

Butlin, R.A. 'The Population of Dublin in the Late Seventeenth Century', in *Irish Geography*, v (1965)

Casey, Christine. *The Buildings of Ireland: Dublin – The City within the Grand and Royal Canals . . .* (New Haven & London: Yale University Press, 2005)

—— ed. *The Eighteenth-Century Dublin Town House: Form, function and finance* (Dublin: Four Courts Press, 2010)

Clark, Mary, and Refaussé, Raymond, eds. *Directory of Historic Dublin Guilds* (Dublin: Dublin Public Libraries, 1993)

Cox, Catherine. 'Women and Business in Eighteenth-Century Dublin: A case study', in Bernadette Whelan, ed., *Women and Paid Work in Ireland 1500–1930* (Dublin: Four Courts Press, 2000)

Craig, Maurice. *Dublin 1660–1860: A social and architectural history* (London: Cresset Press, 1952)

Cullen, L.M. *Princes and Pirates: The Dublin Chamber of Commerce, 1783–1983* (Dublin: Chamber of Commerce, 1983)

—— Shovlin, John, and Truxes, Thomas, eds. *The Bordeaux-Dublin Letters, 1757* (Oxford: University Press, 2013)

Cunningham, Bernadette. *Gentlemen's Daughters in Dublin Cloisters: The social world of nuns in early eighteenth-century Dublin* (Dublin: Dublin City Public Libraries, 2018)

Cunningham, Jessica. 'Dublin's Huguenot Goldsmiths, 1690–1750', in *IADS*, xii (2009)

Dickson, David. 'The Place of Dublin in the Eighteenth-Century Irish Economy', in Devine and Dickson, eds. *Ireland and Scotland 1600–1850*

—— 'Death of a Capital? Dublin and the consequences of Union', in Clark and Gillespie, eds., *Two Capitals*

—— *Dublin: The making of a capital city* (London: Profile Books, 2014)

—— ed. *The Gorgeous Mask: Dublin, 1700–1850* (Dublin: Trinity History Workshop, 1987)

Dudley, Rowena. 'Dublin's Parishes 1660–1729: The Church of Ireland parishes and their role in the civic administration of the city' (Ph.D., University of Dublin, 1995)

—— 'The Failure of Burton's Bank and its Aftermath', in *IESH*, xl (2013)

Dunlevy, Mairead. *Dublin Barracks: A brief history* (Dublin: National Museum of Ireland, 2002)

Eustace, P.B., and Goodbody, O.C., eds. *Quaker Records, Dublin: Abstracts of wills* (Dublin: IMC, 1957)

Fagan, Patrick. *Second City: Portrait of Dublin 1700–1760* (Dublin: Branar, 1986)

—— *Catholics in a Protestant Country: The papist constituency in eighteenth-century Dublin* (Dublin: Four Courts Press, 1998)

FitzGerald, Alison. *Silver in Georgian Dublin: Making, selling, consuming* (Abingdon: Routledge, 2017)

Foster, Sarah. '"Ornament and Splendour": Shops and shopping in Georgian Dublin', in *IADS*, xv (2012)

Fraser, Murray. 'Public Building and Colonial Policy in Dublin, 1760–1800', in *Architectural History*, xxviii (1985)

Gilbert, John. *History of Dublin*, 3 vols (Dublin: James McGlashan, 1854–59)

Gillespie, Raymond. 'Dublin 1600–1700', in Peter Clark and Bernard Lepetit, eds. *Capital Cities and their Hinterlands in Early Modern Europe* (Aldershot: Scolar Press, 1996)

Gilligan, H.A. *History of the Port of Dublin* (Dublin: Gill & Macmillan, 1988)

Gough, Hugh. 'Book Imports from Continental Europe in Late Eighteenth-Century Ireland: Luke White and the *Société Typographique de Neuchâtel*', in *Long Room*, xxxviii (1993)

Griffin, Michael. *Live from the Conniving House: Poetry and music in eighteenth-century Dublin* (Dublin: Dublin City Public Libraries, 2019)

Griffith, Lisa-Marie. 'Social Mobility and the Middling Sort: Dublin merchants, 1760–1800' (Ph.D., University of Dublin, 2008)

—— and Wallace, Ciaran eds., *Grave Matters: Death and dying in Dublin, 1500 to the present* (Dublin: Four Courts Press, 2016)

Hall, F.G. *The Bank of Ireland 1783–1946* (Dublin: Hodges Figgis, 1949)

Hardiman, Nodlaig P., and Kennedy, Máire, eds. *A Directory of Dublin for the Year 1738* (Dublin: Dublin Corporation Public Libraries, 2000)

Henry, Brian. *Dublin Hanged: Crime, law enforcement and punishment in late eighteenth-century Dublin* (Dublin: Irish Academic Press, 1994)

Hill, Jacqueline. *From Patriots to Unionists: Dublin civic politics and Irish Protestant patriotism, 1660–1940* (Oxford: University Press, 1997)

Kelly, James. 'The Impact of the Penal Laws', in Kelly and Dáire Keogh, eds. *History of the Catholic Diocese of Dublin* (Dublin: Four Courts Press, 2000)

—— *The Liberty and Ormond Boys: Factional riot in eighteenth-century Ireland* (Dublin: Four Courts Press, 2005)

Lennon, Colm, and Montague, John. *John Rocque's Dublin: A guide to the Georgian city* (Dublin: RIA, 2010)

Lynch, Patrick, and Vaizey, John. *Guinness's Brewery in the Irish Economy 1759–1876* (Cambridge: University Press, 1960)

McAulay, Eve. 'Some Problems in Building on the Fitzwilliam Estate . . .', in *IADS*, ii (1999)

McCabe, Desmond. *St Stephen's Green, Dublin, 1660–1875* (Dublin: Stationery Office, 2011)

McDowell, R.B., and Webb, D.A. *Trinity College Dublin 1592–1952: An academic history* (Cambridge: University Press, 1982)

McParland, Edward. 'The Wide Streets Commissioners . . . .', in *QBIGS*, xv (1972)

—— *James Gandon, Vitruvius Hibernicus* (London: A. Zwemmer, 1985)

—— 'Malton's Views of Dublin: Too good to be true?', in Brian P. Kennedy and Raymond Gillespie, eds., *Ireland: Art into History* (Dublin: Rinehart, 1994)

—— *Public Architecture in Ireland 1680–1760* (New Haven & London: Yale University Press, 2001)

Malcomson, A.P.W. *Nathaniel Clements 1705–77: Politics, fashion and architecture in mid-eighteenth-century Ireland* (Dublin: Four Courts Press, 2015)

Meredith, Jane. 'Andrew Caldwell (1733–1808): A study of a "guardian of taste and genius"', (M.Litt., University of Dublin, 2005)

Montague, John. 'From Rome to Paris and London: Searching for the European roots of the Wide Streets Commissioners', in *IADS*, xxi (2018)

318

Mullaney, Susan. 'The Evolution of the Medical Professions in Eighteenth-Century Dublin', in John Cunningham, ed. *Early Modern Ireland and the World of Medicine* (Manchester: University Press, 2019)

Murtagh, Timothy. 'Dublin's Artisans and Radical Politics 1779–1803' (Ph.D., University of Dublin, 2015)

O'Brien, Gillian, and O'Kane, Finola, eds. *Georgian Dublin* (Dublin: Four Courts Press, 2008)

Ó Gráda, Cormac. 'Dublin's Demography in the Early Nineteenth Century: Evidence from the Rotunda', in *Population Studies*, xlv, 1 (1991)

Ó Gráda, Diarmuid. *Georgian Dublin* (Cork: University Press, 2015)

Ó Maitiú, Seamas. *The Humours of Donnybrook: Dublin's famous fair and its suppression* (Dublin: Irish Academic Press, 1995)

O'Neill, Thomas P. 'Discoverers and Discoveries: The penal laws and Dublin property', in *DHR*, xxxvii (1983)

Palmer, Stanley. *Police and Protest in England and Ireland 1780–1850* (Cambridge: University Press, 1988)

Phillips, James W. *Printing and Bookselling in Dublin 1670–1800* (Dublin: Irish Academic Press, 1998)

Pollard, Mary. *Dublin's Trade in Books, 1550–1800* (Oxford: University Press, 1989)

—— *A Dictionary of Members of the Dublin Book Trade 1550–1800* (London: Bibliographical Society, 2001)

Prunty, Jacinta. *Dublin Slums, 1800–1925: A study in urban geography* (Dublin: Irish Academic Press, 1999)

Ross, Ian Campbell, ed. *Public Virtue, Public Love: The early years of the Dublin Lying-in Hospital* (Dublin: O'Brien Press, 1986)

Rutty, John. *An Essay towards a Natural History of the County of Dublin* (Dublin: W. Sleator, 1772)

Thomas, W.A. *The Stock Exchanges of Ireland* (Liverpool: Francis Cairns, 1986)

Twomey, Brendan. 'Personal Financial Management in Early Eighteenth-Century Ireland: Practices, participants and outcomes' (Ph.D., University of Dublin, 2018)

Usher, Robin. *Protestant Dublin 1660–1780: Architecture and iconography* (Basingstoke: Palgrave Macmillan, 2012)

Warburton, J., Whitelaw, Rev. J., and Walsh, Rev. Robert. *History of Dublin*, 2 vols (London: T. Cadell & W. Davies, 1818)

Whitelaw, Rev. James. *An Essay on the Population of Dublin . . .* (Dublin: Graisberry & Campbell, 1805)

Wilson's Dublin Directory [for the years 1751–53, 1761–1800]

Wolf, Nicholas M. 'Advocacy, the Enlightenment and the Catholic Print Trade in Mathew Carey's Dublin', in *Éire-Ireland*, xlix, 3/4 (2014)

Woods, C.J. 'The Personnel of the Catholic Convention, 1792–3', in *AH*, lvii (2003); lxvi (2014)

Galway

Cunningham, J.F. 'Patterns of Social Change in a Provincial Capital: Galway, *c.*1800–1914' (Ph.D. dissertation, NUI Galway, 2001)

—— *'A Town Tormented by the Sea': Galway 1790–1914* (Dublin: Geography Publications, 2004)

Hardiman, James. *The History of the Town and County of the Town of Galway*, 2nd edn (Galway: Connacht Tribune, 1926)

Moran, Gerard, and Gillespie, Raymond, eds. *Galway: History and society* (Dublin: Geography Publications, 1996)

Mulloy, Sheila. 'Galway in the Jacobite War', in *JGAHS.*, xl (1985)

Walsh, Paul. *Renaissance Galway: Delineating the Seventeenth-Century City* (Dublin: RIA, 2019)

Kilkenny

Barnard, Toby, and Fenelon, Jane, eds. *The Dukes of Ormonde, 1610–1745* (Woodbridge: Boydell, 2000)

SELECT BIBLIOGRAPHY

Neely, W.G. *Kilkenny: An urban history, 1391–1843* (Belfast: Institute of Irish Studies, QUB, 1989)

Nolan, William, and Whelan, Kevin, eds. *Kilkenny: History and society* (Dublin: Geography Publications, 1990)

Tighe, William. *Statistical Observations Relative to the County of Kilkenny* (Dublin: Graisberry & Campbell, 1802)

Limerick

Ferrar, John. *An History of the City of Limerick . . .* (Limerick: John Ferrar, 1767)

Fleming, D.A. *Politics and Provincial People: Sligo and Limerick, 1691–1761* (Manchester: University Press, 2010)

—— and Logan, John, eds. *Pauper Limerick: The register of the Limerick House of Industry 1774–93* (Dublin: IMC, 2011)

Hill, Judith. *The Building of Limerick* (Cork: Mercier, 1991)

Irwin, Liam, Ó Tuathaigh, Gearóid, and Potter, Matthew, eds. *Limerick: History and society* (Dublin: Geography Publications, 2009)

Lenihan, Maurice. *Limerick, its History and Antiquities . . .* (Dublin: Hodges, Smith & Co., 1866)

Logan, John. ' "Dropped into This Kingdom from the Clouds": The Irish career of Davis Dukart, architect and engineer, 1761–81', in *IADS*, x (2007)

Malcomson, A.P.W. 'Speaker Pery and the Pery Papers', in *NMAJ*, xvi (1973/4)

O'Flaherty, Eamon. 'An Urban Community and the Penal Laws: Limerick 1690–1830', in John Bergin et al., *New Perspectives on the Penal Laws* (Dublin: Eighteenth-Century Ireland Society, 2011)

Sligo

Dickson, David, and Fleming, D.A., eds. 'Charles O'Hara's Observations on County Sligo, 1752–73', in *Anal. Hib.*, xlvi (2015)

Fleming, D.A. *Politics and Provincial People: Sligo and Limerick, 1691–1761* (Manchester: University Press, 2010)

Legg, Marie-Louise. *The Elphin Census, 1749* (Dublin: IMC, 2004)

O'Dowd, Mary. *Early Modern Sligo 1568–1688* (Belfast: Institute of Irish Studies, QUB, 1991)

O'Rorke, T[erence]. *History of Sligo: Town and county* (Dublin: James Duffy & Co., n.d. [1889])

Timoney, Martin A., ed. *A Celebration of Sligo* (Sligo: Field Club, 2007)

Waterford

Cullen, L.M. 'The Overseas Trade of Waterford as Seen from a Ledger of Courtenay and Ridgway', in *JRSAI*, lxxxix (1958)

Dowling, Daniel. *Waterford Streets Past and Present* (Waterford: Waterford Corporation, 1991)

Girouard, Mark. *Town and Country* (New Haven & London: Yale Univsersity Press, 1992)

Lumley, Ian W.J. 'The Georgian Townhouses of Waterford: An architectural assessment', in *Decies*, xxxiv (1987), 49–60

[McEneany, Eamonn, and Ryan, Rosemary]. *Waterford Treasures: A guide . . .* (Waterford: Museum of Treasures, 2004)

Murphy, Liam. *Waterford Merchants and their Families on Distant Shores: Waterford traders in Spain and France 1600–1800* (Dublin: Kingdom Books, 2018)

Nolan, William, and Power, Thomas P., eds. *Waterford: History and society* (Dublin: Geography Publications, 1992)

Smith, Charles. *The Antient and Present State of the County and City of Waterford . . .* (Dublin: Edward & John Exshaw, 1746)

INDEX

Page numbers in italics refer to images.

INDEX